DATE DUE

DEMCO 38-297

SOCIAL EPISTEMOLOGY

SCIENCE, TECHNOLOGY, AND SOCIETY

Ronald N. Giere and Thomas F. Gieryn, General Editors

SOCIAL EPISTEMOLOGY

Steve Fuller

Indiana University Press

Bloomington and Indianapolis

Manufactured in the United States of America

Library of Congress Cataloguing-in-Publication Data

Fuller, Steve   1959-
  Social epistemology.

  (Science, technology, and society)
  Bibliography: p.
  Includes index.
  1. Knowledge, Sociology of. I. Title. II. Series:
Science, technology, and society (Bloomington, Ind.)
BD175.F85 1988   001   87-31056
ISBN 0-253-35227-4

CONTENTS

PART THREE
ISSUES IN THE SOCIAL ORGANIZATION OF KNOWLEDGE

PART FOUR
ISSUES IN KNOWLEDGE POLICY-MAKING

FOREWORD

In this provocative book we see the future of epistemology, or at least one future. This is reassuring, for Richard Rorty, in *Philosophy and the Mirror of Nature*, argued that epistemology has no future; and too many of the dozens of replies to Rorty have defended the honor of the same old questions and answers that we studied at school a decade ago, and five or ten decades ago. To say that the glorious past of epistemology is future enough is really to acknowledge its death as a discipline. Both Rorty and Steve Fuller are intellectually at home on both sides of the Atlantic and even on both sides of the Channel, not to mention both sides of the divide between the two cultures; so this alone will not explain why one asserts what the other denies--the relevance of wider issues to epistemology of science, and *hence* the relevance of the latter to those wider issues. Although no one would mistake him for a quantum logician, Fuller is less poetic than Rorty, and he looks with more favor upon science and upon science policy and science-based public policy.

Disciplines are what Fuller's book is about. His social turn will "turn off" many philosophers, and the manner in which he negotiates his turn will appear reckless to many in the (other) science studies professions--history, sociology, and psychology of science and technology. But the book stands virtually alone in its detailed argument for a social epistemology. It is a rarity among philosophical works in that it *uses* a social conception of inquiry rather than abusing it or at best only "mentioning" it. Happily, the days are past in which philosophers and sociologists spent most of their time together beating up on one another. That is social progress of a modest sort. However, the present book goes well beyond those recent works which favorably mention sociological work and argue that cooperation is *possible*.

A more important "possibility" question is, to what extent are methodological proposals of philosophers socially (and psychologically) possible? Inquiry is a socio-historical process conducted by human beings with the aid of various tools. Many philosophers of science now grant that historical evidence can refute methodological claims. Only a few have seriously asked whether even the leading methodologies are compatible with what we know of the social organization of inquiry. For the majority, it does not really matter. For them methodology may be historically descriptive, to some extent, but it is socially normative in a preemptive way. As for the minority: compatibilism is fine, as far as it goes, but we need specific accounts of how some "causes" can also be "reasons," and vice versa. Fuller appreciates that we need to understand in detail the social realization of the "logic" of inquiry, and the logical upshot of the social organization of inquiry and its products.

In short, *Social Epistemology* lays some of the groundwork, or at least breaks the ground, for a new field of study (or the transformation of an old field). Fuller's endless remarks on disciplinary autonomy, demarcation, the organization of knowledge and of its institutional vehicles, consensus, the locality of research, expertise, tacit knowledge, authority, and so on, are endlessly suggestive. It seems to me that anyone of epistemological bent looking for relevant, new problems to tackle and new fields to explore need look no further.

Thomas Nickles
University of Nevada at Reno

PREFACE

This book is written by a philosopher of science on behalf of the sociology of knowledge. Since I believe that philosophy is primarily a *normative* discipline and that sociology is primarily an *empirical* one, my most basic claim is twofold: (1) If philosophers are interested in arriving at rational knowledge policy (roughly, some design for the ends and means of producing knowledge), then they had better study the range of options that have been provided by the actual social history of knowledge production--a field of study that I assume had originally been explored by rhetoricians and philologists, and more recently, of course, by social scientists. Moreover, if philosophers scrutinize this history fairly, they will then be forced to reconceptualize both the substance and function of their normative theories of knowledge. (2) If sociologists and other students of actual knowledge production wish their work to have the more general significance that it deserves, then they should practice some "naturalistic epistemology" and welcome the opportunity to extrapolate from *is* to *ought*. If these empiricists realized, following Max Weber, that the inferential leap from facts to values is no greater than the leap from our knowledge of the present to our knowledge of the future (a leap that the empiricists would risk in the normal course of their inquiries), they would be relieved of the peculiar combination of fear and loathing which normally prevents them from encroaching on the philosopher's traditional terrain. (A healthy step in the right direction has recently been made in Barnes [1986].) In any case, the alternative is the current state of affairs, whereby science administrators too often justify rather hapless decisions on the basis of some half-digested philosophy of science learned at university.

On the face of it, these claims seem rather reasonable, perhaps even harmless. Yet, the interaction between epistemology and the sociology of knowledge has, in fact, been largely antagonistic. From the standpoint of what I call social epistemology, the reasons for this antagonism are themselves quite interesting, since they raise a whole host questions having to do with the resolution of disciplinary boundary disputes. And not surprisingly, a good portion of this book is devoted to developing some ways of thinking about these questions. For an important decision that the knowledge policymaker will need to make is whether it is better to have one integrated study of our knowledge enterprises (a "Science of Science," so to speak) or the current state of affairs, namely, several mildly affiliated but generally independent fields of inquiry.

The reader should be warned at the outset that, generally speaking, I am not interested in "the problem of knowledge" as classically posed by epistemologists. In other words, the reader will find little in this book that considers whether our beliefs in an external world are veridical or justified. Rather, the key issues for me concern a fairly literal sense of "knowledge production," which includes how certain linguistic artifacts ("texts") become certified as knowledge; the possible circulation patterns of these artifacts (especially how they are used to produce other such artifacts, as well as artifacts that have political and other cultural consequences); and the production of certain attitudes on the part of producers about the nature of the entire knowledge enterprise (such as the belief that it "progresses"). In fact, to draw the contrast with the classical epistemologist as starkly as possible, I would say that most of the issues that I consider would be *exactly* the sort of thing that a Cartesian demon would need to know in order to construct an illusory world of knowledge for some unwitting *res cogitans*.

No doubt, the classical epistemologist will cringe at the last sentence, concluding that there is nothing more to my theory of knowledge than an empirical account of what people in various communities call knowledge. In response, I would first note that our cringing epistemologist usually turns out to be a closet skeptic, for whom my theory of knowledge is inadequate only for the same reasons that everyone else's is, namely, that it cannot reliably demarcate "real" knowledge from mere opinion. But this global negative judgment alone is cause for suspecting that the classical epistemologist has missed the point of inquiring into the nature of knowledge--which is to define, extend, but surely not to *deny*, humanly possible epistemic practices. This must seem a rather obvious point to the nonphilosopher, yet the classical epistemologist's blindness to it may be excused by recalling that the *super*human (in a word, God) has traditionally set the standard of epistemic excellence. Still, I hope that after reading this book, the classical epistemologist will appreciate that I am sensitive to a basic fact that has often animated a skeptical turn of mind: to wit, that our knowledge claims cover less ground with less certainty than we ordinarily realize.

As currently practiced, the branches of philosophy devoted to the nature of knowledge--epistemology and the philosophy of science--rest on a couple of elementary fallacies. On the one hand, philosophers treat the various knowledge states and processes as properties of individuals operating in a social vacuum. They often seem to think that any correct account of individual knowledge can be, ipso facto, generalized as the correct account of social knowledge. For example, the assertibility conditions for a scientific claim are typically defined in terms of the evidential relation that the knower stands to the known, without taking into account the epistemic states of other knowers whose relations to one another and the known would greatly influence the assertibility of the scientific claim. And insofar as this slide from the individual to the social has been implicit instead of argued, philosophers have committed *the fallacy of composition*.

On the other hand, philosophical accounts of the individual knower are sometimes quite perspicuous, but not because they have isolated real features of individual cognition. Rather, these accounts have identified inference schemas, so-called logics of justification, and scripts that have persuasive force in the public exchange of information. Whether these schemas and scripts constitute the structure of belief formation in all rational individuals is immaterial to their social import, which rests solely on members of the relevant cognitive community recognizing that such rationally displayed information commands their consideration. Consequently, philosophers can frequently slip into committing *the fallacy of division* by assuming that a feature of the knowledge enterprise that appears primarily at the level of social interaction is, ipso facto, reproduced (by some means or other) as a feature of the minds of the individuals engaged in that interaction.

Why do philosophers tend to commit these two fallacies when discussing the nature of knowledge? My own diagnosis points to a confusion between what is *intended* and what is *effected* in the course of producing knowledge. When epistemologists commit the fallacy of composition, they suppose that one can predict whether a claim is likely to pass as knowledge in a particular cognitive community on the basis of what most of the community's members believe. Likewise, when epistemologists commit the fallacy of division, they assume that the best explanation for why a cognitive community officially treats a given claim as knowledge is that most of the community's members believe the claim. However, both inferences greatly underestimate the influence exercised by each member's expectations about what is appropriate to assert in his cognitive community, as well as each member's willingness to discount his own personal beliefs and conform to these canonical expectations--if only as a means of maintaining his good standing in the cognitive community. In short, then, in my view epistemic judgment has much of the character of identifying and anticipating trends in the stock market.

Lest the reader think that I have an entirely consensualist approach to social epistemology, I should emphasize that what matters, from the standpoint of the smooth operation of the knowledge process, is that there *appears* to be a conformity in epistemic judgments. However, this appearance need not run any deeper than a similarity in the style in which those judgments are delivered, which can, in turn, be easily monitored by the various gatekeepers of the cognitive community. Not surprisingly, then, as cognitive communities such as disciplines expand in time and space, it becomes more likely that several teams of researchers will assent to the same set of sentences but apply them in ways that suggest that those sentences to have quite different meanings. This leaves us with a picture of the knowledge enterprise which, on the textual surface, seems rather uniform and systematically regulated, but which, at the microlevel of actual usage, is revealed to be only locally constrained. The radical duality suggested here may be encapsulated by the thesis that, because of the ease with which it can conceal epistemic differences, *the communicative process itself is the main source of cognitive change.* When writing in a more "humanistic" idiom, I refer to the consequences of this picture as *the problem of incommensurability,* whereas I refer to it as *the elusiveness of consensus* when writing in a more "social scientific" vein.

The book has been organized in the interest of "today's reader," someone who rarely reads a book cover to cover in one sitting but dips into a chapter here and there (though, of course, the book *should* be read in order of presentation). Consequently, each chapter can be read by itself without too much loss of context, and there are periodic references to earlier and later chapters of relevance. Since particular audiences have particular needs, I also recommend the following reading plans. Everyone should read at least chapter 1, and preferably all of part one. *Humanists* should also read the chapters in part two and Appendix B in part three, while *social scientists* should read all of part three, and *administrators* should read the chapters in part four. *Philosophers of science* will, with some luck, find something of interest everywhere, though *epistemologists* and *philosophers of language* might confine themselves to part two, while *social and political theorists* might prefer parts three and four.

To make the most use out of this text, the reader should regard it, not as the usual monolithic monograph, but as a parcel of provocations, a sourcebook of ideas, and directions for further research. Needless to say, I welcome criticism so as to afford me the opportunity of getting it right in the next book, tentatively titled *Philosophy of Science and Its Discontents* (Westview Press, 1988/9). Footnotes have been eliminated to facilitate reading, though readers will hopefully find the references cited an aid to their own research, especially in suggesting conceptual links between fields of inquiry not normally drawn together. Finally, references to "he," "him," and the like are also a matter of convenience and should thus be understood in a gender-neutral manner.

This book began to emerge in 1983 and was largely completed by 1986. A version of chapter 1 appears in a special issue of *Synthese* devoted to social epistemology, edited by Fred Schmitt, who is undoubtedly the most careful and stimulating philosophical reader that I have yet run across. A portion of chapter 2 was a response to a paper by Margaret Gilbert, delivered at the American Philosophical Association meetings. Chapter 3 is an expanded version of a talk given in the Harvard History of Science colloquium series. Everett Mendelsohn is to be thanked for his generous invitation. (A note of thanks, also, to Hilary Putnam and the Harvard philosophy graduate students, for their challenging and illuminating remarks.) Chapters 5 and 11 were originally delivered at the University of Colorado History and Philosophy of Science Colloquium series. Parts of these two chapters have appeared in *Philosophy of the Social Sciences, Explorations in Knowledge,* and *EASST Newsletter.* Here I would like to thank Patrick Heelan, Gonzalo Munevar, Arie Rip, and Howard Smokler for their informative, encouraging, and sometimes critical, remarks. Part of chapter 6 was delivered at the annual meeting of the International Association for Philosophy and Literature. Appendix B was originally given at the annual convention of the Speech Communication Association. Foremost among my friends in this field has been Charles Willard. A version of chapter 7 has appeared in a special issue of *Pacific Philosophical Quarterly,* while a version of chapter 8 has appeared in *4S Review.* Here I have found Steve Woolgar's writings invaluable. Chapter 9, the only one based on a chapter of my doctoral dissertation, has, in turn, been the basis of a symposium paper given at the Philosophy of Science Association. Ted McGuire and Ken Schaffner are to be thanked for much of the scholarship which graces that chapter.

More general thanks go to my long-standing cronies, David Gorman, editor of *Annals of Scholarship,* and James O'Brien, notes and reviews editor of *The Yale Law Journal,* both for their fierce independence and loyalty in many matters. Ron Giere and Tom Nickles did the most to get this book accepted for publication, while Bob Sloan and the editorial staff at Indiana University Press have since facilitated matters, in conjunction with Jim Roberts of Publishing Resources Incorporated, Boulder. Richard Steele, managing editor for Taylor & Francis Ltd., has indirectly promoted the writing of this book as diligent midwife to a journal I have recently started, also called *Social Epistemology.* The philosophy department at the University of Colorado has been the most pleasant academic environment in which I have so far worked. However, I could always count on Georges Rey to make sure that the pleasant atmosphere did not slip into a dogmatic slumber. In fact, I must confess that Georges has been the only person to make me doubt (albeit, for a few fleeting moments) the fundamental notions in this book. My students have also been a constant source of various forms of stimulation, though a special place must be accorded to my research assistant, Stephen Downes. Finally, my biggest debt is to my mother, who knew all along that this was going to happen.

Steve Fuller
University of Colorado

PART ONE

ISSUES IN DEFINING THE FIELD OF SOCIAL EPISTEMOLOGY

CHAPTER ONE

AN OVERVIEW OF SOCIAL EPISTEMOLOGY

The fundamental question of the field of study I call social epistemology is: *How should the pursuit of knowledge be organized, given that under normal circumstances knowledge is pursued by many human beings, each working on a more or less well-defined body of knowledge and each equipped with roughly the same imperfect cognitive capacities, albeit with varying degrees of access to one another's activities?*

Without knowing anything else about the nature of social epistemology, you can already tell that it has a *normative* interest, namely, in arriving at a kind of optimal division of cognitive labor. In other words, in words that only a Marxist or a positivist could truly love, the social epistemologist would like to be able to show how the *products* of our cognitive pursuits are affected by changing the social relations in which the knowledge *producers* stand to one another. As a result, the social epistemologist would be the ideal epistemic policy maker: if a certain kind of knowledge product is desired, then he could design a scheme for dividing up the labor that would likely (or efficiently) bring it about; or, if the society is already committed to a certain scheme for dividing up the cognitive labor, the social epistemologist could then indicate the knowledge products that are likely to flow from that scheme. I thus follow the lead of Plato's *Republic* and Francis Bacon's *New Atlantis* in conceiving of the "epistemology" in social epistemology as having an interest in describing our cognitive pursuits primarily as a means of prescribing for them.

Yet at the same time, social epistemology is not "utopian" in the pejorative sense that Marx used to distinguish his own "scientific" brand of socialism from those, such as Saint-Simon's and Fourier's, which were based on philosophical ideals that could never be implemented on a mass scale. I take the "normal circumstances" cited in the question to be universal, both historically and cross-culturally, a "brute fact" about the nature of our cognitive pursuits to which any normative epistemology must be held accountable. Moreover, I take this brute fact to be responsible not only for the variety of ways in which knowledge has been pursued, but also for the variety of products that have passed for knowledge itself. Consequently, in so aligning myself with *naturalistic* approaches to knowledge, I reject the Cartesian gesture of withdrawing from all social intercourse as a means of getting into the right frame of mind for posing foundational questions about the nature of knowledge. For even though the social world may appear to be a confusing place from which to deliver epistemic judgments--certainly more confusing than the privacy of one's own study--it is nevertheless the *normal* (and probably the *only*) place in which such judgments are delivered. If you still doubt the wisdom of this move, just recall that only an old rationalist prejudice, one popularized by Descartes himself, ties the adequacy of knowing to the clarity and certainty of thinking.

3

Later in this book (ch. 7) I will argue that a crucial way in which a discipline maintains its status as "science" is by manipulating the historical record so that it appears to be the inevitable outcome of the course of inquiry up to that point. In the first part of this chapter, I attempt a similar legitimating move by showing that social epistemology is a natural development from the history of philosophy since Kant. However, since social epistemology as I conceive it will probably strike many readers as an offspring of rather dubious lineage, I shall then proceed, in the second part of the chapter, to write a different revisionist history of modern philosophy. Here social epistemology, in its incarnation as "the sociology of knowledge," constitutes a radical, if not wholly successful, break with all previous theories of knowledge. But an unwitting combination of philosophers and sociologists nowadays threatens to smother the revolutionary impulse in a spirit of accommodation. Finally, I offer some suggestions as to how the social epistemologist can remain both exciting and relevant to contemporary issues in the theory of knowledge.

1. Social Epistemology as the Goal of All Epistemology

You should now have a rough sense of the conceptual location of social epistemology. But let us proceed somewhat more systematically. First, in calling my field of study social *epistemology* I have identified it as a branch of philosophy, indeed perhaps the main branch of that discipline. Yet a common response that philosophers have made to sociology over the past two centuries is to invoke what Larry Laudan (1977) has called "the arationality assumption," namely, that sociological accounts of our cognitive pursuits are appropriate only when those pursuits fail by universally acceptable standards of rationality. Even Karl Mannheim (1936), who established the sociology of knowledge as a separate discipline in the twentieth century, invoked this assumption when he exempted mathematics and the natural sciences from his field of inquiry. For all their ideological differences, both Laudan and Mannheim portray the sociologist of knowledge as wanting to show that the domain for which a knowledge claim is valid is restricted by the social conditions under which that claim was first made. Thus, unlike the founder of sociology, Emile Durkheim (1961), who, in Kantian fashion, saw the universal features of cognition--space, time, number, cause--grounded in features shared by all societies, Laudan and Mannheim assume that sociological accounts of knowledge, if they have any grounding at all, are grounded in the features of *particular* societies, and hence are, in principle opposed to the philosophical accounts, which are based on appeals to *universal* rationality. Given the uneasy complementarity that has thus developed between philosophy as the study of the universal and sociology as the study of the particular in our cognitive pursuits, it would seem that "social epistemology" has become an oxymoron, a contradiction in terms.

Still, it is curious that for all its current centrality to philosophy, the discipline of epistemology has a distinctly post-Kantian origin. Before Kant philosophers typically understood the nature of knowledge and the nature of reality as two sides of the same coin. The generic philosophical question may thus have been posed: How is reality constituted such that we can know it (insofar as we do), and how are we constituted such that reality can manifest itself to us (insofar as it does)? The point of the Kantian critique--at least as it was taken by Kant's successors--was to detach the question about knowledge from the question about reality, largely by arguing that the question about reality makes sense only as a disguised version of the question about knowledge, and that the answer to the question about knowledge places no discernible constraints on what the answer to the question about reality might be. In this way, it became conceptually possible in the nineteenth century to practice epistemology as something distinct from metaphysics (Habermas 1971, Hacking 1975a).

However, Kant's critique alone was not sufficient to establish epistemology as a *legitimate* philosophical enterprise. After all, if Kant's predecessors had been convinced that knowing about the nature of knowledge told them nothing about the nature of reality, then what would be their motivation for studying knowledge? The nineteenth century provided an answer that was suited to the post-Kantian philosophical sensibility. For once disciplines started to proliferate, claims to knowledge began to be made which were justified solely on *intradisciplinary* grounds but which were clearly meant to have *interdisciplinary* cognitive import. This gave the internal structure of knowledge--quite independent of any link to reality--a new complexity that required study in its own right. The general term coined for these claims was "reductionist," the two most notable cases of which were the attempts to reduce chemical phenomena to atomic physics and the attempts to reduce mental phenomena to a kind of physiological mechanics. The point of studying knowledge, then, would be to arrive at rules for adjudicating the various reductionist claims, which would involve devising a metalanguage for rewriting all such claims so as to display the exact extent of their cognitive authority, often known as their evidential warrant. The normative import of this exercise may be seen in that once the atomic hypothesis was granted cognitive authority in the explanation of chemical phenomena, it was possible to judge the relative "progressiveness" of a research program in chemistry, either past or present, by the likelihood with which it would facilitate the reduction to atomic physics. The ultimate goal of the epistemologist would thus be to map out the structure of cognitive authority among all the disciplines as a means of providing direction for their research--which is precisely the goal of *social* epistemology.

And so, my short answer to the alleged self-contradictoriness of "social epistemology" is that epistemology has been a well-motivated, autonomous field of inquiry only insofar as it has been concerned with the social organization of knowledge. Such had clearly been the case with the first epistemologists, Auguste Comte and John Stuart Mill, and it continued to be the case in the twentieth century with the logical positivists. The continuity of this concern is nowadays lost, however, mainly because logical positivism's legacy has been greater in the techniques it introduced for doing epistemology than in the actual project for which those techniques were introduced.

Consider the ease with which Kuhn, Feyerabend, and Hanson were able to show, in the late 1950s, that the positivist panoply of correspondence rules, equivalence relations, and subsumption strategies could not adequately account for the structure of cognitive authority in the sciences. Indeed, many positivists even granted the more radical critique that these creatures of formal logic had no place whatsoever in the epistemological project. Why? Because the offspring of logical positivism, the analytic philosophers, were coming to the ironic realization that the formal techniques which they had inherited were better suited for the very problems in metaphysics whose intelligibility the logical positivists had questioned. The focus of these problems was the nature of material and logical necessity, in which the work of Georg von Wright, Jaakko Hintikka, Nicholas Rescher, Saul Kripke, and David Lewis has figured prominently. In short, then, contemporary analytic philosophy has let its inquiries be dictated by the available means rather than the original ends.

In spite of the positivists' errant ways, Kuhn and the Popperians have managed to pick up the historical thread and continue the epistemological project into the present day. Although many Popperians would deny it, a constant reminder that this project is still about the social organization of knowledge is the frequent allusions to political theory that one finds in contemporary philosophy of science: Popper's self-styled "open society" vision of the scientific community marks him as a classical liberal, while Feyerabend's emphasis on the "open" and Lakatos' on the "society" aspects of the Popperian vision marks them as, respectively, an anarchist (or libertarian) and a social democrat. And Kuhn, with his talk of normal science being dominated by a single paradigm which can be replaced only by "revolution," is, by all accounts, a totalitarian. These ideological labels should not be taken as merely suggestive metaphors, but rather as literal statements of what the various "methodologies" become, once the epistemologist is transferred from the context of appraising already existent products of knowledge to the context of recommending the scheme by which knowledge ought to be produced (Krige 1980). Indeed, it would not be farfetched to say that, when done properly (that is, when done self-consciously as social epistemology), the philosophy of science is nothing other than the application of political philosophy to a segment of society, the class of scientists, who have special capacities and special status but also make special demands on each other and the rest of society in the course of conducting their activities.

Returning to the positivists, it is well known that their chief ideologue, Otto Neurath (1962), saw the Unified Science movement as, in part, a way of driving out the politically conservative and elitist tendencies of hermeneutical thinking in the "human sciences" (which defined the task of interpretation to be the situating of texts in a clearly defined tradition of readers and writers who saw themselves largely as communicating only with one another) and driving in the more radical and egalitarian, specifically Marxist, politics associated with a naturalistic approach of the "social sciences." Less well known is how Neurath's preoccupation with the status of "protocol statements," those fundamental building blocks of evidential warrant in the natural sciences, contributed to his overall project.

In light of what I have so far said about social epistemology, a clue to the desired link may be found in the work of the historian in residence at the Vienna Circle, Edgar Zilsel (1945), another Marxist who proposed that the decisive factor in the rise of the Scientific Revolution was a shift in the structure of cognitive authority, such that the pronouncements of the scholar class were now held accountable to experimental standards which throughout the Middle Ages had certified expertise in the artisan class. Being experimental standards, they were indexed for such publicly observable features as time and place, which served to open up the knowledge production process to people from all walks of life, even to those who were not trained in the reading of esoteric texts. This change had the effect of not only democratizing the very act of observation, but also of creating a system for efficiently sorting through the various speculations that had been advanced in the past. Neurath's concern with protocol statements, along with other positivist attempts at formulating a principle of verification, may perhaps be seen as raising to self-consciousness the values of *equality* (of the individual knowers) and *progress* (of the collective body of knowers) which were first asserted in the Scientific Revolution.

If, as I have been maintaining, all epistemology worthy of the name has been motivated by essentially sociological considerations, then my thesis should equally apply to the very attempts by epistemologists, such as Laudan, to *dispense* with the social character of knowledge. Our first exposure to these attempts was in terms of the arationality assumption. Underlying it is a distinction, popularized by the positivist Hans Reichenbach (1938), between a knowledge claim's "context of discovery" and its "context of justification" (sometimes called "context of validation"). By distinguishing these two contexts, epistemologists can dissolve the apparent paradox in saying, for instance, that given the appropriate tests, a belief in Newton's Laws could have been justified at any point in history, even though that fact could not itself have been known before Newton's time. On the other hand, by conflating these two contexts, sociologists fall victim to "the genetic fallacy," which leads them to say that the validity of Newton's Laws is, in some way, affected by their origins in seventeenth-century England. It is nowadays popular to soften the blow just dealt to the sociologist by arguing that the nature of the discovery/justification distinction is little more than verbal. Thus, "discovery" captures the novelty normally felt about the most recently justified claim in one's research program, while "justification" describes the logical status of the discovery, once divested of its psychological trappings (Nickles 1980). No doubt this is an astute observation, but it merely neutralizes the distinction without explaining how it too is sociologically motivated. Let us now turn to one such explanation.

As the above examples indicated, the discovery/justification distinction is normally invoked by epistemologists in order to prevent the sociologist from unduly restricting a knowledge claim's domain of validity: Newton's Laws were just as valid before Newton discovered them as afterward, and the fact that we are three centuries beyond Newton does not, in any way, diminish our justification for believing in his laws. The intuitive soundness of these claims rests on conceiving of justification as an idealized discovery procedure--in other words, as a sort of scientific competence that can be abstracted from historical performances of scientific reasoning. Once Newton's Laws are stripped of the socio-historical baggage that might make him hostile to them, even Aristotle could come to have a justified belief in them.

Now consider the epistemologist's strategy itself from a sociological viewpoint: How does it make a difference to the domain of *people* who are eligible to validate Newton's Laws? Taking our cue from Zilsel, the strategy clearly opens up the domain of eligible people by reducing the amount of esoteric knowledge required of the potential validator. In particular, he need not have participated in the cultural milieu of seventeenth-century England, which implies, among other things, that he need not bring to his observations the specialized training that only scientists living at that time would have. Instead, the potential validator would require skills--for example, the ability to perform certain calculations and to focus attention on certain phenomena--that any intelligent and interested human being could be taught at any time or place. Thus, one of the ways in which epistemologists have argued for the universal nature of validity claims is by appealing to the intuition that Galileo, say, could have convinced Aristotle that his account of local motion was in error by conducting free-fall experiments in his presence.

One consequence of regarding the discovery/justification distinction in this manner is that it turns out not to be as ideologically pernicious as philosophers and sociologists have often suggested. A source of the distinction's perniciousness was thought to be that the concept of justification presupposes a Whiggish, or absolutist, conception of epistemic change. After all, while it is clear that Galileo could convince Aristotle of some things, could Aristotle convince Galileo of anything? However, as we have seen, even if Aristotle's and Galileo's persuasive powers turn out to be asymmetrical, that has happened only after both have been limited to justification procedures that are, in principle, equally accessible to all intelligent individuals. In other words, this apparently absolutist end has been reached by strictly egalitarian means.

Even if all the preceding considerations have been enough to persuade you that epistemology is an inherently sociological activity, you may still wonder why epistemologists have been so hostile to the idea. My own diagnosis of the situation points to a rhetorical strategy that epistemologists regularly deploy--and sociologists unfortunately fall for. It involves treating cognitive pursuits and their social organization as if they were two independent entities and then asking how does knowing about the social organization of a particular cognitive pursuit *add* to our knowledge of the pursuit as a *cognitive* pursuit. Of course, the typical answer to this question is that it adds *nothing* to our knowledge of the pursuit as a cognitive pursuit, which leads the epistemologist to conclude that sociology is irrelevant to questions of epistemic status. The sociologist tacitly assents to this conclusion by concentrating his efforts on those features of cognitive pursuits which he himself recognizes as noncognitive. To get a clear sense of the fallaciousness of this strategy, compare the analogous, and historically more familiar, case of someone (perhaps a medieval scholastic) maintaining that knowledge of physiology is irrelevant for knowing about the human being as a *human* being. How would he show this? By arguing that since every creature has a physiology, there is nothing distinctively human about having a physiology, and, therefore, nothing about the humanness of human beings can be learned by studying their physiology.

What the arguments against sociology and physiology have in common may be described as either a logical fallacy or a rhetorical strategy. The logical fallacy they jointly commit is to confuse *the essential features of an object* with *the features that distinguish it from other objects*. As Duns Scotus would put it, the arguers have mixed matters of *quidditas* with matters of *haecceitas*. Most pointedly: several essentially different objects can share some of the same essential properties. The "essential differences" refer to distinctions in species of the shared essential properties. And so, just because human beings are not the only creatures with a physiology, it does not follow that human beings would be what they are without their physiology. Indeed, the science of taxonomy was founded on the idea that a sufficiently fine-grained understanding of physiology would enable one to make distinctions amongst the animal species so as to show that human beings have a unique physiology. Thus, rather than disqualifying them from being distinguishing properties, shared essential properties may provide the basis for making the relevant species distinctions. Likewise, just because cognitive pursuits are not the only activities that are socially organized, it does not follow that cognitive pursuits would be what they are without their social organization. Indeed, the sociology of knowledge was founded on the idea that a sufficiently fine-grained understanding of social organization would enable one to make distinctions among the various human pursuits so as to show that particular cognitive pursuits have unique patterns of organization.

As for the rhetorical strategy deployed by the opponents of sociology and physiology, I will call it, for lack of a better name, negative reification. It consists of a two-step move: (1) Q, the defining structural property of P, is distinguished from P and made into a separate entity; hence, the social organization of knowledge is distinguished from knowledge "as such," and the human physiology is distinguished from the human being "as such." This is the *reifying* move. (2) Even though Q has now been formally distinguished from P, the content of Q remains in P, thereby rendering Q devoid of content. This is the *negative* move. It leaves the impression that one can give an adequate account of knowledge or the human being without referring, respectively, to its social organization or its physiology. However, upon closer scrutiny, it can be shown that the allegedly unnecessary entity is covertly presupposed in the adequate account. Thus, in dualist accounts of the human being, the mind, which supposedly defines the human being as such, is characterized as having a paraphysiology of its own, namely, a system of interdependent functions which regulates the body. Likewise, as we saw when examining the context of justification which supposedly defines a cognitive pursuit as such, a parasociology is presupposed, namely, a normative account of the terms under which one is eligible to participate in the cognitive pursuit. Why hasn't negative reification been more often recognized for what it is? Largely because accounts of both the mind and the context of justification are never discussed with enough specificity to broach the issue of *instantiation*: When has one identified instances of mental activity? Of a justificatory context? Once these questions are raised, one is forced to introduce considerations of, respectively, physiology and sociology.

2.   Social Epistemology as the Pursuit of Scandal and Extravagance

With the founding of the Institute for Social Research at Frankfurt in the 1920s and the publication of Karl Mannheim's *Ideology and Utopia* in 1936, the sociology of knowledge was at first notorious for maintaining that the best way to inquire into the nature of knowledge is by questioning the motives (or "interests") of its producers. Whatever else one might want to say about this program, it was certainly meant as a radical critique and replacement of the epistemological enterprise, especially of its classical task of laying down interest-invariant foundations for knowledge.

Indeed, the sociology of knowledge was conceived as an irreducibly *normative* discipline, integrally tied to social policy-making (Mannheim 1940). Its central thesis was that the social acceptance of a knowledge claim always serves to benefit certain interest groups in the society and to disadvantage others. As a piece of knowledge policy, the implications were clear: if granting epistemic warrant involves, among other things, social acceptance, and a key benefit of being granted such a warrant is the power to make authoritative pronouncements, then *granting epistemic warrant is a covert form of distributing power*.

Putting aside, for the moment, the deliberateness with which this policy normally is (or even *can be*) carried out, the thesis appears most plausible when considering how disciplinary specialization (in law, medicine, business, and the sciences) has removed an increasing number of issues from public debate to the testimony of "experts." These disciplines exercise "power," in the sense that all epistemically warranted opinion in their respective domains requires their certification, which, in turn, forces the warrant-seeker either to undergo the arduous training of becoming such an expert or simply to conserve effort and defer to the experts already in place. Not surprisingly, then, the normative issue of most concern to these sociologists of knowledge, especially their most recent exemplar Habermas (1975), is how to prevent the republican ideal of "civic culture" from totally dissolving, in modern democracies, into a "mass culture" whose members uncritically submit to the authority of experts.

The original scandal created by the sociology of knowledge, then, was to claim that any answer to "What are the sources of knowledge?" presupposes an answer to "How should society be organized?" Classical epistemology appeared to be a viable pursuit precisely because there were thought to be certain knowledge claims whose social acceptance had equal benefit for all-- at least for all rational beings--and hence had no net effect on the distribution of power. This is simply a vivid way of expressing the "value-neutrality" of scientific knowledge: that is, while such knowledge may be *used* to promote a wide variety of values (as in the different policy ends to which economics may be applied), the knowledge itself is not biased toward or against the realization of any particular values. The source of the equality of benefit afforded by these privileged knowledge claims was the equality of access alleged of them--at least when reduced to the ultimate warrants for their assertion. Unlike such traditionally hermetic forms of knowledge as magic and cabalistic theology, the efficacy of natural and social scientific knowledge would seem not to rest on its access being restricted to only a few specially trained individuals; rather, access to the natural and social sciences has always been advertised as (in principle) open to anyone, since its epistemic warrants ultimately rested on the sorts of logical calculations and empirical observations that any rational individual, with a modicum of training, could perform. Indeed, in the revamped version of the classical position defended by Mill, Peirce, Dewey, and Popper, increasing the accessibility to the scientific process was thought to increase the quality of the knowledge produced, since it would increase the level of mutual criticism of knowledge claims, which would, in turn, increase the chance that creeping value biases would be purged from the process. And so, if a "cult of expertise" has developed in modern times, as the early sociologists of knowledge were inclined to think, then the classical epistemologist would interpret that simply as a case in which certain social interests (perhaps of the knowledge producers themselves, in the case of experts) have perverted for their own ends the natural development of knowledge, which promotes equality of benefit and access.

In its first incarnation, the sociology of knowledge remained little more than a scandal. It failed to launch a full-scale conceptual revolution--let alone undermine the project of classical epistemology--because of conceptual confusions at its own foundations. These confusions made knowledge production seem much too contrived, as if the dominant class interest could simply *dictate* what passes for knowledge in the society. After all, if granting epistemic warrant is indeed a covert form of distributing power, does it follow either that granting epistemic warrant *is identical with* distributing power or even that epistemic warrant is granted *in order to* distribute power? The former possibility can be read as a semantic thesis of the sort that emotivists typically make about ethical utterances, transferred to epistemological ones; the latter possibility can be read as describing the motives or intentions of those who grant epistemic warrant, which, in an extreme form, would constitute a conspiracy theory of knowledge. Neither of these possible conclusions necessarily follows from the premise, though the original sociologists of knowledge certainly made it seem otherwise. One omitted possibility is a more indirect and interesting conclusion, namely, that granting epistemic warrant simply *has the effect of* distributing power--thereby leaving open such questions as whether the groups benefitting from this distribution of power are the ones who were originally motivated to propose the particular knowledge claim, whether either the motivators or the benefitters are the ones who make the most use of the claim in proposing other knowledge claims, and so forth. A persuasive defense of this conclusion would be enough to undermine the project of classical epistemology as characterized above, since it would show that there is no method for granting epistemic warrant, including the methods of the natural and social sciences, which does not have an effect on the distribution of power in a society. Yet, at the same time, such a defense would not be forced to assume the extravagant thesis that knowledge is nothing but a myth that the powerful concoct to maintain their power.

At the source of the conceptual confusions that undermined the Old Wave sociology of knowledge was an equivocal reading of the claim that all knowledge is "value-laden" or "interest-laden." Three sorts of groups may be said to have an "interest" in the social acceptance of a knowledge claim:

(a) those who were motivated to propose the claim in the hope that they might benefit from its acceptance;

(b) those who actually benefit from the claim's acceptance;

(c) those who make use of the claim in the course of proposing other knowledge claims.

Let us call (a) *motivators*, (b) *benefitters*, and (c) *users*. The classical epistemologists erred in failing to see that, given the interest-ladenness of all knowledge claims, such groups always exist, and therefore must be taken into account by any normative theory of knowledge production. However, the early sociologists of knowledge were extravagant to suppose that in many (perhaps most) cases of knowledge production, the motivators, benefitters, and users are the same group. If that were the case, then not only would the production of knowledge be reduced to the dissemination of ideology, but the dissemination would prove to be incredibly effective; for the original ideologues would then be shown to have tight enough control over the use of their ideology that only they and their allies benefit.

This piece of extravagance has been revealed by the current crop of empirically-minded sociologists of knowledge to be little more than a rhetorical illusion. The New Wavers (Latour & Woolgar 1979, Knorr-Cetina 1981, Gilbert & Mulkay 1984, Collins 1985), who describe themselves as "social constructivists" or "anthropologists of knowledge cultures," argue that all previous inquiries into the nature of knowledge production--both philosophical and sociological--have erred in concluding that there must be some sort of tight control on the use of knowledge simply because the practitioners of a particular discipline justify their knowledge claims in similar ways (by drawing on the same body of knowledge, employing the same inferential techniques, and so forth). Stated this baldly, the naivete is clear: Why should it be presumed that an account of knowledge production, as might appear in a book or a journal article, represents how knowledge is *actually* produced? After all, the diagnostic tools available to manuscript referees are fairly limited and rarely extend to a comprehensive testing of the knowledge claim under review. Not surprisingly, then, knowledge producers tend to take care in gathering evidence and testing claims only in proportion to the likelihood that the referees will check them. Moreover, an essential part of what makes an account of knowledge production something more than a report of the author's beliefs is that it describes *what ought to have happened,* given the avowed norms of the discipline. Even mistakes and accidents must be accounted for in the right way. Thus, the process by which knowledge is typically disseminated and integrated serves to insure a uniformity in the expression and justification of claims without insuring a similar uniformity in the activities leading up to these moments of textualization.

However, one can be more or less naive about the relation of words to deeds in knowledge production. More naive is the classical epistemologist, who takes the expressed justifications literally as referring to a common method with a track record of getting at an extrasocial reality. A little more astute were the original sociologists of knowledge, who nevertheless continued to think that behind similar forms of expression must lie similar forms of constraint, even if they turn out to be nothing more than the ideological force exerted by a discipline's dominant interest group. To counteract this naive spirit of determinism, the New Wave sociologists like to say that knowledge production is "contingent" or "context-dependent" or "open-ended." Unfortunately, these expressions mask rather than remedy the shortcomings of the earlier accounts, especially that of the Old Wavers. In particular, each of these expressions can imply either

(i) that no knowledge producer can fully predict and/or control how his research will be used by others in their research, or

(ii) that any knowledge producer is relatively free to tailor other knowledge claims to his specific research situation.

The error that the New Wavers make is to interpret (i) as if it were conclusive evidence for (ii), which only serves to make knowledge production seem, once again, too much under the direct control of the producers—the twist being that instead of knowledge production being determined by large corporate wills such as disciplines and other interest groups, it is now said to be determined by somewhat smaller corporate wills such as research teams and even individuals; hence, extravagance returns through the back door.

Sometimes the sociologists (Bloor 1983, ch. 6) try to mitigate these extravagant claims of scientific self-determination by saying that the norms of scientific practice function as a tacit civil code. In that case, the freedom attributed to the scientist in (ii) is constrained by the fact that there are only a certain number of legal ways in which he can appropriate knowledge for his own research. But even this legalistic gloss does not impose quite the right sense of "constraint" on the scientist's activities, since it continues to allow for a charlatan to be successful at the science game. In other words, it is still possible for someone to bring about whatever effect he wishes on the scientific audience by couching his claims in a legally prescribed manner. However, another feature of the legal analogy can be used to block the charlatan's success, namely, that while a law regulates some social activities, one activity that it does not regulate is its own application. Likewise, the would-be charlatan may know all the scientific norms without thereby knowing which are the appropriate ones to apply in his case: to know the right *things* to say is not necessarily to know the right *times* to say them. For example, he may competently write up a (fraudulent) experiment which purports to disconfirm some standing hypothesis, but if other members of the scientific community are writing up (genuine) experiments which provide support for the hypothesis, then the charlatan's ruse will probably either be ignored or suspected (as would any other deviant claim) and perhaps subsequently unmasked. This uncertainty about how norms are to be applied in future cases have led followers of Wittgenstein to speak of the "open-textured" nature of language games. It is an uncertainty that is grounded on the inability of any given social agent to dictate the manner in which his fellow agents will conform to the existing norms; hence, the invalidity of inferring the benefitters from the motivators. Notice also that throughout this discussion, the constraints and ultimate failure of the scientific charlatan have been explained entirely in sociological terms, such that he is undermined primarily because he is unable to track the cognitive movements of his colleagues and only secondarily because his experiments are actually fraudulent.

What we have just attempted here is a *sociological simulation* of the classical epistemic ideal of objectivity. It goes some of the way toward answering scientific realists such as Boyd (1984) who argue that the best explanation for the "success" of science is its access to extrasocial, "objective" reality. In contrast, the method of sociological simulation rests on the assumption that objectivity and the other virtues of knowledge production can be *exhaustively* explained by sociological principles. Notice that this position is the exact mirror image of scientific realism: on the one hand, scientific realism typically does not deny the social rootedness of knowledge claims, only the relevance of that fact to an explanation of the truth or falsity of those claims; on the other hand, sociological simulation need not deny the "real" truth or falsity of knowledge claims, only the relevance of that fact to an explanation of the social rootedness of those claims. The point of contention between the two sides concerns whether claims that exemplify epistemic virtues such as objectivity are best explained as "truth-enhancers" or as "institution-maintainers."

The relevant test case for the scientific realist and the sociological simulator is a situation, perhaps a thought experiment, in which a culture accepts a knowledge claim that we take to be substantially correct but for reasons, or through a method, that we consider highly suspect. In other words, by our lights, the culture has stumbled upon the truth "by accident." A good example here would be the ancient atomist belief in a principle of inertia. Needless to say, Democritus never conducted anything like Galileo's experiments, but his metaphysical picture was conducive, in many respects, to thinking along "proto-Galilean" lines. However, as far as we know, the atomists did not try to verify experimentally their metaphysics, and indeed, given their basic beliefs about the radical contingency of nature, they probably would have balked at the very idea of conducting such experiments.

Scientific realists like to point to examples like this, where a culture gets it right "in spite of itself," as simultaneously illustrating that our inquiries are, in some way or other, directed at fathoming the one reality which we all inhabit and that inquirers fathom that reality with varying degrees of success. The sociological simulator would challenge this conclusion by questioning whether it would be possible to convince the atomists to conduct experiments and thereby get it right by "the appropriate means." For if it turns out that the atomists cannot be so persuaded, then their social practices—especially, the pursuit of pure speculation—will have been shown essential to their belief in an inertia principle, which, in turn, casts doubt on whether it really is like the principle that we endorse.

The realist normally is thought to have the upper hand in the debate because the more cross-culturally and cross-temporally accepted a knowledge claim is, the more difficulty the sociologist has in explaining it simply in terms of the claim's rootedness in several, otherwise quite different, social environments. However, the case of the scientific charlatan shows that the realist's dialectical advantage can be undercut, if the sociologist admits that neither the motivators nor the benefitters of a knowledge claim—nor even the two groups combined—have full control over how the claim is used. In other words, the three sorts of interest groups identified earlier overlap much less than either the Old or New Wave sociologists have been inclined to think. Given a wide enough expanse of history, examples are plentiful. Consider the fate of intelligence testing since 1895. Starting with Binet, the motivators in French pedagogy treated the tests only as diagnostic tools for identifying students in need of remedial education. The users have since included the whole gamut of philosophers of science and social science methodologists who have looked to the tests as evidence for the scientific status of psychology. And since the tests were introduced into Anglo-American psychology through Spearman, the benefitters have ironically been those who believe that IQ refers to an innate intelligence capacity that can be little changed by education (Gould 1983). Therefore, the best sociological explanation for the objectivity of intelligence testing is its versatility in contexts quite unanticipated and even unintended by its originators.

Interestingly, an early step in the direction toward sociological simulation was taken when Popper (1972) introduced World Three, the realm of objective knowledge, whose independent existence emerged as an unanticipated (and usually unintended) consequence of later theorizing about cognitive instruments, such as counting systems, which were originally designed for quite specific practical purposes. For example, the ancients may have developed the study of mathematics in the course of trying to simplify the many measurement tasks performed in everyday life. A general strategy emerged to separate formally the measuring instruments from the measurable things, which led to the invention of a system for representing the natural numbers and, subsequently, to the discovery of properties that the system has independently of how it is used. These properties became the source of problems, such as the nature of irrational numbers, which were sufficiently distant from matters of applied arithmetic to constitute an autonomous domain of knowledge. Yet, at the same time, since this autonomous domain was still thought to underlie all measuring tasks, mathematical experts gained the power to certify the competence of engineers and other professional measurers. At this point, the simulation ends, as the sociologist of knowledge reappears to examine the specific institutional and rhetorical means by which mathematics has maintained this *power* over the years, which, as Bacon would have it, is expressed as *knowledge* of the underlying structure, or "essence," of a widespread social practice like measuring.

The above discussion suggests the following division of explanatory labor between the *psychology* and *sociology* of knowledge. Psychology enters to study the cognitive limitations on one's ability to anticipate the long term consequences following from one's own interactions and artifact productions, as well as to backtrack those consequences once they have occurred. These limitations are the hidden *liability* behind the mind's *capacity* to "economize," that is, to condense and stereotype information so that less of it needs to be stored. We shall later return to this theme. The various performance errors in memory, reasoning, and attribution identified by cognitive psychologists in the laboratory (Nisbett & Ross 1980) can serve as the basis for these studies, keeping in mind that outside the lab the "errors" are rarely caught once they are committed and may be socially rationalized through reifications, such as Popper's World Three. The significance of such cognitive limitations will vary according to the number of individuals and groups whose activities have causal relevance for one another, their distance in time and space from each other, and the technology available for circulating the relevant cognitive artifacts, especially texts. And it is the sociologist's task to study these variables. However, this division of labor is easier said than done, as we shall see in the next section.

3. Nonnormative Social Epistemology and Other Accommodating Banalities

The New Wave sociology of knowledge has not only inherited the scandalous ways of the Old Wavers, but it has also had its brush with banality. The banality comes from recent attempts, within both sociology and philosophy, to divest epistemology of any normative force. Sociologists have long suspected that philosophical talk about how knowledge "ought" to be produced is motivated by a desire to speak with an authority that lies beyond the check of the empirical disciplines. To safeguard against empirical critique, philosophers since Plato and Descartes have typically supplemented their accounts of the idealized rational knower with a story about how he is continually undermined by his own deep-seated passions (Dawes 1976). The same move can be detected in post-Popperian philosophy of science, with Lakatos blaming the actual scientists of the past for being so swayed by special interests and mob psychology that they rarely conform to his rationally reconstructed history. As the sociologists see it, the philosophers have cleverly turned a weakness into a strength: instead of taking the empirical remoteness of the philosophical ideal to mean that the ideal is false, philosophers take it to mean that real knowers are prevented from realizing the ideal by some part of their psychology which they have yet to discipline properly. Thus, the more remote the ideal, the greater the need for Method (capitalized to indicate its epistemically privileged status). And the greater the need for Method, the greater the authority of philosophers, the experts on Method. As these remarks suggest, the banal response to this philosophical ruse is to treat normative epistemology, at best, as an expression of sour grapes that knowledge is not produced as the philosopher would like or, at worst, as an excuse for the philosopher to ignore altogether empirical inquiries into the nature of knowledge production. In both cases, the prescription is clear: the epistemologist should end his normative ways and thereby dissolve the boundaries that currently exist between his work and that of the historian, psychologist, and sociologist.

The philosophical route to banality is quite different in that it portrays the epistemologist as more deceived than deceiver. The *locus classicus* is Quine's (1969, ch. 3) "Epistemology Naturalized," though Rorty's (1979) *Philosophy and the Mirror of Nature* has probably done the most to popularize this picture. The basic idea is that when philosophers from Descartes to Kant proposed a general Method for "justifying" knowledge claims, they were confusing two rather different enterprises: on the one hand, there is the issue of *legitimating* knowledge claims, which is decided by the conventions of a particular culture and will depend on the interests that the culture has in acquiring knowledge; on the other hand, there is the issue of *explaining* knowledge claims, which involves studying their causal origins, a task that Quine, for one, takes to be within the strict purview of behavioral psychology and neurophysiology. By dividing the labor of justification in this manner, the need for a special discipline of epistemology is eliminated: legitimation is best handled by the humanistic disciplines traditionally devoted to cultural criticism, while explanation is a task for which the natural sciences and their emulators in the social studies are best suited. Moreover, once justification has been so divided, the deepest epistemological problem is conquered. This problem, according to Quine and Rorty, is how to account for our ability to generate an indefinite number of theories from the impoverished evidence base afforded by our senses. The twofold way to a solution is, first, to treat how one gets from the evidence to *at least one* theory as a matter of psychological explanation, and then, to treat how one gets from many theories to *only one* as a matter of cultural legitimation. In neither case is there any need for someone equipped with a universally applicable normative theory of knowledge.

There are several problems with these retreats to banality and the spirit of interdisciplinary accommodation that they breed. First of all, the most that either the sociologists or the philosophers have shown is that the methods by which epistemologists justify knowledge claims are not uniquely theirs, though epistemological discourse does its best to obscure any resemblance to the methods of the special disciplines. Suppose *no* case for methodological uniqueness could be made. It still would not follow that epistemologists are not in a particularly good position to make normative judgments about knowledge claims. After all, to speak of "the division of cognitive labor" is to talk not only about differences in the *techniques* used by the laborers but also about differences in the *materials* to which they apply those techniques. And so, even if the secret of the epistemologist's success amounts to nothing more than an idiosyncratic application of the same deductive and inductive canons used by scientists and humanists, the epistemologist would remain distinctive in that he attends to the interrelations among the knowledge claims made by the special disciplines, while scientists and humanists are restricted to the operations of their own disciplines. Another way of making the same point, which echoes themes raised both earlier and later in this chapter, is to say that the critics of normative epistemology have a blurred image of the two strands of positivism which have defined the problem of knowledge since the early nineteenth century: on the one hand, the critics recognize the logical positivist strand and its emphasis on the unity of method, which reduces the task of epistemology to the sort of conceptual housecleaning that practitioners of the special sciences could themselves do, were they not occupied with more important empirical assignments; on the other hand, the critics neglect the Comtean strand and its emphasis on philosophy's unique role of applying the scientific method to the sciences themselves for the purpose of regulating their development.

Still skeptical of the epistemologist's normative powers, the critics may wonder why the special disciplines cannot simply regulate their own activities. Indeed, this laissez-faire attitude is shared by both naturalistically inclined philosophers of science (Laudan 1981) and sociologically inclined critics of epistemology (Bloor 1981), who would normally find themselves at loggerheads. The attitude comes through most clearly in what would seem to be an innocently "pluralistic," even "ecumenical," attitude that the likes of Laudan and Bloor have toward the inclusion of history, psychology, and sociology in any naturalistic theory of knowledge. Presumably, they believe that the philosopher can learn much of value from empirical approaches to knowledge. However, they do not seem to notice that the knowledge claims made by these empirical disciplines are not obviously compatible with one another. Indeed, some of the more interesting claims may be incompatible in a way--call it "incommensurable" if you will--that does not suggest any easy resolution *within* a particular discipline. As prima facie evidence for this incommensurability, consider that, from examining the citation patterns in their relevant literatures, one would be forced to conclude that psychologists and sociologists of science seldom draw on each other's work, even though they are normally lumped together as part of the "science studies" disciplinary cluster (a limited exception is De Mey [1982]). Upon further consideration, this finding should not come as a surprise, since all that ultimately unites the practitioners of "science studies" is a common whipping boy, namely, classical epistemology. Consequently, they have not devoted much effort to challenging each other's claims. Let us now, then, turn to some latent points of confrontation as a means of showing that there is still room for the sort of normative-yet-naturalistic epistemology envisioned by Comte.

One key point of confrontation concerns the degree of *psychologism* that needs to be incorporated in a sociological account of scientific activity. In general, a sociologist is "antipsychologistic" if his account of social interaction does not require that social agents have any private mental contents, such as particular desires or beliefs, distinct from their publicly defined role-expectations. In that case, among sociologists of science, the Edinburgh School (Barnes 1977, Shapin 1982) must be counted as amenable to psychologism, since it typically postulates that social agents have relatively well-defined "interests" which they try to promote by manipulating the course of certain legitimating institutions, such as science. Consequently, the Edinburgh School has tended to present scientific debates as a "superstructure" whose "infrastructure" consists of competing political, economic, and/or cultural interests.

In contrast, the strongest case of antipsychologism may be found among the social constructivists. On their view, derived in part from Wittgenstein and Foucault, an agent's mental contents are themselves socially constructed through institutionalized mechanisms of attribution. If social agents have a specific "interest" on this view, it is simply the interest in maintaining or enhancing one's position in the scientific game; hence, the emphasis that the social constructivists place on the persuasive elements of scientific texts. Indeed, the social constructivists break with both the Old Wave Frankfurt School and the New Wave Edinburgh School in maintaining that the production of scientific knowledge does *not* function primarily as an arena for competing special interests; rather, they believe that "there is no ultimate objective to scientific investment other than the continual redeployment of accumulated resources." (Latour & Woolgar 1979, p. 198) As we shall subsequently see, the capitalist model of knowledge production provides a new slant on the idea that knowledge is pursued "as an end in itself."

Moving from psychologism to psychology, precedent may be found in the history of social psychology (especially in Gestalt and attribution theory) for the incorporation of sociological research. These efforts have focused on the finding that, in an experimental situation open to many interpretations, the presence of several people can enforce closure on how a subject perceives or reasons about it. If we then take "antisociologism" to mean an account of the individual mind that does not include a mechanism for registering the effects that the presence of others might have on his beliefs, desires, or course of action, then the psychology of science experiments conducted in the Tversky and Kahneman (1981) paradigm, which currently dominates the discipline, would have to be called antisociologistic. These experiments (see Tweney, Doherty & Mynatt 1982) typically show that real scientists do not implicitly reason about evidence, hypothesis selection, and so forth according to some norm explicitly upheld by both philosophers of science and the scientific community. The psychologists in this paradigm sometimes codify the implicit reasoning procedures but rarely explain why they diverge so greatly--and so systematically--from the explicit norm. The nearest that they come to a general explanatory principle for the errors is to show that subjects' responses are sensitive to the protocols in which the experimenter frames the problem: frame the same problem in two different ways, and you get two different responses. Not surprisingly, then, scientists are most likely to reason according to the explicit norm when they are asked to solve a problem framed in the "canonical form" usually found in textbooks. This would seem to open the door to some sort of sociologism, perhaps pointing toward the psychological limits of disciplinary socialization: At what point do experimental protocols countervail scientific training in determining the scientist's response? However, antisociologism dies hard among the psychologists of science, who tend to believe that the errors are built into the individual's cognitive mechanism. The result is a picture of human beings as inherently defective computers who, at least when doing science, are subject to external validation checks (Faust 1985).

Interdisciplinary infiltration aside, the incompatibility of psychologism and sociologism also emerges in the form of rival historical hypotheses about the origin and maintenance of disciplines. Though it has been customary to treat disciplines as the point of contact between "the social" and "the cognitive" (roughly, the moment when methodology becomes institutionalized), the most common strategy for explaining their presence has been broadly psychologistic. To get a sense of the difference between a psychologistic and a sociologistic approach (whose exemplar is Foucault) to the history of disciplines, consider the following alternative hypotheses for the rise of biology as a special science in the nineteenth century:

> (d) *Historical Psychologism*--Biology began essentially as an ideological movement by a group of individuals, call them "vitalists," who shared an interest in gaining social recognition for their belief that the phenomena of life could not be exhaustively studied by the methods of the physical sciences.

> (e) *Historical Sociologism*--Biology began essentially as an "opportunity structure," namely, a collection of procedures for observing, describing, and organizing (both people and things) that had proved effective in quite disparate domains but were now made available for use as an ensemble. Individuals with different, and perhaps even radically opposed, agendas realized that it was in their own interest to contest their claims in a forum bound by these procedures.

Given these alternatives, the received wisdom in both the history and the philosophy of science would recommend hypothesis (d). After examining why in each case, we shall consider the change in strategy that an acceptance of (e) would involve.

While the historian would not have a principled reason for preferring (d), it is clear that histories of science tend to have (d)-like scenarios. Take the issue of interdisciplinary borrowing, as in the case of a physicist or economist making use of some mathematical technique. Arguably, a history of conceptual breakthroughs would be exhausted by a history of interdisciplinary borrowing. However, historians frequently understate the importance of such borrowing by focusing on the fact, say, that the mathematical technique contributed significantly to the solution of the physicist's problem rather than on the fact that the physicist had to refashion his problem in order to take advantage of the mathematical technique. Casting the borrowing episode in the former light makes the history of science seem dictated by the intentions of the individual scientist, while casting the episode in the latter light makes the scientist appear constrained by the available resources. And while many histories of science have been written of the successes or failures of scientists' projects, few have considered the extent to which opportunity structures have or have not been utilized.

Philosophers have a characteristically principled reason for preferring a (d)-like to an (e)-like history of disciplines. It turns on a commonly held view about the goal of knowledge production, an issue about which we shall have more to say later. But for now, we need only to attend to the rudiments of this view, namely, that knowledge producers first stake out a domain about which they make claims, which they then test with special procedures to arrive at truths about the domain. Even in this simple account, a psychology is imputed to the knowledge producer which, in turn, tends to favor a psychologistic reading of his activities. The crux of this psychological account is that *theory formation precedes method selection*. Without such an account, it would be difficult to see the motivation for the dispute between realists and verificationists in epistemology. The plausibility of realism rests, in large part, on the alleged psychological fact that we make claims which we believe are true or false, even though we have no way of determining which value. Presumably, according to (d), such claims are often made in the early days of a discipline, when the group has certain beliefs about a domain but no commonly accepted means of testing them. Likewise, verificationism makes sense as an *antidote* to realism insofar as people do indeed tend to theorize first and choose methods later; for then, the verificationist wants to show that the theory becomes cognitively significant (and hence its claims acquire truth values) only once a method has been selected for testing it. In contrast, an (e)-like historiography of science turns the preceding psychological account on its head: domains and theories about them--the very contents of disciplines--are constructed ex post facto to justify the appropriation and successful deployment of certain techniques by a body of individuals (Abir-Am 1985).

So far we have looked at some instances within the history, psychology, and sociology of science which indicate interdisciplinary incompatibility. However, inside the philosopher's own camp, there have also been *epistemological* forms of psychologism and sociologism. Here the incompatibility is overlooked, not out of a spirit of ecumenicity, but simply because there have been no clear rules for conducting philosophical arguments about the regulative ideals of knowledge production, the category under which these forms of psychologism and sociologism normally fall. "Regulative ideal," of course, is a Kantian term for what, in this case, is better called a "cognitive utopia," the optimal social organization of knowledge production--the chief aim of social epistemology. If we use "Truth" as a placeholder for whatever is taken to be the goal of producing knowledge, then the psychologistic and sociologistic utopias, modeled on

Kant and Popper, respectively, may be distinguished in the following manner:

> (f) *Epistemological Psychologism*--The best way for the knowledge process to produce Truth requires that all producers share the same attitude toward the process, namely, they should all intend to produce Truth.

> (g) *Epistemological Sociologism*--The best way for the knowledge process to produce Truth does not require that all producers share the same attitude toward the process, but rather that they evaluate each other's products in the same way.

One reason that the expression "knowledge claim" has been appearing where "belief" normally does is to remain neutral between (f) and (g) as to what the knowledge process is supposed to produce. Putting aside accounts of belief as a disposition to act in a certain way, the production of justified (or reliable) true belief is normally taken to involve a change in the producer's psychology (Goldman 1986). In contrast, a knowledge claim may be regarded psychologistically as the outward expression of an attitude or sociologistically as a move in a language game which may be defended or defeated in certain publicly observed ways. The reader may also notice a resemblance between how the distinction between (f) and (g) has been drawn and how the distinction between the contexts of discovery and justification is normally drawn. In the most general terms, psychologism, like the context of discovery, involves evaluating the frame of mind which the producer brings to the knowledge process, while sociologism, like the context of justification, involves evaluating the consequences of the knowledge process--the actual knowledge products--regardless of the producers' frame of mind. As Durkheim (1938) was the first to realize in his debates with Tarde and LeBon, sociologism had to be distinguished from psychologism in this way in order to prevent sociologism from becoming nothing more than psychologism on a mass scale. To get a sense of the deep-seated differences suggested here between (f) and (g), let us look at how both would respond if the Edinburgh School turned out to be correct in claiming that the knowledge production process is little more than an arena for competing interests.

A proponent of (f) would expect the production of Truth to be thereby arrested, since the individuals are intending Truth only insofar as it serves their particular interests. In order to make the knowledge production process more "productive," the proponent of (f) would have the individual producers aim for the Truth regardless of its social consequences for them or their fellows. This would entail *truly* asserting one's own beliefs in the hope that they are *true* (and treating everyone else's assertions in the same way). One can readily see a role for Method in putting the knowledge producer in the right frame of mind for the arduous task of truly asserting the truth. In contrast, the proponent of (g) is not nearly so Method-conscious, largely because he does not believe that the production of Truth is especially aided by the producers having a special attitude toward the knowledge process, such as "intending to produce Truth." Consequently, the proponent of (g) is more sanguine about the Edinburgh thesis, believing that as the knowledge producers try to maximize their own interests, they will try to undercut each other's claims in the most publicly acceptable way possible--namely, by appeals pertaining to the production of Truth--so as to cover up the fact that their criticisms are motivated exclusively by self-interest. If this process continues long enough, it will be the basis of an "invisible hand" or "cunning of reason" explanation for how the Truth can ultimately be produced by a collection of individuals whose main interests have little to do with producing Truth. Moreover, this explanation is sociologistic in that the individuals are rendered unwitting producers of Truth because the means by which they pursue their interests is dictated by the need to obtain a favorable response from their fellows.

4.   Social Epistemology Rendered Normative and Epistemology Rendered Interesting

Following the example of ethics, there are two standpoints from which one can make normative judgments:

(m) before someone acts, so as to *direct* his action;

or

(n) after someone acts, so as to *evaluate* his action.

The New Wave sociological critique of epistemological practice assumes that philosophers make normative judgments only in sense (n), namely, as critics of an activity in which they themselves do not participate. However, philosophers can equally be read as speaking normatively in sense (m), which would show that, like the original sociologists of knowledge, they follow Marx's dictum that not only must they interpret the world but they must change it as well. Indeed, the truth of the matter may well be that normative judgments in sense (n) about *past* knowledge production are meant as the basis for issuing normative judgments in sense (m) about *future* knowledge production.

Still, we need to give the philosopher's propensity for idealization *some* sociological credibility. A good strategy here may be to treat idealization as an elliptical form of social engineering. The ultimate source of this strategy is Francis Bacon, though its twentieth-century exemplar has been Gaston Bachelard's (1985) theory of scientific experimentation, several versions of which persist to this day (including von Wright [1971], Bhaskar [1980], Hacking [1983], Heelan [1983], and Apel [1984]). The basic idea is this: if we go by ordinary observation alone, nature does not appear to have a lawlike character. What we need to do, then, is to create an environment in which this lawlike character can be exhibited on demand. The instructions for creating such an environment, which are normally left implicit in a law's *ceteris paribus* clause, consist of social practices that would probably have no place outside this context. For example, the social space needed for demonstrating the law of inertia nowadays requires that observations be taken of objects moving in a frictionless medium in a laboratory. As a rule, the social constructivist would want to say that when a scientist claims that some melange of phenomena is "essentially" governed by a particular natural law, all the scientist means is that he knows how to constrain the environment so as to make the phenomena behave in a regular manner. Indeed, attempts have been made (Rip 1982, Whitley 1986) to define disciplines according to the sorts of constraints they require, and perhaps many of the difficulties involved with integrating research from the social sciences are due to these disciplines operating with incompatible constraints (for more on this point, see ch. 8). And so, when philosophers speak of the ideal rational knower, they too may be suggesting that our judgments of knowledge production should be taken in a more restricted social setting, with the philosopher's preferred Method functioning as partial instructions for creating that setting. Thus, we should take seriously as a step toward ideal rationality Descartes' remark, early in the *Meditations*, that his Method cannot be implemented until after one has withdrawn from normal social intercourse.

The only problem with interpreting the epistemologist's normative judgments in this way is that they provide only *partial* instructions. The other part of the instructions, involving the rhetorical, technological, and generally administrative means by which the epistemologist causes his Method to be followed, has rarely been a topic of philosophical discussion. The most immediate sign of this failure has been the lack of interest that epistemologists have generally had in issues of *education* (Dewey being the obvious exception). Instead, the epistemologist has all too often presumed (though some, like Descartes, have been explicit) that his Method is "self-certifying," which is to say, that, if presented with the Method, all rational beings would recognize it for what it is and follow it. This presumption would seem to be enough to convict the epistemologist, at least in the sociologist's eyes, of both arrogance and naivete. However, the epistemologist may try to vindicate himself by arguing that the sociologist has missed the point of his idealizations being clothed in counterfactuals rather than directives, namely, that his interest is restricted to *thought experiments,* cases of methodical abstraction whose validity does not rest on their empirical realizability and, therefore, does not require that the social environment be restructured in any significant way. But even a response of this sort need not satisfy the sociologist, who can always subject the epistemologist to what I shall call *the constructivist's regress,* namely, that as long as there are no self-certifying Methods, and even if what is at stake is simply the conceptual necessity of the outcome to a thought experiment, there will always be a difference between *the epistemologist's Method* and *the means by which the Method's acceptance is brought about,* with the latter requiring some transformation of the social environment--even if only at the level of selecting language that will be persuasive to the intended audience.

Having recovered the normative and social element for the epistemologist, amidst the suspicions of the sociologist, let us now make sure that the naturalistic element remains. Once it is granted that the philosopher makes normative judgments in sense (n), we can then question how those judgments work. Consider two possibilities:

(n1) Every case of knowledge production is evaluated against the best possible case of knowledge production.

(n2) Every case of knowledge production is evaluated as if it were the best possible case of knowledge production.

Given its concern with constructing a method for reaching optimal knowledge production, epistemology has traditionally been normative in sense (n1). However, given what the sociologists have shown to be the suspect motives and inadequate means for following through on (n1), epistemologists might turn to being normative in sense (n2) and thereby practice *panglossian epistemology,* after the character in Voltaire's *Candide* who believed that "this is the best of all possible worlds." The idea would be for the epistemologist to treat what he would normally regard as "interference" in the smooth working of the knowledge production process (fraud, misunderstanding, and other errors) as indicating merely that he has yet to fathom where such "stray parts" fit in the process (Dennett 1971).

In focussing on knowledge as it is actually produced, I do not mean to suggest that the panglossian epistemologist should base his account simply on a snapshot of current practices. Rather, he should identify the historically invariant and regularly varying features of knowledge production which would lead someone to think that it was the sort of thing—a "process" or "system"—to which one may reasonably attribute an overall design. And so, a question in the panglossian vein would be, "Why would the process be designed so that knowledge producers usually explain their success in terms of a particular methodology, even though they rarely do anything rigorous enough to be described as conforming to that methodology?" On the panglossian view, one could grade the adequacy of a classical epistemology by how much of the actual knowledge production process turns out to be dysfunctional in relation to its idealized method. Whereas the classical epistemologist himself would expect a certain amount of dysfunctionality, the best epistemology would now be the one that finds nothing dysfunctional about the process.

At this point, instead of getting excited by our proposal, the classical epistemologist might argue that he too has taken a design stance toward knowledge production, the only difference being that he does not presume that the process is always (or perhaps ever) in perfect working order. Indeed, by presuming that the process is optimally functioning, the panglossian epistemologist seems to commit the naturalistic fallacy, since he not only infers from how knowledge production *is* to how it *ought to be,* but actually *equates* the two. This objection would, thus, charge the panglossian with an embarrassing amount of naivete. In countering the objection, let us start by considering two ways in which an epistemologist might take a design stance toward knowledge production:

(p) Assuming that he already knows the purpose of producing knowledge, he can then determine how and whether the parts of the knowledge production process function to realize that purpose.

(q) Assuming that he already knows that the parts of the knowledge production process function optimally to realize some purpose, he can then determine what that purpose could and could not be.

The classical epistemologist goes the way of (p), which explains his concern for "truth-enhancing methodologies": truth is the goal and (the epistemologist's) method is the means which may or may not be operating in actual cases of knowledge production. But in light of the difference between (p) and (q), how is the classical epistemologist able to assume that he knows the point of producing knowledge, especially since he is the first to admit that there have been few cases of optimal knowledge production? The answer normally given, of course, is that *by definition* knowledge is methodologically sound access to the truth. Consequently, if the classical epistemologist were to learn that most of what passes for "knowledge" was not produced in what he would consider a methodologically sound manner, he would withdraw use of the term in those cases rather than change the definition of knowledge to capture something else that the cases have in common.

Now, if the panglossian claimed to know the point of producing knowledge in the way that the classical epistemologist does, then he would truly be naive; for he would then be denying what both the classical epistemologist and the sociologist of knowledge readily admit, namely, that there are major discrepancies between philosophical idealizations of knowledge production and the actual cases. However, the panglossian takes a design stance, in sense (q), toward knowledge production. It follows that the knowledge production process works optimally toward some end, but it is a matter of *empirical* determination what that end is: What sorts of goals can be realized given the actual structural constraints on knowledge production? On this view, it may simply be a matter of empirical fact that actual knowledge production processes lack any clear indicators for such qualities as retention, accumulation, and convergence, which philosophers of science since Charles Sanders Peirce (Rescher 1978) have associated with the alleged point of knowledge production, progress toward the Truth. (A stronger conclusion would show the unfeasibility of instituting the appropriate indicators.)

The idea that the trinity of retention, accumulation, and convergence might constitute yet another philosophical mythology seems farfetched until we start examining its foundations. All three Peircean qualities draw on the idea that knowledge is not merely transmitted, in a loose sense, from person to person but that some invariant content is preserved in the course of each successful transmission. The task of analytic philosophy in the twentieth century has largely been to arrive at a theory of this stricter sense of transmission, or *translation*. Yet, the historical record reveals only a series of controversial attempts to define the nature of translation in terms of what makes two sentences "synonymous" or "express the same proposition." And, no doubt, much of the inconclusiveness of this enterprise has been due to the lack of "real world" exemplars for any stricter sense of knowledge transmission, outside the standard cases of truth-functional equivalence in formal logic. On the basis of this record, the panglossian epistemologist concludes that whatever may be the point of knowledge production, it does not need to involve an activity as illusory as the analytic philosopher's sense of translation.

As a result, the panglossian is skeptical of two images of the knowledge product that presuppose a strong sense of translatability. First, he doubts that knowledge can be regarded as a storehouse whose contents are expanded and contracted at appropriate moments. This picture often informs the view that unequivocal judgments can be made about the relative size of two bodies of knowledge, and it is central to the belief that knowledge is essentially cumulative. The logical conception of translation assumed by the storehouse picture becomes especially clear in attempts to render scientific revolutions "rational." For example, Isaac Levi (1984) has argued that in the course of such revolutions, the knowledge base must contract before expanding, and not vice versa, because were a revolution to start by expanding the knowledge base, a contradiction would be harbored. The "must" in the argument seems to be invested with transcendental status--at least if the history of science is to be rendered rational. Thus, we should expect that the parts of Aristotelian physics in potential contradiction with Newtonian mechanics were fully excised from the early eighteenth-century knowledge base before Newtonian physics was added. But clearly this was not the case historically. This implies that the same knowledge production process can incorporate incompatible bodies of knowledge, which, in turn, suggests that real knowledge processes are, at best, imperfect monitors of their own logical coherence. We shall later return to this point, when looking more closely at the knowledge process as a "system."

The panglossian epistemologist also doubts that the knowledge product is realistically regarded as a deductively closed network of commitments. Whereas the storehouse picture tried to account for the expansive and contractive properties of knowledge, the network picture attempts to capture some of knowledge's other alleged properties, such as the power of propositions to explain their logical consequences, and of those consequences to confirm the propositions from which they were derived. Logical positivism was dedicated to elaborating this picture. One telling feature is that it typically defines rationality in terms of the knower believing all the logical consequences of the propositions to which he is explicitly committed (Dennett 1978, part 2). The principle sources of irrationality, then, come from the knower either not making the right inferential moves from one proposition to the next or simply not having a comprehensive enough grasp of his own knowledge base to know what he knows. If historical reality undermined the first image, psychological reality undermines the second; for if knowledge were a deductively closed network, then rationality would be exclusively the property of *artificial* intelligences, since what passes for irrationality in the network picture is the norm for human beings and their knowledge production processes (as seen above in their tolerance for contradictions). This observation shows that the network picture violates the panglossian's methodological stricture that the point of knowledge (and rationality a fortiori) be empirically determined by studying its naturally occurring instances (Cherniak 1986).

Having just given the panglossian critique of the two images of the knowledge product that presuppose a strong, logician's sense of translatability, it must now be admitted that both have become very much bound up with ordinary conceptions of knowledge. Thus, the burden remains with the panglossian to come up with an alternative image that is true to the knowledge product in its "natural state." To meet the classical epistemologist's challenge, we shall provide the panglossian with a composite image of knowledge production, drawn mostly from the Marxism, Structuralism, and Systems Theory that is current among French philosophers and sociologists of science. It is a somewhat sanitized synthesis of proposals put forth by Pierre Bourdieu (1975), Michel Serres (1972), and Latour & Woolgar (1979). (Fuller [1984] places this image in the context of contemporary European social theory.) Yet, as the following theses make clear, the sociological simulation marks a radical break with how the classical epistemologist has handled such matters.

(A) It is misleading to regard knowledge as something that could, at least in principle, be accumulated indefinitely by all knowledge producers. Rather, knowledge production is an "economic" process, which means that the more knowledge had by one producer, the less had by another. Therefore, the key issue in regulating knowledge production is not how to accumulate more but how to redistribute more equitably.

(A1) The knowledge production process "economizes" at two levels: at the micro level, each new knowledge product (say, a journal article) redistributes the overall balance of credibility (see [B]); at the macro level, a relatively constant amount of knowledge is circulating in the process, which means that relatively little of the knowledge produced is preserved in the long run; rather, it is "translated" (see [B1]).

(B) "Having knowledge" is not a matter of possession, as the having of a mental representation typically is in classical epistemology. Rather, it is a socially ascribed status that a knowledge producer can (and normally wants to) earn in the course of his participation in the knowledge process. A producer "has knowledge" if enough of his fellow producers *either* devote their resources to following up his research (even for purposes of refutation) *or* cite his research as background material for their own. The producer continues to "have knowledge" only as long as these investments by his fellows pay off *for them*. Thus, "having knowledge" is ultimately a matter of *credibility*. But given the numerous ways in which producers can draw on each other's work, the fact that there are centers of credibility in the knowledge production process does not necessarily imply that the producers agree on anything more than on who the credible knowledge producers are.

(B1) The sense of "translation" relevant to knowledge production is limited to the design of functionally equivalent texts, which facilitate the distribution of credibility in the knowledge process. Since more knowledge is produced than could ever be preserved (footnotes do not accumulate in proportion to the footnotable material available), a premium is placed on works which can render redundant much of what is already in circulation. Thus, what are normally called "interpretations," "synopses," and "glosses" pass as translations. These works accrue credibility for their producers and diminish, if not entirely subsume, the credibility of the producers whose works are replaced. Thus, the relevant sense of "translation" is that of substituting and eliminating texts, though without the presumption that the exact contents of those texts are retained along the way. That retention is really as spotty as this account suggests may be seen in the extent to which the contents of a text can be lost without ever having been definitively refuted, only to be recovered at some future date to revolutionize the particular knowledge production process.

CHAPTER TWO

SOCIAL EPISTEMOLOGY AND SOCIAL METAPHYSICS

1. Drawing the Distinction

We have argued that perhaps the crucial step in making epistemology an autonomous activity was its separation from metaphysics. In that case, it would make sense to spend some time distinguishing *social epistemology* from *social metaphysics*. A standard definition of metaphysics is "the study of what there really is." Although some have been overwhelmed by the idea of such a discipline, others have failed to be impressed. Why can't one satisfy the demands of metaphysics simply by giving a careful and exhaustive description of what is perceptually available to us? A discipline of this kind, call it "phenomenology," would maybe require a keen eye, but, as disciplines go, it would be more like art than science. A ready response to this challenge, popularized by Descartes, is to say that our perceptions may be in error, a possibility that can be put to rest only by metaphysically grounding those perceptions in something indubitable. However, the phenomenologist may well prefer, as did Ernst Mach, to forego the metaphysical grounding and simply be very conservative in the conclusions he draws from the phenomena he observes. For example, he would not license the inference from a chair-like sensation to the existence of a chair or a collection of molecules or any other entity that requires supplementing the original sensation. In that way, both the problem of error and its metaphysical solution can be avoided at the same time.

Nevertheless, the need for a discipline of metaphysics can be seen by interpreting the threat of perceptual error in a slightly different light. After all, in the Cartesian story, the fear of error is the fear that an evil demon may be the ultimate source of the various phenomena we perceive. That is to say, the real worry is that there might be a much simpler (and more unsavory) account of reality than the exhaustive description of phenomena would suggest. The diversity might disguise an underlying unity, and the phenomenologist's project might therefore be an unnecessary waste of effort. The relevant error, then, is not that our perceptions may themselves be *false*, but rather that they may be *superficial*. This is a charge to which the phenomenologist is certainly open and which can only be met by engaging in some additional enterprise, metaphysics, which aims to reduce the world's complexity to a minimum. *Indeed, metaphysics is really nothing more than the study of the world's natural economy.* Thus, a methodological constraint on how metaphysicians arrive at their accounts of reality is that they explain the *most* phenomena by appealing to the *least* number of principles. This still leaves room for the many different systems that have populated the history of metaphysics. At one extreme is Neoplatonism (Plotinus) and Absolute Idealism (Hegel), which purported

31

to explain everything in terms of just one thing. At the other extreme may be found our phenomenologist, who argued that any attempt at reducing the world's apparent complexity—however useful that may be—in fact distorts the underlying reality, which is equally complex.

Now that the practice of metaphysics has been motivated, what reason is there to think that such a practice could be "social"? To answer this question we first need to consider what it is about human beings that makes them capable of doing metaphysics. A naturalistic inquiry of this kind, which would most easily find its home in the period since Marx and Darwin, was in fact suggested as early as Peter Abelard in the twelfth century. Abelard is generally known as one of the first medieval nominalists, but he also speculated about the origin of the claims expressed by his opponents, the realists, who argued for the existence of "universals" underlying particular phenomena. Abelard's basic position, which would be echoed centuries later by that other great nominalist John Stuart Mill, was that *the metaphysician does reflectively what memory does unreflectively.* To clarify the meaning of this maxim, I will now turn to an example around which subsequent discussion of social metaphysics will center.

One of the natural functions of memory is to eliminate the differences among particular phenomena so that they can be more easily stored and recalled. In the course of this systematic forgetting, the uniqueness of the phenomena drops out and all that remains are certain general properties that the phenomena share; hence, universals are *distilled* from particulars. The realist focuses on the fact that memory always functions in this way. Another capacity, one which permanently preserved particular phenomena in their uniqueness, might be quite useful but it would not be *memory.* The nominalist replies that just because universals are always distilled from particulars, it does not follow that they must be distilled in just one way. The nominalist then proceeds to emphasize the conventional element in how one goes about distilling universals from particulars, even though the distilling is itself universal. In a later chapter, I will argue that an institutionalized version of the distillation process occurs when a discipline engages in an historiography of *reification*, which legitimates the discipline's current activities by revealing them to be the realization of a goal shared by related practitioners throughout history.

We see, then, that the metaphysician's discipline consists in his ability to attend systematically to certain features of naturally occurring phenomena and to ignore others. This is how universals are distilled from particulars, with the universals picking out the "necessary" or "essential" features of the particulars. Writ large, metaphysical practice results in the schemes that societies design for classifying their members. The political aim of these schemes is to exchange individual uniqueness for the equality and interchangeability that comes from receiving the same classification. Thus, they ground the possibility of treating like cases alike, and hence the possibility of at least a formal sense of justice. Indeed, the "collective representations" which Durkheim originally identified as the distinct subject matter of his brand of cognitive sociology were, in our sense, a species of social metaphysics. The main Durkheimian examples of these representations—namely, the basic legal categories expressed in totems and taboos—govern the segregation and integration of individuals in a society by defining each individual in terms of what Levi-Strauss (1964) has called a "dual code," half *natural* and half *cultural.* That is, regulations on individual conduct simultaneously articulate theories about the individual's *natural* capacity to behave in a socially acceptable manner and confirm the truth of those theories through *culturally* constituted agencies; hence, slaves are permitted only limited interaction with citizens because of the slave's inherently limited capacities, which are reinforced by police efforts to segregate the slaves from the citizens.

In recent years, Michel Foucault (1979) has carried the idea of "law as social metaphysics" to great lengths, revealing moreover the conventions by which individuals are fitted into various medical and penal schemes. The fitting process invariably requires a restructuring of the physical environment and the addition of new technologies, all designed to make the signs of membership in the relevant classes more evident to the trained eye. This fact should come as no surprise, and indeed, it explains why a metaphysics worthy of the name must be social: namely, if a metaphysics is to appear as an account of "how things really are," then its categorical distinctions should seem "natural" even to the perception of someone who is unlikely to understand or accept the theoretical justifications for that metaphysics. In other words, in order to cover up the socially constructed character of reality, it is important that any potentially discontented individuals be made to feel that they must bear the burden of proof, should they ever become suspicious of the regnant social metaphysics. For example, Foucault himself writes of the "discipline" that both a psychiatrist and a patient must undergo before the psychiatrist can classify the patient as having a certain mental disorder. For his part, the psychiatrist must learn to focus his attention—his "gaze" Foucault calls it—on specific behaviors manifested by the patient that are to be treated as "symptoms," even if, in a different social context, they would appear quite normal. Likewise, the patient must learn to interpret his own behavior in this way and thereby admit that the psychiatrist better understands what sort of person the patient is than the patient himself does. In thus submitting to the psychiatrist's authority, the patient contributes to the standardization of the scheme for classifying mental disorders and, hence, to its objectivity.

One way of making the move at this point from metaphysics to epistemology is to have the metaphysician locate himself within his own scheme. Suppose, for instance, that the psychiatrist reflects on the psychiatric status of his own behavior and concludes that he manifests enough symptoms of mental disorder to have himself legitimately committed to an asylum. Assuming that the psychiatrist holds steadfastly to the validity of his scheme, he now faces the fundamental epistemological question of how to reconcile appearance and reality: Why has the essentially pathological nature of his own behavior eluded him (and others) all these years?   Appropriate answers would include references to "false consciousness," "self-deception," "systematic distortion," and other processes that fall under the general rubric of *ideology.*

For our purposes, an ideology is an explanation of some phenomenon that also serves to justify the phenomenon's presence. On this definition, then, ideologies can, but need not be, false; rather, they serve mainly to explain phenomena so as to make them appear "normal," or at least not in need of further examination. There are two common forms of ideological reasoning:

> (a) *Functional explanations,* which account for phenomena in terms of their beneficial consequences for some overall social design. It would be rash to claim, at   least without further argument, that they are always false, though it is noteworthy that they forestall easy falsification by allowing the possibility—as in the case of "invisible hand" explanations of the capitalist market—that the agents who generate the phenomena in question do not know (and perhaps would even object to) the beneficial consequences that follow from them.

> (b) *Transcendental arguments,* which purport to show that if a particular state of affairs did not obtain, some well-grounded phenomenon would be rendered unintelligible. While an argument of this kind looks as though it is supposed to explain the well-grounded phenomenon, it in fact serves to establish the credibility of the state of affairs necessary for the phenomenon's presence; for usually this state of affairs is something like causality, which is metaphysically more obscure than the well-grounded phenomenon of the world having spatiotemporal regularity.

In short, ideologies are designed to prevent criticism and revision. Certainly, this would be the import of whatever reasons the psychiatrist had offered in the past for being excepted from his own scheme of mental disorders. For example, the psychiatrist may have believed for many years that he was sufficiently reflective about his mental states to know that he was not motivated by any of the impulses that typically motivate patients who act in a similar manner. True to this explanation's ideological form, it is by no means clear how one would go about challenging it without appealing to a still deeper, and correspondingly less falsifiable, cognitive level at which the psychiatrist was simply "rationalizing" rather than "reasoning." But recall that we have stipulated that the psychiatrist *does* eventually challenge and overturn this explanation. For the moment that the psychiatrist identifies and evaluates his explanation's ideological character, he becomes an *epistemologist.*

And where in a social metaphysics are ideologies most likely to be found? The key sites are in the regions of what the anthropologist Mary Douglas (Bloor 1979) calls "boundary maintenance." No matter what the social metaphysical scheme, individuals cannot always be easily classified. Moreover, individuals who fall "between" or "beyond" a particular set of categories threaten the legitimacy of the entire scheme by undermining its chief claim to authority, namely, its comprehensiveness. The point of boundary maintenance, then, is to neutralize the effects of these anomalies on the scheme's legitimacy, ideally leaving the social metaphysics stronger than ever. By considering two sorts of examples, we will be able to see how, in the first case, this strength travels under the guise of flexibility, and how, in the second case, it appears as sheer force.

As for flexibility, most legal systems incorporate some principle of *equity*, which permits judges discretion in particular cases to take exception to "the letter of the law" in order to satisfy "the spirit of the law." However, in Anglo- American legal procedure, the appeal to equity has been so extensive as to make one wonder why this fact is not taken to be symptomatic of the conceptual inadequacy of Anglo-American legal procedure. Rather, equity is seen as pointing to the "mercifulness" of the judges who preside over a flexible legal system, which, in turn, gives one the impression that the law is not an ironclad authoritarian scheme. But, of course, the chances that such a legal system will ever be substantially revised is greatly diminished, precisely *because* exceptions can so readily be taken in particular cases.

As for the dark side of ideology in action, consider a situation first noted by Durkheim (1951) and since played up by Foucault. It might be thought that a significant and regular occurrence of deviant behavior—primarily criminal and psychiatric disorders—would prove that the regnant social metaphysics was dysfunctional. However, the authorities can readily turn this apparent "minus" into a "plus" by arguing that all it shows is that the deviants recognize themselves as falling under the relevant categories in the scheme and thus deliberately try to avoid the various forms of incarceration that would count as "formal subsumption." Clearly, this ideological move bolsters the regnant social metaphysics by justifying more extensive surveillance as the deviants prove to be that much more elusive than originally expected.

The epistemologist's role in all this is to locate the boundary maintenance strategies of the ideologue. Using our original case of the psychiatrist as a paradigm, we are now ready to ask two questions of the sort which distinguish the epistemological enterprise from the metaphysical one:

(c) What allowed the psychiatrist's ideology to survive as long as it did, given its falsity?

(d) What allowed the psychiatrist to discover the falsity of his ideology, given its survival value?

Without even beginning to answer these questions, we are still able to conclude that *the epistemologist is interested in evaluating the metaphysical scheme of the individuals that his own metaphysical scheme classifies.* As it happens, the psychiatrist's case is reflexive, since he is trying to situate *himself* inside his scheme of disorders. But the epistemological enterprise as such need not be reflexive and, in fact, is generally motivated by a *lack* of reflexivity on *everyone's* part, both the individuals classified by the epistemologist's metaphysical scheme and the epistemologist himself. To put it bluntly, my epistemology is parasitic on someone else's (perhaps, as in the case of the psychiatrist, my earlier self's) ideology. An illuminating and provocative way of restating this point is to say that there would be no need for epistemology, if the metaphysician simply submitted to the authority of the individuals classified in his scheme by treating their metaphysics as his own.

Once stated in these terms, the *authoritarian* character of epistemology is brought into sharp focus. The epistemologist can either authorize the metaphysicians under study to speak on his behalf or himself be authorized to speak on their behalf. The first possibility is realized in cases, well known to anthropologists, where the epistemologist decides to "go native" by simply assuming that the tribal metaphysics represents how things really are. This is also the stance implicitly taken by philosophical *relativism*. The second possibility arises under the more usual situation in which the epistemologist finds it necessary to reinterpret a tribal metaphysics in terms of his own metaphysical scheme in order to render the tribe rational, that is, as making reasonable errors. This is the strategy behind much of philosophical *absolutism*. In either case, the practice of epistemology invites us to consider the general issue of which individuals have the authority to *represent* which other individuals in matters of knowledge. Indeed, what does it mean for an individual (person or thing) to stand in a relation of "representation" to some other individual (person or thing)?

2.   Transcendental and Naturalistic Approaches to Representation

Starting with Thomas Hobbes and continuing throughout the Age of Reason, language was regarded as ordering the world of things just as law was regarded as ordering the world of persons. In the case of Hobbes and the materialists of the French Enlightenment, the legal order was understood simply as a special case of the linguistic order, and, more interestingly perhaps, the legal order was regarded as the best case study of the linguistic order at work (Foucault 1970, ch. 4). The concept that subsumed both the linguistic and the legal cases was *representation*: namely, elected representatives are granted the license to speak on behalf their constituency in a manner that is more closely circumscribed than, but not fundamentally different from, the way in which competent members of a linguistic community are granted the license to speak on behalf of the world.

In political theory, two conceptions of representation are typically treated, each corresponding to one of the approaches to linguistic representation outlined in this section. On the one hand, a representative may be empowered by his constituency to act with absolute authority when conducting its affairs. In that case, whatever voice the constituency has is only through its representative. This is the position of the Hobbesian sovereign. Interpreted as a theory about the cognitive control that speakers exercise over the world in virtue of speaking correctly, this conception of representation suggests the asymmetrical approach of the *transcendentalist*, who claims, in effect, that whatever cannot spoken *for* cannot be spoken *about*.

On the other hand, the *naturalistic* approach favors a more democratic conception of the representative as someone who is accountable to his constituency, a primus inter pares ("first among equals"), as the Romans put it, in a somewhat different context. Since words are themselves a sort of thing, there is no reason to think that the structure of their relations is any more stable than the structure of the things whose relations they represent. And so, just as things may change without a speaker either intending or expecting it to happen, likewise words may change in a similar manner as a result of causally interacting with the things they represent. The appropriate political analogy here is with the representative who unwittingly loses his seat because he manages to say something which upsets his constituency (Pitkin 1972).

I am in broad sympathy with the Enlightenment project of bridging the legal and the linguistic by examining common "structures of representation." One consequence of this view, however, should be mentioned at the outset, lest you think that I now intend to talk about language in the disembodied (that is, decontextualized) manner so characteristic of contemporary philosophy. When I speak of "drawing valid inferences" or "making legal moves" in a language game, you should not automatically think that these inferences and moves could simply be made by *anyone* in the linguistic community. For example, in Foucault's scenario, the patient's submission to the psychiatrist's authority is by no means enhanced by his ability to reason exactly as the psychiatrist would about his condition. On the contrary, such "simulations" of rational discourse would tend to underscore the depth and complexity of the patient's mental disorder. Thus, not only must a psychiatric diagnosis be articulated according to a fixed set of rules, but it must also be articulated by someone who has been authorized to issue a diagnosis of that kind. And so, it is crucial to the patient's having submitted to the psychiatrist's authority that he remain silent while the psychiatrist speaks on his behalf.

Let us now turn to a more systematic consideration of the two senses in which language/law can "order" things/persons. As we have seen, the general name for this ordering relation is *representation*, and, for ease of expression, I will call the role that language/law play in representation, the *repraesentans* (Latin for "that which does the representing"; the plural is *repraesentantes*), and the role that things/persons play, the *re-praesentandum* (Latin for "that which is represented"; the plural is *repraesentanda*). In that case, the repraesentans may be seen as either (i) regulating the repraesentanda from outside its domain or (ii) constituting the repraesentanda from inside its domain. (i) describes a *transcendental* approach to representation, whereas (ii) describes a *naturalistic* one. Although the more usual approach to representation is transcendental, I shall defend a naturalistic approach instead.

On the transcendental approach, a repraesentans neither causally affects nor is causally affected by a repraesentandum. Simply put, the order of words is independent of the order of things. The intuitions behind this approach are easy enough to identify. For example, there is no one *physical* relation in which all speakers stand to the world, simply in virtue of saying "Newton's *Principia Mathematica* was published in 1687." Rather, there seems to be a set of situations, more or less well defined by the conventions of the English language for uttering the sentence "correctly" (that is, as stating a contextually relevant truth). Indeed, depending on the state of knowledge in the particular linguistic community, what we would regard as the best explanation of the fact that Newton published *Principia Mathematica* in 1687 may turn out *never* to be an appropriate reason for speakers in that community saying "Newton's *Principia Mathematica* was published in 1687." Yet, at the same time, the causal independence of words and things allows *both* the order of words to act as the frame of reference from which the changing order of things may be "mirrored" or "mapped" *and* the order of things to act as the frame of reference from which the order of words may be tested and perhaps even replaced. Thus, whether it be in his incarnation as an Anglo-American theorist of meaning or as a continental semiotician, the transcendentalist notoriously holds that there is a *nonphysical* relation in which all speakers stand to the world when they utter correctly, variously called *reference* or *signification*. To know a language, then, is to know how to find one's way around the world, to know the sorts of things to which one can and cannot "refer" or "signify."

In contrast, the naturalistic approach proposes that a repraesentans may causally interact with a repraesentandum: the order of words is part of the order of things, language a part of the world. The evidence for this view is rather subtle, relying on the observation that no matter how hard one tries to contain the effects of changing either language or the world, it is virtually impossible to change one without, at least unintentionally, changing the other. Philologists have long noted that language change has an "internal dynamic" contrary to the wishes of the actual speakers, as in the tendency for similar sounding words to acquire similar meanings, which, in turn, creates new categories into which cases can be fitted all too easily. In fact, it is precisely because such changes are largely *unintentional*, and hence detected only in retrospect, that language appears to have the autonomy and structural stability that make the transcendental approach seem so compelling.

To get at the contrast here, consider two ways of explaining the recurrence of "justice" and its cognates in the history of Western philosophical discourse. One explanation—the transcendental one—points to a "nature" of justice, which all theories of justice have tried to capture. The fact that these theories have been very diverse indicates that the nature of justice is deep and complex, and that perhaps some of the theories are in error. Moreover, the fact that the fortunes of these theories have risen and fallen during their history does not, in any way, alter the nature of justice itself. Another explanation—the naturalistic one—diagnoses the situation somewhat more modestly, namely, that "justice" is a word that has been recycled many times to capture many different paradigmatic usages, which when taken together really have little more in common than use of the same word. Of course, there are, so to speak, "historical reasons" for why "justice" gets transferred from one context of usage to the next. But if we continue to think that "justice" ultimately picks out something with a deep and complex nature, that is only because we needlessly suppose that more than simply some accidental causal links tie these contexts together.

Although most contemporary theories of language (with the possible exception of Marxist ones) presuppose transcendentalism, the debate with naturalism was quite alive a century ago in two rather different quarters: *philology* and *logic*.

In philology, naturalism had been the received view from the German historicist school of Franz Bopp and August Schleicher, and, by the 1890s, had combined with Darwinian notions to produce a view of languages as species undergoing variation and selection according to principles outside the control of its speakers. Indeed, since the philologists had come to believe that linguistic evolution was sufficiently independent from the wills of actual speakers, such that they could at best "anticipate" future states of their language, claims began to be made for philology being a *natural science* (Aarsleff 1982, ch. 10).

Interestingly, the transcendentalist reaction began with Michel Breal (1964), who reversed the grounding for the "autonomy" of language, and hence philology: language is indeed independent, but not as an impediment to expression having a life of its own, but as a versatile tool facilitating expression. Thus, Breal reinterpreted the proposed laws of language change, with an eye toward the new possibilities for expression they opened rather than the old possibilities they closed. The result was a proposal to make "semantics" (a word of Breal's coinage) the foundational discipline of the *human sciences*. And with Ferdinand de Saussure's work, Breal's functionalist strategy was crystallized in the transcendental approach that currently characterizes scientific linguistics. For once it was accepted that the mere presence of a language attests to its speakers finding it capable of representing their world, it was no longer clear that a diachronic study of the language would usefully supplement a synchronic study in trying to explain how words represent things (Aarsleff 1982, ch. 14).

Turning now to logic, despite the clear winner in these debates, the two approaches to representation seemed, at the time, to be on more or less equal footing. Of particular interest here are the differences between the "idealist"

F.H. Bradley and the "realist" Gottlob Frege (Passmore 1966, chs. 6-7). As the scare quotes suggest, the metaphysical labels are potentially misleading: on the one hand, Bradley's idealism is an example of the naturalistic approach, in that it involves a view of language as itself a part of the reality it tries to represent; on the other hand, Frege's realism is of the Platonic sort, which portrays language—once stripped to its logical form—as the transcendental conveyor of propositions whose truth or falsity is independent of the fact that they are materially embodied. Frege believed that logic was a particularly good analytic tool for getting at the structure of reality because, as something fundamentally detached from matter, logic could represent distinct "senses" of a referent that, in the material world, appeared as a solid whole (as in the case of Venus not being materially distinguished from its being the Morning Star and its being the Evening Star). In contrast, Bradley saw Fregean claims for the representational power of logic as little more than rationalizations: the abstract character of the "structure of reality" simply refers to its incompleteness and hence its falsity, which follows from the fact that a part of reality is being enlisted to articulate the whole.

As for their respective views on the capacity of language to convey truth, Frege is, of course, famous for maintaining that language was necessary for the expression of truth, which occurred whenever the truth conditions of a sentence were "satisfied" by a state of affairs. It should by now come as no surprise that Bradley disavowed any such views. Instead, he held the interesting position that all sentences have indeterminate truth values ("degrees of error") because, even in the case of a sentence whose truth conditions have been satisfied, nothing in the nature of reality itself required that that sentence *and not some other* had to be the one uttered. In short, then, because Bradley regarded language from the standpoint of the world (and not vice versa, as Frege did), he was sensitive to the radically contingent character of utterance, a key feature of the naturalistic approach that has since been exploited by social constructivists in the study of scientific discourse.

Despite my general lack of sympathy for the transcendental approach to representation, it nevertheless captures a fairly basic intuition about the language/world relation, namely, that if truth is defined as the correspondence of words to things, then there must be a language-transcendent conception of the world. On the naturalistic approach, it is not clear how the world at least *appears* to have this sort of conceptual distance from the language representing it. In response, let me offer two ways in which the naturalist might gloss Wittgenstein's (1961, prop. 5.6) cryptic remark, "The limits of my language mean the limits of my world," which can be easily understood as the transcendentalist's motto. For reasons that will soon be made clear, I call the two glosses the *straight* and the *cunning* reading of the remark. Both are naturalistic in the sense that they account for the apparent causal independence of words and things by treating words as simply another sort of thing in the world. In considering the naturalistic glosses, you should notice that they focus on language's role in *facilitating* and *impeding* the expression of content, rather than in absolutely *permitting* and *prohibiting* its expression, which is, by contrast, typical of the transcendental approach. Indeed, the Wittgenstein remark is usually glossed, quite transcendentally, as that whatever I cannot say I am simply *prohibited* from meaning.

The straight reading of the remark is as instructions for making one's way around the world. If a sentence turns out to be true in a particular language, then it must be true in virtue of satisfying verifiability conditions expressed in that language. If that is the case, then there is an explicit procedure for coming to understand the truth of that sentence that can be, in turn, used as the basis of effecting a translation from the language in which the truth was first expressed to another language in which it remains unexpressed. If, say, the first language is Newtonian mechanics and the second is Aristotelian mechanics, then translating the law of falling bodies may be a cumbersome task since Aristotle's language does not lend itself to an easy articulation of this truth. Perhaps concepts used in verifying the law, such as inertia, may have to be represented as an inference that one is licensed to draw when presented with evidence expressed in an observation language basic enough for even Aristotle to understand. And so, while it is *unlikely* that Aristotle himself would have ever discovered the law of falling bodies, it is nevertheless *most likely* that he could be persuaded of its truth by being taught how to express it as a truth—that is, to verify it—within the language of his own mechanics. The upshot, then, is that languages differ only with respect to their relative ease of articulation and comprehension, the source of which is the uses to which the languages have been commonly put. These differences, which are most clearly manifested in attempts at translation, are, in turn, the source of the intuition that some languages come closer than others to representing a language-transcendent world.

Apropos its name, the cunning reading of Wittgenstein's remark slightly shifts the emphases of the straight reading to arrive at the idea that language should be regarded as the only thing that stands in the way of representing whatever one wants about the world. The cunning reader starts with the seemingly innocuous observation that the only truths expressible by language are truths *in* language, namely, inferences that are valid in virtue of being derivable from premises (which are themselves derivable from still other premises whose validity have been similarly established). However, these truths *merely* orient the speaker around the world, without necessarily specifying what it is about the world that allows these truths to orient him successfully. It is in this lack of specification that the cunning reader maneuvers.

Paul Feyerabend's (1975, ch. 11) Galileo fable is a good case in point. Here we have someone, Galileo, who in fact violates many of the accepted rules of inference for the scientific language game of his time—and for other times as well, since he fakes the evidence used in verifying his claims). He is, in turn, justifiably persecuted by the authorities of the day, the Papal

Inquisition, yet he ends up—in the hands of Newton—to have said something that we can now say is essentially correct about the world. The irony is compounded in Feyerabend's telling, since it is not clear that Galileo was even motivated by some intuition of "the Truth" that lay beyond the expressive powers of his language, which could have served as an apologia for faking the evidence. Instead, he was most likely using language, *just as every other speaker uses it*, to express and satisfy his interests, which, in his particular case, required that the language be *misused*, namely, for asserting claims even when they were unwarranted. Nevertheless, all these ad hominem arguments against Galileo add up to admitting the substantial truth of his terrestrial mechanics, precisely *because* there was no reason to think that his underhanded methods would have yielded lasting results— unless, of course, those results just so happen to represent how the world really is, regardless of method or language. The persuasiveness of this argument is what would have made Newton, in Feyerabend's fable, a cunning reader of Galileo. At least, that is how cheating in a language game can be made to simulate the presence of a language transcendent world.

Since the naturalist holds that words are just a kind of thing, the distinction between words and things is a *functional*, not an *ontological* one: there are things *with* which and *to* which one refers. And as the semioticians are fond of noting, given the appropriate code, anything can be made to signify anything else. The puffs of air and scrawled letters that normally pass for words have the special advantage of permitting the economical expression of the repraesentanda. In particular, some marks on a page may capture the essential features of a thing, which, for whatever reason, would be impossible to inspect directly. More explicitly: *a repraesentans is a thing whose use is efficient enough, in terms of the energy the user needs to expend vis-a-vis the cognitive benefit he receives, such that it is more worthwhile to use it than the repraesentandum itself.* The question most clearly suggested by this definition is, "How efficient is 'efficient enough'?" The answer will be in terms of the overall function that the representational system serves in the community. Thus, we can address how a community should distribute things between the two categories of representation so as to reach some level of what I shall call *cognitive economy*.

At one extreme, the "speaker" (meant in the sense of the person doing the representing) may use a silent or invisible repraesentans, which expends the least energy but also offers the least cognitive benefit, since an audience would be unable to determine what is being represented. Such a speaker would simply let the repraesentandum "speak for itself" and hope that telepathy is a viable form of communication. One is reminded here of the pregnant silences of the Zen Buddhist master which leave his students in an equally pregnant and silent state of bewilderment. Clearly, the role that a representational system of this sort would play in its community would primarily *not* be that of communication in the usual sense.

At the other extreme are the inhabitants of the island of Laputa, whom Gulliver encounters on his travels: the Laputians talk only about things that are either within sight or reach, which is to say, they can refer *to* only what they can refer *with* (Swift 1960, part 3). In that case, maximum cognitive benefit is gained, insofar as an audience can perceptually fix on the repraesentandum as it is being used as its own repraesentans. But maximum effort is also expended, for no matter how equivocal a repraesentans the word "table," say, may be, it is nevertheless much easier to use, for most purposes, than the actual table itself. Furthermore, although the Laputian audience may reap the cognitive benefits of knowing exactly what a speaker is representing, their language would probably place severe limitations on the number of things they could know so exactly. The brute identity of the repraesentanda as spatiotemporally extended individuals could certainly be known, as well as some of their grosser perceptual properties to which one could readily refer by ostension. But since there is no privileged set of repraesentantes—such as sentences or pictures—that could be used to represent the thing under different descriptions, it would be difficult to express the various subtle features that the thing may share with other things.

It might be thought that the cognitive economy of a community tends toward one of these two extremes, which correspond to familiar caricatures in the epistemological literature. The first extreme, minimum work and minimum benefit, may be seen as an example of *radical skepticism*, which presupposes that the representational capacity of any language is sufficiently impoverished to always render the repraesentanda cognitively underdetermined by the repraesentantes. Thus, no matter how explicit or graphic I try to be, I will never be able to specify exactly what I am talking about, in which case I might as well not try at all. The second extreme, maximum work and maximum benefit, may then be taken as a case of *naive realism*, in which the repraesentanda are cognitively determined in full by the repraesentantes because each repraesentandum is its own repraesentans. If the two extreme positions were the only available options, then language would be useless as the means by which the cognitive structure of the community is represented, mainly because communication would be undermined: radical skepticism makes communication impossible, while naive realism makes it redundant.

However, there is another way of looking at the cognitive economy of a community, namely, in terms of things regularly passing from being repraesentantes to being repraesentanda, and back again, so as to maintain a rough "equilibrium" between the things assigned to the two categories. Perhaps an example will make my meaning plainer. Let us start by taking something that is self-evident, such as a table in Laputian, since it is both a repraesentandum and its own repraesentans at the same time. This is reasonably regarded as the naive realist view that we have of the table in ordinary life. Now let us imagine that the Laputians find that they talk about tables so much, that it stands in so many significant relations with other things in their world, that it would be much more convenient simply to be able to do something a little less strenuous than move a table into view whenever they wanted to refer to one. They also realize the trade-off that would be involved in having tables, from now on, mediated by some other repraesentans, such as the few puffs of air it takes to say "table": namely, efficiency has been bought at the price of cognitive underdetermination, since "table" can now be used to refer to things other than literal tables, and it may not be clear simply from a given utterance of "table" which one of those things is intended by the speaker. However, this may itself not be all bad, since with cognitive underdetermination also comes the possibility for the sort of semantic richness associated with metaphor, irony, and other nonliteral forms of speech. To put it in a nutshell, then, the introduction of the word "table" into Laputian can be construed as trading off a *gain* in efficiency at the level of the repraesentans (that is, the word is easier to use than the table itself for representing the table) against a *loss* in efficiency at the level of the repraesentandum (that is, the word is not as clear and distinct a representation of the table as the table itself). And it is precisely this balancing of representational gains and losses that I mean by "equilibrium" in a cognitive economy.

While the vividness of the Laputian example may have clarified the concept of equilibrium in a cognitive economy, it has perhaps failed to demonstrate the general need for such a concept in a naturalistic account of representation. To bring out this need, let us assume that at least part of the community's activities is devoted to the revision and extension of the knowledge base—in other words, that there is an institution functionally equivalent to science. One clear long-term effect that scientific activity has on a community's representational system centers on the passage of things between being repraesentantes and repraesentanda. It is epitomized in the question, "How much theoretical mediation does something require in order to be known?" And by "theoretical mediation" I mean the extent to which a repraesentandum is made accessible through the distinct set of repraesentantes we normally call a "theory." I take it to be a characteristic of increased theoretical mediation that it makes the ordinary individual's access to a repraesentandum more *indirect*: perhaps he must now master a special discourse, which requires considerable training, before being permitted to speak authoritatively about the repraesentandum. Conversely, decreased theoretical mediation opens up access to the repraesentandum to more individuals in the community. Therefore, we can imagine two kinds of passages occurring. On the one hand, what used to be self-evident, an object of ordinary observation like the Laputian table, may later be known only as a complex of inferences drawn from one or more scientific theories; on the other hand, an object that was once known only through much theoretical mediation, such as the hidden eighth planet (Neptune), which tugged at the orbit of Uranus, may have now become sufficiently integrated into ordinary observation that one need only point to the planet in order to make clear and knowledgeable reference to it.

The thesis that cognitive economies tend toward an equilibrium is simply the idea that *any attempt at decreasing theoretical mediation at one point in*

*the representational system is compensated for by an increase in theoretical
mediation at some other, perhaps as yet undisclosed, point.* In other words,
not only does theoretical mediation make access to a repraesentandum more
indirect, but increased theoretical mediation is, to a large extent, itself
indirectly (unintentionally) caused. And so, harking back to an earlier
example, while it is indeed true that Aristotle could express Newton's self-
evident primitive concept of inertia only in a highly mediated form, and
hence only indirectly and clumsily, this is compensated by the fact that
aspects of terrestrial motion which both commonsense and Aristotelian
mechanics can express with relatively little theoretical mediation turn out
to be highly theorized complex objects in Newtonian mechanics. The bite of
the equilibrium thesis thus lies in the implication that unless a
representational system is radically restructured, there is no clear sense in
which a community could now have, say, a "more" theoretically mediated
understanding of the world than it had at some earlier point in its history;
rather, such apparent cases of increased theoreticity are better seen as nothing
more than local occurrences within the representational system, only to be
offset by decreased theoreticity elsewhere.

I assume that, at this point, the thesis of cognitive equilibrium is itself
less than self-evident, and so, in order to motivate it, I will draw on two
cases—one relatively concrete one from anthropology and one relatively
abstract one from systems theory—in which the thesis is assumed in the
course of explaining what is happening. If nothing else, these two cases
will afford us the opportunity of illustrating the difference between the
transcendentalist and naturalistic approaches to representation.

2.1. Naturalism among the Savages

Well into the twentieth century, anthropologists had taken "the savage
mind" to exhibit patterns of reasoning inferior to those of the "civilized"
Westerner. Indeed, it was popular to argue, on the basis of the apparent
similarity between the mentalities of savages and Western children, that the
savage was an evolutionary precursor of the Westerner, not quite deserving
the title *Homo sapiens.* One alleged case of the savage's primitiveness was
his inability to distinguish abstract concepts from concrete objects, as shown
in his frequent conflation of talk about words (or concepts, the two will
used be interchangeably) with talk about things. For example, a shaman
might claim to be "thinking with animal parts" in order to decipher a
message from the gods, even though it looks to the anthropologist as though
he is arranging those parts, which have already been assigned meanings, in
order to trigger some associated religious concept, which is, in turn,
probably an implicit command for the shaman's community to act in a
certain way. The animal parts then are not what really get manipulated in
thought, just as the beads of an abacus are not what really get manipulated
in arithmetic: both the parts and the beads are merely concrete models of an

abstract process, thinking, whose success or failure is conceptually unrelated to whether the models are manipulated especially well.   If the anthropologist understands the shaman in this light, then, after seeing that there are implicit rules for decoding the animal parts, he will wonder why the shaman and his community regard each "correct" (according to the implicit rules) decoding as an empirical discovery and why the community does not suspect the shaman's authority when he gives patently "incorrect" decodings.

The anthropologist is puzzled here because he is a transcendentalist, while the shaman and his community are naturalists.   For the naturalist, no category mistake is committed in saying that thought is conducted with animal parts rather than with concepts or words.   In contrast, the transcendentalist presumes that every use of an object must be mediated by a distinct set of concepts, which implies that an ontological distinction is made between what can count as repraesentantes (namely, concepts) and what can count as repraesentanda (namely, objects).   The repraesentantes function, then, as meanings, what Frege called "senses," which are assigned by the linguistic community to fix the identity of the object so that it can be referred to on a regular basis.   The naturalist denies this picture, of course, claiming that concepts and objects can function as either repraesentantes or repraesentanda.   Indeed, consider what it would mean to "allow an object to represent some concept," as in the case of the animal parts representing a divine message, according to the shaman's community: to wit, that the object is taken by the language user as self-evident and hence not in need of any further mediating concept.   On the naturalist view, something counts as part of the medium of thought, or set of repraesentantes, if it cannot be conveyed by some more primitive medium of thought, or represented by some more primitive set of repraesentantes: that is, to think (or speak, or refer) with x is to regard x as self-evident.

Furthermore, when it looks to the anthropologist as though the shaman is covering up error and thereby breaking his own rules, the shaman (and his community, insofar as they agree) is in fact renegotiating the representational function of some aspect of his practice.   For example, if the shaman denies the divine message that would normally be read off the animal parts, he is, in effect, claiming that what was previously the repraesentandum (namely, the usual divine message) should now itself be taken as the repraesentans of some heretofore unknown repraesentandum (namely, another divine message).   The animal parts would then be, so to speak, "doubly inscribed."   To balk at this move as just an obfuscatory piece of ad hoc reasoning is to suppose that some straightforward interpretation of the animal parts is being suppressed by the shaman.   Admittedly, the shaman may be suppressing what the transcendentalist would like him to say, namely, that he made a mistake.   However, for the naturalist, as we presume the shaman to be, it does not follow from this suppression that his community is not receiving as straightforward an understanding of the animal parts as possible—at least if the thesis of cognitive equilibrium holds sway. To explain this point, suppose that the shaman *does* confess error. Whatever clarity is gained by keeping the rules uncomplicated by exceptional cases is lost as the shaman's word can no longer be taken at face value. In other words, *the shaman's discourse itself* becomes doubly inscribed: *apparently*, he is issuing commands from the gods; but *really*, his comprehension of the gods is fallible, and so the community may need to put forth independent arguments for following the commands that do not invoke the shaman's authority.

2.2. Naturalism among the Systems

Three demons have possessed the Western imagination in the modern period: Descartes', Laplace's, and Maxwell's (Schweber 1982). In many ways, however, they are the same demon: namely, the knower who is able to know without causally affecting the known. In Kantian epistemology, this knower was called "the transcendental ego," and we have been contrasting its manner of expression, the transcendental approach to representation, with that of the naturalist approach. The Cartesian demon was encountered earlier when motivating the enterprise of metaphysics. Its claim to transcendentalism rests on the idea that the demon does not leave a mark of its presence in the world of phenomena, though its presence (or some benign version, such as God) may be presupposed if the world of phenomena is to be understood as some unified whole. The Laplacean and Maxwellian demons are incarnations of eighteenth- and nineteenth-century physical science, respectively. Laplace's was a creature of optimism, while Maxwell's turned out to be one of pessimism. This difference in attitude toward the possibility of the two demons reflects a shift in the physical scientist's representational system from transcendental to naturalist. In considering the shift we will get a vivid sense of how the thesis of cognitive equilibrium can be interpreted as a model of how conceptual change occurs.

Cybernetics has been divided into the study of two types of systems: the *deviation-counteracting* type, in which noise can be eliminated from the system without introducing new noise, and the *deviation-amplifying* type, in which noise can be eliminated only by introducing new noise, which then has to be eliminated, and so on (Maruyama 1968). The laws governing the first type are temporally reversible, which is to say, that an earlier state of the system can be regained simply by reversing the operation of the laws, while those governing the second are temporally irreversible. And so, if we regard the physical universe as a system, then the laws of classical mechanics would model the universe as the first type, while the principles of entropy and evolution would model it as the second. In the first universe lives Laplace's demon who, just given the universal laws and any set of initial conditions, can compute what happens at any point in spacetime *without the computation itself making a difference to the state of the universe*. In the second universe lives Maxwell's demon who—try as it may to approximate the transcendental aloofness of the Laplacian demon—is able to bring about a local reversal of the statistical tendency toward entropy *only at the cost of generating entropy elsewhere in the universe.* Indeed, the more structure that the Maxwellian demon succeeds in imposing on the motion of molecules in a specific region, the more likely that the rest of the universe will exhibit a random distribution of molecules. To put the point somewhat paradoxically, the very process of conferring order on the universe has, as one of its unintended consequences, the generation of disorder. Clearly, a being that finds itself so inextricably bound to the universe it wants to represent is a product of naturalism (Watzlawick 1977, ch. 18).

Laplace's demon is the ideal classical epistemologist, whose efforts at gaining information about (or eliminating noise from) the world-system does not require any loss of previously gained information. On the classical approach, information acquisition was presumed to be perfectly cost-effective: the Laplacian demon's computations succeed in producing new knowledge without "consuming" any old knowledge, which is to say, that the new knowledge does not invalidate the old. This image is responsible for much of the rhetoric of classical epistemology:

(e) the observer unobtrusively representing the world-system (even when the mode of representation involves instruments, such as telescopes and microscopes, that alter both perception and the objects perceived);

(f) the overall progressive nature of knowledge (whether it be toward greater verisimilitude, certainty, or simply the accumulation of more facts);

(g) the so-called *parametric* nature of scientific rationality.

If these rhetorical points reflected the reality of the scientific enterprise, then the thesis of cognitive equilibrium would clearly be shown false. But, as it happens, over the last fifty years the points have been shown to be *little more* than rhetoric. Phenomenological philosophies of science, starting with Gaston Bachelard's (1985) pioneering *New Scientific Spirit,* have countered point (e) with the slogan "No representation without transformation (of the Lifeworld)." We shall later make more of this slogan. Kuhn effectively shattered point (f) by showing that any information gained during a scientific revolution must be paid back by some retraction of the old knowledge base. We will shortly illustrate this observation, which the Lakatosians have dubbed "Kuhn Loss," for it provides the historical basis for our cognitive equilibrium thesis. Finally, the contemporary French philosopher of science, Michel Serres (1972, 1982), has responded to point (g), which I shall now discuss in some detail, to draw out the implications of the cognitive equilibrium thesis for the theory of rationality.

The term "parametric" is normally a term in decision theory. A decision maker may try to optimize his situation in either a *parametric* or a *strategic* environment (Elster 1983). The decision maker of concern to us here is the scientist who optimizes his situation by obtaining a fully determinate (completely informative, noisefree) representation of the world-system. The classical epistemologist presumes that he operates in a parametric environment: that is, he has no reason to think that Nature intends to keep her secrets from him by deliberately confounding his hypotheses. Nature may be difficult to fathom, but not because of fickleness. For once the scientist proposes a correct hypothesis, Nature easily submits to his rule. Less sexist (that is to say, less Baconian) versions of this image of Nature may be found in Aristotelian potencies, Kantian matter (the "receptive" mode), and the Hegelian in-itself. It is an image that Serres counters by portraying the scientist's environment as strategic, with Nature just as interested in revealing the scientist's secrets as the scientist is interested in revealing Nature's. As the scientific enterprise becomes truly a game one plays with Nature, the approach to representation shifts from transcendental to naturalistic.

A scientist such as Newton intends to eliminate the noise, or "anomalies," in the Aristotelian world-system by providing a unified and mathematized theory of motion. He operates on the assumption that his strategy will solve more problems than it creates and, thus, will count as a step toward total knowledge. However, given his finite intellectual resources (great as they may be), Newton cannot survey all the possible states of the world-system that may result from each of the courses of action available to him. Consequently, he acts like Maxwell's ill-fated demon: in the immediate vicinity of the problems he is trying to solve, such as those concerning the motions of the planets, Newton makes striking advances over Aristotle. Indeed, the advances are so striking that they divert the public's attention from the massive noise being generated at the other conceptual end of the world-system. For once Newton divested physics of teleology, man no longer had a purpose, or "natural place," in the universe, except as another moving body. Arguably, the magnitude of this problem matches the one Newton succeeded in solving. And so, despite this implicit cost, the Newtonian Revolution was at first very much seen as a net gain in information, as witnessed in the continuation of Aristotelian modes of speaking about "man's place in the universe" by various eighteenth-century personalities, including Newton himself.

What are we to make of this blithe incoherence? In words borrowed from the deconstructionist critic Paul De Man (1971), the continued talk of man's place in the universe revealed the "blindness" unintentionally generated by the "insights" of the Newtonian Revolution. Serres would personify this blindness in terms of Nature having successfully outfoxed the scientist at his own game by getting him to construe a loss as a win. The success of Nature's long term strategy is revealed in philology, as the expression "man's place in the universe" subtly shifted meaning so that it ultimately became difficult to argue that Newton had failed to represent a significant portion of reality without appealing to the "old" use of the expression in Aristotle's cosmology. A key moment in covering over the sense of Kuhn Loss occurred when Kant characterized those non-Newtonian elements of the human condition—purpose and morality, especially—as having a *para-Newtonian* nature. Thus, Kant distinguished between man's *phenomenal* being, governed by laws beyond his control (namely, those of Newton's universe), and man's *noumenal* being, governed by laws that are self-legislated. After this distinction was made, the burden of proof lay squarely with someone who wished to argue that an account of the *physical* universe was radically incomplete if it did not provide an account of "man's place."

By way of indicating exactly how the savages and the systems illustrate the cognitive equilibrium thesis, we might start by explaining why I call it an *equilibrium* thesis. After all, both thermodynamicists and their followers in cybernetics are fond of saying that what counts as a "system," and whether it is in a state of "equilibrium" or "disequilibrium," depends on how one frames the point and scope of the activities under consideration. For example, the anthropologist focused on divination as a self-contained practice, and consequently found the shaman's ad hoc reasoning about the animal parts to increase the level of systemic disorder, since it seemed to complicate the implicit rules of divination for no apparent reason except to save the particular case. In contrast, the savages situated the shaman's reasoning in a larger system of representation, namely, one which included not only the animal parts, but the shaman himself, as representantes. The question for them, then, was whether to complicate their interpretation of how divination works or their interpretation of how the shaman works. The savages decided on the former, which effectively increased the level of theoretical mediation required for an observer to understand divination, since now not only must he grasp overt regularities in the practice, but he must also know those crucial junctures when deviation is allowed. One consequence of this move is to place more authority in the hands of the shaman over the interpretation of his own actions. Notice the upshot, namely, that the savages, as opposed to the anthropologist, realized that there are no absolute gains or losses of order in their representational system: in this regard, they implicitly subscribed to the cognitive equilibrium thesis.

Similarly, we might think of Newton's Enlightenment enthusiasts as acting like the anthropologist, only this time being impressed with the increased *order* in our understanding of the physical universe brought about as a result of Newtonian mechanics. However, this sign of scientific progress is seen by the critical historian as a purely local phenomenon in the representational system of eighteenth-century European culture, since it only made it that much more difficult to understand the nature of human beings: again the trade-off characteristic of the cognitive equilibrium thesis. Indeed, contrary to what one might have expected, the theologians of the time were able to take comfort in the emerging "man-the-machine" motif, since it embodied a paradox worthy of a divine genius. As Antoine Arnauld first noted, even if it is true that man himself is just another machine, man is nevertheless such a sophisticated machine that it will always remain a mystery how God was able to combine the rather simple laws of physics to design him (Vartanian 1973). Notice also that this case clearly brings out how cognitive equilibrium is maintained: not only is one's access to human nature made more indirect with the rise of Newtonianism (insofar as human nature can be understood only through the theoretical mediation of mechanics), but also *this indirectness is itself indirectly caused* (insofar as the mysteries of the man-the-machine motif were the unintended, and often unrecognized, consequences of the introduction of Newtonianism).

3. Explaining Transcendentalism Naturalistically: Bloor on Popper

We now turn to a sustained examination of an attempt to explain the transcendent-appearing features of representation in purely naturalistic, and specifically sociological, terms. In a series of writings starting with a review of *Objective Knowledge,* David Bloor (1974) has attempted to shift the locale of Popper's mysterious World Three—the realm of knowledge without a knowing subject—from a Platonic heaven to a Wittgensteinian language game. For all its mystery, World Three is nevertheless the very epitome of the transcendental approach to representation. We shall see that while Bloor succeeds in showing how much of what ordinarily passes as signs of objectivity may be understood as the product of normatively constrained social action, he fails to sociologize precisely what Popper and other thinkers have considered to be most emblematic of our sense of the objective: namely, *something (an anomaly or a problem) achieves objective status in virtue of resisting our efforts (understood either individually or collectively) at conceptualization and anticipation.* Yet here too a sociological translation is possible. According to my diagnosis, Bloor's reliance on Wittgenstein causes him to neglect the historical dimension of knowledge transmission. Remedying this deficiency suggests a role for Foucault's "archaeological" approach in fortifying Bloor's "Strong Program in the Sociology of Knowledge."

In "Epistemology without a Knowing Subject," Popper (1972, ch. 3) offers a "biological" argument for doubting that minds and bodies exhaust all the entities inhabiting the human world. Not only is man a conscious animal, he is also a being whose communicative capacity has evolved to the point of being able to describe and criticize his encounters with the world. The products of these distinctive efforts—books, artworks, and other textualized or symbolically coded items—have a peculiar ontological status: they are neither knowers nor, strictly speaking, knowns; rather they are *knowables.* To coax our intuitions into admitting this third world, Popper asks us to imagine a situation in which we have lost both the mental and material products of our encounters with the environment. Thus, we no longer have our individual subjective stores of information accumulated from years of experience, nor to do we have such artifacts as machines, tools, and buildings. Yet, so Popper claims, as long as the items in World Three and our ability to decode them (presumably, a general linguistic competence) remain, we will be able, after much hardship, to reconstruct our culture. In a stronger version of this story, even the human beings are eliminated, and sufficiently competent Martians are imported to reconstruct the human world. The fact that feats of this kind would be possible leads Popper to conclude that there is an autonomous realm of "objective knowledge."

The reader may already sense that we are on some tricky ground. In the first place, the very premise of Popper's thought experiment is controversial: namely, that aliens *could* reconstruct our culture by developing a linguistic competence in a way that does not involve actually interacting with us. It is clear why Popper wants this premise, since it drives a wedge between our beliefs (World Two) and the aliens' ability to know them (World Three). However, Alasdair MacIntyre (1984, pp. 1-5) has recently enlisted alien anthropologists in the cause of making sense of our moral discourse with much less success. MacIntyre supposes that anything short of *perfect* linguistic competence is bound to give the aliens a systematically distorted picture of the point of having moral discourse. Indeed, insofar as we in the present appear alien to Aristotle and the other great ethicists of the past, we have similar problems; hence, the thesis of *After Virtue*. (In part two, I shall address the problems raised by MacIntyre and resolve them in a way that he, but not Popper, would find salutary.)

But there are other problems with Popper's conceptualization of World Three. First, to say that World Three is the realm of the "knowables" is to capitalize on an equivocal "-able." Though Popper is less than completely open on this point, what seems to mark off the texts in World Three from the tools in World One is that texts can intervene in any of the three worlds. A text can be used to intervene in World One, if it is interpreted as a set of instructions for maintaining or transforming the physical environment. The same text can also be used to intervene in World Two, if it is interpreted as a set of propositions that purport to represent one of the worlds and, hence, a candidate for the reader's assent. Finally, and most obviously, the text can be used to intervene in World Three, if it is interpreted as a set of remarks that defines the significance of some other text. The equivocation in "knowable" enters once we observe that a text is, therefore, not only an object that can be known in several different ways (that is, "knowable" in the sense of interpretable as a set of instructions or propositions or remarks), but also itself a medium for knowing the objects of the different worlds (that is, "knowable" in the sense of something that can be used for knowing something else).

Now, readers who have been influenced by the likes of Marshall McLuhan and Umberto Eco will find this definition of World Three excessively narrow, since contemporary studies of technics and semiotics tend to collapse World One and World Three into a realm of "mutually signifying objects." Thus, on this current view (which is intuitively most plausible in the archaeological contexts), texts in the conventional sense, linguistically coded bits of matter, do not have a privileged status as "representers" or "signifiers" of reality—any artifact will suffice. But a charitable reading of Popper demands that the difference between Worlds One and Three be seen as *functional* rather than as ontological. In other words, a text may simultaneously be in the two worlds, but in World One it functions as a material object, while in World Three it functions as a knowable. This functional distinction is important, since Popper's elaboration of a realm of knowables is probably the most successful attempt yet at saving the intuitions that have traditionally motivated Platonist and other transcendentalist ontologies. Moreover, as will be noted in our critique of Bloor, these intuitions are easily lost on the modern mind.

Bloor enters the picture once we start to wonder about the exact contents of World Three. While Popper's thought experiment may have succeeded in carving out a metaphysical space for objective knowledge, clearly more work needs to be done in order to fully specify its contents. For example, if *Don Quixote* is to be found in World Three, then it certainly does not appear there as some bound printed pages on a library shelf, nor as the set of particular interpretations gleaned by particular readers: the former would be found in Popper's World One and the latter in World Two. Whereas Popper at this point resorts to Platonic ideas, Hegel's Absolute Spirit, and Fregean propositions, Bloor offers the more down-to-earth suggestion that World Three is simply the social world—or, more precisely, the set of permissible moves of the language games that constitute a "form of life." In that case, *Don Quixote* appears in World Three as the language game one must play in order to pass off an interpretation of the text as legitimate to a given community of readers. Among the components of this game would be knowledge of what counts as a proper citation from *Don Quixote*, what counts as a proper argument in support of a particular interpretation of the text, and so forth. Contra Popper and other closet Platonists, Bloor's World Three does not contain "the best possible reading" of *Don Quixote*— say, all the true propositions concerning Cervantes's intentions in writing the text.

This last point is important for Bloor because, like Wittgenstein, he stresses the *open-textured* nature of such concepts as "proper citation" and "proper argument," which implies that the social order defined by a set of language games constrains an agent's possibilities *only* through the actions taken by other agents in particular situations (Waismann 1951). Thus, what counts as a permissible interpretation of *Don Quixote* at one point in history might not have appeared that way at an earlier point, even though in both cases the interpreters seem to have been playing the same language game. When Popper (1972, p. 155) claims that World Three can interact with the other two Worlds only through World Two, he makes largely the same point. However, as Bloor observes, since Popper models World Three, at least in part, on an immutable Platonic heaven, he underestimates the open-textured, and hence sociogenic, nature of its contents. But as we shall now see, Bloor goes to the opposite extreme and underestimates the autonomy, and hence, objectivity of World Three.

Bloor (1984, p. 229) claims that his sociological construal of World Three captures the chief aspects of objectivity, which he identifies as "the *impersonal* and *stable* character that attaches to some of our beliefs, and the sense of reality that attaches to their reference." Bloor (1982) normally credits the idea to Durkheim, though Durkheim never quite expressed it the way Bloor does. Instead of speaking of *beliefs* as having a social origin, Durkheim (1961) generally referred to collective *representations*. The difference is subtle, but nevertheless crucial for understanding the source of Bloor's difficulties.

Like Popper, Durkheim and his followers in French and British social anthropology have treated beliefs as irreducibly subjective and hence outside the domain of an inquiry devoted to objective knowledge (as sociology was supposed to be). Indeed, it was on these grounds that Durkheim had dissented from Gabriel Tarde and Gustave LeBon, who argued that the collective representations studied by sociology were reducible to a summation of the "sentiments" of the constitutive individuals, which would be the proper subject matter of an intersubjective psychology (Sorokin 1928, ch. 11). Although Durkheim himself was less than explicit on this point, a close study of the Durkheim School's use of "collective representation" would reveal that such an entity arises not when everyone has the same beliefs, nor even when everyone believes that a belief has been accepted by the group; rather, it arises when everyone tacitly agrees to express *whatever they may happen to believe* in terms of specific linguistic and other symbolic practices. This is certainly how Saussure construed Durkheim in the course of presenting structural linguistics (that is, *langue*) as a study of collective representations (Dinneen 1967, ch. 7). In other words, the attitude emergent on *belief* once epistemologists ascend from the individual to the social level is *conformity*: individuals believe, groups conform. In the most thorough study to date of Durkheimian epistemology, Rodney Needham (1972, p. 155) underscores this point by observing that in modern societies, the legal system comes closer than any particular set of beliefs to exemplifying a collective representation.

More like Foucault than Popper, the Durkheimians go so far as to deny any cross-cultural (let alone, ontological) import to the category of belief. They point out that beliefs inhabit personal psychologies, which are, in turn, the invention of modern European culture (Mauss 1979). Consequently, the anthropologist runs a great risk of misinterpreting an alien culture if he tries to sort out its epistemology in terms of the "beliefs" that members of the culture hold. Needham (1972, ch. 2) beautifully documents this claim, as in the case of the Nuer, who do not have a word for belief, not because their psychological lexicon is not sufficiently discriminating, but because the contexts in which the Nuer evaluate assertions never require that they treat an assertion as expressing a belief. In other words, there simply are no situations in Nuer culture where one would be interested in evaluating an assertion in terms of its fit with the asserter's background knowledge: the typical context in which we would evaluate a belief. Even in our own culture, the evaluation of beliefs in this sense is relatively recent. The Latin source of the concept, *fides*, originally had to do with loyalty, a willingness (or "disposition," as epistemologists would now say) to act on behalf of the object of belief, especially in the case of God. However, the concept of belief as the unit of a personal knowledge, whether the object be God or "medium-sized dry goods," came into general English usage only in the nineteenth century (Smith 1977).

However, to put Bloor on the right track, we do not need to decide here whether belief is a cross-culturally valid category of knowledge. The point he needs to take from the Durkheimians is, vividly put, that beliefs are the "messages" that individuals of a society send to each other, while representations are their common "medium." Thus, a belief may be represented linguistically in various ways, each conveying the sense of the belief more or less successfully. The rules of a language game may be such that certain beliefs—in virtue of being readily expressible—are more easily justified than others, but that does not preclude the possibility that a hard-to-justify belief may someday have its burden of proof borne successfully by a skillful player of the game. Thus, what Bloor may have mistaken for a collective belief is, in fact, a *presumption* under which members of the society have agreed to operate. To return to our original example, it is not that the more farfetched readings of *Don Quixote* are impossible to defend, but rather that they require satisfying probative standards much more stringent than interpreters would probably undertake. Consequently, the farfetched interpretation is de facto, though not de jure, excluded by the community of readers as a legitimate belief about the meaning of *Don Quixote.*

The same applies to episodes of theoretical change in science. However, like most of his antagonists who do "internalist" history of science, Bloor errs in thinking that during such episodes what generally happens is that *beliefs* change. At least, this is an error if Bloor intends on saving the appearances of Popper's World Three within a Durkheimian framework. Popper is quite adamant that beliefs are purely subjective matters that belong exclusively to World Two, and, as we saw, World Three appears in World Two as the display of certain, mostly linguistic competences (especially the ability to read) which would allow for the successful reconstruction of our culture after a global catastrophe. Once Bloor is given a more strictly Durkheimian gloss, the role of language games in sociologizing World Three becomes clear: namely, they define the situations in which these competences can be displayed, which is exactly how they provide the normative structure of social action. Bloor sometimes actually espouses this position, as when he says, the connection between the stable features of the social system and the stable features of the knowledge system is perfectly clear cut. One is not an arbitrary correlate of the other. As we arrange the conventional pattern of our relations we are, at the same time, arranging the framework upon which our cognition must depend. This should occasion no surprise once we realize that we do not have a choice between arranging our beliefs according to reality, and arranging them according to social convention. We know *with* our conventions, not in spite of them. Our conventions represent an unavoidable condition for, and vehicle of, knowledge. To yearn after a reality unmediated by convention is like wanting to see better by getting our organs of vision out of the way. [Bloor 1984, pp. 239-240]

Nevertheless, Bloor fails to maintain this position consistently, perhaps because he runs together two meanings of *convention*. In politics and linguistics, conventions are contrasted, respectively, with contracts and grammars, in that a convention is a practice that has emerged largely without design yet continues to be maintained in virtue of the beneficial consequences accrued to the individuals who adhere to it. Conventions in this sense, the subject of David Lewis' (1969) influential book, are often said to be *naturally* occurring. But there is also a more *artificial* sense of convention associated with "conventionalism," a doctrine formulated by Henri Poincare about what confers validity or legitimacy on a theoretical statement, namely, that it follows from some earlier explicit agreement about definitions and assumptions. As Hilary Putnam (1975, ch. 9) first observed, conventionalism's metaphysical consequences are stronger than they seem, since the doctrine implies that the validity of, say, a mathematical theorem follows from *nothing but* the set of axioms from which it can be derived. Now, most of Bloor's examples of theoretical change in science involve explaining the adoption of a set of theoretical beliefs in terms of how those beliefs would promote the interests of a group of interest-seeking scientists. Sometimes the emphasis is placed on how the scientists can ex post facto benefit from beliefs which happen to gain the approval of the greater scientific community: this suggests the first sense of convention. However, on other occasions, the emphasis is placed on the scientists originally deciding to hold a certain belief in order to promote their interests, which suggests the second sense of convention.

Bloor's failure to distinguish these two senses of convention becomes most apparent when we try to parse the concommitant "arranging" of "our relations" and "the framework upon which our cognition must depend." Even granting that Bloor is correct when he says that whenever we engage in science we are also engaging in a social practice, it does not follow that what makes for good science policy also makes for good social policy (and vice versa). If we regard science as a naturally occurring convention, like the capitalist marketplace in the Popperian manner, then the temptation is to let science be as science does, which is not necessarily beneficial for the society at large. On the other hand, if science is regarded as an artificially constructed convention, like a game in the ethnomethodological vein, then there may be the temptation to erect and dismantle the institutional structure of disciplines with the sort of ease normally reserved for fashions. Thus, until Bloor is forthcoming with a theory of conventions, it by no means clear how showing the "conventionality" of our knowledge enterprises is supposed to explain or justify them.

Nevertheless, Bloor's convention-and-interest explanations have been taken as competing with the accounts offered by internalist historians of science, who try to explain the very same theoretical beliefs in terms of evidence and background information (or misinformation, as the case may be) available to the relevant scientists.   Neither type of explanation requires a clear demarcation of World Three from World Two. In particular, they lack the sense of normative constraint that a sociologized version of World Three is supposed to provide (Lukes 1982b). To remedy matters, Bloor would be wise to avoid focusing on how individual scientists tailor their beliefs to serve their social ends; rather, he should try to show how scientific language games impede or facilitate the articulation and legitimation of certain beliefs, *regardless of who might be interested in advancing them.* And so, to borrow Bloor's favorite example, while it may be true that Boyle and Newton would not have put forth corpuscularian natural philosophies had they not been interested in staving off religious sectarians, this at most gives a sociogenic account of how their beliefs attained *subjective* status—that is, beliefs which they personally found worthy of pursuit.   To explain sociologically how these beliefs attained *objective* status would be to identify the arbiters of scientific competence in seventeenth-century England and the forms of linguistic representation (especially the kinds of arguments) they took as signs of such competence, and offer an assessment of the relative ease with which corpuscularian beliefs could be conveyed in this medium.

And so we see that the source of Bloor's difficulties in constructing a social theory of objectivity may be traced to his usual portrayal of social agents as relatively unconstrained manipulators of the contents of World Three. As a result, Bloor is unable to show how objectivity transcends the judgments of a collection of psyches, denizens of World Two, without reverting to some traditional identification of the objective with the physical—that is, part of World One. Ironically, this weakness in Bloor's position is most glaring in what he takes to be his biggest advance over Popper's account of World Three. A key Popperian argument for the independent existence of World Three is that all theories have logical implications unknown to the original theorist which are recognized, and hence *discovered*, by later theorists.   These unanticipated theoretical consequences then become the basis of problems, which for Popper are the only source of genuine intellectual growth. Bloor dismisses this argument as a kind of mystified Platonism, offering in its stead the following explanatory strategy:

> We would have to say that, really, logical implications do not pre-exist: we construct them as we go along, depending on nothing but the dispositions that we possess naturally or have been given in the course of

our training. This will have to be the reason why we agree to the extent that we do on such matters as the implications of our premises. Our tendency to *say* that the consequences of our premises pre-exist then becomes a facet of our behavior that calls for special explanation. The explanation might be that certain feelings attend our drawing of inferences—say, feelings of compulsion. Or the explanation might be that this way of talking is a way of trying to justify our (really unjustifiable) tendency to say one thing rather than another. It is our way of creating a continuity between our current and our past verbal practices. [Bloor 1984, pp. 234-235]

Notice that the kind of explanation Bloor suggests for "our tendency to say that the consequences of our premises pre-exist" is, broadly speaking, teleological. The last three sentences of the quote may each be understood as "teleological" in three distinct senses:

(j) each may be describing the *intentions* of certain individuals whose interests are served by being logical;

(k) each may be using logical compulsion to *rationalize* certain otherwise inexplicable psychological tendencies found in all human beings;

(l) each may be giving the *function* that being logical serves in maintaining the social order, regardless of whether anyone intended it that way or even realizes that such a function is served.

But do any of these accounts explain the sense of objectivity that *the social agents themselves* attach to the logical implications of a theory? Another way of putting this point is to ask, assuming that there is some validity to (j), (k), and (l) as explanations of our tendency to be logical, why then are most agents intuitively skeptical of the adequacy of these very explanations? For we routinely reaffirm our belief in the objectivity of logical implications *in the course of doubting sociological explanations of the very kind Bloor proposes.* Somehow, we vaguely suspect, there must be more to logic than just a set of conventions established by social agents to behave in a certain way. While Bloor may ultimately be right that all these intuitions and suspicions are instances of false consciousness, they are exactly the sorts of thing which constitute *the appearance of objectivity* and thus need to be saved—or reduced—by a social theory of objectivity. (We shall consider this point in more detail in ch. 10.)

For a somewhat different perspective on Bloor's inability to keep the identity of World Three distinct from Popper's other two worlds, let us briefly look at Bloor's most extended attempt at showing how agents negotiate the unanticipated consequences of a theory. It appears in a review of Lakatos' *Proofs and Refutations.* Here Bloor (1979) argues that a theory can retain its claim to representing reality inspite of failed predictions and unforeseen counterexamples, just as long as its proponents agree to deploy a set of devices—Lakatos' negative heuristic—designed to neutralize the destabilizing effects of anomalies. Bloor then shows that the tendency to use one such device more than another—say, monster barring over exception taking—is indicative of how the particular research community is organized. But can these efforts at theory maintenance be taken as the source of the theory's *objectivity*? As before, the best strategy for answering this question is to consider the point at which the objective intuitively diverges from the social. While the classification of an anomaly is readily seen as socially negotiable, the very presence of the anomaly—whence comes the *need* for classification—seems quite independent of the social order, largely in virtue of its not having been anticipated. Even Bloor is of this opinion: "The natural order provides the external stimulus, and the social order the terms of the response." (Bloor 1974, p. 76) Yet Popper himself refuses to let objectivity slide back into its traditional place in World One, as Bloor now seems to suggest. Indeed, as we shall now see, it appears that inclusion of both theories *and their unanticipated consequences* keeps all the objects securely in World Three.

Let us consider two somewhat analogous cases, one firmly rooted in the animal kingdom and the other quite distinctly human. Suppose some jungle animals want a drink of water from the local pond. Since this is their sole desire, they take the shortest route to the pond, plowing through the underbrush and leaving traces of a path which can be later used by other animals. Though clearly an unanticipated consequence of the interest in water, the path will soon become an object of interest in its own right, as its existence creates problems, which if not addressed could seriously upset the animal ecology. For example, should the path have free or restricted access, and what if one animal tries to restrict passage to members of its own kind? That the animals feel compelled to address these problems in some way indicates to Popper (1972, p. 117) that their behavior is constrained by World Three.

Now suppose the ancients, reflecting on the many measurement tasks they perform in everyday life, decide to economize on effort by clearly distinguishing the measuring instruments, which can be used repeatedly, from the various things that can be measured. This leads to the invention of a system for representing the natural numbers. However, it is soon noticed that these symbols do more than just facilitate practical tasks. On the one hand, the number system has peculiar properties of its own, which generate the kinds of problems mathematicians discover and try to solve; on the other hand, once the number system is recognized as mediating all measurement tasks, knowledge of at least some of its properties becomes necessary for competence in measuring, which ultimately leads to mathematics becoming an essential part of the training of, say, engineers. The former consequence, stressed by Popper, establishes the autonomy of mathematics as a body of knowledge, while the latter consequence, stressed by Foucault (1975, p. 118) as "the principle of rarity," authorizes mathematicians to judge the competence of engineers whenever they engage in measurement.

From these two cases of how animals and humans unexpectedly—indeed, unintentionally—cause World Three, we may draw some conclusions about the nature of the link between unanticipated consequences, objectivity, and the social order:

First, the consequences of creating the path and the number system were unanticipated in that their creators had no idea of the various ways *others* would use them. This implies that for unanticipated consequences to arise, there must be a collection of individuals drawing from a common pool of artifacts (including systems of representation), but for purposes that are not always closely monitored and thus allow for divergent uses. Had there been close surveillance of the individuals, then it would have been possible to anticipate, and thereby perhaps control, the range of uses to which the path and number system could be put. As Robert Merton (1936) originally observed, virtually every classical social theorist—including a "methodological individualist" like Adam Smith (one might add Popper [1957] as well)—located the origin of the social in the constraints that these unanticipated consequences placed on the possibility for future action.

What makes a collection of individuals difficult to monitor, and hence their actions difficult to anticipate, is either their sheer numerosity or their distribution over great expanses of space and time. Had the inventor of the number system thought that his scheme would make it easy later to pose the problem of irrational numbers, he might have come up with some other way of separating out the measuring from the measured, or he might even have scrapped the idea entirely. But of course, once the number system left his hands, these options were no longer available. Foucault's (1979) relevance here is to bring out a sociological counterpart to "Nature abhors a vacuum"—to wit, *Power abhors ignorance.* Whenever it is impracticable to monitor the activities of a vast array of individuals, the unmonitored individuals constitute themselves as a monitored group, or "discipline." And so we see that not only do the mathematicians study the unanticipated consequences of the invention of the number system, but they also embody a special competence which allows them to monitor the activities of the engineers (Smart 1983, pp. 108-137).

It is clear, then, that unanticipated consequences are intrinsically socio-historical phenomena. Both Popper and Bloor miss the point, though for different reasons. Popper, perhaps because his paradigm of World Three is the set of mathematical objects, unnecessarily falls back on a Platonic picture of the consequences of a theory "pre-existing" their discovery. After all, Popper (1972, pp. 128-140) first presented the three worlds picture as a critical tribute to the mathematical intuitionist L.E.J. Brouwer. Brouwer believed (i) that the only real mathematical objects are those constructible (by some direct proof procedure) by the finite human mind, (ii) that these objects exist solely as mental constructions, and (iii) that their objectivity is maintained only by our ability to construct them *at will.* Popper introduced World Three largely as a means of refuting Brouwer's belief that (i) entails (ii) and (iii). The positive thesis to issue from this refutation was that mathematical objects cannot be purely mental constructions, or intuitions, because all the problems arising from them cannot be anticipated by the finite mind.

Bloor, who alters the nature of theories from sets of propositions to language games, rightly criticizes Popper for overreacting to Brouwer and, thus, retaining a Platonist's sense of "pre-existing" mathematical forms. Still, the sociologist is not thereby forced to render, say, the realization of a contradiction as either a matter of pure convention or a sign of brute nature impinging on the theory. Rather, he need only say that Lakatos-style anomalies arise once a theory is used to represent a domain which the original theorist(s) did not fully anticipate—or maybe even intended. However, in creating the theory, the originator also created *the potential* to be used that way. (The model for such a substantive notion of potential is, of course, Aristotle's *dynamos*, which has been revived in social theory by Bourdieu [1977].) Only some of the potential consequences of a theory are ever articulated, while others will forever remain silent as other theoretical language games emerge.

What makes the emergence of unanticipated consequences possible is also what makes their emergence difficult to detect. Ordinarily, actions are evaluated in terms of the consequences that their agents intend and anticipate. Byproducts of the actions are rarely taken into account unless they are fairly noticeable in their own right or relatively contemporaneous with the intended/anticipated consequences. However, if these byproducts do not make themselves felt until long after the initiating actions—and then in a rather different context compounded with the byproducts of other actions—they are unlikely to be perceived as causally related to the original actions. Foucault's (1975) "archaeology of knowledge" aims precisely to recover this often obscure chain of accidents, for the inability to specify the socio-historical origin of a concept or practice has often been taken as a sign of its timelessness and immutability—in a word, its objectivity. Thus, in *The Order of Things*, Foucault (1970) starts with the curious fact that while "the problem of man" has generally been regarded as a perennial one for our culture, the idea of an inquiry specifically devoted to it does not arise until Kant's coinage of "anthropology" in 1795. Foucault then goes on to show, among other things, how the potential for anthropological discourse was created by the roughly simultaneous appearance in the mid-eighteenth century of quite independent lines of research in natural history, philology, and political economy. Unlike Bloor, who usually seems to draw episodes from history without demonstrating an awareness of the *flux* of history, Foucault realizes that to identify the objective with the social is not to make what passes as objective knowledge any less resistant to the intentions and expectations of individual social agents.

PART TWO

ISSUES IN THE LANGUAGE AND HISTORY OF KNOWLEDGE PRODUCTION

CHAPTER THREE

REALISM, THE MOVING TARGET OF SCIENCE STUDIES:
A TALE OF PHILOSOPHERS, HISTORIANS, AND
SOCIOLOGISTS IN HOT PURSUIT

Is whether a sentence is true or false, or whether a state of affairs obtains or not, relative to our state of knowledge? "No," says the *realist*. "Yes," says the *antirealist*. Setting the debate in such stark terms makes the difference of opinion seem quite straightforward. And, indeed, it would be, were it not for the fact that the dispute arises at many points in Science Studies—points between which there are no clear connections. In other words, we follow Michael Dummett (1976, ch. 10) and Jerry Fodor (and oppose the more popular W.V.O. Quine and Donald Davidson) in seeing the problem of realism decided differently in different contexts of inquiry. It is a mistake to simply *presume* that the problem must be resolved in one way for all contexts. Admittedly, the standard procedure in metaphysical disputes has been to attempt all-or-nothing solutions. But this procedure encourages a sort of "in principle" or "a priori" style of argumentation, which, because it is designed to cover all cases, tends to be conducted at so abstract a plane that it becomes difficult to judge the validity of the particular arguments made. We shall see an example of this style in the transcendental arguments for scientific realism, which are so abstract that it is no longer clear how the historical evidence should be interpreted.

Before we begin tracking down the various contexts in which the problem of realism arises, a quick survey of the conceptual terrain is in order. For the sake of convenience, I shall state these as a list of dicta:

(1) You cannot participate in the scientific realism debate—even as an antirealist—unless you are an historical realist. All parties believe that the history of science bears decisively on the outcome of this debate, largely because they presume that historical inquiry is as epistemologically sound as any other empirical inquiry. This even goes for Kuhn and Feyerabend, both of whom are more concerned with how historical agents constructed their worlds than with the more strictly hermeneutical issue of how historians construct the historical agents. In fact, given his reluctance to abstract from the "brute facts," the scientific antirealist may be *especially* committed to historical realism.

(2) Although sociologists of knowledge are, understandably, antirealists about the entities produced by physicists and other natural scientists, they need not be antirealists about social entities as well. For example, they may believe that there is "a fact of matter" about why a certain set of individuals are said to belong to a certain category. But whereas the scientific realist would ideally say that the

fact has to do with properties that these individuals have in common (an "essence"), the sociologist would, first, show that the individuals really do not share the alleged common properties and, then, explain the individuals being "conventionally" grouped together in terms of the relevant social facts about the context of categorization.

(3) The modern realist debates are analogous to the scholastic dispute over the existence of universals. Corresponding to the defenders of universals are regulative realists, who believe that if something is an x, then it is an x in virtue of certain properties that all x-type things are said to have. Corresponding to the nominalists are constitutive realists, who believe that there are certain brute individuals (things, events), in virtue of which words refer, but which do not in any way depend on the words for their existence. The point to be noted here is that these two realisms are logically independent of one another. For example, both positivists and social constructivists are typically constitutive realists but regulative antirealists, while Kuhn and most Platonists are regulative realists but constitutive antirealists. Of course, scientific realists are realists on both scores, though the thought that one *must* hold the same view on both regulative and constitutive matters has led to much confusion in the debates over whether alien cultures are "really" rational.

(4) Insofar as scientific realism is committed to the gradual accumulation of knowledge over time, it presupposes that knowledge can be retained, which, in turn, entails that the content of a given knowledge claim can be preserved intact in a later body of knowledge. Now the realist has two options as to how this perfect translation occurs: either by preserving the entities to which the original claimant thought he was referring (pluralistic, or many-worlds, realism) or by preserving only the evidence that originally caused the claimant to refer as he did (monistic, or one-world, realism). The difference is represented by Kuhn and Quine, respectively. Here the antirealist holds that neither of the realist options provides an entirely satisfactory account of how translation occurs. Instead, each case of translation involves a contextually determined trade-off between the two approaches to translation.

1.   Realism: Who's Got the Burden of Proof?

There was a time, three hundred years ago, when Bishop Berkeley could argue a priori that realism was unintelligible on the grounds that counterfactual claims about the state of the world independent of knowers were neither true nor false, since by definition such claims could not be verified; hence, Berkeley argued that our "intuitive" belief in the existence of

God was grounded in our equally "intuitive" antirealism toward the world, which required the presence of an ever vigilant verifier. But those days are long gone. Nowadays, in arguing about realism, philosophers frequently start with the claim that we have realist intuitions, that realism is commonsense, or that realism is the natural attitude. Claims of this kind are intended to shift the burden of proof from the realist to the antirealist. Yet, despite the fact that such claims preface detailed arguments for scientific realism, they are typically based on an equivocation.

In common parlance, "regarding the world realistically" or "having a realistic attitude toward the world" is best glossed, in philosophical jargon, as knowing the probabilities of certain states of affairs obtaining under the conditions most likely to obtain in the agent's world. Thus, people who are ordinarily described as "realistic" are *not* ones who know the theories that best explain how and why things happen as they do (something that a scientific realist would know), but people who can anticipate what is and is not likely to happen, both in light of and in spite of whatever they might do. The ordinary realist then is a devotee of practice not theory, *phronesis* not *episteme*, *savoir* not *connaissance*.

It would seem, then, that the "realist" of common parlance is indifferent to the philosophical problems of realism. Indeed, we can imagine a scientific realist whom ordinary folks would regard as anything but a paradigm case of a "realist" in their sense. For example, this scientific realist may be equipped with all the best theories available for explaining everything that is of interest to him, but because these theories must be combined in rather complicated ways when applied to particular cases, our realist has great difficulty accessing the information he needs to predict what is going to happen next. To be concrete, let us say that he knows all the best theories of terrestrial mechanics, optics, and perceptual psychology, but nothing about the "folk" psychological and physical theories implicit in our ordinary understanding of the world. It would hardly be surprising then if our scientific realist ends up bumping into walls and doing all the other sorts of things that would mark him as an "absent-minded professor" rather than as a "realist" of common parlance.

Irony aside, this example should make us sensitive to the fact that even if we knew the "real principles" governing the behavior of some domain of objects, it would not follow that those principles would be of much use in answering the questions that interest us about that domain. More to the point, it would not even follow that those principles would be of much use for *scientific research itself*, unless we had already established (through independent argument) that the search for real principles is one of the aims of science. This point would have been obvious to a positivist/fideist like Pierre Duhem (1954), who argued that since the principles then typically proposed as "real" were metaphysical and theological in nature, knowledge of them was clearly beyond the methodological strictures of science. However, the point is now much subtler, insofar as we might want to include among the "real principles" entities derived from the application of scientific technology, such as quarks and other creatures of microphysics, whose relevance to the human condition seems minimal and whose interest to scientists may entirely depend on the search for real principles being one of the aims of science. (Admittedly, the scientific realist may have an "escape clause" here, if he can show that these real principles are necessary for the production of certain humanly beneficial byproducts.)

Someone unsympathetic to what I have said so far will remark, "All that you have managed to show is that 'realism' is a word with many different meanings. The fact that philosophical realists like to piggyback on the ordinary sense of the term only shows that they shouldn't be allowed to do that. It certainly doesn't show that any form of philosophical realism is false or untenable." True, but, for better or worse, it is the *word* "realism" that makes literary critics and historians of science perk up their ears and start taking an interest in what philosophers are doing. And given that the terms of the realism debate have shifted over the years, it is still very much an open question as to what is the *interesting* issue that hovers around the word "realism."

To give you a sense of how drastically the terms have shifted over just the last twenty years, consider that back in the days when the debate was presented as "realism vs. instrumentalism," the burden of proof was placed on the *realist* to explain why science could not go about its business without supposing that the terms mentioned in its theories had real referents. The presumption was that the positivist theory of science was both correct and exhaustive: namely, that science aims toward greater prediction and control of the world and that the relative value of theories can be measured exclusively in terms of how they contribute to that goal. Traditional virtues of scientific theories such as explanatory power, fertility, and analogy remained virtuous only to the extent that they served as indirect indicators of increased instrumentality. It should be noted that the realist of common parlance would probably feel quite comfortable with the sentiments of the *instrumentalist* who, after all, is not denying that the terms of scientific theories refer; rather he is denying only that the ends of science are enhanced in any way by knowing whether or not they refer. Thus, just as the ordinary realist is indifferent to the issue debated by current philosophers, the instrumentalist, as, so to speak, "the conscience of common scientist," was indifferent to the issue that greatly exercised his opponent twenty years ago (Nagel 1968, ch. 6).

From a rhetorical standpoint, the scientific realist was originally at a disadvantage because the debate was framed in instrumentalist terms: that is, the realist had to give an *instrumentalist* defense of realism, namely, by showing how realism enhanced the ends of science. With the deck so stacked, it is perhaps not surprising that convincing realist responses were not forthcoming. There has been great confusion over the significance of this dialectical state of affairs in the 1960s and early 1970s, again largely due to the fact that historians and philosophers have not been careful in specifying exactly what "realism," "instrumentalism," "positivism," and the like are supposed to characterize. Take the roles that Kuhn and Feyerabend are thought to play in all this. In my view, while Kuhn and Feyerabend were beneficiaries of "the instrumentalist presumption" then operating in philosophical debate, they themselves were not instrumentalists. Indeed, they were committed to rather exotic forms of realism (Kuhn to a many-worlds ontology and Feyerabend to a one-world ontology that resists any possible epistemology) which would quickly discourage the scientific enterprise *if anything scientific hinged on knowing whether or not the terms of our theories had real referents*. And, of course, this is the very point that instrumentalism denies.

2. Why Is It Now So Difficult to Defeat the Realist?

As we would expect of any dialectic, the pendulum has now swung so that the current philosophical debate over realism places the burden of proof squarely on the shoulders of the realist's foe, now called the "antirealist," which already suggests that the foe's very position makes sense primarily in terms of its opposition to realism. There are two ways of posing the question that the antirealist must now answer, which are not strictly equivalent, but which are similar enough to highlight the difference in style between Old Wave Metaphysicians and New Wave Philosophers of Science. In the Old Wave: Is there any way that the success of science can be rendered intelligible other than by saying that (most of) the terms of its (most recent) theories have real referents? In the New Wave: Is there any better way of explaining the success of science than by saying that (most of) the sentences of its (most recent) theories are true? The Old Wave dares the antirealist to refute a transcendental argument to the effect that a realist interpretation of scientific theories must be presupposed conceptually if the history of science is to make any sense at all. The New Wave argues in a somewhat more empirical vein, hypothesizing that once we collect all the data about scientific practice and situate it a general theory of our attempts to make sense of reality, we will find that the best explanation of why science is so notably successful is that its theories are true representations of reality. The difference between the Old Wave and the New Wave Realists, then, boils down to the difference between Kant and Peirce.

Yet, for all their differences, both Waves of Realists agree on what the antirealist needs to account for as well as they can: namely, the *success* of science (Boyd 1984). Expressing the contested phenomenon in this way nicely captures the extent to which the realist now controls the terms of debate, such that the antirealist is asked, in effect, to provide a realist defense of antirealism. "Success" is simply the realist's discreet way of saying "progress," the long term net accumulation of knowledge as measured by increasingly better explanation, prediction, and control over more phenomena. If success in this sense is taken to be a brute fact about the history of science, then notice the sorts of explanatory avenues that are closed off to the antirealist. Take, for instance, this argument: if we compare what, say, Aristotle was interested in explaining, predicting, and controlling with what we currently are, it would not be so clear that relative to our interests we have advanced that much further than Aristotle did relative to his. The antirealist cannot make this argument because the realist's concept of "success" allows any relativistic maneuver to be reinterpreted by saying, first, that Aristotle was essentially engaged in our project when doing what he called "science" and, second, that Aristotelian sentences can be translated into our own and then evaluated for their truth-values.

Another line of attack closed to the antirealist is this: as major conceptual changes occur in science, cognitive interests shift so as to render entire bodies of knowledge obsolete, not because they have been shown false, but because they cannot be easily fitted into the new conceptual scheme. As a result, scientists simply stop talking about such matters. This is the phenomenon that Lakatosians call "Kuhn Loss," which is most clearly illustrated in the loss of *telos* as a constitutive feature of nature after the transition from the Aristotelian worldview to the mechanical world-system. Clearly, the antirealist wants to show by this argument that it is difficult to make out the claim that there has been a net *gain* in knowledge, except from the standpoint of what currently interests us. However, realists easily block this move by what is known, after Kripke and Putnam, as *the causal theory of reference* (Schwartz 1977). The general strategy here is to say that just because Aristotelians thought that there were *teloi* ("purposes") about which one could make true or false claims, it does not follow that sentences which mentioned *teloi* were really about the intended entities. Rather, the Aristotelian sentences really refer to whatever entities in the best scientific theory (with ours, of course, acting as surrogate) would best explain their uttering those sentences. The envisioned explanation would then show how the Aristotelians systematically misidentified the properties of some real entities as *teloi*.

In blocking this last argument, the realist claims to be making a point about the relation of meaning to reference: namely, a theory of reference for a language need not admit what speakers of that language "mean" or "intend" by their sentences; it need only admit the entities (as identified in the best scientific theory) which caused the speakers to utter those sentences. However, to the antirealist, this simply looks like a subtle way of begging the question in favor of realism, since it presupposes that there is a fact of the matter about the reference of particular sentences, independent of the linguistic categories in which the world is conceptualized. Yet, this presupposition is supposed to be the bone of contention that divides the realist and the antirealist. Befitting the current "realist presumption," philosophical debate over the causal theory of reference has centered largely on making the proposal conceptually coherent and on specifying the implications of cases in which the referent is not easily identified. There has been little discussion about the general empirical feasibility of such a theory

(Do we have the sort of resources it would take to determine the reference of sentences in this manner?) or whether it approximates our actual referring practices. Now, is there any way that the historian of science can open up some new avenues of inquiries and thereby save the antirealist from his dialectical disadvantage?

Let us start with the Old Wave Metaphysician, who makes a transcendental challenge to the antirealist. At first glance, it might seem that the empirically minded historian has little to offer in the antirealist's defense. But such a judgment would be much too premature. Recall that the transcendental argument purports to show only the *conceptual* necessity of a realist interpretation of the history of science. And it is at least arguable that it would be very difficult indeed to understand the history of science as a history of *science* if its trajectory did not exhibit the kind of progress lacking in the histories of other cognitive pursuits, such as religion and common sense. However, just because there is this conceptual limitation in *our understanding* of science, it does not follow that the history of science *really* exhibits the conceptually necessary progress. It may simply be that a certain way of writing the history of science has become so entrenched in our culture—one whose narrative structure includes a "Scientific Revolution" in the seventeenth century and the increasingly successful attempts of the special sciences over the last three centuries to emulate the virtues of classical mechanics—that we systematically ignore or explain away any evidence which would impede this particular historiography.

Notice that we have just provided the basis for a *realist* refutation of Old Wave Realism that is, at the same time, a defense of antirealism. More to the point, it is a dialectical strategy in which the skills of the historian of science are essential. His main role here is to "demystify" or "deconstruct" the narratives normally used for recounting the history of science by revealing the "facts" (construed as a realist would) that are systematically omitted because these narratives perform the latent function of legitimating the cognitive interests which motivate current scientific inquiry. If the historian finds the exemplars of this method—Marx, Foucault, Derrida— rather obscure masters to follow, that is only because the masters have been unwilling to presuppose historical realism in the course of defeating historical theses advanced by the realist. Marx and Foucault may be exceptions here, but they certainly do not follow through on their realism consistently. Indeed, one of the biggest tactical blunders committed by the deconstructionists has been to focus exclusively on the reflexive implications of their radical antirealism, which leads them to produce texts that "deconstruct themselves," while remaining oblivious to the fact that on the current dialectical scene realism is most forcefully refuted on its own terms. However, the realists have not been oblivious to the significance of this blunder, which is that carried to its extreme, antirealism could not ground the kind of communication theory that is presupposed by science preserving the truths that it accumulates over time.

Somewhat more sure-footed in its willingness to presuppose historical realism is the methodology of Quentin Skinner (1969), who, armed with Austin's speech-act theory, has systematically shown the vast disparity between how Machiavelli, Hobbes, and Locke were understood by their intended audiences (which, as Skinner is at pains to observe, is something other than how they intended to be understood by those audiences) and how we understand them as voices in "our political tradition." Moreover, the most significant feature of this disparity is *not*, say, that Hobbes' audience understood him as asserting one proposition, while we understand him as asserting another; rather, they often understood Hobbes as performing some speech act other than *asserting*, which is the speech act we typically understand him to be doing all the time. I direct this point about Skinner's methodology specifically to historians of science, since among the facts they may unearth to refute the realist is that the scientists in question were not originally understood as making assertions, but rather speech acts which do not involve the assignment of truth values.

Before going any further, it should be made clear that the historian of science needs only to presuppose historical realism *dialectically* in arguing against the scientific realist, who, after all, will accept only arguments with realist premises. Nothing I have said should be taken to suggest that historical realism is *generally* a desirable philosophical position. But in all fairness to the scientific realist, I should also say that he would be able to fend off the attacks of the historian of science, if he could neutralize the significance of the facts that he has been "systematically" omitting. Briefly, such a possibility would consist in the realist somehow managing to abstract the "purpose" of the history of science—namely, to attain the maximally coherent and comprehensive theory of the nature of things—and then showing how the events he identifies are *essential* for realizing that purpose, while the ones identified by the historian are *accidental* and need not have taken place.

In recent philosophy of science, the Popperians, especially Imre Lakatos (1970), have been masters at this sort of counterfactual teleologizing. However, in writing such a history, the scientific realist must be careful not to fall prey to a fallacy first noted by Max Weber (1964), which would involve confusing the *value significance* of realism with its *causal significance*. Although the value significance of scientific realism is undeniably great insofar as major scientists, such as Aristotle, Galileo, Newton, and Einstein, made sense of their own work in this way, such a commitment to realism may well turn out to have had relatively little impact in determining the actual course of events in the history of science. Indeed, given the causal complexity of history in general, it is well within reason to suppose that the operative causal factors have been incidental to the value commitments of the historical agents.

Now on to a more direct confrontation between the historian of science and the New Wave Realist. You will recall that the New Waver thinks of himself as being a sort of scientist of history whose theory of reference will help him establish what scientists in the past were really talking about and how right they were in saying what they said about it. Now if the New Wave Realist fancies himself to be a scientist, or at least someone who proposes realism as an *empirical* hypothesis about the "success" of science, then the hypothesis must be systematically testable. Admittedly, since the New Wave Realist is—needless to say—a realist, he may still be right even if there turns out to be no way of testing his hypothesis. He may simply follow the Old Wave line and claim that the causal theory of reference is part of what must be presupposed if the history of science is to make any sense at all. However, in that case, the New Waver would also have to give up any pretense of being scientific or empirical. And so, he is forced to play the game of *verifiability conditions* in the antirealist's ballpark: namely, to what extent can *we* determine the reference of past scientific discourse such that *we* are able to tell how much of it is true?

3. Putting Scientific Realism to the Historical Test

From reading Putnam (1975, ch. 13; 1984), one could easily get the impression that the requisite verifiability conditions are easily satisfied. Much of the argument has what can only be called a "pseudo-empirical" feel. For example, we are told that the Bohr-Rutherford 1912 description of what they called "electron" *approximately fits* the quantum mechanical description of what is today called "electron," in virtue of our electron playing many of the same conceptual roles that their electron was intended to play. The way Putnam wishes to verify this claim is by applying "the benefit of the doubt principle" to Bohr and Rutherford (in their 1912 frame of mind), which implies that if Bohr and Rutherford were shown (what we now know to be) the mistaken beliefs that informed their 1912 description of the electron, they would gladly accept today's formulation. The pseudo-empirical feel of all this does *not* stem from Putnam's mere reliance on counterfactual history. Actually, I think such a history can be quite valuable for the historian of science who wishes to take part in the realism debates—as long as its methodology is somewhat more substantial than an appeal to naive intuition, which, I fear, is all that is operating in Putnam's case.

Where naive intuition is lurking, transcendental concerns cannot be far behind. And indeed, Putnam goes on to argue that the Bohr-Rutherford electron *must* approximately describe the referent of our term "electron," in order for the history of science to be rendered intelligible. His striking way of making this point is by claiming that the rationality of science depends on the following induction being blocked: *just as no scientific theory held fifty years ago (or at some other suitably distant time in the past) is today taken to be true, likewise in another fifty years no theory that we now take to be true will enjoy that status.* Putnam's worry seems to stem from a view that has become prevalent among historians influenced by Kuhn and Feyerabend, namely, that alternative scientific theories are not simply better or worse ways of making sense of a common body of data but rather are actually constitutive of different bodies of data. It follows on this "holistic" approach that to replace one scientific theory with another is also to replace one body of data with another. Consequently, since theories are accepted and rejected as wholes, nothing is preserved and transmitted in the course of history, which means that the key indicator of scientific progress, cumulative growth (at least in the body of data accounted for), is eliminated.

Now if one holds that scientific theories are designed *exclusively* to attend to the cognitive and practical demands of a particular period, then radical holism of this sort does not cause any problems. But as Richard Boyd, one of Putnam's students, has observed, the succession of theories in the history of science appears to have an implicit *direction*, namely, toward the subsumption of more data (Putnam 1978, ch. 2). Boyd believes that this tendency occurs by the latest theory accounting for data that an earlier theory failed to do, while retaining most of the data that allowed the earlier theory to replace a still earlier theory. Notice here that Boyd's concept of directionality allows us to distinguish a *stronger* and a *weaker* version of scientific realism. The stronger version, one endorsed by Peirce, Popper, and the early Putnam, takes the tendency toward increasing data subsumption, or "phenomena saving," in the history of science as evidence for science aiming for (and ultimately arriving at) the best possible account of how things really are. On this view, the history of science has both a direction and a goal: scientific activity is both purposeful in its own right and has a purpose other than its own pursuit. In contrast, the weaker version attributes to science a direction but not necessarily a goal, namely, the subsumption of ever more data without the process having to converge on the ultimate picture of reality. Such a view would be palatable to a positivist, has actually been endorsed by Bas van Fraassen (1980), a theoretical antirealist who is also an *empirical* realist, and seems to be lurking in Putnam's (1983) most recent writings.

Because Putnam's work encompasses both versions of scientific realism, it makes a good touchstone for launching critiques of the general position. I shall proceed by attacking the stronger version on four grounds, then launching one attack on the weaker version, and finally criticizing any scientific realism that relies on a causal theory of reference.

The first criticism is launched at the supposed need to block the induction that worries Putnam. As was noted, *only* a scientific realist has such a need. Either of his major opponents, the instrumentalist or the more generic antirealist, can not only accept, but also explain why the induction *should* go through. Recall that the whole point of instrumentalism is that the success of science is not tied to the truth-value of its claims (or even whether they have truth-values), since scientific theories are nothing but elaborate sets of *instructions* for predicting and controlling the world. The realist's worries would thus seem to stem from having too narrow an understanding of the different functions that language can perform: surely they include more than just representation or description, since (so claims the instrumentalist) the linguistic practice of scientists does not function primarily in either manner. The more generic antirealist would take a slightly different tack, granting (at least for the sake of argument) that scientific discourse is primarily representational or descriptive, but then arguing that as the cognitive interests of the scientific community change, so too do the sorts of things about which one needs to have true theories. On this diagnosis, then, the realist is worried only because he holds the unwarranted belief that there are some historically invariant cognitive interests—alluded to earlier as the "purpose" of the history of science—in terms of which one may speak of "increasing success" over time.

My second critical remark is directed at Putnam's appeal to "approximate truth." Unlike most philosophers who criticize this notion, I am not so much concerned with either the conceptual point that "approximate truth" may have no useful meaning if the truth is not already presumed to be known (as Putnam and other realists more or less do) or the factual point that no method has yet been devised for ordering scientific theories according to how closely they approximate the truth. My own concern is with taking seriously the metaphor which guided Popper's original conceptualization of "verisimilitude," the prototype of all recent theories of approximate truth. Popper likened the idea of theories successively approximating the truth with mountaineers climbing a mountain shrouded in fog. An implication of the metaphor to which I would draw your attention is that several mountaineers may be *the same distance from the summit but coming at it from different directions.* This makes matters somewhat messy for the scientific realist, unless he has reason to believe that there is a *preferred direction* to the top (compare Haack [1980]).

To drive home this last point, consider the roles that the mystical Johannes Kepler and the mechanistic Rene Descartes played in the development of Newton's world-system. (In using the word "development," I am trying to tell the scientific realist's story in as much of his own terms as possible.) Kepler was correct about the elliptical shape of the planetary orbits and about the existence of an attractive force over the planets that decreased in inverse proportion to the square of a planet's distance from the sun. Unfortunately (from the standpoint of Newton), Kepler believed that the physical source of this force was the sun and that the force itself was the embodiment of the Holy Spirit. Now Descartes was correct about minimizing the explanatory significance of God and about the existence of another force in the universe, namely, the one inherent in bodies that pushes them toward one another. But while Descartes, therefore, had a clear conception of inertia, he lacked any sense of gravitational attraction. Moreover, he continued to think that the planets moved in circular orbits. This comparison of Kepler and Descartes suggests that if there is no preferred direction to the truth, then Kepler and Descartes, despite their radically different orientations to science, approximated the truths expressed in Newtonian mechanics to roughly the same degree, since the work of these two "natural philosophers" represents complementary theoretical strengths (and weaknesses) from the standpoint of Newtonian mechanics.

While none of the above, strictly speaking, contradicts scientific realism, the realist would still find it a rather undesirable possibility because scientists would then appear a bit too unwitting in their contributions to the progress of science. It is one thing to claim, as Putnam and realists normally do, that past scientists wanted to know about roughly the sorts of things that now interest us and therefore are rightly said to have provided, in many cases, approximate descriptions of what we can now provide true descriptions. It is quite another thing to claim, as we have shown to be permissible by the concept of approximate truth, that past scientists can provide descriptions that approximate our own even if they had no interest whatsoever in knowing about the sorts of things that now interest us.

This brings us to my third critical remark, which concerns Putnam's appeal to "the benefit of the doubt principle." As the Bohr-Rutherford example illustrated, Putnam assumes that showing a rational agent that some of his beliefs are false is sufficient for his changing those beliefs, specifically *to the ones that his critic suggests*. Now such an assumption might be appropriate in Putnam's chosen example, since it is historically probable that Bohr and Rutherford were engaged in a project that contemporary quantum mechanics has brought to fruition. However, in general, it is important to countenance two sorts of situations, whose likelihood increases the farther back in history we go, in which we would still want to claim that the agent was rational:

(a) the agent grants that some of his beliefs would be false, were he engaged in some modern project, which he is not, and so the criticisms are not applicable;

(b) the agent admits that his beliefs are indeed false, but corrects them so as to retrench his own cognitive interests, rather than to conform more closely to the beliefs of his modern critic.

A couple of thought experiments will perhaps jar your intuitions in the right direction—that is, away from indiscriminately applying the benefit of the doubt principle. Start by supposing that Galileo tried to convince Aristotle through a series of experiments that he confused average and instantaneous velocity. Why might Aristotle not be impressed by the demonstration? Perhaps Aristotle would refuse to pay attention to the results of a science that uses Galileo-style experiments, or maybe, seeing that the distinction in velocities boils down to a difference in their mathematical representation, he would deny their intelligibility. Now let us suppose that a thoroughly agnostic Newtonian (that is, *not* Newton himself) tried to convince Kepler that universal gravitational attraction, and not the sun's luminescence, was the best explanation of the inverse square law. Whereas the Newtonian would understand his arguments as being exclusively about physical principles, Kepler would interpret them in terms of their consequences for conceptualizing God's power and would thus judge the Newtonian's arguments accordingly.

I do not want to suggest by these examples that Aristotle and Kepler could *never* be brought around to taking Galileo's and the Newtonian's criticisms as they were intended. However, a conversion of that kind would involve persuading Aristotle and Kepler that their *projects* are not as sound as those of their critics. Moreover, I believe that there can be rational argument even about such normative matters. All I wish to point out here is that the critic would then have to appeal to something more than the simple falsity of his interlocutor's beliefs.

My fourth critical remark, which was suggested by some things I earlier said about approximate truth, addresses the realist claim that "truth" is the best explanation for the success of science. Even if we grant that the overall goal of the history of science is the maximally true representation of reality, it does not follow that the best explanation for the success of any *particular* scientific theory is that it is true. To license such a conclusion would be similar to arguing that because the market *functions* to benefit all its participants, it follows that each participant *intends* to benefit the others, even though, as Adam Smith showed, what allows the market to be self-regulating is precisely that its participants intend to benefit *only themselves*. In general, to think that the truth of the whole implies the truth of its historically constitutive parts is to commit the fallacy of division. I take this logical point to underpin the Hegelian thesis that if history is "rational," or purposeful, then it is probably "cunning" as well, in the sense that its agents unwittingly bring about this purpose (Elster 1978, ch. 5).

Depending on his attitude to the history of science, the realist may find the Hegelian thesis either comforting or distressing. He would find it comforting, if he sees the history as providing an empirical test of his explanation for the success of particular theories. On the one hand, an increasing number of historical and sociological studies show that if we equate the "success" of a scientific theory with its survival value, then it is probably false to say that the most successful theories have been the ones whose claims to truth have been most closely scrutinized (Shapin 1982). Still, on the other hand, as a Hegelian, the scientific realist can dismiss these potentially falsifying cases and claim only "truth in the whole." And perhaps his story would not be entirely implausible. If a scientific theory typically survives because, say, it serves the cognitive interests of its time, then those parts of the theory that are retained throughout history must serve several, perhaps quite different, cognitive interests. How is that possible? Maybe because interest-invariance is the leading empirical indicator (or practical consequence, to put it more robustly) of truth.

But notice the price that the scientific realist has to pay for telling this story—and here he starts to find the Hegelian thesis distressing: to wit, the realist becomes irrelevant to the sorts of issues that interest historians of science, which typically concern the fates of particular theories. Moreover, even when the historian is concerned with explaining the survival of theories through major changes in cognitive interests, the realist must contend with the alternative accounts more likely to be favored by the antirealist and instrumentalist: whereas the antirealist might try to show that the change in cognitive interests caused subtle shifts in the meaning of the theory's terms which render the old and new versions little more than homonyms, the instrumentalist might well just fall back on an appeal to human resourcefulness in adapting old theories to new ends.

The weaker version of scientific realism would seem to be less open to criticism, since it purports to render science rational without referring to any goals outside of the practice of science itself. Indeed, there is a way of elaborating this view that makes it compatible with social constructivist approaches to science, which are normally regarded as antirealist. Whereas Putnam only hints at such a view, it has been more fully articulated by Ian Hacking (1983, chs. 9-14) in *Representing and Intervening*. The basic idea shared by Putnam and Hacking is that Boyd's sense of directionality in the history of science became possible only once units were designed for measuring levels of accuracy and precision—in particular, the accuracy of fit between predicted and actual observations and the mathematical precision with which both sorts of observations can be characterized (Laymon (1984) applies this thesis to Newton's light experiments). To put it bluntly, the concept of scientific progress, especially the idea that one can approximate the truth by degrees ("verisimilitude"), was a byproduct of the invention of certain instruments that allowed the relevant sorts of measurements to be taken and compared. Not surprisingly, these instruments—including the telescope, microscope, and pendulum clock—were introduced in the late Renaissance, roughly the time of the Scientific Revolution.

To get a feel for the fit between the realist and constructivist strains in this version of scientific realism, consider some general claims that a proponent of this position would make about the history of science:

(c) Before the design of accuracy and precision metrics, it was impossible to speak, in any modern sense, of one theory being "better" than another for a given range of phenomena.

(d) The only circumstance in which it makes sense to say that one theory is "better" than another is when they both measure the same range of phenomena (and one theory provides more accurate and precise measurements than the other).

Neither of these claims is particularly surprising: (c) reflects the constructivist and (d) the realist strain in this weaker version of scientific realism. However, the litmus test for the position arises in answer to this question: Does it make sense to say that a measurable theory is "better" than a theory without provisions for measurement? Here is another way of putting it, which clarifies what exactly is at stake: *Does the "invention" of scientific progress itself constitute a moment of progress in the history of science?* The realist strain (dominant in Putnam) says "Yes," while the social constructivist strain (dominant in Hacking) says "No." Either response is problematic, however, because the weaker version of scientific realism cannot generally make good on the connection between its own sense of "scientific progress" and "the growth of knowledge," without begging the question.

As we suggested earlier, the weaker version of scientific realism is compatible with positivism. And herein lies the problem. Boyd assumes that successive theories are able to subsume more data because they have greater explanatory power, which, in turn, derives from each successor isolating deeper causal factors than its predecessor. This is clearly a realist account, indeed the only one that works, according to Boyd. However, there is an alternative, antirealist account for the.directionality of the history of science: namely, in terms of a tendency for instruments to be used to the point of maximum efficiency (Elster 1983, part 2). This tendency may be regarded as either relatively autonomous, as in the pursuit of technical virtuosity for its own sake, or tied to a goal outside scientific practice proper, as in the application of scientific techniques to social problems whenever the opportunity arises. The pursuit of technical virtuosity is an especially interesting option because it captures, to a large extent, how the "pure scientist" conceives of his own activity (Polanyi 1957). In that case, the purposefulness of, say, using a telescope to make very precise observations is comparable to the purposefulness of playing a trumpet to make highly nuanced sounds. This comparison is a good reminder that pursuing science for its own sake is logically independent of pursuing science for the sake of Truth. Indeed, the realist would need an empirical argument to establish that pursuing science for its own sake—rather than, say, pursuing science for the sake of increasing wealth or power—is the best means of pursuing Truth. Moreover, it is entirely open whether such an argument is ever likely to work.

For the episode in the history of science that epitomizes the antirealist line, interpreted both aesthetically and instrumentally, one need only turn to the development of Alexandrian science in late Antiquity, which produced Euclid's geometry, Ptolemy's astronomy, Galen's medicine, Diogenes' grammar, and Callimachus' prosody—all distinguished by the perfection of technique, a concern for application, and a disdain for speculations beyond the phenomena. Indeed, the motivation for building the Library of Alexandria was, contrary to realist expectations, *not* to centralize all knowledge in order to facilitate further study and synthesis. Rather, the library's ever increasing size symbolized a key dimension of power at which the Pharaoh was unsurpassed. Indeed, while comprehensive, the library was not particularly well organized (Thiem 1979, Fuller & Gorman 1987). Notice that this great era of measurement and technique took place over 1,500 years before the Scientific Revolution. Again contrary to realist expectations, the observations made during the Scientific Revolution were, for the most part, less accurate and precise than those made by the Alexandrians. (Of course, this is not to deny the realist claim that the *explanations* of these phenomena "improved" during the seventeenth century, at least in that they began to approximate our own.) To take a vivid case, the utility of Ptolemy's *Almagest* for navigation was not surpassed until Laplace's *Celestial Mechanics* of 1799 turned Newtonian mechanics into a convenient device for computing the positions of the stars and planets (Toulmin 1972, p. 378).

Finally, let us consider whether it is empirically feasible to test the causal theory of reference as an explanation for the continuity apparently exhibited by the history of science. To take a concrete case, what would a historian with realist sympathies need to know in order to show both that Archimedes was interested in discovering the nature of what we call "gold" and that he would accept the atomic weight of gold as a better description of its nature than the one he proposed 2,500 years ago? My perhaps surprising answer is that he would need to know *at least* what some other historian would need to know in order to show that Archimedes was *not* interested in discovering the nature of what we call "gold" and, consequently, would *not* accept the atomic weight of gold as a better description, etc. We might imagine this second historian to be a supporter of Kuhn or Skinner, who is a scientific antirealist but a historical realist. In other words, our second historian believes that Archimedes is talking about whatever his intended audience understood him to be talking about and that there is a fact of matter as to how his audience understood him.

But regardless of their stands on scientific realism, both historians would need to know what Archimedes (or his intended audience) thought he was talking about. This may seem to be a rather trivial point of convergence, yet it highlights the fact that just because the scientific realist does not grant the Archimedean conceptual framework any *authority* in determining what Archimedes was really talking about, it does not follow that the realist can do without knowing how that conceptual framework picked out objects for Archimedes. As Kripke (1977) would put it, Archimedes' description of what he called "chrysos" performs two distinct functions: it both *defines the meaning* and *fixes the reference* of "chrysos." Whereas a follower of Skinner or Kuhn might tend to conflate these two functions, the scientific realist wants to be able use the description so as, first, to identify what in the world Archimedes is talking about (that is, fix the reference of "chrysos") and, second, to determine whether what he says about it is true (that is, to see whether what he means by "chrysos" is the same as what our best scientist means by "gold"). Indeed, we might see the reference-fixing aspect of the episode as exhibiting the *performative* character of the description; for even once it turned out that Archimedes had defined the meaning of gold incorrectly (that is, on the basis of a false theory of elements), the *act* of definition itself remained as the historical trace grounding subsequent attempts at a definition.

It should be clear, then, that, if anything, the historian with scientific realist sympathies needs to know *more*, not less, about Archimedes' original context of utterance than his opponent, since the Skinnerian historian, in a flourish of Kuhnian many-worlds realism, could simply conclude that whenever Archimedes said "chrysos" he was (of course) talking about the entity chrysos—something that occupies a more or less well-defined space in the Greek conceptual framework—and not feel that he was missing anything important by never having observed Archimedes hold up a sample of what he called "chrysos." While this may appear to imply a defense of the thoroughness required of a historian with scientific realist sympathies, keep in mind that the issue here is not *thoroughness* but *feasibility*. Your philosophical position in the current realist debates should keep you believing that the history of science is both doable and worth doing. As we have just seen, however, it is not clear that the causal theory of reference supports such a belief, since, on this view, what makes the history of science worth doing is that it allows us to determine how close to the truth past scientists got, yet the way historians are supposed to determine this is by *observing* how the reference of past scientific terms were fixed. Of course, much turns on how strictly one interprets "observing." On a radical empiricist reading, which makes observation something inherently of the *present* (as in the case of sense-data language), the historian would be blocked by logical impossibility in his attempt to show the continuity of scientific inquiry over time. But even if we were to count as "observations" the textbook reports of authoritative individuals naming or sampling objects, we would still be faced with the fact that the relevant evidence is not systematically available. In other words, once we regard language from an empirical standpoint, there is no reason to think that the reference of every term in a language is initially fixed in the manner suggested by Kripke, nor that the reference of each term is transmitted by a "teacher" reenacting the original naming episode for the benefit of a "pupil."

Now this last objection may strike the reader as begging the question against the realist, since it slides from commenting on our knowledge of reference fixing episodes to commenting on the very existence of such episodes. Only an antirealist, it would seem, can slide from epistemology to ontology merely with "in other words" rather than with extensive argument. The missing premise here, which complicates the realism issue even further, is that reference fixing is a *social fact*, as in the case of a contract or a promise. That is to say, a major part of what makes an event "a reference-fixing episode" is its being officially designated as such an episode. In one sense, then, social facts are clearly creatures of antirealism: namely, they are brought into existence by the appropriate group recognizing them as such. For even if it is reasonable to suppose that every term had an "original" use in the sense of "temporally first," that original use is its reference-fixing episode only if it has been canonized as the standard by which subsequent uses are evaluated as (im)proper applications, extensions, and so forth, of the term. No doubt, this point is often missed by an equivocation on "origin," which, like the Greek *archai*, can mean either "temporally first" or "ultimate principle." Thus, as Searle (1969, pp. 50-53) would put it, people often confuse the "brute fact" and the "institutional fact" of origin.

But social facts are creatures of realism, too, in that the answer to whether a reference-fixing episode exists for a given term is independent of our *current* historical knowledge. Indeed, to say that a fact has been "socially constructed" is *not* to deny either its objective status or its ability to persist in the face of human efforts at changing it—points made, in recent times, by Popper (1972) and Sartre (1976), respectively. Rather, to call a fact "social" is simply to remark on the fact's origin, which may well be quite significant in its own right—especially if the fact in question is one generally regarded as not having an origin, or more precisely, one generally regarded as not needing to have originated when it did in order to enjoy the epistemological status that it does. (The relevant examples here are mathematical facts and other allegedly "necessary" or "universal" truths.) In that case, identifying the social origins of these facts can be the first step toward showing the various long term cultural commitments that had to be made in order for their social character to be erased. More relevant to our concerns here, a realist attitude toward social facts is necessary in order to distinguish between terms for which we no longer have the evidence as to how their reference was fixed and terms which simply never had their reference fixed. For as we shall see below, it is the second half of this distinction that figures in the most damaging critique of *scientific* realism.

If there is some truth to what we have been saying, then why has there been relatively little criticism of the causal theory of reference? One reason, no doubt, is that the sort of reference-fixing events to which the causal theorist, or historian, would need access are the relatively mundane ones that occur whenever, say, a master introduces a novice to a technical term or a parent teaches a child a new word. Because we frequently witness such events happening, and indeed often participate in them, there is a tendency to think that we can simply infer by analogy what would have occurred in past reference-fixing episodes. However, reference fixing is a transparent activity only for competent speakers of the language whose terms are being fixed, since a speaker understands how the reference of a new term is fixed by being able to locate its meaning in the conceptual space mapped out by his language, which will, in turn, enable him to individuate the referent from other things in the world. Now the realist historian's task would be greatly aided if cultures typically recorded their principles of individuation: that is, if they made explicit both how much of the world is meant to be picked out whenever they used a name and which are the clear and borderline cases of using the name correctly. However, typically no such records are systematically kept, thus giving rise to the problem which Quine (1969, chs.

1-2) has famously called, "the inscrutability of reference." Drawing on Whorf's account of the ontology implicit in the Hopi language, Quine illustrates the inscrutability thesis by having a native say "Gavagai" and point to what looks to the anthropologist to be a rabbit and then asking how would the anthropologist be able to tell whether "Gavagai" means rabbit, rabbit part, or even the fly that always follows rabbits around. Needless to say, the situation is much more desperate for the historian who cannot take the liberty to conduct experiments on dead "natives" to test these interpretive possibilities.

Given the obvious importance of individuating principles for turning the abstract conceptual framework of a language into a concrete practice, it might be thought that a record of them would be useful not only for the realist historian but for the native speakers as well. Why, then, do they go unrecorded? A question of this kind—namely, of why something *isn't* the case—is, of course, unabashedly speculative. Still, thinking about it may remind us of some basic facts, especially that *you cannot become a member of a culture by taking a correspondence course.* More precisely, the knowledge amassed by a culture is encoded not merely in the sentences which fill the pages that historians typically read but in the habits that one comes to learn by interacting with other members of the culture. I submit that the main habits learned by natives which mark them as "competent speakers" consist in how to individuate objects through their language.

But having said that, *could* these habits of individuation, at least in principle, be recorded in writing, so that a historian, many years and miles away, would be able to develop a competence in the native language without ever having to make contact with the natives themselves? After all, the main reason why the natives fail to articulate their individuation principles may simply be that they do not have an interest in belaboring with words what gives them no difficulty in practice. However, I suspect that the reason runs much deeper, namely, that although the natives are constantly being given feedback about whether they have used some term or other correctly, it does not follow that there are any strict principles governing *how* that feedback is given. Returning to Quine's example, the fact that the natives themselves discriminate between right and wrong uses of "Gavagai" does not allow the anthropologist to conclude that their judgment calls are determined (even implicitly, in the sense of a Chomskyan deep structure) by a set of grammatical rules. The general point, then, is that just because the linguistic behavior of the natives is *locally constrained,* that does not mean that their behavior is also *systematically regulated.*

So far I have argued that one reason why the causal theory of reference has not been criticized for being unverifiable is that the facts it relies on are rather homely and therefore thought (fallaciously) to be readily available. Another reason, I shall now maintain, is that the causal theory probably functions as a transcendental condition for our understanding the present as historically continuous with the past: that is, the intelligibility of history would be substantially undermined, if it proved impossible to render what past speakers were talking about in terms of things that we might talk about today. But as we noted earlier when criticizing realism as a transcendental condition for the intelligiblity of science itself, even if the causal theory of reference is *conceptually necessary* for our making sense of history, it does not follow that it cannot be *empirically dubious* as well.

Indeed, if we are correct in claiming that relatively few words have had their references canonically fixed, then it is likely that most of the time the historian has no way of knowing how to characterize, in his own language, what some past speaker was talking about, unless he has quite detailed knowledge of the actual context of utterance. Moreover, as our remarks in the second to last paragraph suggest, even in the cases of words whose references have been canonically fixed, the mere presence of canonical usage does not guarantee that the canon will be applied in a systematic fashion. Thus, the later Wittgenstein (1958, 1967) was right to maintain that even well-defined concepts (that is, a system of semantically related words) are "open-textured" with regard to their application in specific cases, which means that there is no fact of the matter about the correct application of a concept in a given case prior to the native speakers actually letting the application pass as correct. And so, even if the historian were able to cross-examine the original historical agents about their usage, he would probably discover that they had no principled knowledge about it. In short, despite its admitted transcendental status, *it is doubtful that the sort of knowledge required by the causal theory of reference has ever existed.*

Let me explain what I mean by this last claim. Of course, I am not denying that speakers of a language fix the reference of their terms or that they get into "habits of referring," so to speak, which allow them to individuate objects in new situations with relative ease. What I reject is the idea that a culture has any authoritative means of ensuring that all these activities proceed in a systematic and consistent manner: while language games have many local referees, they have nothing analogous to a supreme court or a bureau of standards. As a result, there are probably many cases in which, say, one group of ancient Greeks permitted a certain use of "chrysos" to pass as correct, while another group of Greeks refused to allow a similar use of the word to pass. If the two groups do not soon afterward meet up to decide which usage is correct, then "chrysos" starts to acquire a complex referential function, which, in the long term, will lead to the subtle shifts in meaning that philologists have found to be ubiquitous in language, and which are, in turn, the source of much of the "incommensurability" studied in this book. Given its rather low level of self-regulation, a language is then hardly the ideal mechanism for storing, transmitting, and retrieving information. *Therefore, we must take seriously the possibility that a language is simply not well designed to do the sorts of jobs—storage, transmission, and retrieval—that the scientific realist requires of it.* If a final blow is ever dealt to scientific realism, it will be on these grounds.

4. Kuhn and the Realism of Many-Worlds

On the face of it, my last pronouncement seems patently false, at least on semantic grounds: What else is a language but a means by which knowledge is stored, transmitted, and retrieved? True enough—but one can say that language was designed to perform particular cognitive functions without being committed to saying that it performs those functions particularly well, or even that those are the functions that it performs best. Indeed, the point of this section will be to show that poor self-regulation is the price that language pays for being a rather exceptional means of lending continuity, and hence legitimacy, to whatever happens to be the current state of affairs. As our subheading suggests, this phase of the inquiry will examine a new and strange brand of realism.

Despite what I have said about the design features of language, I am far from skeptical about the possibility of our having any historical knowledge. After all, there may be a fact of the matter as to whether a culture had a certain concept (that is, whether it applied a set of semantically related words in a range of cases) without there being a fact of the matter as to whether the concept is applied correctly in a particular case. The problem with the causal theory of reference is that it is realist on both scores, even though relatively few words have had their references fixed in a way that would provide either the native or the historian grounds for judging the correctness of usage, aside from the brute fact that, in particular cases, the use happened to go challenged or unchallenged. Not surprisingly, historians take into account this absence of canonical facts about usage in the course of their practice, and, indeed, this feature of their practice explains why *philology* has traditionally been the flagship discipline of the "historical sciences." Say I want to know the extent to which the ancient Greek "chrysos" overlaps in meaning with the modern English "gold." As an historian, I start by getting a clear sense of the conceptual space mapped out by "gold," namely, the category it belongs to, the kinds of predicates ascribed to it, the registers of discourse it occupies (technical, colloquial, etc.), the implicitly contrasting terms, and its typical figurative uses. I would probably need to rely on a dictionary, a thesaurus, an encyclopedia, and some writing samples. Next, I go through a similar routine for "chrysos." Finally, I compare notes for the extent of overlap. Notice that all this can be done without my ever having observed a correct application of "chrysos."

While the procedure outlined above is well within the limits of verifiability, you might wonder whether it exhausts everything that a historian needs to know in order to understand a culture. After all, shouldn't he know *something* about how words in the native language were used in particular cases? In an important sense, the historian already does, since if, in a particular case, an ancient Greek was deemed correct in his use of "chrysos," then the historian knows the reason that the Greek (or his audience) would have given for his having used "chrysos" on that occasion: namely, that the particular stuff to which the speaker referred was deemed to have the properties that anything called "chrysos" is defined as having. This sort of information, which could be gained from a somewhat idealized dictionary of ancient Greek, does not predict, or perhaps even explain, why *that* particular stuff on *that* occasion was identified as an instance of chrysos, but it does *justify* the significance of that event to the ancient Greek audience.

In discussing matters of methodology, as we have in the preceding example, it is always tempting to claim that historians focus so much on the linguistic features of a culture because only those features are readily available to them. However, instead of assuming that historical methodology is simply a matter of making the best of a bad situation, we can take it to suggest an account of how language works different from the one implicit in the causal theory of reference. Rather than "chrysos" being directly attached to samples of the stuff we call "gold" through episodes of reference fixing, *this account would suppose that both "chrysos" and the sample are alternative ways of identifying a concept which serves a particular function in legitimating the practices of ancient Greek culture.* If the reader suspects that I am trying to impute a socialized version of Platonism to the historian, then he has followed me so far.

Let us consider an alternative way of making the same point that will be familiar to readers of Wittgenstein's *Remarks on the Foundations of Mathematics* and *Philosophical Investigations.* My knowledge of, say, the Peano Axioms and all the theorems of arithmetic—the sorts of universal principles that mathematicians study and formalize—is never sufficient to determine which arithmetic principle I am applying when I am trying to complete a number series like "2, 4, 8,..." Moreover, when the mathematical realist (or "Platonist") claims that there is a fact of the matter as to how the series goes, he may well be correct, but that piece of information offers small comfort to the person counting, who is interested in finding out exactly *which* fact is being referred to. What is missing, of course, is the background knowledge that forms the context for this particular case of counting. And, so Wittgenstein famously concluded, if one is interested in discovering what grounds our mathematical knowledge, in this ground-level sense of knowing how to continue the series, then he had better look to the social function served by the particular counting practice, which will render certain ways of continuing the series legitimate and other ways illegitimate. Notice that Wittgenstein has not so much shown Platonism false as *irrelevant* to the regulation of our actual counting practices, which, in the final analysis, are constrained only on a context-by-context basis (Bloor 1973).

Our only difference from Wittgenstein is that we have no special interest in underplaying the legitimating role of Platonism. For no matter how the series turns out to be completed on a particular occasion, its completion will be justified in terms of its conformity to one of the infinitely many valid mathematical formulae that are normally said to inhabit the Platonic Heaven or some other suitably objective realm. And unlike Wittgenstein's philosophical anthropologist, historians can study the local application of constraints only with great difficulties. Likewise, when it comes establishing the canonical use of "chrysos," while its usage is not defined in a way that would enable the historian to predict its applications, it is defined so that once something is said to be an instance of the "chrysos," the historian he can infer the properties in virtue of which that thing is properly called "chrysos."

There is one sense in which I would go so far as to claim that the historian is not missing any essential information about ancient Greek culture by never having observed a Greek fix the reference of his words, namely, insofar as the historian supposes that sentences in ancient Greek are better designed for manufacturing the culture of ancient Greece from moment to moment than for either describing reality or, indeed, communicating actual events across long stretches of time to the historian. Without repeating my earlier remarks, the general reason why he would suppose that the design features of language are as I have suggested is that he can obtain reliable information about the conceptual framework underlying ancient Greek culture by knowing its language, while his ability to extract from the language information about the exact history of the culture (that is, the actual events to which particular sentences refer) is much less certain. I do not take this to be a surprising result, since a crucial feature of how a culture maintains its identity over time is by publicizing, through the repeated use of sentences in its language, the similarity of current episodes in the its history to those in its past. However, given that the culture is likely during an appropriately long period to have undergone many changes, it is therefore important that language use be quite versatile, even to the point of allowing subtle changes in word use, a so-called "slippage in reference," to go unnoticed. Admittedly, subtle changes of this kind make it difficult, if not impossible, for the historian to sort out what actually happened in the culture. But then again, the point is that the culture's language was not designed primarily with the historian's task in mind.

All this is by way of bringing Kuhn back into the picture. I have so far vacillated between labeling Kuhn an "antirealist" and labeling him a "realist" who believes in many realities. I would now like to argue that he is fruitfully understood as being *both*, and thereby distance him somewhat from the position of "historical realism" that I have been attributing to Quentin Skinner and have pitted against the scientific realist throughout most of this paper. To get at what I take to be Kuhn's intriguing metaphysical position, let us start by identifying what Kuhn calls a "paradigm" or "disciplinary matrix" with a language's implicit conceptual framework, as discussed above. Now let us recall three parts of Kuhn's (1970a) notorious *incommensurability thesis:*

(e) that scientists in different paradigms inhabit different worlds;

(f) that the claims of two different paradigms cannot be compared;

(g) that scientists in one paradigm tend to systematically misunderstand the claims made by scientists in another paradigm.

There is also a fourth part to the thesis which is often neglected, but which nevertheless factors in Kuhn's rather traditional views on the objective stance of the normal scientist:

(h) that the scientists themselves are generally oblivious to the truth of (e), (f), and (g), which is to say, they believe that there is only one world and many paradigms, that they can compare claims made by different paradigms, and that they can understand what scientists from another paradigm are saying.

Our question, then, is what is the best way to understand this complicated state of affairs.

If Kuhn were a pure antirealist—say, a social constructivist of the Latour & Woolgar (1979) variety—he would have characterized the boundaries between paradigms as *fluid* rather than *rigid*, the subject of constant negotiation by concerned parties. Admittedly, Kuhn is very much the social constructivist when he claims that there is no fact of the matter as to whether, say, *a specific sample* of gas is oxygen or dephlogisticated air. Very much will depend on which scientists are in the vicinity at the time, and which one ends up persuading the other to identify the gas as an instance of one or the other substance. In short, it will depend on the actual history of the situation, much of which will be unavailable to the historian and thereby the source of the sorts of misunderstandings associated with incommensurability. Yet Kuhn also seems to believe that there *is* a fact of the matter as to whether oxygen or dephlogisticated air *as such* exists: the answer is, notoriously, that *both* exist. I take this simply to mean that each substance performs a definite role in a specific system of concepts, or paradigm, which may be invoked correctly or incorrectly relative to that system. Thus, once the two scientists have agreed to discuss the gas sample in the language of oxygen, a set of opportunities for uttering truths and falsehoods have been opened up (compare Hacking 1982). As parts of conceptual systems in this robust sense, oxygen and dephlogisticated air enjoy a Platonic existence, which is to say, that they are part of the permanent possibilities for articulating the structure of reality. An ironic way of summarizing our reading of Kuhn's position on realism is to say that he believes in the independent reality of all scientifically possible worlds (that is, paradigms) except the actual one, whose reality depends entirely on what the relevant group of scientists negotiate.

We may, of course, resort to less ironic terms. To borrow a distinction introduced by the philosopher of law, John Rawls (1955), Kuhn seems to be a *regulative realist* and a *constitutive antirealist*. As Rawls portrays this Kant-inspired distinction, regulative rules are drafted by legislators and appear as statutory laws: for example, "All wrongdoers must be punished." Notice that this rule is stated as a universal principle, but it does not mention which cases count as instances of the principle. The latter problem is the business of adjudication, which works by applying constitutive rules. These rules determine how and which particular cases should be constructed under the principle, usually on the basis of tacit criteria for which a judge's opinion provides ex post facto justification. On the basis of Rawls' distinction, we can make sense of the idea that a rule can be universally applicable without itself specifying the universe of cases to which it may be legitimately applied. Thus, a judge may believe that there is a body of law to uphold in his decisions, without believing that the corpus determines which particular law applies in the case he is currently deciding. However, if he exercises discretion to decide that a particular law does apply, then that law specifies reasons (precedents and statutory interpretations) justifying his decision. Likewise for Kuhn's understanding of the "rules" governing the language game of phlogiston chemistry: although the rules do not determine whether phlogiston talk applies to the next experimental outcome, if it turns out (through negotiation) that such talk applies, then it delivers a specific description and explanation for the outcome.

5. Regulative and Constitutive Realism in the Human Sciences

Armed with Rawls' distinction and a general sensitivity to the different contexts in which the problem of realism arises, we may now turn to elucidate the rather complicated debates about ascriptions of rationality in the *human* sciences. As we shall see, the complications are the result of the contesting parties failing to distinguish between issues about whether there are real rules in terms of which we must justify our ascriptions of rationality (the *regulative* issue) and whether there are real rules for identifying that a certain behavior is or is not rational (the *constitutive* issue). This confusion colors the rationality debates, insofar as, in each of the versions discussed below, one party (generally, the Wittgensteinians and the sociologists) realizes that a theory of rationality is not complete without addressing these two distinct issues, while the other party (generally, the Popperians and the Davidsonians) realizes that you can believe that there are real regulative rules for justifying ascriptions of rationality without believing that there are any real constitutive rules (or even holding any obvious view on the issue). Moreover, as the details reveal, the confusion of rules and realisms cuts across the usual battle lines of *relativism versus universalism* and *scientism versus humanism*.

The surest way to get partisans of Popper, Wittgenstein, Davidson, and the sociology of knowledge into open debate is by asking them how they would determine whether the beliefs of an alien culture or historical period were rational. The Popperians started the debate a quarter century ago as an attack on Peter Winch's (1958) Wittgensteinian *Idea of a Social Science* (Wilson 1970). The more recent exchanges have been dominated by Davidsonians centered at Oxford picking apart the Edinburgh School's "Strong Program in the Sociology of Knowledge" (Hollis and Lukes 1982). All the contending camps lay claim to a "naturalistic" theory of rationality—one that accounts for the judgments that a philosophically astute observer would make in situations actually faced by anthropologists and historians. And since each camp's theory of rationality is presented as an extension of its general position, it would seem that we have the perfect setting for the empirical testing of philosophical theories. But no such luck. For despite the often dazzling polemics launched by the various partisans, one is forced to conclude that they have been shooting past each other. Still, so I shall now argue, there is a method to their collective misfirings, which once identified will allow us to place subsequent debate over this version of "epistemology naturalized" on a more secure footing.

To start, let us draw the battle lines separating the four camps by specifying how each would determine the rationality of an alien belief.

The Wittgensteinians would simply check whether the belief can be expressed as a legal move in an alien language game. Since the rationality of a belief is relative to the rules of a particular language game, the very same belief—say, in the efficacy of witchcraft—may be rational in the context of an alien culture, yet still be irrational in the context of our own. Moreover, the Wittgensteinians claim that all language games are created equal, suited as they are to their respective forms of life. In that case, it follows that all belief systems, once properly contextualized, are equally rational (Winch 1958, Bloor 1973).

The Popperians would check whether the aliens tend to revise their beliefs in response to criticism, especially from someone not sharing the overall belief system. For example, the critic may be the philosophically astute observer himself, who points out that what the aliens are trying to accomplish by performing witchcraft—say, healing—may be more effectively brought about by medical techniques currently used in his culture. Since Western culture has historically been the most open to criticism of this kind—and hence cognitively the most progressive— Popperians argue that our beliefs tend to be held more rationally than those of the aliens (Jarvie 1970, Gellner 1970, MacIntyre 1970).

The Davidsonians would check whether, given the interests, background beliefs, and evidence available to the alien, the philosophically astute observer would himself hold the belief. This test presupposes that all cultures share a core set of rules for licensing beliefs, which include basic patterns of deductive and inductive inference, as well as a correspondence theory of truth. These universals of rationality permit a "bridgehead," as

Martin Hollis (1982) puts it, for the observer to conclude that an alien—no matter what he currently believes—has the cognitive potential for holding our beliefs: the alien just needs to be provided with *our* interests, background beliefs, and evidence (Davidson 1984, Lukes 1982, MacDonald & Pettit 1981).

The Sociologists would check whether the alien is sensitive to the social factors that maintain the justifiability or legitimacy of his belief even to the exclusion of other beliefs that could be made to appear, at least in principle, equally justified or legitimate—simply by extending the evidence base, challenging some background beliefs, reorienting cognitive interests, etc. Thus, irrationality becomes the limitations on one's cognitive horizon associated with the "false consciousness" sense of ideology. And insofar as both scientists and shamans engage in inquiries which (at least indirectly) maintain their respective social orders, both are equally irrational on this account. Though they rarely articulate it, the sociologists conceive of rationality as the realization that no single system is ever likely to incorporate all potentially justifiable beliefs: to justify some, others must remain unjustifiable (Bloor & Barnes 1982, MacIntyre 1970, Mannheim 1936, Lukacs 1971).

Three notes. First, each camp has been presented as an "ideal type," since its members—one thinks of David Bloor and Alisdair MacIntyre—occasionally break rank and adopt the tactics of the other camps. Second, and more significant, we have been using "belief" in a sense that fails to discriminate between the disposition to assert a proposition and the disposition to act as if the proposition were true. Though we shall shortly want to distinguish these two cases, for now we shall follow the custom of our four camps and blur the distinction. Third, our four camps represent two general senses of "naturalistic" that may be appropriate to a theory of rationality. On the one hand, the Wittgensteinian and the Davidsonian observers evaluate the rationality of a belief within the context in which it "naturally" arises. On the other hand, the Popperians and the sociologists base their judgments on observations that approximate a "natural-scientific" standpoint, namely, one in which the relevant categories of evaluation need not be native to the culture whose beliefs are under study.

Although as we originally observed, our four camps have split into two more or less separate battle fronts, a similar dialectical strategy has characterized both fronts, which, in both cases, has resulted in an impasse to any further debate. It is to this strategy that we now turn.

Consider Winch's typical rebuttal to the Popperian charge that his Wittgensteinian theory of rationality does not really capture the sense of what it is to be rational. Ian Jarvie, for example, argues that to be rational is to have an interest in pursuing one's ends as effectively as possible. Consequently, the rational being is someone who would gladly be shown in error if it promises a still more effective means for pursuing his ends. Winch may be read as offering a twofold response:

(j) The members of a culture may have an interest in pursuing their ends without having an interest in pursuing them as effectively as possible. Instead, they may be constrained by other interests incompatible with the pursuit of "effectiveness." Thus, as long as it appears that the language games that the members play have a point, they constitute a rational form of life.

(k) Even if members of a culture have an interest in pursuing their ends as effectively as possible, it doesnot follow that what we would consider an improvement in effectiveness would be so considered by the members. Thus, while the members may admit being receptive to criticism, it is not clear that they would count anything the Popperian might propose as genuine cases of criticism, since instances of criticism must themselves be expressible as legal moves in a language game played by the members.

Closet relativists and universalists reveal their true selves when presented with response (j). Relativists find it *obviously true*, since only modern Western culture professes an overriding interest in the pursuit of "instrumental rationality." To ascribe this interest to other cultures is to foster a most misleading ethnocentrism. However, universalists find (j) *obviously false,* since they think it impossible to conceive of pursuing ends without smuggling in a sensitivity to effectiveness. The fact that the sensitivity remains latent in most cultures does not disturb the universalist, for he is confident that without it their pursuits would soon be terminated.

Although much ink has been spilled in assessing the relativist and universalist reactions to (j), I fear that their differences are not easily resolved, largely because the two reactions form something like a Kantian antinomy. That is, what the relativist and universalist are ultimately arguing about are the rules for conducting the naturalistic study of rationality. The relativist, in effect, is recommending a *strict* policy of ascribing cognitive dispositions to individuals on the basis of behavioral evidence. Thus, if the members of a culture do not manifest virtually all the behaviors—including verbal cognates—that we associate with a certain disposition, then the observer is to conclude that some other, perhaps distinctly alien disposition is being expressed. In contrast, the universalist advises a *lax* policy of ascribing cognitive dispositions which explains away differences between what the observer would ideally expect and what the alien actually does as the result of mitigating circumstances in the alien's environment. The universalist justifies this move on the grounds that he, unlike the relativist, believes that he can distinguish the essential from the nonessential features of a social practice. And not surprisingly, then, a strict policy of ascribing cognitive dispositions encourages the relativist to stretch his imagination in trying to make sense of the alien's behavior in unfamiliar terms, whereas the universalist's lax interpretive policy serves to restrict his imagination, compelling him to argue that the alien could not be understood as doing or thinking anything other than what we would do or think under similar circumstances.

We shall have more to say shortly about the nature of these differences, but now let us sum up what has so far transpired. We might say that in proposing (j), Winch stalemates the rationality debate because there is no commonly accepted procedure for ascribing cognitive dispositions which would allow the contesting parties to treat (j) as an empirical hypothesis. On the one hand, if the alien actually needs to assert a belief in the value of effectiveness in order to be properly ascribed such a belief, then the relativist—with whom Winch normally sides—will almost always win. But if, on the other hand, the alien only needs to manifest some minimal nonverbal behavior to demonstrate the same belief, then the universalist—who is more closely associated with Jarvie—will more often prove victorious.

While (j) brought out the *regulative* aspect of a naturalistic study of rationality, (k) highlights the *constitutive* aspect. And once again, Winch's response creates an impasse to further debate that is nevertheless instructive. In effect, Winch is now challenging Jarvie to try to constitute his criticism of an alien belief as a legal move in one of the alien language games. Winch seems to be motivated by the suspicion that Jarvie cannot make good on the challenge because the Popperian theory of rationality is purely regulative, and thus carries no empirical expectations for the observer of particular instances of alien belief. Winch (1970) himself has a catchy way of putting this: whereas Popperians are concerned exclusively with *the rationality of criteria* that the aliens would use when evaluating beliefs (Do these criteria conform to the Popperian ideal?), Winch and his fellow Wittgensteinians want to identify *the criteria of rationality* that Jarvie, the aliens, or anyone else would rely on when judging certain beliefs to be rational and others not. These criteria would vary among cultures, each centering on a few paradigmatic uses, which are then extended by analogy to new situations. And so, Winch might argue, since the Popperian paradigms of criticism are two distinctly Western cultural developments—Socratic dialectics and Baconian crucial experiments—it would probably be very difficult for the Popperian observer to recognize an alien practice as an instance of criticism. This could mean either that the observer finds most alien cultures to be uncritical and hence irrational, or that he is forced to loosen his own criteria of rationality so that just a vague receptiveness to "learning from one's mistakes" becomes sufficient for ascribing rationality to the aliens. The latter possibility, indicative of a universalist approach to rationality, seems to be the tack taken by Jarvie and other Popperians. This explains the watered-down version of Popperianism to which they hold the aliens accountable.

However, in pursuing this lax interpretive policy, the Popperians gingerly avoid meeting Winch's challenge. For example, the aliens are never asked the cognitive status of their vaguely defined critical practice within their own language games: Is it as significant as the Popperians make it out to be? Moreover, would the aliens accept just *any* sharpening of their critical practice by a Popperian observer as an improvement, or would the suggested change be considered "unnatural"? Winch and other Wittgensteinians suppose that the Popperians have no choice but to answer no to both questions. In that case, either the criticizability criterion is not as universal as the Popperians thought, or the aliens are not as rational as they first seemed to be. To sidestep these equally unsavory options—so the Wittgensteinians argue—the Popperians would have to develop the constitutive aspect of their theory of rationality, which would, in turn, force them to come to terms with the differences in situations and attitudes that call for "criticism" in particular language games.

In the 1980s the Wittgensteinians and the Popperians have taken a backseat to the sociologists of science and the Davidsonians, respectively. Admittedly, some of the terms of our dispute have changed. Nowadays the relativist is more likely to favor the scientific standpoint of the sociologist, while the universalist leans more toward the humanistic perspective of the Davidsonian. Contrast this with the humanism of the Wittgensteinians *versus* the scientism of the Popperians. In addition, the opposing camps have become more extreme in their claims. Whereas, for the most part, the Popperians proposed only modus tollens as a universal criterion of rationality, the Davidsonians have added to that the other principles of natural deduction, Mill's canons of induction, and various substantive metaphysical assumptions. Indeed, from reading Davidson, one would think that *all* that separates us from any alien culture is the store of empirical knowledge on the basis of which beliefs are licensed. Similarly, the sociologists outdo the relativism of the Wittgensteinians: Bloor explicitly assimiliates the laws of logic and mathematics to social conventions, and others have suggested that the course of natural science may be charted, not by watching some internal necessity working itself out in history, but simply by looking at who makes the key decisions in the relevant bureaucracies. Still, the impasses are much the same as before, as we shall now see.

In defending the value of thought experiments to historical understanding, Kuhn (1981) imagines a situation in which Galileo tries empirically to convince Aristotle that his concept of velocity is contradictory, such that he fails to distinguish the average from the instantaneous speed of a body. Kuhn likens this episode to one of Piaget's children who is brought to the threshold of the next cognitive stage by being made to have contradictory intuitions about how a particular experiment will turn out. As it so happens, Kuhn seems to want to use this situation to show that there are ways of having one's paradigm penetrated from "the outside." This would make him—just this once—the darling of the Davidsonians, since the success of Galileo's and Piaget's demonstrations depend on them and their respective subjects sharing a fairly extensive set of principles of reasoning. However, what goes for Kuhn need not go for the hardline sociologist, such as Bloor, who, in response to the Davidsonian claim that Aristotle's rationality hinges on his capacity to see and correct the incoherence of his conceptual ways, would probably make the following two arguments:

> (m) Aristotle might well see the point of Galileo's experiments and yet not be swayed by the argument that self-contradictoriness alone is sufficient grounds for revising a concept. Admittedly, logical consistency was a virtue touted by Aristotle himself, but it is far from clear that he touted it as the virtue to pursue *before all others*. Indeed, the fact that none of Aristotle's rather diverse philosophical contemporaries had pointed out this problem that Galileo can demonstrate so easily suggests that the Greeks were not nearly as concerned as we are about the internal consistency of a conceptual scheme.

> (n) Even if Aristotle took the elimination of contradictions to be one of his primary concerns, it is not clear that he would identify them in the same way that we (or Galileo) do, nor even that he would correct the contradictions he identified in a manner that we would consider appropriate. Much will depend on Aristotle's general attitude toward conceptual anomalies, and especially his sense of which types have the greatest potential for undermining his projects, for those would be the ones targeted for official "elimination" and not simply ignored. Thus, the sociologist is forced to the ironic conclusion that the robust conceptual constraints postulated by the Davidsonians add relatively little to the constraints already placed on Aristotle's behavior by his social interests.

The astute reader will no doubt see a parallel both between (m) and (j) and between (n) and (k). But I shall confine my discussion to the first parallel. The Davidsonians and the sociologists appear to differ ultimately over the correct policy for interpreting Aristotle, an issue that cannot be resolved simply by appealing to certain facts about Aristotle. However, a crucial disanalogy between (m) and (j) is that, in (m), the scientist (the sociologist) is a relativist, whereas the humanist (the Davidsonian) is a universalist. For example, in (j) the universalist's lax interpretive policy enabled him to abstract invariant principles of rationality from the immediate cultural context. By contrast, in (m) the Davidsonian is more interested in using his own sense of rational conduct as a subjective model for rendering Aristotle's conduct rational than in identifying specific principles which objectively unite himself and Aristotle in one rational discourse. In other words, the desired outcome of the universalist's inquiry is no longer an explicit method, such as the criticizability criterion, by which the rationality of aliens may be evaluated, but an implicit one, such as *Verstehen*, which is applied with the aim of rendering alien conduct rational.

Likewise, in (j) the relativist's strict interpretive policy was designed to do justice to the full range of the alien's social experience.   But once the Wittgensteinian yields to the sociologist in (m), the point of a relativist policy has also changed, for it has now become the consummate *outsider's* perspective.   This shift in the status of relativism starts to make sense once we consider our own ability to tolerate a certain amount of deviation in how people in our own culture conduct themselves.   Indeed, one of the defining features of our being "insiders" to our own culture is that we know what is essential and what is not essential to understand about the conduct of our fellows in order to understand the point of what they are doing.   In this respect, the methodology of *Verstehen* is an attempt to regard everyone as essentially an insider to his own culture. However, the objective relativist does not believe that he can take these sorts of interpretive liberties, and, as a result, judges the appropriateness of his own pursuits in terms of his ability to identify systematic value differences between his own and the alien culture.   And certainly, this is how anthropologists in the twentieth century have tried to prove their scientific credentials (Rosenthal 1984, part 3).

6.   The Ultimate Solution to the Problem of Realism

This chapter has proceeded on the assumption that there is no *one* problem of realism that our best metaphysics will ultimately solve. Nevertheless, it is tempting to suppose that there is a maximally general version of the problems of realism that we have been considering. If there is such a version, it may be best expressed as a problem of *translation*. After all, one way of seeing the point of contention between any realist and any antirealist is in terms of whether there is something that remains constant in spite of radical changes in human knowledge. Translating between the languages of two radically different cultures fits this condition: Is there some "content" that can be conveyed intact? If the cultures are temporally ordered and roughly coextensive in space (as in "The History of Europe"), the question then becomes one of knowledge retention, which grounds the concept of scientific progress, to which the scientific realist is, in turn, committed. Moreover, the question of "conveying content" is ultimate in the sense of being indifferent to the two major realist ways of characterizing content, namely, as propositions in a Platonic realm or observation sentences in an empirical realm.

Translation has played a key role in scientific theory selection, as understood in the analytic philosophical tradition, since the early days of positivism. Ideally, before the scientist can decide which of two theories is better, the philosopher must "reduce" or "parse" each theory into its "cognitive content." Positivists have traditionally suspected that much of the actual debates over scientific theories have not been about differences in content, but merely differences in the ideological connotations of certain verbal formulations of the theories. For our purposes, a bit of parsing is in order, since we want to examine whether it is possible to extract real "content" from a theory that can then be added to the storehouse of knowledge. If so, then realism in some "ultimate" sense has been vindicated.

At the outset, we should keep in mind that there is a conceptual difference between how the problem of realism arises for the philosopher trying to parse a scientific theory and how it arises for the scientist trying to decide between two parsed theories. In particular, even if the philosopher gives a realist parsing of two rival theories, the scientist may still be an antirealist in the course of making his decision. Having a "best" interpretation of each theory is, at most, only a necessary condition for making a "best" decision between two theories. Moreover, this point has a further complication. Over the last generation, analytic philosophers have usually cited *Quine's underdetermination thesis* and *Kuhn's incommensurability thesis* as reasons for thinking that there is no fact of the matter as to which of two theories represents reality better, and hence no grounds for the scientist being a realist. Indeed, the two theses have been often linked together in argument as if they were mutually compatible products of an antirealist parsing of scientific theories. However, as we shall now argue, their parsing strategies are neither antirealist nor compatible, though the general antirealist conclusion they supposedly support turns out to be correct.

Let us return to the standard example of phlogiston-based chemistry and oxygen-based chemistry as the two rival chemical theories in the late eighteenth century: Why is it so difficult to decide between them? In effect, the underdetermination and incommensurability theses answer this question by parsing the theories in such a way that their alleged rivalry is eliminated. In the case of Quine's thesis, the philosopher would reduce the theories to their evidential bases, then realize that they save the phenomena equally well and make similar predictions (that is, once their defenders are forced to formulate the predictions solely in terms of their observational consequences). In the case of Kuhn's thesis, the philosopher would parse the two theories in terms of the objects to which they were meant to apply, and then realize that the objects do not correspond to one another on a type-for-type basis (for example, there is no entity in the oxygen-based chemistry that answers to all the properties had by phlogiston). While in both cases, the rivalry between the two chemistries has clearly been eliminated, the elimination strategies are diametrically opposed: on the Quinean strategy, the two theories end up being alternative ways of articulating roughly the same content, whereas on the Kuhnian strategy, the theories end up representing domains with mutually exclusive contents.

From the standpoint of the problem of realism, this is an interesting conclusion, especially since, *taken alone*, neither the Quinean nor the Kuhnian elimination strategy is antirealist: the Quinean reduces to a version of empirical realism, while the Kuhnian reduces to a version of many-worlds realism. Yet, the scientist cannot be satisfied with either strategy because by eliminating the element of rivalry between the two chemistries, each has also eliminated the need for a decision to be made between them, which was, after all, the original reason for wanting to parse the two theories. However, *taken together*, the polar tendencies of the Quinean and Kuhnian strategies suggest that before being able to decide between the two chemistries, the scientist will have to adopt a *metastrategy* for selectively applying each parsing strategy. For example, if the chemist is clearly a "modern," he will probably want to parse "phlogiston" in a Quinean manner, namely, in terms of the evidence for its assertion, and "oxygen" in a Kuhnian manner, in terms of its intended referent. More generally, the chemist will want to treat some of the sentences in the two theories as straightforwardly meaningful utterances (Kuhnianly) and others as simply behaviors that are produced whenever certain data are regularly presented (Quineanly).

Not surprisngly, these two ways of treating the sentences correspond to the two central and complementary approaches to translation identified by practicing translators: formal (Kuhnian) and dynamic (Quinean) equivalence (Nida 1964). More to the point, practicing translators believe that there is no one "best way" of negotiating this complementarity, except to make the trade-off in a way that is best suited to the point of wanting the translation in the first place. Insofar as something similar can be said about the nature of the metastrategy for trading off the two realist theory parsings, antirealism would seem to be the ultimate solution to the problem of realism. We shall pick up on these points in chapters five and six.

CHAPTER FOUR

BEARING THE BURDEN OF PROOF:
ON THE FRONTIER OF SCIENCE AND HISTORY

This chapter explores the point where the epistemology of science and the epistemology of history meet, namely, the evidence base which allows the historian to attribute knowledge states to a scientific community. A key presupposition of this inquiry is that the central problems in rationalizing our epistemic history do not concern changes in belief, but *changes in orthodoxy*. It is one thing to ask what each member of a community should believe for himself: an essentially Cartesian question. It is quite another thing to ask what the members should take to be the dominant beliefs of their community. This second question considers the relative burden of proof that their beliefs should bear. Moreover, it is not obvious that the answer to the first question constrains the answer to the second question in any significant way. Even if the vast majority of members of the community hold a certain belief, that is no indication of whether they would allow it to pass in open forum without strenuous argument. On various long-term methodological or ideological grounds, the members may have an interest in keeping certain of their widely held beliefs from gaining general social currency (that is, from acting as licenses or warrants in their language games). Consider this vivid case: for all we know, a majority of scientists may still believe in God, yet the belief must bear an enormous—perhaps insurmountable—burden of proof before it can be used to justify a scientific claim.

Another such case may be the beliefs that scientists (and humanists as well) have of one another's "real reasons" for conducting certain lines of research. Sociologists of science have no doubt accurately captured the "interest-laden" nature of these reasons. But given the scientific community's overriding interest in the long-term maintenance of our knowledge enterprises, it has erected many probative barriers that prevent the sociologists' findings from gaining general credence. Not the least of these barriers are alternative, more orthodox explanations for the seemingly "interest-laden" behavior. Indeed, if Jon Elster (1979, ch. 2) is correct, a key reason why the orthodox view does not necessarily coincide with the majority view is that by distinguishing the orthodoxy from the majority, a community is afforded an indirect means for changing its undesirable yet widespread beliefs, namely, by making them so difficult to express (since they must bear such a large burden of proof) that the members of the community are effectively discouraged from holding the beliefs (Fuller 1985a, ch. 2). Thus, through adequate training, scientists may come to believe that there is a sharp distinction between theoretical (interest-free) and practical (interest-laden) reasoning. And so, we see that although answers to questions of personal belief may not resolve questions of orthodoxy, answers to questions of orthodoxy may be used to resolve (at least indirectly) questions of personal belief.

However, these last two paragraphs have been something of a teaser, since I do not intend to discuss the interesting *normative* issues they suggest about epistemic change. My task here is the propaedeutic one of showing how the epistemic historian goes about identifying orthodoxies, or presumed truths, and beliefs that bear varying burdens of proof. This task is set against the backdrop of debates in the philosophy of science, my purpose being to highlight the inadequacies had by all sides.

We start by considering Feyerabend's attacks on positivism and conclude that his own version of realism lacks the key virtue of positivism, namely, a well-developed theory of "verification" or evidence. This problem becomes especially acute in the case of incommensurability, which is defined here in terms of two theories having different verifiability conditions but the same truth conditions (so as not to get into any needless debates with the scientific realist). On our account, two theories have different verifiability conditions when they do not bear the same burden of proof. We claim that our account of verifiability conditions, based on the socio-historical variable of burden of proof, renders the history of science more intelligible than other accounts. Moreover, rendering the history of science intelligible is taken to be an essential condition for any adequate theory of science to meet. We thus adopt a strategy of *Minimal Hegelianism,* whereby the presence of a sufficient reason is presumed for whatever happens in history. In this chapter, language is treated as the something that "happens" (a performance), which then allows us to draw on Grice's Quantity Maxim and Quentin Skinner's historical methodology to fashion a principle for judging burden of proof: namely, the historical figures who say more (in defense of their claims) needed to say more, since they bore a greater burden of proof for their claims. Minimal Hegelianism is then used to interpret Kuhn's distinction between the tacit knowledge of paradigms and articulated methodological rules. In the end, we draw on resources from the positivist theory of law to bear out Kuhn's claim that paradigms cannot be reduced to rules.

1. Feyerabend and the Problem of "Rival Yet Incommensurable" Theories

In his 1951 doctoral thesis, "An Attempt at a Realistic Interpretation of Experience," Paul Feyerabend (1981a, ch. 2) set out for the first time the metaphysical strategy that, within a decade, would mark him as the most potent philosophical foe that logical positivism has ever had. Feyerabend considered two paradigms: *positivism* and *realism*. We shall begin by laying out these paradigms, partly following Feyerabend's argument and partly expanding its scope to incorporate more recent developments in the positivism/realism debate.

According to positivism's proponents, Russell and Carnap, observation sentences derive their meaning from one-to-one correspondences with atomic sensations or combinations of such sensations. Feyerabend called this the *Stability Thesis,* presumably after the positivist tenet that meaning was possible only because, at the most basic level of observation, words had some stable attachment—call it "correspondence"—to the world. As subsequent papers showed, Feyerabend took this thesis as the source of the positivist claim that scientific theories may change without the meanings of theoretical terms undergoing a change. This was the notorious *Meaning-Invariance Thesis* that allowed for the comparison of scientific theories and, thus, for judgments about their relative merits. Moreover, on the positivist view, the set of sentences constituting a theory is nothing more than an economical means for inferring observation sentences.

The last point about positivism may be taken in two ways (not distinguished by Feyerabend). On the one hand, it may imply that theory adds neither to the empirical content claimed of the world nor to the meaning of the observation sentences. The "nor" follows from the "neither" by the positivist "criterion of cognitive significance," namely, that a sentence's meaningfulness is exhaustively defined in terms of its empirical content. On the other hand, the positivist stance on the role of theory in science may be taken to imply that the empirical content of a theory exceeds that of its observation sentences, if the theoretical sentences are understood as making use of terms denoting, say, middle-sized objects, which are constructed from infinitely many atomic sensations. But in that case, theoretical sentences are, strictly speaking, undecidable, since we can never determine the total evidence for the presence of one such object. On the first reading, positivism is a species of "antirealism" in Bas van Fraassen's (1980) sense, which is informed by scientific practice; on the second reading, positivism is "antirealist" in Michael Dummett's (1976) sense, which is informed by ordinary linguistic practice. Both readings, however, share the view that whatever hidden causal mechanisms seem to be invoked in theoretical sentences can be justifiably regarded as no more than heuristic fictions.

According to realism, the position taken by Feyerabend himself, someone may be *caused* to utter an observation sentence whenever he has a particular sensation without that sensation conferring *meaning* on the sentence. The distinction between the causal and semantic sources of utterances is blurred in the positivist use of sensations as its metaphysical starting point, which, in effect, conflates third and first person perspectives on an individual's behavior. The behavioral scientist can correlate the speed with which a subject linguistically responds to the exposure of a physical stimulus. The subject himself immediately identifies his sensation of the stimulus as a meaningful object. Contrary to the connotations of "sensations," "speed" cannot be equated with "immediacy," for the speed of response stems from the conditioning history of the subject, while the immediacy of identification stems for the observation sentence being derivable from a comprehensive theory that defines the sensation as evidence for some higher-order entity or process. Feyerabend suggests that the positivist conflation may arise from a subject possibly being so well conditioned to respond within one theoretical language that he cannot conceive of the sensation as evidence for some other entity. However, this inconceivability should not be confused with the supposed *infallibility* of the observation sentence, for, once again, since the sentence derives its meaning from a theory which posits entities, if those entities turn out not to exist, then the sentence may turn out to be false.

Feyerabend's arguments were originally aimed at Niels Bohr, who claimed that it was "psychologically impossible" for a physicist to understand the world as clearly through quantum mechanics as through classical mechanics. Classical mechanics is, so to speak, the "ordinary language" of physics. Bohr is interesting because, while he believes that the meanings of sensations are conferred by a subject's entire theoretical language, he also believes that only *one* such language is uniquely isomorphic with the totality of our objects of perception—namely, the world of middle-sized objects of classical mechanics. Feyerabend, thus, sees in Bohr a veiled endorsement of the Stability Thesis. In contrast, the realist treats the entities posited by a theory as the putative causes of a subject's linguistic behavior, such that the behavioral scientist and the subject may be regarded as offering rival theories of the same "phenomena" (which, in turn, will be described in the language of the theory that turns out to be true). This suggests that a realist theory of reference would be identical with the latest physical theory, or at least the best available account of the causes of linguistic behavior, regardless of whether most actual language users know (the best theory of) what their observation sentences are true of. Again in contrast, a positivist theory of reference would group together observation sentences uttered by individuals in different languages that were triggered by sensations of the same type. It would thus depend crucially on the possibility of intersubjective agreement among language users.

Although he has shown the advantages of a realist over a positivist paradigm of experience for doing the kinds of activities (such as searching for hidden causal mechanisms) that normally fall under the rubric of "science," Feyerabend nevertheless realizes that his own account of meaning, which relativizes meaning to particular theories, obscures, if not renders incoherent, the sense in which two theories may be regarded as offering rival interpretations of "the same phenomena." For even in 1951, he had already renounced the possibility of a crucial experiment deciding between them. Yet the cogency of realism as a genuine alternative to positivism rests on making sense of the concept of *rival yet incommensurable* theories. As we shall see, this problem is hardly a stranger to positivism.

One of the more unsavory features of positivism has been precisely its inability to provide sufficient reason for the theory choices that have occurred in the history of science, let alone why theoretical issues should appear more significant than empirical ones. On the sort of antirealism espoused by van Fraassen, there is nothing to choose from, since theoretical languages are merely notational variants for expressing the same empirical content. At best, then, the prominent disputes in science turn out to be arguments about heuristics: to be a Newtonian or an Aristotelian is simply a matter of how one's scientific research is to be organized. At worst, scientific theory disputes become exercises in the emotive uses of language or, more charitably, "ideological conflicts": to be a Newtonian or an Aristotelian is simply a matter of identifying the interest group of which one is a member. On the sort of antirealism espoused by Dummett, there may be a real choice, but never adequate warrant for making it, since, short of total evidence, legitimate doubt may remain about whether or not the putative object of some theoretical term really exists. This, of course, is one of the many guises under which the *problem of induction* has traveled. And, as Nelson Goodman's (1955) "grue paradox" has shown, the scientist's predilection for theorizing with one of two terms that save the phenomena equally well will depend on which term happens to be better integrated with other terms in the scientist's language. Ironically, throughout his career, Feyerabend has resorted to these positivist maneuvers to account for both the apparent groundedness of established theories and the real ungroundedness of new theories. Indeed, he may easily be taken to have endorsed the following argument:

(P1) If theory choice can be explained by positivist maneuvers,

(P2) And theory choice (as opposed to, say, data gathering) is the most significant feature of science,

(C) Then science does not live up to its rational self-image.

However, nothing said so far forces us to accept (P1).

Larry Laudan (1977), for one, has tried to get around the "rival yet incommensurable" problem by denying that two theories must be commensurable in order to be rivals. The general strategy is to decide in favor of the research tradition that has solved more of the problems it has set for itself. However, this strategy is less helpful than it first seems, since it is not clear how such decision would be made. Assuming that the decider can individuate problems within each research tradition, he must then weigh and tally them, not unlike a utilitarian calculus. But it is difficult to imagine the mechanisms of such a weighting without supposing that the research traditions are much more commensurable than Laudan would have them be. Indeed, Bentham's own calculus was motivated by the idea that qualitatively different goods were reducible to the net magnitudes of pleasure and pain that they gave the same result to either the decider or those for whom the decision was binding. Thus, we can conclude that at least Laudan's attempt to sever rivalry from commensurability will not do. Notice that we have so far supposed, as have most philosophers of science, that incommensurability is an *obstacle* to any possible rivalry between two theories. Laudan's strategy was to circumvent the obstacle. But perhaps incommensurability is *integral* to understanding the sense in which two theories may be rivals. However, there are several senses of incommensurability. We shall first look at a radical sense of incommensurability, to which we would normally be attracted, but which is too radical for our current purposes.

One strain in the positivist tradition traces all seemingly significant disagreements—namely, those over higher-order concepts like truth, goodness, and beauty—to mutual misunderstandings by the disputants. Let us call this the *Babel Thesis*. The Babel Thesis appears in the view that two theories of equal empirical adequacy are merely notational variants, as well as in the Quine-Davidson position that optimal translation makes most of the sentences in the translated language come out true (Follesdal 1975). The idea is that given the same evidence, and the same background knowledge, all rational individuals would license the same inferences. And so, if two disputants agree on the premises but not the conclusion, then this disagreement may be attributed to some misunderstanding: perhaps one party erroneously presumed that the other party had the same background knowledge, or perhaps the other party's conclusions have simply been mistranslated. Applied to science, the Babel Thesis implies that the only *epistemic* reason why it appears that *choices* between theories must be made is that the proponents of the two theories do not quite understand what each other is claiming and/or about what they are claiming it; hence, rivalry implies incommensurability in a rather strong sense. Our only real epistemic duties, then, are to effect a translation that maximizes consensus where the two proponents are making claims about the same domain of objects and to specify where the two proponents are making claims about different domains of objects.

Notice that the Babel Thesis does not deny that there are good *social* reasons necessitating theory choice: perhaps resources are limited, and the language of one theory (especially its metaphors) suggests applications that the other does not, even though there is no difference in empirical content. The implications of the Babel Thesis are far-reaching. For if the very need for theory choice is "social" rather than "epistemic" (in the way that a classical philosopher is likely to draw the distinction), then there is something to the thesis, advanced by both Feyerabend and Foucault, that to believe that established scientific theories are entities "commanding" our assent and "constraining" our assertions about the world is to mix the epistemic and social import of those theories. However tantalizing it would be to explore this implication here, the reader must turn to the next chapters. For present purposes, the Babel Thesis does not offer the right account of "rival yet incommensurable," since the reading of the history of science that it presupposes raises too many foundational questions.

2. The Missing Link: Burden of Proof

ᴵⁿˢᵗead, our account of "rival yet incommensurable" turns on the idea that two theories are incommensurable because they do not bear the same *burden of proof*. Admittedly, considerable normative force is attached to the idea that two theories bear the burden of proof equally, as in the case of a crucial experiment, whereby the same outcome is said to verify one theory and falsify another. This approach to burden of proof suited the positivists, who generally conceived of theories as closed logical structures. As a result, they have been unable to make sense of the intuition that evidence bears only on *parts* of theories, and on different sized parts of different theories (Glymour 1980). However, in order to give burden of proof a more "realistic" flavor, followers of Karl Popper have refined the idea of crucial experiment so that the outcome of such an experiment need not bear on each of the theories equally: one theory may have a high-level principle falsified, while the other may, at the same time, have only a low-level theorem corroborated. Imre Lakatos (1970) introduced the idea of "negative heuristic" in order to determine just what aspects of a theory may be tested by what pieces of evidence. And Doppelt (1982) has even attempted a partial explication of Thomas Kuhn's concept of incommensurability in terms of two theories having widely divergent senses of the relative significance had by particular pieces of evidence.

Nevertheless, to say that the evidence does not bear on two theories equally is *not* to say that the two theories do not bear the burden of proof equally. In order to identify the condition necessary for the two theories not bearing the same burden of proof, imagine that one predicts that some event will happen (O) and the other predicts that the event will not happen ($-O$). The burden of proof would be different, then, only if the *kind* of evidence that is adequate for showing the truth of O is not also adequate for showing that -O is false. A typical case would involve proponents of one theory needing only to assert "O" as evidence for O because the truth of O is so well entrenched that mere assertion commands assent, while advocates of an opposing theory need to go through a great many arguments and experiments in order to persuade the scientific community that -O is really the case: mere assertion of "-O" may command little more than incredulous looks.

The role played by the kind of evidence has been underscored because in discussions of the possibility of crucial experiment, and how evidence bears on theories in general, "evidence" is usually taken to be *sentences* describing the outcome of some empirical inquiry. Until Hacking's (1983) recent work on experiment, little attention had been paid to the kinds of procedures used for generating this evidence. In fact, it may even be suspected that much of the importance that Lakatos and Laudan attach to empirical adequacy and theoretical promise as principles of rational theory choice would be diminished if a clear distinction were made been the sheer *quantity* of evidence (that is, the number of verified claims) *possessed by* two theories and the *quality* of evidence (that is, the kinds of procedures for verifying claims) *demanded of* the two theories. In that case, the Lakatosian dictum "All theories are born refuted" may be replaced by *All theories are born plaintiffs* as the problem for which an account of theory change in science would be the solution.

No doubt, the impoverished sense of evidence normally found in the philosophy of science can be traced to the lingering effects of positivism, especially its historical role in explicating "the conditions of verifiability" for an observation sentence, the unit of evidence. In brief, the strategy has been as follows. The truth conditions of an observation sentence are defined by the Tarski Convention; hence, "O" is true if and only if O. O's verifiability conditions are, in turn, defined as a reduction of O to the set of atomic sensations warranting the assertion "O" (for more, see Hacking 1975a, ch. 12). Notice that verifiability conditions are defined *not* as a procedure for generating O but merely as the appearance of O that licenses the assertion "O." This explication of the conditions of verifiability goes little beyond the Stability Thesis. Indeed, by identifying verifiability with a simple phenomenal analysis of truth conditions, the positivists did not distinguish the two conditions sharply enough for thinking about one independently of the other. This is a major point for us, since, in saying that two theories bear unequal burdens of proof, we want to draw the following distinction that would be difficult for the positivist to express:

(a) Given two theories, one of which entails O and the other -O, if O is true, then ipso facto -O is false.

(b) Given the same two theories, if E is the kind of evidence that would verify O, then E is not necessarily the kind of evidence that would verify -O.

Whereas (a) claims that the two theories have truth conditions for their respective observation sentences, (b) claims that the two sentences do not necessarily have common verifiability conditions, since one theory may bear the burden of proof and thereby require more elaborate procedures for establishing the truth of its claims than the other, whose claims are (for the time being at least) presumed true. The positivist would deny (b) because the kinds of evidence required to verify O and -O are the same, namely, the observation of whichever happens to be the case. Notice also that (a) and (b) contribute to saving the appearances of Feyerabend's realism, in that the independence of (a) from (b) secures the minimal condition of realism: the truth-value of a sentence obtains irrespective of the means by which the value is determined. Furthermore, (b) simply states that the two theories bear unequal burdens of proof, our gloss on the concept of incommensurability. Finally, (a) shows that at least partial translatability is allowed between the two theories, so that we do not depend on the the the Babel Thesis.

As soon as it became clear that no theory could be verified in the positivist sense of verifiability, the possibility was opened for the concept of burden of proof to be articulated in one of two ways. On the one hand, the concept could be articulated in terms of the degree to which a given claim has been confirmed or corroborated, such that, if the observational consequences of one theory are more confirmed than another, then the more confirmed theory is presumed true and the burden of proof is placed on the less confirmed theory to make its case. On the other hand, the articulation could be in terms of the number of problems solved or phenomena saved, such that the burden of proof is placed on the theory that accounts for less. However, by focusing on what we previously called "the quantity of evidence," positivists have had notorious difficulties in converting their definitions of verifiability (suitably amended) into procedures for reading the history of science. If verifiability is defined as degree of corroboration, how are such degrees to be identified for particular claims made in history, which, at least in the more interesting cases, do not advertise their statistical status on their surface structures?

But is this a fair criticism of positivism? That depends on whether we can provide an account of verifiability—especially that aspect of the concept concerning how two theories bear the burden of proof—from which "instructions" can be derived for reading the history of science. As successive editions of A.J. Ayer's (1952, ch. 8) *Language, Truth, and Logic* amply illustrate, verifiability has been developed more with an eye toward satisfying certain logical demands than historical ones. Thus, we should not be surprised if an adequate definition of verifiability turns out to have no obvious bearing on how history is read. And perhaps this is how it *should* be, especially if one takes the Popperian line that the philosophy of science stands in relation to science just as ethics does to human action in general (Popper 1981). In that case, since the philosophy of science is an exclusively normative discipline, it is under no obligation to develop concepts that make the phenomena of the history of science easier to save; for it might well be that science, like human action in general, has been exemplary only during sporadic "revolutionary" episodes.

If philosophy of science is not to become indistinguishable from mere descriptive history, the only strategy other than Popper's would seem to involve showing that the history of science is *inherently* norm-governed. He would try to vindicate Hegel's maxim: "the real is rational and the rational is real." More to the point: the more history that comes out rational by one's philosophical account, the closer one has come to discovering the identity of the governing norm (or set of norms). Thus, *in principle,* greater knowledge of history begets better normative judgments. We have introduced these global concerns in order to point out that, insofar as we are interested in defining one aspect of verifiability—burden of proof—as a philosophical concept that implies a method for reading the history of science (rather than as a philosophical concept against which the history of science is then judged), we are implicitly endorsing a Hegelian rather than a

Popperian approach to the normative status, or "rationality," of history. This is, to say the least, a controversial move (one, however, which echoes the move toward "panglossian epistemology" in ch. 1). And while I do not intend to show that Hegel should be endorsed over Popper, I do intend to show that Hegel is at least as worthy of endorsement. Interestingly, given the generally ecumenical spirit of our times, it has become necessary to make my point by showing that Hegel is something other than Popper dressed up for a nineteenth-century audience. In other words, we must address the question: Is there a *genuine difference* between the Popperian who argues that most of history does not conform to his norms and the Hegelian who argues that all of history conforms to his?

One reason why we might at first suspect that there is no real difference is that the Hegelian sense of history, the "world-historic," excludes most of what would otherwise be considered historical phenomena—much in the manner of a normative account of historical rationality. Among contemporary philosophers of science, Ian Hacking (1981b) has most forcefully pressed for this sort of similarity between Popperian and Hegelian sense of historical rationality. At the outset, Hacking admits that the differences between Hegel and the Popperian Lakatos stand out. On the one hand, Lakatos held that judgments of an agent's or an act's rationality were essentially retrospective, which implies that history is rational only in the sense that a modern can claim that he would have done what some historical agent did, had he been in the same situation, given the agent's set of beliefs and interests. On the other hand, Hegel believed that, in some objective sense, history itself was governed by sufficient reason. Hacking argues, however, that Lakatos was forced to adopt a retrospectivist approach to rationality because his paradigm of rationality, the hypothetico-deductivist methodology of the positivists, constituted a style of reasoning alien to the styles in which most scientific activity has been conducted. Consequently, Lakatos found it difficult to *identify* instances of rationality in history and had to resort to "rationally reconstructing" past episodes.

Hacking, nevertheless, endorses these historiographical maneuvers because they readily support his pet thesis that any attempt to show the rationality of history will issue *either* in massive omissions of what actually happened (so as to preserve the rationality of the account) *or* in many judgments to the effect that various historical agents did not act in an optimally rational fashion (simply because we cannot easily "make sense" of what they did). Hacking believes that Hegel took the way of the "either," while Lakatos took the way of the "or." Admittedly, Hacking's argument is grounded in a Foucauldian premise, namely, that any account of historical rationality constitutes a "rationalization" (in Freud's sense) and hence a falsification of history. But whatever one makes of the cogency of this premise, the argument still poses a challenge that deserves to be met.

Let us start by returning to the Hegelian claim that there is sufficient reason for whatever happens in history, such that the philosopher does not so much impose norms as discover them. If we treat the utterances of historical agents as situated actions (as, say, a speech-act theorist or a Marxist would) rather than as verbal icons of the external world (as a positivist and most others would), then the Hegelian claim can be translated into Paul Grice's (1975) Maxim of Quantity for Conversational Implicature. Since this conclusion must appear to be drawing a rabbit out of a hat, the link should be made more explicit.

Grice's project is to articulate what "speakers" (understood most generally to include any language users) must presuppose in order for communication to be a rationally grounded activity. His strategy is to identify heuristics that a speaker uses to supply the background against which his interlocutor's utterances are to be understood. One of Grice's four main heuristics, or "maxims," is Quantity: *everything that is said needs to be said.* In conversation, this maxim works by each speaker presuming of the other that everything they say is necessary for mutual understanding to occur. One says neither too much nor too little. The same can be applied to the historical record, so that whenever it seems that argumentative points are being belabored by an historical agent, the historian is instructed to presume that the figure did not take for granted that his intended audience would understand what the historian now finds so obvious. Notice, therefore, that the Quantity Maxim is presumed to operate between the author and his intended audience, but not necessarily between the author and the historian. It also follows that there may be points that the author need never articulate, since he and his audience take them for granted, even though without having them made explicit the historian runs the risk of seriously misunderstanding the author.

To draw out the consequences of this line of reasoning would lead us back to the Babel Thesis. But in order to apply the Gricean account to the history of science, we shall limit our horizons. Our model will be Quentin Skinner's (1969, 1970) appropriation of J.L. Austin's (1962) speech-act theory, which was first introduced in chapter three. In particular, we shall restrict the concept of "understanding" to the audience being sufficiently informed by the speaker that it can decide whether his claim is true or false; that is, we are accepting a verifiabilist account of meaning. In that case, we can speak of the *threshold of decidability* for a claim as the extent to which a speaker must inform his audience before it can make a decision: How explicit must he be? What follows is a tentative ordering of thresholds from claims that are either presumed true or presumed false until otherwise shown (A) to those that place the entire burden of proof on the speaker to reverse the presumed truth-value of the claim (E):

Question—What must an author/speaker do so that his intended audience can determine the truth-value of his claim?

(A) Mere assertion of the claim is sufficient for immediate acceptance or rejection. Indeed, if the audience hesitated over accepting or rejecting the claim for no stated reason, then the audience's competence would be justifiably thrown into doubt. This may be regarded as the speech-act version of so-called analytic truths and synthetic truisms. Furthermore, (A)-type claims may be so "self-evident" that they remain unsaid as the speaker addresses his audience; hence, they are the ones most likely to elude the historian and distort his understanding.

(B) An assertion of the claim must be accompanied by explication or verbal argument, for while the claim may be inferred from those already accepted by the audience, it is an inference not often (or perhaps ever) drawn.

(C) An assertion of the claim must be accompanied by a "loose" statement of evidence, that is, associated considerations (for example, circumstantial evidence, analogous decidable claims) which by themselves do not demonstrate the truth-value of the claim, but nevertheless provide enough information so that the audience, given the claims it already takes as decidable, will be able to decide this one as well.

(D) An assertion of the claim must be accompanied by a "strict" statement of evidence, that is, a procedure for demonstrating the truth-value of the claim that uses "techniques" (in the broad sense, to include unaided perception and mental computation, as well as the more obvious cases) accepted as reliably representing reality (if empirical) and/or preserving information across operations (if logico-mathematical).

(E) An assertion of the claim must be accompanied not only by a strict statement of evidence, as in (D), but also by an account of why the audience, without having undergone the stipulated procedure, might think that the claim has the opposite truth-value from the one demonstrated.

The methodological upshot of what may be seen as our *Minimal Hegelianism* is that the history of science is a tale of burdens of proof shifting from a claim to one of its many possible denials, with incommensurability arising when the threshold of decidability for some claim O is at (A) and the threshold for -O is at (E). Roughly, incommensurability lessens as the thresholds for O and -O draw closer together, with the two claims being commensurable only if both have (C) as their threshold and thus bear the burden of proof equally. Furthermore, the thresholds may be adjacent, as in the case of (A) for O and (B) for -O, which would arise if someone who speaks for -O could show that what the audience takes as a natural consequence of its body of accepted claims, O, in fact does not logically follow those claims. This is the sort of position in which the ordinary language philosopher finds himself whenever he claims to have "discovered" a mistake in usage. No claim is ever definitively shown to be false, but rather, the burden of proof it must bear becomes so overwhelming (an extreme case of [E]) that no one is inclined to take up the challenge in its defense. And, in accordance with the Quantity Maxim, the claim falls into the oblivion of tacit rejection (that is, [A]). Not surprisingly, then, a "revolution" occurs when someone successfully bears the burden of proof of a claim whose threshold is (E), and so, a "paradigm switch" would amount to a reversal of the burden of proof for a large body of claims.

3. Burden of Proof as Tacit Knowledge: Rule-Governedness

Although we have just borrowed liberally from the Kuhnian lexicon, points of contact have yet to be made with the account of scientific change given in Kuhn (1970a). First, a "paradigm" may be identified with those claims whose threshold of decidability is (A). However, they do not constitute all the claims made by the members of a scientific community, since many of their claims may have decidability thresholds at (C). And in the case of "anomalies," the two incompatible claims accounting for the anomaly would have their thresholds at (C), making it impossible to decide between them. Notice that even though two such claims would be "commensurable" in *our* sense because they bear an equal burden of proof, they could also be symptomatic of another sense of Kuhn's "incommensurability," namely, the one normally described as Quine's (1960) "underdetermination of theory by data." On our account, Kuhn's thesis about scientific revolutions states that once enough claims and their denials have (C) as their threshold of decidability, claims whose threshold is (A) will be successfully denied by claims whose threshold is (E). For our purposes, the historical validity of this thesis is not so much of interest as the reading of the history of science that would be required for testing the thesis. This is not an idle consideration. For if Kuhn's (1977b) own replies to his critics are to be believed, a great deal of the misunderstanding that philosophers have had of his thesis stems from a profound misunderstanding of how the history of science works. Admittedly, Kuhn has never plumbed these depths to anyone's satisfaction, and it may be thought that his remarks are merely self-serving. However, read charitably, the issue seems to center on chapter five of *The Structure of Scientific Revolutions,* where Kuhn maintains "the priority of paradigms" over methodological rules in reading the history of science. An interpretation of this assertion will now be offered that turns it into an extension of our own Minimal Hegelianism.

In chapter five, Kuhn most closely associates "paradigm" with "tacit knowledge," the key features of which are captured by a scientific community's claims whose threshold of decidability is (A). Since such knowledge is "self-evident" or "natural" to the scientists, it will probably go unarticulated, as the Quantity Maxim would have it, and thereby prove elusive to the historian. This much has already been admitted. But Kuhn seems to make a stronger claim about tacit knowledge that compounds the historian's difficulties: tacit knowledge is *never* articulated, that is to say, not even to novice scientists. A novice is said to learn the trade exclusively through the negative feedback of instructors once a textbook example has been misapplied to a new case. Kuhn is rather careful *not* to say that the novice learns a certain bodies of *beliefs*; instead, he learns a rough-and-ready way of talking about what he is doing which consists of appeals to the similarity between his actions and the ones prescribed, again, by textbook examples. Kuhn even seems to suggest that a scientific community has no way of maintaining that its members hold similar beliefs about what they are doing, only that they "pass" as competent performers—whether it be in the lab or at a conference. And so, Kuhn concludes that while it should be possible to determine the paradigm of a scientific community from examining the historical record, there is no reason to think that any assertion concerning a communal commitment (say, to a particular methodology) made by a member of that community will capture it. In fact, such assertions tend to be made only once the self-evident nature of the paradigm has been called into question.

Kuhn's claim may be initially understood as a reassertion of the Hegelian over the Popperian line on historical rationality. If the methodological rules uttered by a member of the scientific community could capture the subtle nature of the paradigm, then much of the historical record would be rendered *superfluous*. Philosophers of science could simply take what their favorite scientist had to say about scientific practice as an adequate synopsis of that practice, without studying how the scientific community actually did their work. Hacking showed that philosophers in fact do just that. However, in so doing, they do not carefully distinguish *the intended application* of methodological rules (a theory of optimal scientific activity) from their *illocutionary force* (the activity performed in uttering the rules). Unless the historical record overtly contradicts the methodological pronouncements, the philosopher is inclined to take them as intended—that is, *not* as actions on par with other aspects of scientific practice, but as privileged representations of that practice which allow the philosopher to safely ignore those other aspects. (Recall our critique of "transcendentalist" approaches to representation in ch. 2.) Kuhn's point would then be that the illocutionary force of asserting communal commitments is to indicate that the scientific community is entering a period of *dissensus* over such commitments—a point that would be easily missed on the Popperian approach to historical rationality. In contrast, such a point would vindicate the Hegelian approach, since it would go to show that methodology does not merely recapitulate practice but has a distinct function of its own—that is, there is a sufficient reason for its being uttered.

At this point, it would be instructive to integrate the discussion of Kuhn with the issues raised about Feyerabend at the beginning of the paper. At that time, we pointed out that if realism is to be regarded as a genuine alternative to positivism, it must overcome positivism's inability to provide sufficient reason for theory choices that have occurred in the history of science. We then saw that Feyerabend failed to meet the challenge. However, our reading of Kuhn may offer aid to the realist. First, as someone interested more in the performative than in the representational nature of language, Kuhn would claim that all theory disputes amount to methodological disputes over how and/or whether certain concepts apply. Next, as a Minimal Hegelian who discovers "reason in history" (Hegel 1964), he would *presume* that there is a *deep* paradigmatic structure to the history of a scientific community that cannot be simply inferred from the *surface* utterance of methodological rules. Furthermore, just as the positivist maintained that theories are heuristic fictions, Popperians, we have seen, make similar claims about accounts of historical rationality—which Kuhn, of course, implicitly denies. Indeed, Kuhn's (again implicit) critique of the Popperian approach to historical rationality parallels the one originally made by Feyerabend against the positivist concept of experience. Whereas the positivist conflated the situation that gave rise to an individual uttering an observation sentence (which could be determined by some third party, such as a behavioral scientist) with the meaning he conferred on that sentence (which would be determined by the theoretical framework of the observer himself), the Popperian is taken to have conflated the historical situation that gave rise to the utterance of methodological rules (namely, communal dissensus) with the interpretation that the utterer would have his audience attach to those rules (namely, that this is how science is and should be practiced). However, having said this much, we have yet to indicate wherein lies the difference between tacit knowledge and articulated methodology.

Given our previous analysis of the Quantity Maxim into thresholds of decidability, it follows that methodological rules do not merely state what was obvious to the scientific community of the time. Were the rules so obvious, they would not need to be *stated*; they would simply be *shown* in practice. On the contrary, the assertion of methodological rules is warranted only when there is sufficient doubt about the regulation of scientific practice. From these considerations it might be concluded that methodology is nothing but ideology. In other words, scientists start talking about their practice only as a means of deferring attention from what they are really doing, which is much more complicated than a neat set of rules would indicate. Furthermore, it would be practically impossible to enforce such rules, even if they constituted an adequate description of the best science, since scientists practice their trade in diverse locales. How would one then be able to control the judgment calls on what counts as a correct application of a particular concept or a correct extension of a particular theory? However, by uttering methodological rules, scientists aim to persuade their colleagues to read the history of their discipline in a way that allows them to *evaluate* previous practice, supposedly (given the unlikelihood that such methods could be rigorously enforced) with an eye toward subsequent practice. In effect, the *perlocutionary force* (that is, the practical import) of methodological utterances is to *make* scientists Popperian historical rationalists. Not surprisingly, then, Popper favors episodes of "crisis" in the history of science precisely because only then are scientists licensed to make the kinds of judgments—one always being made by philosophers of science—that he thinks are most appropriate for bringing out the rationality of science.

However compelling this conclusion may be, it still would not satisfy someone who believes that there is a point at which ideology ends and knowledge begins. Even though Kuhn may *in fact* be right that scientists have given inadequate accounts of the principles governing their practice because they are really trying to serve some other purpose by asserting such principles, that fact in itself does not preclude the *possibility* of a reflective scientist someday articulating an adequate account of the principles governing his practice. Kuhn offers no reasons for thinking that tacit knowledge must remain tacit forever, or else be distorted in articulation. However, Kuhn *does* seem to want to make this strong claim. One way to make good on it would be to show that the tacit knowledge of paradigms is different *in kind* from the methodological rules articulated by scientists. That is to say, the two do not "govern" scientific activity in the same sense, and so one cannot be reduced to the other. This somewhat cryptic strategy may be illuminated by discussing the two kinds of norms we have in mind.

If we take at face value Kuhn's account of how novices learn the scientific trade, largely through negative feedback (which is also how colleagues keep checks on one another's work), then the application of concepts to new data and the extension of theories to new domains would seem to be definable only in terms of what the philosopher of law Herbert Hart (1948; Baker 1977) has called *defeasibility conditions.* Hart's main example is a situation in which a judge must decide whether a contract has really existed between the two litigants. As in Anglo-American legal matters generally, the burden of proof is on the party who wants to deny the presumed state of affairs, namely, the one wants to claim that what initially passed as a contract between him and the other party should be invalidated as having never existed. Hart points out that the judge decides the matter not by seeing whether the transaction under dispute falls under a well-defined concept of contract (that is, a concept with specifiable necessary and sufficient conditions for application), but by seeing whether the complaint conforms to one of a more or less well-defined set of defeating conditions, as in the misrepresentation of the terms of the contract or incompetence of one of the parties. This practice may be traced to the case law tradition itself, where no codes are present that actually give a legal definition of a term like "contract." Hart then makes greater, Wittgenstein-inspired claims for defeasibility, especially that all mental concepts are defeasible in nature. Thus, there are no defining characteristics for intentional activity; rather, specific intentions are *presumed* of human beings unless otherwise shown in behavior.

For our purposes, Hart's defeasibility conditions are interesting because they provide an alternative way of thinking about what it means "to apply a concept." On this view, misapplications may have more in common than correct applications, in that the former cases are defined by specific defeasibility conditions, while the latter cases simply share the fact that they have not been defeated as applications of the concept. Defeasibility conditions may thus be the key to understanding how a scientific paradigm can be pedagogically constraining yet liberal enough to permit innovative scientific work. The historian of science searching for the defeasibility conditions for applying a paradigmatic concept would ideally proceed to find two apparently similar situations where a concept is applied, but in one case the use is taken as unproblematic, while in the other it is taken as "problematic," either in that the scientist is taken to have erred or that he is taken to have made a radical move which challenges how other concepts are subsequently applied. Articulating the difference that allowed the first application to pass unnoticed but not the second would amount to a codification of tacit knowledge. The precise nature of this codification awaits further inquiry. But if negative feedback is indeed essential to scientific practice, then some insight may be gleaned from philosophies of law, especially Hans Kelsen's (1949), that attempt to define a legal system as a pattern for imposing sanctions on law-breakers. And while Kelsen's approach has been criticized for, in effect, reducing legal systems to decision procedures that judges follow upon recognizing an illegality (Moore 1978), it may be exactly the right starting point for modeling the norms governing a scientific paradigm.

We have been proposing that the historian codify tacit knowledge through defeasibility conditions, on the assumption that the negative cases are easier to characterize than the positive ones. Yet scientists themselves tend to utter methodological rules that take the form of a hypothetical imperative, flanked by a *ceteris paribus* clause. Thus, one is instructed to apply concepts or extend theories in certain ways, granting that the appropriate background conditions obtain. In the archetypal case of a scientific *law*, the force of inserting the *ceteris paribus* clause is to indicate that the background conditions presupposed in a fair, or ideal, test of the law are so numerous and varied that one is better off simply asserting the outcome that would be expected in the fair test—however *improbable* its occurrence outside an experimental context—than specifying the expected outcome of testing the law under less than ideal conditions (Suppes 1962). In other words, the presence of the *ceteris paribus* clause presumes that the positive case is easier to characterize than the many possible negative ones, thereby *inverting* the strategy behind specifying defeasibility conditions.

When transferred from the statement of scientific laws to that of methodological rules, the ideal test case becomes the optimally rational science that occurs only during selected periods in the history of science, with the rest of science deviating from it in ways too numerous and varied to be codified. Of course, on this account, much of the content of the rules will be determined by the episodes collected together as exemplary by the methodologist. Whatever resemblance statements of methodology have borne to one another in the past would then stem from the same cases being collected together. Hart (1961) also noted this kind of reasoning in the legal sphere; for even though judges decide cases on the basis of whether a challenged presumption withstands defeasibility claims, the reasons they offer for their decision will be stated in the form of a rule said to be exemplified in selected instances from the body of case law. And as in the case of scientific methodological rules, the judge is more interested in his decision being taken as a precedent for subsequent decisions than as a faithful record of how decisions were rendered in the past, *even though it is only by appealing to history that his decision can have the desired impact.* Consequently, Hart espouses a principle of *judicial discretion,* whereby the judge is under no obligation, other than logical consistency, to collect cases together in a particular manner in the course of justifying his decision.

Although methodological pronouncements seem to be subject to a much narrower sense of "discretion," insofar as the exemplary cases of scientific activity are more readily agreed upon than that of judicial activity, the upshot nevertheless remains the same. Because tacit knowledge effectively defines the threshold of scientific competence (below which defeasibility conditions obtain), while methodological rules define the ideal cases of scientific competence (whose rarity is offset by *ceteris paribus* clauses), tacit knowledge underdetermines methodology. As a result, methodological disputes would seem to be *both* inevitable and insoluble by appeals to the nature of tacit knowledge.

CHAPTER FIVE

INCOMMENSURABILITY EXPLAINED AND DEFENDED

Hanson's death, Feyerabend's fall from intellectual grace, and Kuhn's quick and easy concessions to the opposition have proved a deadly combination for any serious consideration of the incommensurability thesis. Notice that I have carefully omitted "critics of incommensurability" from this autopsy, since due to either uncharitable readings or a bit of incommensurability on their own part, the critics have so far failed to see the point of arguing for such a seemingly perverse position. I shall attempt to portray two versions of incommensurability, *ecological* and *textual*, both of which take Kuhn's *Structure of Scientific Revolutions* as their "inspiration." Following the convention of Kuhn's critics, I shall use the name "Kuhn" as what may be dubbed a "rigid evocator," as opposed to a rigid designator, for the mere mention of "Kuhn" never fails to evoke enough strong feelings so as to obscure whatever interest one what might have in finding out what he actually said. The aim of this chapter is neither to offer knockdown arguments on behalf of incommensurability, nor even to explicate whatever relation the two versions of the thesis might have to each other. Instead, I aim to arrive at a set of instructions for thinking about the incommensurability thesis. Is it merely, as Kuhn's critics have suggested, a (false) *empirical hypothesis* about the history of science? Or, is the thesis better treated as a *methodological guideline* for reading the history of science?

1. Ecological Incommensurability

Appropriately enough, both the promise and the problem of the incommensurability thesis are summed up in the famous duckrabbit illusion, a line drawing that, depending on its background, appears to portray either a duck or a rabbit. On the one hand, Hanson (1958), Feyerabend (1975), and Kuhn (1970a) follow Wittgenstein (1958) in highlighting the fact that the rather incommensurable images of the duck and the rabbit cannot be read off the drawing at the same time, thereby forcing the viewer to perform a "Gestalt-switch" as he goes from one image to the other. Insofar as these Gestalt-switches may be regarded as small-scale paradigm shifts, they are literally shifts in world view as well. On the other hand, the critics highlight the fact that the two incommensurable images are merely two ways of reading the same text—namely, the line drawing—that may be described in some language sufficiently neutral to a duck viewer and a rabbit viewer that each can explain to the other what features of the drawing cued his reading. Presumably, the Gestalt psychologist himself adopts such a stance toward the duckrabbit illusion.

However, the critics (Shapere 1981, Kordig 1971, Field 1973, Kitcher 1978) have been more concerned with how "meanings" and/or "referents" are read off the terms in scientific discourse than with how animal images are read off Gestalt figures. Nevertheless, the strategy remains largely unchanged. Indeed, there are even versions to suit the tastes of scientific realists and instrumentalists. The realist proposes to redescribe the discourse of the two incommensurable parties so that not only can he determine what they are really talking about but also whether what they are saying about it is true. Let us call this move toward what is *signified* in the discourse of the incommensurable parties the semiotic *ascent* strategy. It plays on our historical presumption that the more recent the theory the better it represents reality, and hence the better position it places us for understanding what others have been previously arguing about to no avail. And so, the parties are shown to have been "really" talking about the observable properties of some entities currently recognized as existing by a community of scientists.

In contrast, the instrumentalist proposes to seek "lower" neutral ground for translation and evaluation of two incommensurable theories. He aims at redescribing the discourse of the two theories in terms of an observation language that would satisfy both sets of adherents. As in the original duckrabbit example, the instrumentalist wants to determine which perceptual cues in the environment (or "lifeworld") common to the two incommensurable parties triggered such radically different theoretical responses. And so, let us call this move toward uncovering the otherwise subliminal *signifiers* that perceptually cue the discourses of the incommensurable parties the semiotic *descent* strategy. Evaluation in this case may not be so much an adjudication of truth claims, as the realist would have it, but rather, a judgment as to which of the two incommensurable parties responds to sensory stimulation more closely to the way we do—comes closer, as it were, to sharing our worldview.

Insofar as they are interested in motivating the emergence of particular theories, historians of science are more likely to make the semiotic descent, whereas the normative impulses of philosophers of science predispose them toward making the semiotic ascent. But it may be that one cannot semiotically ascend without first making a semiotic descent. In other words, it must be known what at the bottom of Priestley's flask stimulated his retina, before it is decided that, regardless what he may have thought, it was definitely *not* phlogiston.

Although the two critical strategies just outlined differ in interesting ways, they are similar in several important respects. Both involve a thought experiment in which the historian or philosopher acts as arbitrator between two incommensurable parties. If we alter the situation so that the historian or philosopher is himself one of the incommensurable parties, then something like Quine's (1960, ch. 2) radical translation episode in *Word and Object* has been approximated. The historian or philosopher would then be playing the part of an anthropologist trying to reconstruct the language of a tribe (of scientists) about which he knows little (except how they designate the logical connectives) but which nevertheless is cooperative enough to provide a native speaker who will name objects as the anthropologist points to them and correct the anthropologist whenever he misnames objects in the tribal language. We shall have more to say about the heuristic value of the radical translation episode later, but for now just notice how the realist and the instrumentalist play slightly different variations on Quine's theme.

The realist would try to decode, say, a phlogiston chemist's discourse in order to show ultimately where he went wrong in analyzing what is now known to be oxygen and nitrogen. Indeed, the realist would be able to tell that his translation has succeeded by his ability to then persuade the chemist *in the chemist's own terms* to abandon talk of phlogiston. Such a criterion of success may seem a little paradoxical, since, it stipulates that a translation has been effected once the translated language is recognized as defective by its native speaker. However, we must not forget that translation, for the realist, is only a *means* toward evaluating claims made in the translated language. Moreover, if we suppose (as philosophers, justifiably or not, tend to do) that it is a mark of rationality for someone to relinquish their beliefs upon being shown good grounds for accepting alternative ones, then the realist's criterion makes sense. Indeed, Kuhn (1981) has cast Galileo's experiments for showing the self-contradictory nature of the Aristotelian concept of "velocity" (which conflates the senses of "average speed" and "instantaneous speed") somewhat in this light. But of course, unlike our realist, Galileo had not yet fully worked out the alternative language in which such confusions would not arise. For, rather than being a radical translator, Galileo was still very much a native speaker of Aristotelian physics.

In contrast, the instrumentalist seems to fit the intent of the radical translation episode more closely. However, this is not to make the task any easier, for reasons of what Quine (1969, chs. 1-2) calls "the inscrutability of reference." In brief, even if the anthropologist never errs in uttering "Gavagai" whenever the native points to a rabbit, it does not follow that "Gavagai" means "rabbit," for it may instead mean "rabbit-part" or "rabbitlike spacetime slice," depending on the tacit ontology governing the native's language. But unless the anthropologist has ways of testing these other possible referents, Ockham's Razor would have the anthropologist presume that the native's ontology is the same as his. Returning to the instrumentalist, it is hard to say whether the inscrutability of reference would be a real problem for him as he tries to make sense of how the sensory stimuli present in the eighteenth-century laboratory were encoded by the phlogiston chemist. On the one hand, we are tempted to pull out Ockham's Razor once again and declare that, unless he has reason to think otherwise, the instrumentalist should simply presume that the phlogiston chemist subscribes to the same tacit ontology as he does. Yet on the other hand, if the Gestalt psychologists were right in thinking that our perception is triggered by subliminal contextual cues that sensitize a viewer to, say, the ducklike features of an ambiguous line drawing rather than its rabbitlike features, then we must take seriously the possibility that a scientist exposed to an eighteenth-century environment, which houses its flasks in Rococco architecture, would perceive the world in a significantly different manner from a scientist exposed to a twentieth-century environment which contextualizes the very same flasks in Bauhaus buildings. (Among the many twentieth-century research programs to study worldviews, the *Arcades* project of the Frankfurt critic Walter Benjamin was unique in taking this possibility seriously. See McCole [1985].)

What is being suggested here is that we may be able to retain Kuhn's original robust sense of incommensurable worldviews by presuming that the configuration of artifacts in an individual's environment will determine what he perceives. Such a suggestion, however, should not be taken as a counsel of despair for the instrumentalist trying to understand the phlogiston chemist. Instead, he is simply being instructed to look at the kinds of things that the chemist must have looked at when the term "phlogiston" was first introduced and used. But the instrumentalist's task by no means ends here, since the thought experiment dictates that he communicate with the phlogiston chemist to make sure that he is seeing things in the eighteenth-century way. It would be misleading, though, to think (as Quine tends to do in his more behaviorist moments) that this communication amounts to little more than confirming proposed translations of the phlogiston chemist's utterances. For the whole point of the semiotic descent strategy is to *negotiate* a language in which both parties can describe what they are seeing. In other words, the instrumentalist and the phlogiston chemist jointly *fabricate* an observation language that wrenches, say, a flask from the different artifactual contexts in which it would normally be perceived, just as the duck viewer and the rabbit viewer can fabricate a language of line drawings for communicating how their perception is being triggered by a common stimulus.

The point of working through the radical translation thought experiment for the realist and the instrumentalist has been not merely to show that both have plausible strategies for eliminating incommensurability, but more importantly, to show that those strategies succeed only if at least one of the incommensurable parties relinquishes his worldview. The phlogiston chemist's discourse is successfully translated by the instrumentalist only if he and the chemist can communicate in an artificial language that takes both out of their respective worldviews. I take it that such a conclusion would be to the liking of the defenders of incommensurability, since it shows just how difficult and how reconstructive the translation task really is—a point not readily brought out by the idea of translation as a finished list of correspondences between syntactic items in the two languages. We shall eventually return to the two senses of translation suggested here, but first something should be said about these worldviews which are allegedly so incommensurable.

Since Fred Suppe's (1977) introduction to *The Structure of Scientific Theories*, it has become common to suppose that the incommensurability thesis is wedded to a worldview approach to scientific activity. We have so far taken "worldview" in its most literal sense as the way in which people view, or see, the world. However, there is a somewhat looser sense of worldview (*Weltanschauung* in German) associated with nineteenth-century and early twentieth-century German schools of historiography, particularly the followers of Wilhelm Dilthey. In this sense, the members of a worldview are said to hold, perhaps unconsciously, a core set of beliefs and attitudes that can be detected in the various expressive media of their culture, such as art, philosophy, literature, and science. The task of the historian, then, is to identify the different expressions of these constant cultural forms. Since virtually no one in the culture can think beyond the core set of beliefs because they appear self-evident, chances are that the core is much less articulated than its importance would seem to merit. On account of this presumed inscrutability, the historian must read the culture's texts "deeply" in order to reenact the thought processes of their authors. This method, generally called *hermeneutics*, is often prescribed as the means for obtaining access to what Kuhn and others have characterized as the "tacit knowledge" that allows a scientist to be recognized by his colleagues as one of their own.

However, while tacit knowledge may indeed remain unarticulated within a scientific community, it does not follow that it constitutes some set of unconscious beliefs held in common by its members. As we saw in the last chapter, Kuhn typically discusses paradigms in the sense of tacit knowledge in pedagogical contexts, where novices generally learn to apply textbook examples competently to new cases through the negative feedback of instructors. No one ever actually tells the novice what constitutes a competent performance; instead, it turns out to be whatever passes the community's critical scrutiny. In that case, tacit knowledge is rarely, if ever, articulated because there is no pedagogical need to say what is already shown in practice.

Another important aspect of tacit knowledge is that scientists learn the proper way of talking about what they are doing. But it does not follow that they are adopting a common set of beliefs in the process. Rather, we should say that certain ways of talking make it easier to articulate some beliefs and not others. Contrary to what a hermeneutician might say, there is nothing in the Kuhnian concept of tacit knowledge that precludes the possibility of, say, Aristotle conceiving of inertia, though given the cumbersome linguistic expression that would be involved, the possibility would be most unlikely. Indeed, there may be an advantage in having the thought of a scientific community underdetermined by its language in that genuine disagreement among its members would then be allowed. But underdetermination by itself does not guarantee that whatever disagreements are expressed will reflect deep-seated cognitive differences. In fact, much of what passes as differences of beliefs may be just a failure by two parties to understand the sensory cues to which each is responding. It would be as if, once the Gestalt psychologist walked out of the lab, the duck viewers and the rabbit viewers took their mutually exclusive perceptions to indicate some deeper logical incompatibility, when actually each viewer has merely been trained to regard different features of the same line drawing as significant. It should come as no surprise that Niels Bohr characterized the "complementarity" of the wave and particle theories of light in a somewhat similar manner, for, as we saw in the last chapter, it was in the course of considering this and other Bohrian principles that Feyerabend first arrived at the incommensurability thesis.

To sum up our discussion so far, much of the suspicion surrounding the possibility of incommensurable worldviews may be traced to the radical subjectivism associated with traditional hermeneutical approaches to the topic. Moreover, the very philosophers most likely to endorse the incommensurability thesis—namely, those who claim that observations are theory laden—are also the ones most likely to think that incommensurability on the perceptual level implies incommensurability on some deeper cognitive level. Indeed, the original proponent of theory-ladenness, Russell Hanson (1958), tended to a treat a scientific theory as little more than the linguistic codification of the scientist's belief structure. In that case, to return to the duckrabbit illusion, the difference between seeing the duck and seeing the rabbit would be attributed by a philosopher like Hanson to a difference in the beliefs of the two individuals that psychologically predisposes one toward seeing the duck and the other toward seeing the rabbit. And while it may indeed be true that one's beliefs, unconscious or otherwise, color everything one sees, this need not be an hypothesis made by the historian who wants to take seriously the incommensurability thesis in its original robust form.

It would be worthwhile, at this point, to consider an extended and rather extreme example of ecological incommensurability, drawn from Patrick Heelan's (1983) *Space-Perception and the Philosophy of Science.* Trained originally as a quantum physicist, Heelan is clearly a hermeneutical phenomenologist in his approach to the philosophy of science, yet he resists the radical subjectivism normally associated with that position. Heelan argues that, starting in the fifteenth century, certain artifacts were introduced to the European lifeworld which gradually restructured spatial perception so as to make the emergence of the scientific worldview in the seventeenth century a natural outcome. In particular, he maintains that whereas Europeans before 1500 tended to perceive space as having a hyperbolic geometry, after that date they gradually came to perceive it as having a Euclidean geometry. One of the most significant features of Heelan's thesis is that, although it involves a rejection of radical subjectivism, it still implies a radical relativism—indeed, as we shall see below, one much more radical than hermeneuticians have traditionally advocated. However, to see how such a position is possible, we first need to recall the outlines of Dilthey's uncompleted life project (Makkreel 1975).

Dilthey's hermeneutical program can be read as having two parts. The more famous part consisted in a "Critique of Historical Reason," which, like Kant's *Critique*, would systematically lay out "categories of the understanding"—only, this time, relative to various historical epochs. Thus, Dilthey envisaged that in differnt epochs, people constructed the causal order differently, had different views of how properties adhered to substances, and so forth. The less famous part consisted in developing a method that would allow the historian to make sense of these different epochs, namely, by taking advantage of the fact that, despite the many forms that human expression has taken, they have all been responses to a recurrent set of life problems that arise from man's need to survive in his physical environment. Thus, the process of *Verstehen*, which enabled the historian to traverse incommensurable worldviews, was grounded in the biological unity of man. Biologism of this kind was widespread at the turn of the century, appearing, for example, in Ernst Mach's explanation for the growth of knowledge (Munevar 1981, ch. 6). It was supported by a conception of animal intelligence informed by evolutionary theory: namely, that the adaptiveness of an organism must be judged relative to what its nervous system can pick up from the environment and constitute as its "world." Dilthey deviated from this doctrine only in his speculation that human beings are distinguished by the range of worldviews that they can construct from their biological endowment, which, in turn, makes human history a more interesting endeavor than the history of other organisms. In the twentieth century, Dilthey's biologism was purged of its scientistic trappings and repackaged in the form of *Lebensphilosophie* (Schnaedelbach 1984, ch. 5).

Notice that, for Dilthey, the diversity of worldviews occurs at a fairly high level of cognition, namely, at the cultural equivalents of Kant's categories. However, at the level of Kant's "sensibility," bare spatial and temporal perception, Dilthey is a believer in psychic unity, since that is tied most closely to man's unchanging biological inheritance. Heelan differs from Dilthey in relativizing even this level of cognition to culture. Dilthey would find Heelan's radical relativism difficult to grasp, for if man's psychic unity does not run as deep as spatial perception, how can we make any sense of other cultures, indeed, how can we make sense of them as *human* cultures? This question would trouble Dilthey because, like most philosophers who have struggled with the issue of "psychic unity vs. cultural diversity," he assumes that the scope of a psychological universal cannot include the specification of environmental conditions. To put the point less abstractly, consider two candidates for a psychological universal:

(a) It is true of all human beings that, no matter the environment, they perceive space as having a Euclidean structure.

(b) It is true of all human beings that, if they are placed in certain sorts of environments (to be specified), then they will perceive space as having a Euclidean structure.

Dilthey could think of psychological universals only as having the form of (a). In contrast, Heelan believes that while, for example, the basic ability to perceive depth and direction is universal in sense (a), the geometric structure assumed by our perception of depth and direction is universal in sense (b), which is to say, the very geometry of human perception is sensitive to changes in the environment. And so, if the distinction between (a) and (b) is a valid one, and (b)-type universals run as deep as Heelan thinks, then it would seem that human cognition has an innate tendency toward cultural relativism! And despite its paradoxicality, this conclusion has had a distinguished, albeit somewhat peripheral, lineage in the psychological literature (Segall, Campbell & Herskovitz 1966; Gibson 1979).

This last point is important because it brings out the lack of subjectivism in Heelan's account. Hermeneuticians, Dilthey included, frequently talk about changes in worldviews as if they were alternative ways of hallucinating a structure for a world whose environmental cues are inherently impoverished. On this account, it would seem quite appropriate to introduce such subjectivist considerations as "choice." However, this realm of choice is never said to extend to the subject's spatial perception, since that would involve deciding, presumably through an act of will, to reorganize the most fundamental parts of one's experience, the parts least susceptible to any systematic conscious control. Now Heelan likes to talk about the difference between hyperbolic and Euclidean spatial perception as involving a "cultural choice" about how distances should be measured. This, I would maintain, is an unfortunate turn of phrase. For, as we shall see in the examination that follows, the most that Heelan needs to maintain is that one can *indirectly* choose a geometry for his spatial perception by changing the configuration of artifacts that cue his perception. And even this mode of choice assumes that the person both knows which configurations cue which geometries and can coordinate the activities of others in his vicinity to maintain the required configurations. Needless to say, our talents at social engineering have yet to reach such godlike proportions!

The difference between hyperbolic and Euclidean spatial perception can be illustrated by considering what happens when each geometry is imposed on our primordial experience of nearness as visual clarity and distance as visual ambiguity. Each geometry supplies a "rule of congruence," whereby distances are assigned to intervals by comparing them to a standard unit interval. The Euclidean rule of congruence is captured by the "rigid ruler" whose physical dimensions do not change as it is transported through space, thereby rendering the viewer's location irrelevant to the measurement task. In contrast, the hyperbolic rule of congruence is defined solely in terms of the visual estimation by a viewer relative to the significant objects in his immediate vicinity. One way of looking at this distinction is in terms of the one regularly drawn in psychophysics between units of physical stimulus (compare Euclidean) and units of sensory response or just-noticeable-differences (compare hyperbolic). Another way is in terms of the distinction between first (hyperbolic) and third (Euclidean) person perspectives.

While both geometries lead viewers to assign roughly the same measurements to nearby objects, the hyperbolic viewer tends to estimate distant objects as closer and flatter than his Euclidean counterpart, resulting in the kinds of "distortion" seen in the paintings of van Gogh and Cezanne. Heelan maintains that these pictorial images appear distorted only because Euclidean perception is the cultural norm. However, once the contextual cues for Euclidean perception are removed, as in the case of optical illusions, viewers tend to issue perceptual judgments that more closely conform to a hyperbolic metric. Indeed, natives of non-European cultures persistently issue hyperbolic perceptual judgments even when the cues are present. These considerations, together with evidence drawn from ancient and medieval art, suggest to Heelan that hyperbolic perception was common even among Europeans until artifacts were constructed that allowed the viewer to correct for perceptual "distortions" resulting from the viewer being at a particular point in space. A common feature of these artifacts—reflected in the design of post-Renaissance buildings, streets, and paintings—is a series of equally spaced physical markers (such as columns and lamp posts), which cue the viewer to interpret what he sees according to the principles of Euclidean pictorial perspective and thereby effectively impose a Cartesian coordinate system (that is, a "grid") on his perceptual horizon.

Precedent for Heelan's project may be found in Gaston Bachelard's (1985) *New Scientific Spirit* of 1934, which attempted to account for the emergence of the scientific worldview (from Galileo to Dalton) in terms of an "epistemological rupture," namely, the temporary suspension of one's natural attitude to the world that results when a new instrument of perception is introduced to the lifeworld. The rupture is gradually closed as the instrument is integrated in the lifeworld (especially once a theory is offered for why the instrument works), the net result being a reconstitution of one's perceptual horizon. Bachelard's best example of this process concerns the telescope, which, once it became "naturalized" in the European lifeworld, was taken to provide an access to the world as immediate as that provided by one's unaided senses. In short, the telescope became what Bachelard calls a *phenomenotechnique*. Heelan's somewhat more illuminating expression is *readable technology*: just as one directly reads the meaning off words without lingering over their physical presence on the page, so too (say Bachelard and Heelan) one directly sees the moon without reflecting on the fact that the main evidence is a telescopic image.

Bachelard was so taken by the relative ease with which several hundred years of Aristotelian objections to mediated perception were overcome that he regarded the optical theory accompanying the telescope's introduction as something akin to a Freudian defense mechanism. In particular, the theory repressed the primordial intuition of the telescope's artificiality in order to allow the instrument to be used unproblematically. Not surprisingly, then, Bachelardian philosophy of science—as practiced by Georges Canguilhem (1978), Louis Althusser (1970, part 2), and Michel Foucault (1975)—has been devoted primarily to a psychoanalytic study of ecological incommensurabilities, in which epistemological ruptures function as traumas sustained by the Western collective unconscious.

Difficulties for Heelan arise once we consider where he *differs* from Bachelard. Unlike Bachelard, Heelan is more concerned with the worldviews on either side of the rupture than with the rupture itself. In this sense, he joins Dilthey and the early Karl Mannheim (1971) in presenting a typology of *Weltanschauungen*. And like these "historicists," Heelan never gives the reader a sense of what Bachelard would have called "the dialectics of historical change." For example, the telescope plays a relatively slight role in Heelan's account, even though the issues generated by its introduction were instrumental in grafting Euclidean spatial perception onto scientific inquiry. As Alexandre Koyre (1964, ch. 3) has shown in *From the Closed World to the Infinite Universe,* Kepler was able to supply much of the optical theory for Galileo's telescope and yet perceive space in terms that Heelan would consider largely hyperbolic. And while Heelan readily admits that the history of the transition from hyperbolic to Euclidean spatial perception has yet to be written, it is not clear that such a history would entirely vindicate his position. In particular, Heelan is vulnerable to a fallacious line of reasoning, all too common among phenomenologists, that attempts to derive free choice from historical contingency. In this case, he wants to use the fact that Euclidean spatial perception had a clear historical origin to show that we can alter our spatial perception at any subsequent point in history.

Once Heelan has shown that an alternative to Euclidean spatial perception exists, and that it was in fact dominant in pre-Renaissance Europe, he concludes that we Euclidean perceivers are in a position to adopt that alternative geometry for more than just simple Gestalt-style experiments. Indeed, Heelan believes (for reasons which will not be discussed here) that the trend toward "dehumanization" that has attended the rise of the scientific worldview can be stopped by partially returning to a hyperbolic perception of space. Though interesting, the proposal remains as unpersuasive as any conventionalist claim that we actually *decide* on what geometry to use for purposes other than constructing proofs and other formal operations. Heelan's problem here is that he follows phenomenological usage in defining the thing that a geometry structures, a "possible world," not as a linguistic construct, but as an object of introspection, which is to say, an object that exists for consciousness under certain specified conditions. At this point, it is easy to fall into the trap of concluding that such objects of consciousness can themselves be objects of conscious control.

However, the conditions under which an object can exist for a lone Cartesian consciousness are not those under which it can exist for a "collective consciousness," so to speak. The structure of a community's spatial perception is not the product of individuals deliberately performing phenomenological experiments. And if a community can even be said to "have" a spatial perception, it would be as a result of the activities of every individual being coordinated in space. It would then seem unlikely that the relevant individuals could be motivated in the same way to alter their spatial perception in such a deliberate manner, not only because of the wide variety of interests those individuals would likely have but, more importantly, because the alleged benefits of adopting a Euclidean view of the world are genuine benefits only for individuals who are already willing to radically alter their preference structure, thus reflecting the incommensurability of the hyperbolic and Euclidean worldviews. (Heelan suggests how values of "locality" can be traced to a hyperbolic worldview, while values of "globality" can be traced to a Euclidean one.)

A more likely explanation for the transition in geometries would need to invoke some indirect causal factors, the so-called *invisible hand*. For various political and economic reasons, European princes commissioned the engineering projects from which the modern theories of perspective and optics were eventually drawn. With the institutional rise of science, these theories, in turn, came to be enforced as the European cultural norm. There is no reason to think that the interests of the princes, the theorists, and the pedagogues coincided, though their activities were individually necessary and jointly sufficient for the emergence of the Euclidean perceptual horizon. Furthermore, a new geometry of spatial perception may well be one of those states of affairs that can arise *only* as the unintended consequence of the activities of many individuals (Elster 1984, Fuller 1985a). Indeed, the invisible hand account may also explain why individual philosophers and scientists, Kant most notably, have perennially found it impossible to *intend* their way out of a Euclidean framework.

Let us finally consider the viability of ecological incommensurability as a research program in the history of science. Rather than explain different responses to the same stimulus in terms of different background beliefs, the historian may make the simpler assumption that the two individuals have largely the same psychic makeup but that their environments are sufficiently dissimilar so as to trigger sensory cues leading one to see a duck and the other a rabbit. In that case, the historian may confine his study of worldviews to three rather objectively defined areas:

(c) the canonical language in which scientists must articulate whatever beliefs they happen to hold;

(d) the configuration of artifacts comprising the sensory environment of the scientific community;

(e) situations in which either a novice or an expert is judged to have made incompetent linguistic or sensory performances (along with any remarks that may attend the judgment); a faulty argument and an illicit inference would be examples of incompetent linguistic performances, while the misuse of experimental apparatus and failure to attend to the "significant" features of one's experimental set up would be examples of incompetent sensory performances.

A major consequence of this objectified construal of worldviews is that the friends and foes of incommensurability may be reconciled at least tentatively. Foes, such as Donald Davidson (1984), are granted the validity of such principles of rationality as "charity" and "humanity," which presume that, ceteris paribus, all human beings are sufficiently similar in how they process linguistic and sensory cues so as to act in largely the same manner under the same circumstances. The friends of incommensurability also have no trouble with accepting these principles, just as long as "the same circumstances" is taken to mean the same with respect to the three aforementioned areas of historical inquiry, so that scientists of different periods are distinguished only by different sensory and linguistic cues. And so, just as theory-ladenness does not bother the rationalist follower of Davidson, neither should it bother the incommensurabilist follower of Kuhn.

So far we have seen that taken in its robust sense, incommensurability need not imply some deep structure of thought that prevents one worldview from coming to terms with another. On the contrary, we may understand the Kuhn thesis as calling for a shift of focus in the history and philosophy of science from largely mentalistic concerns for "beliefs" and "meanings," which (as Popper [Jarvie 1984] had already realized) underpinned much positivist talk of "theories," to more objective inquiries into the sensory and linguistic cues that constitute the normative boundaries of the scientific community. In closing this section of the chapter, let me note that, in running together his views with Feyerabend's, Kuhn's critics tend to inject much more talk of beliefs, meanings, and theories than Kuhn himself was ever inclined to do. They seem to take Kuhn's reluctance to use the positivist vocabulary as either a gesture toward the ineffable qualities of tacit knowledge or the mark of a historian's humility in the face of philosophical issues, *when in fact he may be challenging the legitimacy of pursuing those very issues.*

2. Textual Incommensurability

At first glance, the second type of incommensurability seems so implausible that no rational being would ever think of espousing it, let alone refuting it. However, like the skeptic's challenge, the implausibility of textual incommensurability is matched only by its irrefutability. In essence, it is the notorious Babel Thesis introduced in the last chapter. It arises from rather humble conceptual origins. Since there are no commonly accepted methods for proving that we have understood what someone has said, and since communication is essential to any sustained human endeavor, we are forced to presume that we have understood our interlocutor until a misunderstanding has been brought to our attention. This seems to be a reasonable strategy, one that has supported many years of successful human interaction. However, it rests on the assumption that any misunderstanding would be detected at some point in the discourse and, furthermore, that it would be detected *as a misunderstanding,* that is, as the result of one party's failure to have understood the other party. But we can imagine misunderstandings that persist for long periods because the parties are using much of the same language, yet to mean systematically different things. The longer the discourse proceeds unchecked in this way, the more the misunderstandings accumulate, until some "crisis" emerges, which causes a breakdown in communication. However, this crisis is not then diagnosed as the result of compounded prior misunderstandings, but rather as following from some deep conceptual problems that none of the current interlocutors seem able to solve to everyone's satisfaction. Knowing the linguistic origin of the crisis, we would not be surprised to learn that these deep problems appear either as an inability to apply a concept to an anomalous case or as a paradox whose solution requires a more finely grained lexicon. In the end, the discourse community fragments into schools, paradigms, and disciplines—quite in keeping with the biblical tale of the Tower of Babel. Notice that for this entire scenario to be true, *nothing in the historical record would have to be different.*

We have so far presented the Babel Thesis as a thought experiment, but our intention is to suggest that it may provide the best explanation for what Michael Oakeshott and Richard Rorty (1979) have called "the conversation of mankind," the seemingly interminable debates that have transpired for the last 2,500 years in the West over the natures of Truth, Goodness, Beauty, and the like. When considering the incommensurable accounts that have been proposed for understanding the nature of Beauty, W. B. Gallie (1957) referred to Beauty as "an essentially contested concept." An even clearer case of such a concept is Truth, which has led philosophers not only to contest a wide variety of seemingly unrelated theories (correspondence, coherence, redundancy, and pragmatism—to name the leading contenders), but also the metaissue of whether the goal of these theories should be to provide a definition or a criterion of Truth (Haack 1978, ch. 7). For all its radicalness, the Babel Thesis never strayed far from the minds of the positivists, who were quite willing to attribute many higher-order conceptual disputes (especially the ones associated with empirically equivalent scientific theories) to a difference in language use rather than a genuine difference in beliefs. But perhaps the most flagrant endorsement of the Babel Thesis may be found in the writings of the deconstructionists—Jacques Derrida, Harold Bloom, Paul De Man—who, persuaded by Marxist and Freudian claims, have shifted the burden of proof to someone who believes that he understands how even *his own* language is being used (Fuller 1983a). And, finally, in a report on "the state of knowledge" in the West, Jean-Francois Lyotard (1984) has observed that a key feature of the "postmodern" attitude is the realization *both* that the Babel Thesis is an inevitable outcome of knowledge production being so decentralized in contemporary society *and* that this radical incommensurability has the unexpected benefit of fostering innovation at a faster rate than ever before.

Despite the robustness of the Babel Thesis' pedigree, we should not lose sight of the fact that it is still very much a minority opinion about the nature of knowledge production. In fact, analytic philosophers of language, such as Quine and Davidson, make a point of arguing that the thesis *must* be false, if translation is to be possible at all. Clearly, in order to make such a strong claim, these philosophers must have ways of talking about the transmission of knowledge that systematically prevent the Babel Thesis from being expressed as an intelligent alternative. We shall examine Quine's radical translation episode with this thought in mind, in particular four of its features that indirectly serve to make the Babel Thesis less plausible: *first*, how the idea of translation is construed; *second*, how the idea of linguistic rule is construed; *third*, the role of speech as the paradigm of language use; *fourth*, the implicit aims of constructing a translation.

First, the theory of translation implicit in the radical translation episode is quite unlike the one presumed in the actual practice of translators. Indeed, this implicit theory reflects Quine's training as a formal logician in the heyday of logical positivism. To see the difference we are suggesting here, consider two general strategies for effecting a translation:

(T1) The translator renders an alien text in sentences that are nearest in meaning to ones that speakers in his own language would normally use, even if it means losing some of the ambiguity or nuance in the alien text.

(T2) The translator renders an alien text in sentences that are nearest in meaning to ones that, though grammatically possible in his own language, require a suspension of normal usage, perhaps including the introduction of neologistic terms and distinctions that capture semantic subtleties in the alien text.

In short, then, translation proceeds in (T1) by the translator adjusting the alien language to fit his own, while in (T2) it proceeds by the translator adjusting his own language to fit the alien one. Quine's episode can be seen as a case of (T1) in that the anthropologist translates the native by having him simply respond to specially selected test cases that reflect semantic distinctions drawn in the anthropologist's language.

When treated as a general account of translation, (T1) implies that a set of noises or marks does not constitute a meaningful utterance unless it can be translated into one's own language. The model of this position is Wittgenstein's (1961) *Tractatus*, which argues that the limits of translatability cannot be recognized as such: either one is able to give a complete rendering of the propositional content of an alien text in one's own language or one is forced into silence. The historical sources of (T1) are Russell and Carnap, who gave the name "translation" to the task of isolating the propositional content of sentences in natural languages and reproducing that content in a formal language. And even though this project of translation—championed by logical positivism—was abandoned thirty years ago, Quine (as well as Davidson) continues to privilege the translator's language as the nonnegotiable basis for making sense of the native's utterances. Quine manages this point rather subtly by claiming that all languages are implicit theories of physical reality, with the anthropologist's language differing from the native's only in terms of its relative richness. This move commits the natives to, among other things, having many of the same interests as the anthropologist in using language (namely, the interests associated with representing reality). Thus, the fact that the anthropologist needs to force the native to respond to specially designed situations can be interpreted as demonstrating that the native's language is less adequate to its own goals than the anthropologist's language.

Moreover, the anthropologist has at his disposal a repertoire of linguistic distinctions that conceal this tacit evaluation without causing him to worry that he might be misreading what the native has said. The two most frequently used distinctions of this kind are probably *cognitive vs. emotive* and *propositional vs. performative*. Any aspect of the native's utterance that the anthropologist cannot readily check against the semantic categories of his own language becomes a candidate for the second half of each dichotomy. However, these distinctions start to look suspiciously ethnocentric, once it seems that *most* of what the native says turns out to be emotive or performative (Sperber 1982). Indeed, the principle of charity itself may be read as a covert statement of ethnocentrism, since it instructs the anthropologist to interpret the native either as saying something that the anthropologist already knows (and perhaps can articulate better) or as erring because the native lacks some background knowledge that the anthropologist has. In other words, charity does not allow the possibility that the anthropologist and the native may have a legitimate, cognitively based disagreement.

In contrast, (T2), the practicing translator's implicit theory of translation, affords him the opportunity to strike a critical stance toward his own culture. The opportunity arises whenever the translator confronts fluent native expressions that can be rendered in his own language only with great difficulty, as witnessed in the number of neologisms he must construct. Moreover, the awkwardness of these neologisms is readily noticed, giving the translation a distinctly alien quality, quite unlike how the original expression must have seemed to the native. For the philosophically minded reader, a most vivid example is Heidegger's (1962) attempt, in *Being and Time,* to recapture in German the metaphysical distinctions drawn by the ancient Greeks, who were, of course, noteworthy for engaging in a discourse much more publicly accessible than Heidegger's "faithful" rendition. In this case, we see that unlike the (T1) translator, the (T2) translator recognizes the limits of translatability *in the very act of translation;* for the more attentive he is to the semantic distinctions drawn in the original (as Heidegger was), the more he also emphasizes the "otherness" of the native language and, hence, the inability of the native language to serve a function outside its original context. To put it bluntly, if a translation attempts to be too "close" to the original, it ends up defeating the overall purpose of translation, which is to render the foreign familiar. Eugene Nida (1964), perhaps the leading theorist among practicing translators (and an influence on both Quine and Kuhn), has noted this irony, characterizing it in terms of complementary "equivalences" between which the translator must strike a balance. An example from Nida's own field of expertise, biblical translation, will make the point.

Biblical translators are typically beset by two conflicting goals. As the most significant historical document of early Western culture, the books of the Bible should be rendered in a manner that is semantically faithful to the original Hebrew, Aramaic, and Greek. Nida calls this sort of equivalence *formal*, and he associates it with *biblical exegesis.* Yet, the Bible is also the canonical text for several major living faiths, and so a good translation should also render the "spirit" of the original in a way that makes its message as relevant now as it was two thousand years ago. Nida calls this sort of equivalence (lacking in Heidegger's approach) *dynamic*, and he associates it with *biblical hermeneutics.* Moreover, it is no less "faithful" to the original than a formally equivalent translation. Indeed, in aiming for dynamic equivalence, the translator wants to capture the fact that when originally uttered, the native text performed a specific social function for its intended audience, as indicated in the behavioral response that the audience subsequently produced. In order to elicit a similar response in our own culture, the translation may need to deviate sharply from the original, as in the case of the Broadway play *West Side Story* having the same sort of popular appeal as Shakespeare's original *Romeo and Juliet.* A more extreme example is E. V. Rieu's rendering of the Homeric epics as mass-consumption novels written in several English dialects. Indeed, Quine himself seems to have understood the dynamic equivalence sense of translation quite well, since one of his criteria for an adequate translation is that it elicits the appropriate behavioral response, regardless of whether the native would accept the terms employed by the translator as formally equivalent to his own.

Clearly, then, to maximize one goal of translation is to minimize the other, since formal equivalence tends to emphasize the difference between the translator's and the native's languages, while the dynamic tends to emphasize their similarity. Depending on their specific goals, translators resolve this tension in a variety of ways, but it should be noted that *in each case some information contained in the original is lost.* And while some of this lost information can often be recovered by returning to the original text and setting new translation goals, for reasons of economy attempts at recovery are rarely made, and never systematically. This means that to a large extent, the knowledge that our culture has gathered and transmitted over the centuries has been captive to the ever-changing aims of translators, which, in turn, is the basis for whatever truth there is in the Babel Thesis.

In fact, given Nida's analysis, we can construct the Babel Thesis as a trade-off that the (T2) translator must negotiate. On the one hand, if he believes that philosophers who have argued about the nature of, say, Truth over the last two millenia have been bewitched by their language, then in order to explain their linguistic behavior, he must suspend an assumption that he would never suspend in his own case, namely, that the philosophers know what their words mean. On the other hand, if the translator believes that the philosophers are very much like himself and thus not susceptible to deep semantic errors, then the Babel Thesis cannot possibly be correct. We can thus summarize the difference between the (T1) and (T2) approach to translation in the following manner. Whereas Quine, Davidson, and other "charitable" (T1) translators would claim that the latter alternative, the route of dynamic equivalence, is the only available one, (T2) translators maintain that one alternative must always be traded off against the other.

The *second* way in which the radical translation episode conspires against the Babel Thesis may be captured by the following question: Just how are linguistic rules to be characterized, regardless of whether they appear as a generative grammar designed by a computational linguist in his office or a translation manual constructed by an anthropologist in the field? In either setting, the rules are normally conceived of as positive directives for arriving at syntactically and semantically correct utterances. However, in Quine's episode, the only evidence that the anthropologist has for native discourse being governed by some rule or other are the native's negative responses to his incorrect utterances. Quine is fully aware of this fact and plays it up as *the indeterminacy of translation thesis,* which, in effect, claims that no amount of negative feedback from the native will ever be enough for the anthropologist to determine what positive rules he has been breaking. Thus understood, Quine's thesis locates the "indeterminacy" in the epistemic gap between the native's positive understanding of the rules and the anthropologist's indirect, negative understanding of them.

But suppose that the linguistic rules were themselves inherently indirect or, as Wittgensteinians like to put it, "open-textured." In other words, the anthropologist never seems to get enough evidence for inferring the native grammar only because the rules themselves are nothing more than *negative* directives defining what *cannot* be meant by a certain expression in a certain context, but otherwise leaving open what can be meant. In that case, indeterminacy is not merely a consequence of the anthropologist not being a native speaker, but rather, a feature built into the very structure of language itself, whose constraints on its users would be more ill defined than normally supposed. We would not be surprised then at the native himself not being able to articulate the rules governing his own discourse, or, at least, not being able to articulate rules that are consistent with the judgment calls he would make on what counts as "correct usage." Linguists in fact constantly run up against such discrepancies when testing the psychological validity of a grammar (Greene 1972). But the idea of linguistic rules as negative directives would illuminate not only these discrepancies but also the pragmatic sources of terms imperceptibly shifting their meanings and referents over time, as evidenced in etymologies, which has been a cornerstone of the incommensurability thesis.

Third, in the Quine episode, since the native is in the presence of the anthropologist, he can correct mistranslations immediately after they occur. This is one feature of speech as a linguistic medium that distinguishes it from writing, whose communicativeness does not lie with the author constantly attending his text. However, there is little actual face-to-face contact among the people relevant to either the making or the recording of the history of science. Admittedly, there is much face-to-face contact among members of a school of thought or a scientific community confined to, say, one academic institution. Indeed, this constant, and largely speech-based, interaction ensures the formation of strong normative bounds on what can be said and done. But such bounds do not normally extend to other institutions, the work of whose members is encountered almost exclusively through the written media of journals and books. In that case, members of one community regularly take their ability to incorporate the work of another community in their own research as evidence for their having understood the nature of the other community's activities. This is hardly a foolproof strategy for the kind of translation Quine's anthropologist wants. Yet the curious historical trajectories often taken by disciplines may be explained in part by this failure to distinguish clearly between *understanding* and *using* someone else's work. As long as this distinction is not made by a community of researchers, incommensurability remains a viable possibility. There is more to say on this matter, but we should just note here that incommensurability may be intimately tied to what Max Weber (and more lately Lyotard) has taken to be be the "rationalization" of knowledge in a literate society having a complex division of cognitive labor. In other words, as the boundaries of scientific communities become restricted to narrower subject matters, the scientist needs to turn to written media for his information on a wider range of topics, which have may the net effect of proliferating uncorrected misunderstandings. Many such sociological hypotheses have been proposed and tested about the rise of bureaucracies, but only recently have they been fruitfully applied to the dissemination of knowledge in the network of scientific communities

(Collins 1975, ch. 9; Whitley 1986). We shall have occasion to examine these issues in more detail in chapter 9.

The *fourth* and final feature of the radical translation episode that casts doubt on the incommensurability thesis concerns the goals of translation itself, specifically whether all attempts at translation have at least one goal in common. However, as was suggested in our first objection to Quine's episode, it is not clear whether the episode or the thesis is the less plausible. Quine assumes that there is some intuitive sense in which understanding someone else's discourse can be pursued as an end in its own right, namely, as the project of *semantics*. This assumption accounts for why Quine's reader is never told why the anthropologist would want to translate the tribal language in the first place, aside from preserving the content of tribal utterances (which itself must be understood in terms of preserving the *reference*, not the sense, of the native utterance). However, an adequate understanding of another's discourse is usually a means for one's own cognitive ends. And depending on the nature of the ends and the constraints placed on how they may be achieved, various translations may pass as an adequate understanding. The point here is analogous to the one made by Bas van Fraassen (1980, ch. 5) about the nature of explanation in *The Scientific Image:* just as there is no privileged explanation called "scientific" that is the best answer to all requests for an explanation, so too there is no privileged translation called "semantic" that is the best answer to all requests for a translation (compare LePore 1986, part 6).

One type of constraint peculiar to requests for translations is dictated by the probability that the author of the translated discourse, or such surrogates as scholars and disciples, will criticize misunderstandings of what he has said. On the one hand, if we do not expect an opponent or one of his agencies to respond to how we have rendered his positions, we will characterize them with only as much fidelity as will serve our polemical purposes. For example, Granger (1985) and Sacksteder (1986) show this to have certainly been the case for key words in Aristotle. The same applies to an author such as Kuhn(!) whose obscure discourse makes virtually any interpretation look reasonable. On the other hand, we would have to take more care with figures such as Aristotle and Newton. But let us now leave the state of nature of the "Hobbesian Hermeneutician" and turn briefly to the Roman orator Cicero, who is credited with originating what analytic philosophers, at least, generally take to be the *only* theory of translation: namely, that the sense of the translated language should be preserved in the translating language (Bassnett-McGuire 1980). For we shall find that Cicero's motivations were not quite as they seem to modern eyes.

Cicero did not advance the sense-preserving view of translation in order to curb the tendencies of readers solely interested in the use-value of texts. On the contrary, he held that a sense-preserving translation offered the most effective means for preserving and transmitting the accumulated wisdom of the Greeks. In more general terms, then, Cicero took maximum understanding as necessary for making the most use of another's discourse.

This is a proposition that no one today would hold as particularly rational, especially once we measure the time needed for fully understanding what someone meant against the likely payoff of this understanding for our own research. But of course, Cicero presumed the view, strong even during the Scientific Revolution, that intellectual progress consists in showing how one's current research, whether speculative or empirical, illuminates some ultimate source of knowledge, usually some Greek, Hebrew, or early Christian text, whose meaning remained obscured in the mists of antiquity. A key wedge in dividing what we now call "the sciences" from "the humanities" occurred in the eighteenth and nineteenth centuries, when the sciences lost the Ciceronian sensibility, which is responsible for our current inability to see any problems in our using someone's ideas (that is, paraphrases of his text) even if we cannot fully see what he had intended when he first articulated them.

Moreover, if you think that even outside its original practical context, some "sense" can be made of sense-preserving translation, then the history of translation theory since the late seventeenth century should make you think again. For example, John Dryden, who was noted not only for his poetry and criticism but also for his translations of Vergil, predated Nelson Goodman's (1949) critique of the idea of similarity (and its linguistic version, synonymy) by likening the translator's task to that of the open-air painter of nature: both work in a medium different from the original without being given any cues from the original as to how it should be represented. Dryden's analogy suggests that the difference between two natural languages is as great as the difference between a three-dimensional "living" nature and its two-dimensional representation on canvas. It is ironic that Dryden should have mounted such a persuasive attack on the idea that every utterance has a sense that may be rendered in any language, since he himself was the first major defender and exemplar of a "clear," non-Latinate prose style in the English language. Perhaps the best explanation for this irony is that Dryden had a strong (T2) sense of translation.

One common literary construal of the sense-preserving thesis that has escaped the notice of analytic philosophers is the *genre-preserving* translation, which requires that the translator capture not only the "content" of the original but also some sense of how its syntax indicated the kind of work it was to its original audience. To take some simple examples: works originally composed as poems should look like poems in translation, histories should look like histories, science like science. Since we are far from a general theory of stylistics capable of distinguishing histories, sciences, and other so-called cognitive discourses from one another, it is not clear exactly what changes would need to be made in actual translation practices. However, E. D. Hirsch's (1967) *Validity in Interpretation* takes the first steps in the right direction, back to a systematic *Geisteswissenschaften* on the late nineteenth-century model. In the more restricted domain of the metaphysical and theological aspects of seventeenth-century scientific discourse, Koyre's (1969) sophisticated stylistics set the stage for what remains some of the best work being done in the historiography of science.

The *reductio* of the stylistic strategy is captured in the idea that not only should the translator represent the syntactic features that made a text accessible to its original audience but also those features that make it inaccessible, or at least alien, to its current audience. In formulating the hermeneutical enterprise, Friedrich Schleiermacher argued that the only way in which the reader is encouraged to seek out the tacit presuppositions (and hence underlying meaning) of a previous discourse is through a translation whose obscurity forces the reader to question even the most elementary thought processes of the author (Hirsch 1967, ch. 5). The maxim assumed here, that difficult expression (by the author, or his translator) begets deep thinking (by the reader), may be repugnant to the instincts of analytic philosophers. Nevertheless, we should not lose sight of the fact that Schleiermacher's counsel of obscurity was followed not only in Germany, but it also served as the major criterion of adequacy for translation during the Victorian period, which led translators and other conveyors of distant cultures (including Carlyle, Browning, Pater, and Fitzgerald) to render that "distance" stylistically in an archaic, stilted English prose.

Notice that the hermeneutical strategy turns Quine's principle of charity on its head. For, rather than minimize the number of sentences in the translated language that turn out false or strange, Schleiermacher proposed to *maximize* their number. Quine would, no doubt, respond by pointing out that the hermeneutical strategy actually removes the most crucial check on the adequacy of a translation, namely, that it renders the author rational. However, Schleiermacher would probably then respond that the "rationality" of human beings lies not in their recurrent—perhaps even universal—patterns of conduct, but rather in their ability to render meaningful largely unrepeatable—perhaps even unique—situations. Moreover, this response would not be merely a function of Schleiermacher's susceptibility to Romanticism's emphasis on the individual, but it would, more importantly, reflect the major alternative tradition in the history of rationality, starting with Aristotle's discussion of judicial discretion, which locates the paradigm of reason in the practical rather than the theoretical (Brown 1978).

The point, then, is that even if philosophers such as Quine and Davidson are correct in regarding a theory of translation as a covert theory of rationality, that is, at best, to give only a functional, not a substantive, definition of "rationality." In other words, the analytic philosophers should be taken, not as having argued for any particular theory of translation or theory of rationality, but only for a logically necessary connection between the two *sorts* of theories, regardless of their particular content. In that case, incommensurability again looks plausible, if only because *the very idea of sense-preserving translation has itself been subject to changes in sense* and *the very idea of rationality has itself been exemplified over the years by individuals who would not consider each other rational.*

But suppose we grant Quine that the optimal translation strategy is to take the principle of charity as a regulative ideal. Does it then follow that misunderstandings will tend to be minimized and incommensurability eliminated? In arguing against the coherence of construing conceptual schemes as self-contained, incommensurable discourses, Davidson (1984, ch. 13) seems to presume an intuitive answer of yes to this question. However, outside the artificial setting of Quinean concerns, the attempt to minimize the number of sentences in the translated language that turn out false or strange could be quite easily seen as a strategy for co-opting the author's beliefs into the translator's set of beliefs and smoothing over whatever real differences remain.   In other words, the principle of charity might be designed to promote a form of Whig History, where the historical figures have the chance of either giving inchoate expression to our current beliefs or simply being deemed irrational.

The impalatability of these alternatives has moved Michel Foucault to devise an historiography of science that does away with the principle of charity and presumes incommensurability as a regulative ideal of historical inquiry (Hacking 1979). Foucault's strategy, roughly, has been to take the apparent strangeness of past discourse to indicate a genuine break from our own discourse. The intent is to methodologically curb the sovereignty that we ultimately exercise over how the past is interpreted. The benefit is to maintain a distinction that is often blurred in Quine-Davidson-type discussions of translation. Following Gilbert Ryle's (1949, p. 130) distinction, we are pointing to the difference between "translate" as a *task verb* and "translate" as an *achievement verb*. The "achievement" refers to the list of syntactic correspondences constituting the translation manual of Quine's anthropologist, while the "task" refers to the activities that must be performed in order to achieve a translation, as well as the criteria indicating that the translation has been achieved.

As we have seen, translation as a task is a rather difficult issue about which incommensurability has much to offer. For, properly understood, our second version of the incommensurability thesis does not say that translations can never be achieved, but rather that we should not assume that any strategy that aims a translation is ipso facto likely to succeed. In that case, incommensurability is not so much an empirical hypothesis about the history of science as a methodological directive for the historiography of science.

CHAPTER SIX

THE INSCRUTABILITY OF SILENCE AND THE PROBLEM OF KNOWLEDGE IN THE HUMAN SCIENCES

The aim of this chapter is to identify and analyze (but, alas, not solve) an epistemological problem, perhaps the fundamental one, that besets anyone who tries to obtain a systematic understanding of human beings and wishes to rely on their utterances as evidence. The problem concerns *the criteriological status of silence.* More explicitly: Is silence a mark of the familiar or the alien? Still more explicitly: If a "concept" (that is, a belief, desire, or other intentional state using the concept) familiar to the humanist is missing from "the record" of a culture, should he conclude that the culture found the concept so familiar as not to require mention, or that the culture simply lacked the concept? As we deal with this problem—which we may call, with all due respect to Quine, *the inscrutability of silence*—it will become clear that the final verdict has yet to be delivered on the incommensurability thesis. Indeed, we shall see that, far from refuting the thesis, Donald Davidson's transcendental argument for the translatability of alien discourses is quite compatible with it.

Before we begin our inquiry, we should say why we intend to use "translation" and "interpretation" interchangeably. Simply stated, the reason is that there is no agreement as to which term is the more primitive. Whereas analytic philosophers tend to view the construction of a translation manual as a precondition for interpreting particular alien speakers, practitioners of the human sciences tend to treat interpretation as a largely prelinguistic understanding of an alien culture that often never advances to the stage of explicit translation. If there is one clear difference in usage between the two terms, it is that "interpretations" are more open to disagreement than "translations," much as "theories" are generally taken to be more contestable than "observations." Indeed, the analogy suggested here may run deeper, since just as observations tend to be of atomic sensations, translations tend to be of relatively small, well-defined units of discourse, such as words or sentences. And similarly, both theories and interpretations tend to be of more holistic entities: respectively, systems of objects and complete texts.

1. Inscrutability and the Analytic Philosophy of Language

For our first look at silence, let us consider a case adapted from Paul Feyerabend (1975, ch. 17). The Homeric epics mention various parts of the human body without ever mentioning the body as a whole. Does this mean that the archaic Greeks had no concept of the body qua unit, or, as we might normally think, that they intended the concept as implicitly understood in their discourse? A question of this sort is *fundamental* to the epistemology of the human sciences in that it forces us to *justify* a maxim without which no systematic understanding of human beings would seem to be possible: namely, for two speakers A and B, if A says something that B understands as *p*, then, unless B has reason to think otherwise, A may be taken as intending all that is normally presupposed by *p*. Of course, "normally" needs specification, but, just given our example, if Homer appears to be speaking of limbs and organs, then it is clearly "normal" for the classicist to understand Homer as presupposing at least a whole body of which those limbs and organs are parts. Moreover, since it is difficult to imagine an interpretation of Homer in which the presupposition turns out to be misattributed, the classicist would first want to find evidence, such as anomalous utterances, that suggests an alternative interpretation. All this seems to be sound humanistic practice—that is, until we try to *justify* it.

As Paul Grice (1957, 1975), among others, have pointed out, B is justified in attributing certain "implicitly understood" presuppositions to A, only if A is understood as *addressing* B. It is important to see why this is so, since the classicist may be fully aware that Homer is not specifically addressing him, yet persist in believing that it makes sense to attribute the concept of body qua unit, alleging that the concept is a "primordial intuition" common to all human beings. Yet this alone would not explain why the concept is never articulated, since primordial intuitions are often discussed and sometimes even formally studied. Indeed, our own concept of bodily wholeness is a topic in the psychology of perception, namely, "proprioception." In contrast, a Gricean account *could* explain how Homer *possessed yet never mentioned* the concept of bodily wholeness: to wit, Homer was addressing an audience for whom mention of the concept would have been gratuitous; thus, he would be seen as obeying the Quantity Maxim of conversational implicature: namely, that speakers should say no more and no less than is needed to be perfectly understood by their intended audiences. And indeed, a Gricean account *would* be true, were Homer addressing *us*, which he clearly is *not*. In fact, as Matthew Arnold famously pointed out, we know less about Homer's intended audience than about Homer himself (Newmark 1981, ch. 1). And even if the classicist knew the identity of Homer's audience, since Homer himself would not recognize the classicist as one its members, the classicist ends up engaging the Homeric text in an epistemic role of a spectator to an exchange—between Homer and his audience—in which none of the utterances are intended for the classicist. In short, his role is reduced to that of an *eavesdropper*.

Thus, the classicist cannot justify his taking silence as a mark of the familiar by appealing to the standard philosophical account of communication represented by Grice. This is not to say that the classicist must therefore conclude that Homer did *not* have a concept of bodily wholeness. Rather, the classicist's epistemic stance does not permit him to decide between the two interpretations. And while the Homer example is extreme, the same problem can be refashioned for all cases in which an author did not intend the humanist interpreter as part of his audience.

Besides highlighting the inscrutability of silence, the above example functions as a kind of "duck-rabbit" Gestalt for the problems of interpretation that have recently vexed philosophers of language and science: Does the inscrutability of silence illustrate *the indeterminacy of translation* or *the incommensurability thesis*? As Ian Hacking (1975a, chs. 11-12; 1982) has suggested on several occasions, these two theses offer contrary diagnoses of what can go wrong during interpretation. On the one hand, the human scientist may arrive at several incompatible, but equally adequate, interpretations of an alien discourse; on the other hand, he may be faced with not even one adequate interpretation of the alien discourse. And, interestingly, while most philosophers have found the former thesis, indeterminacy, the more compelling, most practitioners of the human sciences (especially literary critics and anthropologists) seem to have been pulled toward the latter thesis, incommensurability. On the surface, then, these two positions appeal to quite divergent intuitions about the nature of interpretation. However, we shall now argue that, like the "duck" and "rabbit" faces of the famous Gestalt, indeterminacy and incommensurability are themselves just complementary ways of interpreting the inscrutability of silence.

First notice the difference in the kinds of arguments used to justify the two contrary theses. From reading Davidson's (1984; Rorty 1972) articles on interpretation, it becomes clear that the indeterminacy thesis is a consequence—intended or not—of a *transcendental argument* for every language being translatable into our own. Davidson argues by asking us to conceive of a situation in which we could identify some collection of signs as a language without at least having implicitly interpreted them. Since Davidson believes that such a situation is inconceivable, he concludes that translatability is a necessary condition for our recognizing the signs as a language. Beyond that point, however, Davidson is not much concerned with *which* interpretation we confer on those signs. Given his concept of translatability, this attitude makes sense, since Davidson does not offer the interpreter much of a choice. In particular, he defines translatabilty as the interpreter's ability to show that most of the sentences in an alien discourse are true and that the rest are understandable errors. And so, even when the alien speaker sounds his strangest, the human scientist must still opt to interpret him either as having false beliefs forged from familiar concepts used familiarly or as having true beliefs forged from familiar concepts used idiosyncratically.

But even if Davidson were interested in resolving this indeterminacy, his reliance on transcendental argumentation would be of no help. The reason, simply put, is that transcendental arguments typically establish that X must be the case without (and perhaps instead of) establishing how one would identify instances of X being the case. For example, why does a Humean remain unimpressed after hearing a Kantian transcendentally argue that our experience of the physical world would be inconceivable if every event did not have a cause? The answer, of course, is that such an argument, even if valid, would not help us determine the *particular* causes of *particular* events, which is the Humean's problem. We see then that a positive transcendental argument about the general case—cause per se—is quite compatible with a skeptical empiricist argument about causes in actual cases. Not surprisingly, we shall now find that the incommensurability thesis typically appears as the outcome of skeptical empiricist arguments about particular cases of failed or impeded translation drawn from the annals of native and scientific cultures.

To illustrate the incommensurabilist's role as "Humean Hermeneutician," consider how Peter Winch reconciles his view that native cultures can be understood only from the inside (that is, complete translation into one's own discourse is impossible) with his view (which he shares with Davidson) that there are cross-cultural principles of interpretation and rationality:

> I never of course denied that Zande witchcraft practices involve appeals to what we can understand as standards of rationality. Such appeals also involve behavior which we can identify as "the recognition of a contradiction." What I was arguing, though, was that we should be cautious in how we identify the contradiction, which may not be what it would be if we approach it with "scientific" preconceptions. [Winch 1970, p. 254]

The key words here are "recognition" and "identify." The Zande and the anthropologist may assent to exactly the same inference rules of deduction, but make totally different judgment calls on whether or not particular natural language arguments are valid by those rules. Failure to see this point stems from a failure to appreciate the inscrutability of silence. For example, the anthropologist may identify an argument uttered by a Zande speaker (assuming, probably contrary-to-fact, that "arguing" is a legitimate Zande speech act) as invalid simply because he failed to supply the suppressed premises that would be readily supplied by the speaker's intended audience. A much less studied but more interesting case would involve the anthropologist, much to the consternation of the Zande audience, treating an argument uttered by a Zande speaker as valid only because he had read into the argument *more* than was warranted by the speaker's actual utterance. In either case, whether out of parsimony or charity, the anthropologist has shown his failure to master how the Zande language (its particular syntax and semantics, along with universal principles of rationality, such as deductive logic, that equip the language to convey truths) is converted into timely and efficient pieces of discourse by its speakers. In short, the anthropologist has failed at Zande pragmatics.

Upon turning to the history of science, we find Thomas Kuhn making the incommensurabilist's point. In the following passage, he argues that even if we allow the positivists and Popperians that the great scientists have evaluated theories by appealing to the same criteria, and even if we allow them that the nature of science itself hangs on the universality of these criteria, it still does not follow that the historian will have enough information to retrodict particular evaluations made by particular scientists.

Moreover, it does not eliminate the possibility that scientists from two different paradigms may apply the same criteria in radically different ways:

> When scientists must choose between competing theories, two men fully committed to the same list of criteria of choice may nevertheless reach different conclusions. Perhaps they interpret simplicity differently or have different convictions about the range of fields within which the consistency criterion must be met. Or perhaps they agree about these matters but differ about the relative weights to be accorded to these or to other criteria when several are deployed together. With respect to divergences of this sort, no set of choice criteria yet proposed is of any use. [Kuhn 1977a, p. 324]

Kuhn's last sentence tips us off to the Humean Hermeneutician's dissatisfaction with a Kantian approach to interpretation. Moreover, the factors that Kuhn cites as rendering the Kantian approach inadequate are of the kind whose "presence" would be difficult to detect in a particular scientist's text precisely because such factors allow him to economize on what he needs to say to his intended audience.

Consider the following example. A scientist addressing the members of his research community need not explicate the sense of "simplicity" that makes his theory the simplest, nor explicitly argue that his theory is the best because it satisfies the "important" criteria sufficiently well to compensate for the theory's failure to satisfy the "unimportant" criteria. For Kuhn, such silence is justified because the members of the research community would understand the import of a theory reaching their forum (say, a professional journal) as a license for them to judge that theory by the virtues commonly thought to be exhibited by theories considered "exemplary." In that case, all the scientist needs to do is to articulate his theory in enough detail so that his readers are provided with the evidence they need for judging that his theory does indeed exhibit the virtues of a commonly recognized exemplar. And so, to take an extremely simple case, if one of the virtues of an exemplar is that its arguments are deductively valid, then the scientist needs to show his readers that his own arguments are likewise deductively valid. However, in the interest of not boring his readers, the arguments presented in his text are likely to be enthymematic and would almost certainly not be accompanied by the metalinguistic remark, "This counts as a deductively valid argument." Yet, to the historian who is not part of the scientist's intended audience, knowledge of these boring details is crucial to penetrating the research community's discourse. Consequently, Kuhn has stressed the historical value of studying elementary textbooks, designed as they are to initiate the novice to the tacit conventions of the community.

Having noted the difference between the Kantian strategy of the indeterminist and the Humean strategy of the incommensurabilist, we should not be surprised to find Hilary Putnam, one of Davidson's partisans, trying transcendentally to refute the incommensurability thesis. After endorsing Davidson's stance on translatability, Putnam poses the following problem:

> Once it is conceded that we can find a translation scheme which "works" in the case of a seventeenth century text, at least in the context fixed by our interests and the use to which the translation will be put, what sense does it have *in that context* to say that the translation does not "really" capture the sense or reference of the original? [Putnam 1982, p. 116]

Putnam goes on to claim that, unless its proponents can answer this question, the incommensurability thesis will have been proven vacuous. However, Putnam's question is not nearly as formidable as it seems, and may be answered in the course of addressing another question: Why are Whiggish interpretations and rational reconstructions of past science considered *historically* suspect?

Notice first that such interpretations and reconstructions have their uses, normally in introductory science texts and in the normative counsel of positivist and Popperian philosophers of science. In order for a text, such as Newton's *Principia Mathematica,* to become canonical in a research community, and thus applicable (as an exemplar) in various research contexts, it must be removed from its original context of utterance. This occurs as successive scientists imagine themselves to be Newton's intended audience, which allows them to attribute presuppositions to Newton that makes his text usable. Among these presuppositions may even be counterfactual conditionals to the effect that had Newton known of subsequent research, he would have altered some of his original utterances. Indeed, the construction of such counterfactuals is the hallmark of Imre Lakatos' (1981) method of rational reconstruction. And in the form of Whig history, this method can be a very effective pedagogical device. For even though we may *know* that *Principia Mathematica* was not written with our current interests in mind, we still have difficulty *understanding* it unless concern for such issues is attributed to Newton.

Yet, what amounts to perfectly sound practice in *natural science* is of no use to the *human scientist.* The reason, of course, is that the natural scientist has systematically substituted his own tacit presuppositions for the ones that were in force when Newton addressed his audience three hundred years ago. As far as the human scientist is concerned, this systematic substitution involves as much an alteration of the text of *Principia Mathematica* as would be involved were the scientist to systematically substitute his own up-to-date sentences for Newton's seventeenth-century ones. In other words, just as there is a fact of the matter as to what is *said in Principia Mathematica,* which is discovered in a rather direct manner by looking at the original text, there is also a fact of the matter as to what is *not said* in Newton's text—though it is discovered in a rather indirect manner by identifying the communicative context of Newton's original utterance. And though the "not-said" is less palpable than the "said," it is no less real and no less indicative of how, why, when, and for whom *Principia Mathematica* was written.

Thus, the incommensurabilist should answer Putnam's original question by pointing out that all interpretations seem to be created equal, and all texts seem equally pliable to an interpreter's interests, only if we suppose that the only "phenomena" that the interpreter needs to "save" are the actual sentences on the text's pages. In that case, he can fill in the silences (or "white spaces") as he pleases. However, if the interpreter regards those sentences as the most economical means of communicating with an intended audience, then he will need to consider the exact nature of the omissions; for while such information would have been obvious to both author and audience, it might prove quite alien to an interpreter for whom the text was not intended. In fact, if the interpreter is as indifferent to the criteriological status of silence as Putnam seems to be, and hence regards the human scientist's interpretation as, in principle, no more adequate to *Principia Mathematica* than the natural scientist's Whiggish one, then he becomes susceptible to the subtle form of incommensurability that comes from *systematically* misunderstanding a text.

Let us retrace our steps and move forward a bit. We originally claimed that the indeterminacy and incommensurability theses are just complementary ways of interpreting the inscrutability of silence. We then saw that Davidson believes that the problem of interpretation has been solved once it is shown that *at least one* interpretation is possible for any given text. This he shows by transcendental argument. However, we also saw that the incommensurabilists, echoing Hume, believe that the problem of interpretation only *starts* once it seems that we can go no further than to provide a *transcendental* argument. In effect, they highlight Davidson's failure to show that any given text has *exactly one* interpretation. Next we saw in the cases of Winch and Kuhn that incommensurability is a very subtle, if not impossible, problem to solve. In any case, it requires that the human scientist empirically specify the communicative context of the text he aims to interpret. And as we just saw in Putnam's attempt to refute incommensurability, a key reason why Davidson and his partisans do not explicitly derive the incommensurability thesis from their own failure to overcome the indeterminacy thesis is that they regard the sentences of a text as the sole objects of interpretations, thereby neglecting the silences that allowed those sentences to function as an *economical* expression of thought when originally uttered. In short, the Davidsonians commensensically, but fallaciously, equate the unsaid with the unspecified.

But how did this error arise? As we saw in the last chapter, one obvious source is the way in which the problem of interpretation was originally posed in analytic philosophy, namely, through Quine's (1960, ch. 2) radical translation episode. Since Quine stipulated that the anthropologist had to translate the native's discourse from scratch, the episode was not presented as an especially communicative one (even though the native had to have at least recognized the anthropologist as his intended audience when answering "yes" or "no" to various analytic hypotheses). Quine envisaged the task of radical translation as one of correlating the native's utterances with what appeared to the anthropologist as the evidence which prompted those utterances. Later Richard Grandy (1973) employed largely the same setup as the basis of a *general* theory of interpretation. His main example (that of mistaking water in a martini glass for a martini) involves one native speaker silently but observantly trying to interpret the utterances of *another native speaker* that do not seem to be well grounded in the available evidence. Interestingly, Grandy never explains why the first native speaker couldn't just *ask* the second the meaning of what he said.

But perhaps the best example of interpretation being artificially severed from communication is provided by Davidson himself:

> If you see a ketch sailing by and your companion says, "Look at the handsome yawl," you may be faced with a problem of interpretation. One natural possibility is that your friend has mistaken a ketch for a yawl, and has formed a false belief. But if his vision is good and his line of sight favorable, then it is even more plausible that he does not use the word "yawl" quite as you do, and has made no mistake at all about the position of the jigger of the passing yacht. We do this sort of off the cuff interpretation all the time, deciding in favor of the reinterpretation of words in order to preserve a reasonable theory of belief. [Davidson 1984, p. 196]

The last sentence is a bit disingenuous, since instead of trading off idiosyncratic word use against false beliefs, it would be even *more* plausible for "you" to *ask* your companion what he meant by calling the ketch a yawl. However, as Davidson sets the scene, you do not actually address your companion after he makes his peculiar assertion, though he probably would not have made the assertion were you not present to hear it. In other words, although you are your companion's intended audience, and hence targeted by him as a potential respondent to whatever he says, he is not your intended audience. ("You" seem to be talking to the reader.)

While it is easy to see how the above setup would permit several possible interpretations of your companion's assertion, it is not so easy to see why this setup should be the basis on which to draw conclusions about the nature of interpretation. Perhaps Quine, Davidson, and Grandy would argue that since interpretation is a more primitive concept than communication, communication cannot be presupposed in any account of the nature of interpretation. This would be an interesting response, if only because the incommensurability thesis denies the possibility of interpretation, *unless* the communicative context of an utterance can be recovered. Thus, it would be natural for Feyerabend, Kuhn, and Winch to react to Quine's radical translation episode by saying that it is no longer recognizable as an episode in *translation*. And here, it would seem, the indeterminist and incommensurabilist have reached a genuine point of disagreement.

2. Inscrutability as a Neglected but Persistent Theme in the History of the Human Sciences

If the inscrutability of silence is indeed the fundamental epistemological problem of the human sciences, why then has it gone relatively unnoticed? I shall propose three reasons.

First, philosophers have traditionally regarded negative attributes— ineffability, nonexistence, privation, nothingness— as points at which to stop, not start, inquiry. The criteriological status of silence would thus seem hopelessly unapproachable. One source of this attitude may be a sort of analogical inference that philosophers make from the indeterminate sense of *negative statements* to the indeterminate sense of simply *not stating*. For example, just as no other particular color is implied in just saying that the table is not red, likewise, it might be thought, no other particular action or thought is implied in not saying anything at all. However, this analogy is misleading in at least one respect, recently elucidated by Bernard Harrison (1979, ch. 7), who has taken his cue from Wittgenstein's *Philosophical Remarks*. The analogy suggests that the sense of a positive statement is more determinate than the sense of a negative statement. Yet, as Harrison observes, the sense of "The table is red" is determinate only on the assumption that we have correctly attributed to its utterer the range of alternative utterances that he intends *not* to make. Our competence in making such attributions seems assured until we consider whether the speaker would utter "The table is red" is the face of certain ambiguously table-ish and reddish things (and the ambiguity may be functional rather than structural, as in the case of a very table-looking object that serves hardly any of the functions of the table). Does he intend to utter the statement under those circumstances?

There is no reason to think that questions of this kind cannot be answered. Indeed, in the heyday of logical positivism, Rudolf Carnap (1956, supp. D) and Arne Naess drafted sample questionnaires expressly for this purpose. All we are suggesting, then, is that the sense of making statements is no more determinate than the sense of not making statements, since any interpretation of an utterance presumes an account of the utterer intends not to say. But since such accounts tend to represent what the interpreter would himself intend under the circumstances—thereby making silence the mark of the familiar—the value of articulating what is left unsaid appears negligible.

The second reason why the inscrutability of silence has been unduly neglected may be traced to an essential ambiguity in the very aims of humanistic inquiry. Despite attempts to distance itself from the natural sciences' exploitive use of its past, humanistic knowledge has in fact rarely been pursued for its own sake, but rather as a means to increase the storehouse of "practical wisdom" (Aristotle's *phronesis*). And at the turn of the century, the height of the humanities' prestige in the German and American university systems, practical wisdom included such normative projects as legitimating nationalist ideologies (Hofstadter & Metzger 1955, ch. 8). In its most general form, the normative project of the humanities proceeds, roughly, by identifying and preserving the good in our past, while improving upon or eliminating the bad.

An example of the humanistic orientation just described is Larry Laudan's (1977, ch. 7) reaction to the sociology of knowledge, which aims to explain all beliefs—both true and false, rational and irrational—according to the same kinds of causal principles. Laudan's "arationality assumption" is a typically humanistic move in suggesting that it is less important to give a systematic account of all beliefs than to give a systematic account of only those beliefs held rationally. Moreover, Laudan is typically humanistic in thinking that his normative enterprise is enhanced by an accurate account of the history of science. Consequently, he has taken Lakatos and other Popperians to task for their use of "reconstructed" histories. Yet, if an "accurate account" includes identifying a scientist's intended audience, then it is not clear how this rather major piece of history contributes to *phronesis*, especially in light of our earlier remarks on the utility of recontextualizing scientific utterances.

Of course, since the philosopher does not require a complete historical account for his purposes, he can argue that the intended audience of a scientist is dispensable. Still, what remains is not so much an historical account that is accurate within the philosopher's "selection constraints" on the data, as an account in which both selection and *replacement* occurs. In other words, the scientist's intended audience is not merely eliminated, but another audience is presumed in its place, namely, those sharing the philosopher's intuitions about rationality and interpretation. In an obvious sense, adding the new audience vitiates the accuracy of the philosopher's history, yet Laudan, for one, does not think that his history is vitiated enough to be called *in*accurate. But this belief only serves to obscure the criteriological status of silence. Since Laudan presumes that the accuracy of his account is tested simply by its compatibility with the scientist's *utterances*, he cannot distinguish between the silence that arises from correctly attributing presuppositions to the scientist and the silence that arises from systematically misunderstanding the scientist, as suggested above in our discussion of Putnam.

The third, and final, reason that will be offered for the criteriological status of silence not receiving its due attention turns on philosophical attitudes to the humanities as a form of inquiry. In particular, analytic philosophers have rarely treated the humanities as having any *unique* epistemic problems. One immediately recalls that Carl Hempel's (1965, ch. 9) deductive-nomological model of explanation was first presented as a model of *historical*, not physical, explanation. Hempel's main epistemic problems were the standard positivist puzzles about the confirmation of universal hypotheses. Moreover, Hempel's examples of "historical" explanation, drawn almost exclusively from the social sciences, make it clear that by "history" he simply meant statements about the past—a category which is both more and less inclusive than the hypotheses that are proposed in the course of humanistic inquiry. Not surprisingly, positivists have regarded Wilhelm Dilthey's candidate for the distinctive humanistic method, *Verstehen*, as either a heuristic for generating social scientific hypotheses or a literary device for inducing the reader to accept the historian's point of view (Nagel 1968, chs. 13-14).

A more subtle analytic-philosophical tendency has been to reduce humanistic inquiry to a form of commonsense or everyday interaction. For example, Hempel's critics have given ordinary language analyses of how "cause" is used in historical discourse, which emphasize its event-specific (Scriven 1958) and evaluative (Dray 1957) character. Such analyses are supposedly relevant to the humanities because, as Strawson (1959, p. 11) put it, ordinary language codifies "the massive central core of human thinking which has no history." Presumably, this means that the concepts articulated in ordinary language can act as a lingua franca between episodes in our history. Dilthey himself suggested as much in justifying *Verstehen* on the grounds that there has been a limited range of life problems and solutions— born of a world populated by persons and things—which have confronted all people at all times. In spite of the intuitive appeal of such doctrines, they seem to be based on the dubious notion that adopting someone else's point of view presupposes that the other person shares at least part of our point of view—again, the hermeneutical idea of fusing horizons. Admittedly, believing such a notion may enhance history's contribution to *phronesis*, but, as we have seen, that is quite different from enhancing historical accuracy per se, which is at the root of silence being so inscrutable.

Perhaps the best way to grasp the unique epistemic problems of the humanities is to examine the methodological concerns of the humanistic disciplines just before the rise of the social sciences. In the case of history, we may contrast the concerns of Max Weber and Emile Durkheim with those of their respective university mentors, Theodor Mommsen and Fustel de Coulanges. We would want to see which issues present in the writings of the mentors (circa 1875) either disappear or mutate in the writings of the students (circa 1900). One such issue that bears directly on the criteriological status of silence is *the problem of objectivity*. By 1900 Europe had witnessed a Kantian revival which identified the objective with the noumenal: Can the past be known as it actually happened, or does the inquirer's own concepts and values necessarily vitiate his understanding? If the latter is the case, can methods be devised for identifying and eliminating the inevitable distortions? The problem of objectivity in the social sciences is still largely posed in this manner. However, in 1875, objectivity was a matter of compensating for the biases in previous historical accounts of an era. This view nicely captured the humanist's ideal of progress through successive commentary and critique. In earlier times, the historian would improve on his predecessors by bringing to light facts that escaped their notice and thus biased their accounts. But by the end of the nineteenth century, the archival approach seemed to have virtually exhausted the available facts, yet many omissions and ambiguities remained in the historical record. How were these silences and equivocations to be interpreted? Mommsen and Fustel epitomized two opposing approaches, the former regarding history as *tradition* and the latter as *antiquity*. Not only was their influence felt by the founders of modern sociology, but also (and more directly) by the authors of the two classic manuals on the historical method: Mommsen's student Ernst Bernheim wrote *Lehrbuch der Historischen Methode*, while Fustel's students Charles Langlois and Charles Seignobos wrote *Introduction Aux Etudes Historiques*. In what follows, it should be kept in mind that both Mommsen and Fustel regarded themselves as practitioners of a discipline whose claim to "science" was its "rigorous methodology" (Stern 1956, chs. 11-12).

Both Mommsen and Fustel criticized the tendency of past historians to mythologize Roman wisdom as having founded the modern model of politics, republicanism. Mommsen attempted to demythologize these accounts by showing that if the Romans arrived at conclusions similar to our own, it was only because the problems and solutions facing them were also similar (Cassirer 1950, ch. 15). *Verstehen* would thus be deployed in interpreting the silences. However, Fustel noted that once the Romans are seen as part of our tradition, *their* culture loses its own unity and becomes instead an incomplete version of ours, full of "proto-institutions," "functionally equivalent concepts," and "inchoate expressions." And so, in trying to make the Romans seem more ordinary, Mommsen succeeded in making it difficult to see how they could have experienced their culture as a stable and integrated whole rather than as the anticipation of some future social system (Cassirer 1950, ch. 18). Not surprisingly, such gratuitous teleologizing occurred as the historian filled the gaps in the historical record. For example, if a practice of subsequent import seemed to have arisen by accident, then the utterances of its designated founders would be fraught with preconscious awareness of the future. In contrast, Fustel demythologized the Romans by "defamiliarizing" them, through what he suggestively termed "the Cartesian method of doubt." And so, to return to the previous example, Fustel would argue that if there is no obvious record of the intentions we so readily attribute to the "founders," then we should assume that they had no such intentions. Moreover, this lack of evidence should cause us to question the interpretation of the evidence we do have that led, in the first place, to the unwarranted attribution.

In taking silence, not as an occasion for imaginatively supplementing the historical record, but as a falsifying instance of the standing interpretation, Fustel's strategy is a clear ancestor of the deconstructive histories of science recently written by Foucault (1970) and Hacking (1975b). For example, two features of Foucault's method, especially evident in *The Order of Things*, mark him as a descendent of Fustel. First, in order to control for the systematic misunderstanding that may easily arise from dealing exclusively with figures who still have practical value for us, Foucault typically focuses on personalities, quite famous in their own time (such as the philologist Franz Bopp and the biologist Georges Cuvier), who have since fallen into oblivion. These figures often appear very old-fashioned, yet their currently esteemed contemporaries undoubtedly had more in common with them than with us. A systematic way of achieving this effect would be to divide one's study of an historical period in proportion to the citations received by an author in that period from his contemporaries.

A second telling feature of Foucault's method is that, unlike Kuhn, who explains the need for paradigm shifts in terms of the old paradigm's inability to resolve standing anomalies, Foucault notoriously offers *no* account of why or how one *episteme* (roughly, "paradigm") replaces another. Foucault's silence here probably reflects a concern to distinguish between a scientist who intentionally solves a problem which has the unintended consequence of contributing to a paradigm shift and a scientist who solves a problem as the means by which he intends to effect a paradigm shift. Despite Kuhn's (1970a, ch. 11) talk of "the invisibility of revolutions," his account sounds too intention-driven, which Foucualt would ascribe to an artifact of the historian's hindsight, another case of gratuitous teleologizing.

In his own day, Fustel de Coulanges was criticized for making the past seem too remote to be useful. (It should come as no surprise that Fustel's own research centered on such topics as the pagan religion of the ancient Greeks and the political structure of early medieval France, whereas Mommsen was the founder of the study of German constitutional law.) But as we have suggested, his antiquarian approach appears to be more sensitive to the criteriological status of silence than an approach, like Mommsen's, which more easily conflates the use and truth of history. Furthermore, Foucault's deconstructive history shows that a Fustelian strategy may not be so useless after all, since it serves as a methodological reminder that many of our "established" practices and concepts may have pedigrees much shorter than we would like to think.

3. Conjuring Up Inscrutability in Thought Experiments

Seeing that our purpose in this chapter has been to identify and contextualize—but not solve—the epistemological problem of the human sciences, it is only fitting that we end on a skeptical note. Specifically, we shall present a three thought experiments aimed at shattering some rather entrenched intuitions that make the humanist's task seem easier than it really is. Not surprisingly, these intuitions are born of a failure to appreciate the inscrutability of silence. The first thought experiment attempts to show that the meaning of even the most careful writer is bound to be transformed by successive readers. The second questions the criteria that the humanist would take as indicative of his having correctly interpreted a text. The third thought experiment questions the technique that he would use, under the best of circumstances, for arriving at the communicative context of the utterance.

The first thought experiment starts by imagining a discursive practice in which the meanings of technical terms are stabilized through explicit definition. As testimony to the success of Richard Rorty's (1979) debunking efforts, the practices that most readily come to mind in this regard are analytic philosophy of language and epistemology. The aim of using explicit definitions, of course, is to focus the reader's attention on just the sense of the term intended by the author and no other that the reader may have previously run across. However, very often the analytic philosopher explicitly defines a term whose sense the reader would have understood as appropriate, even without the author's definition, because the author intends either ordinary or some canonical philosophical usage. Under those circumstances, following Grice's rules of conversational implicature, the reader seems forced to make a decision as to how the author intends Grice's Quantity Maxim to be taken in his text: Has the author temporarily suspended the Maxim in order to conform to his self- imposed stylistic dictates (which, because they involve explicit definition, would force him to spell out the obvious)? Or, has the author continued to obey the Maxim, so that what appears to the reader as a familiar sense of the term really involves some subtle variation that demands further scrutiny? In short, the reader must decide whether the analytic philosopher intends to have his specific stylistic practice overrule general discursive practice. It is clear that more explicit definition won't help, since there are no unique set of definitions that would eliminate for *all* readers the author's ambiguous stance toward the Quantity Maxim.

If the history of analytic philosophy over the last two generations is any indication, it would seem that the reader has normally opted for the interpretation that imputes to the author continued obedience to the Quantity Maxim. At least, this conclusion would account for the fact that the lexicon of analytic philosophy consists almost entirely of ordinary words whose senses become more diverse and sophisticated as the trail of journal commentaries lengthens. Two consequences follow from this observation. First, in attempting to adopt a style that would permit the progress of philosophy through conceptual clarification, the analyst has unintentionally generated a new "jargon of authenticity," to borrow Adorno's (1973) phrase for a philosophical style (such as Heidegger's) which claims to bring the reader closer to an extralinguistic truth but only succeeds in placing him in yet another hermetically sealed universe of discourse. The second consequence of note is that this new jargon has resulted from the reader effectively subordinating the analytic philosopher's *specific* intention (which may indeed be through progressive clarification) to the *general* intentional structure of the communicative act (which obeys the Quantity Maxim).

Moreover, the unwitting generation of this new jargon parallels the ironic use often put to a so-called realistic sense description in order to *defamiliarize* the reader from what is described. This point, first made by Viktor Shklovsky (Lemon & Reis 1965, ch. 1) in "Art as Technique" and subsequently emblematic of Russian Formalist criticism, highlights the fact that the text has an economy of its own, in terms of which all extratextual elements must be transacted. For example, the effects of this economy are especially striking when the information contained in an instantaneous glance is converted into discursive prose. Care for the kind of detail that could be registered in a glance may generate an exaggerated response in the reader: either a sense of the grotesque (as in Gogol's extended physical descriptions) or a sense of the belabored (as in Proust's extended psychological descriptions). But in neither case does the reader's response in any way diminish the author's claim to realism. Rather, the reader's response is simply the product of the literary author's intended realism "refracted" through the medium of the text—much in the same way as the reader's tendency to sophisticate the analytic text is the product of the philosophical author's heightened sense of explicitness filtered through the Quantity Maxim, which the reader presumes the author's writing to obey.

To set the stage for the second thought experiment, recall that one of Galileo's main accomplishments in *Dialogues Concerning the Two Chief World-Systems* was to demonstrate that Aristotle had treated the concepts of average and instantaneous velocity as though they were one. But if Galileo were suddenly to appear in Aristotle's presence, would he be able to convince Aristotle that his concept of velocity was based on such a confusion? Although it might take a while for Aristotle to catch on to the background knowledge presumed in Galileo's presentation, our intuitions strongly suggest that, if Galileo were clever enough in how he designed his experiments, Aristotle should come to see the errors of his ways. Indeed, we may follow Kuhn (1981) in likening Aristotle's newfound insight to a Piagetian child who had just been "shown" the conservation of volume.

But what if Aristotle balked at Galileo's mode of presentation? After all, Aristotle might think that Galileo's easy appeal to bodies moving in a vacuum distorted the way bodies "naturally" move. Again, our intuitions do not find this obstacle insurmountable. Galileo would be able to show that his way leads to better (more precise and accurate) solutions to Aristotle's own problems. But what if Aristotle continued to resist Galileo's conclusions, arguing that he was interested in a general, largely qualitative account of motion per se, not simply a quantitative account of local motion? Well, Aristotle's own distinction would then answer his objection. In other words, Galileo's presentation would have forced Aristotle to define his own project more clearly: in particular, to distinguish between what he was trying to do and what he was *not* trying to do. If, at this point, Galileo were to press Aristotle to pass judgment on his presentation, Aristotle would probably admit that Galileo had proven his point, given his beliefs, evidence, and the problem that he was interested in solving. Moreover, Aristotle would admit that while Galileo had not succeeded in falsifying any of his original beliefs, he had convinced Aristotle that his own project needed more careful articulation.

At first glance, the thought experiment seems to vindicate Davidsonian reasoning about interpretation. What must have initially appeared to Galileo as a bizarre, if not confused, use of concepts by Aristotle was resolved once Aristotle was made to define his project in terms of Galileo's. As Davidson would have it, Aristotle had the option of either revising his beliefs in light of Galileo's presentation or admitting to an aim different from, yet compatible with, Galileo's. But on closer inspection, the *counterfactual* nature of the thought experiment only serves to render the *actual* history more mysterious, and thereby to render suspect the Davidsonian approach to interpretation.

If our intuitions tell us that Aristotle would feel compelled to make conceptual concessions in light of Galileo's presentation, then why didn't Aristotle (or his intended audience, for that matter, including antagonists) get the concept of velocity straight when he was practicing natural philosophy in fourth-century B.C. Athens? To find this question frivolous is to overlook the difference between, on the one hand, asserting or denying a truth and, on the other hand, failing to assert a truth. Ever since Quine, analytic philosophers have taken the main obstacle to translation to be that the translatee often seems to deny truths and assert falsehoods. In the thought experiment, Aristotle was cast as originally denying a conceptual distinction that Galileo and we assert. However, this casting is purely an artifact of the thought experiment, which turns an act of interpretation into *an act of communication*. In historical fact, Aristotle did not *deny* a distinction in velocities; rather, he *failed to assert* such a distinction. It would not have even made sense for Aristotle to deny a distinction that no one in his intended audience was entertaining, let alone defending. It would likewise be seriously misleading for today's interpreter of Aristotle's *Physics* to conclude that Aristotle "implicitly denied" the distinction, for that would be to suggest that fourth-century B.C. Athenians commonly presumed that a distinction between instantaneous and average velocity was spurious—when, once again, no such thought is likely to have entered their minds.

And so, as soon as the human scientist makes the criteriological status of silence problematic, and hence refuses to assimilate failure-to-assert to either implicit assertion or implicit denial, the incommensurability thesis starts to look more plausible. In fact, the philosophical problem raised by incommensurability may be usefully defined as the task of reconciling two rather polarized, though not incompatible, intuitions—only the first of which has been recognized by the Davidsonian interpreter:

(a) If Galileo were in Aristotle's presence, then it would be rational for Aristotle to concede at least that his concept of velocity required some clarification and perhaps even that he had been laboring under false beliefs about the nature of motion.

(b) Unless Galileo, or someone like him, were in Aristotle's presence, there would be no reason for Aristotle to clarify his concepts or revise his beliefs in the manner that Galileo would have him do.

The methodological moral of this thought experiment for the human sciences is clear. The more readily we can "Davidsonize" an alien author, such as Aristotle, by imagining the steps we would take to persuade him that he has made a conceptual error, the *more likely* that we have misinterpreted that author's text. At the very least, we have created a mystery about the communicative context of the text's original utterance. If the errors are *in principle* so easily remedied, then why were they *in fact* not so remedied? It is not enough to say that Aristotle pursued interests different from our own and that, in some sense, those interests "prevented" him from originally seeing the errors of his ways. For how exactly does the pursuit of a qualitative sense of motion *prevent* one from pursuing the quantitative sense of motion that Galileo and we now recommend? Although the two pursuits are certainly different, they are neither logically nor practically incompatible. In other words, the humanist cannot simply *cite* the cognitive interests of fourth-century B.C. Athenians as an adequate explanation for their overlooking certain conceptual points that we take to be obvious and easily demonstrated to rational beings (for recall that the incommensurabilist endorses intuition [a] as well as [b]). Instead, the humanist must show how Athenian interests conceptually excluded our own. But the evidence for such conceptual exclusion is bound to be indirect, since we have already supposed that our distinction in velocities never crossed the Athenian mind, let alone in rejection. By "indirect" we mean to suggest that the evidence would pertain to features of Athenian discourse over which its speakers thought they had little choice but to accept, as in the case of so-called analytic truths. Perhaps then Galileo's ideal of thoroughly mathematized account of motion would have been conceptually out of court to Aristotle, as it violated the very *definition* of motion, mathematics, or some other related concept. That would certainly explain why such an ideal never attracted *or* repelled the Athenians.

Still, none of this tells against Galileo's ability to make his point to Aristotle. What we have done, however, is to open up the possibility that Aristotle would regard Galileo's point to be as much a product of *semantic manipulation* as of empirical demonstration—Galileo's very attitude toward Aristotle! In other words, Aristotle may have no trouble grasping Galileo's point, but he may have trouble accepting the point as anything more than a win in a Galilean language game. In that case, Aristotle would be unable to see how Galileo could sincerely believe that his distinction in velocities has any import *outside* the rules of his game.

Now on to the third thought experiment. To set the stage here, consider the feature of lexical meaning that linguists (Lyons 1977, pp. 305-311; Halliday 1982, pp. 31-35) call *markedness*. Take the lexical opposition: good/bad. If A has no idea of whether the play that B saw last night was *good* or *bad*, which lexeme is A most likely to select when asking, "How _____ was the play?" Our intuitions strongly suggest that A would select *good*. In that case, *good* is the *unmarked* member of the opposition, the item that would normally be used in interrogative contexts, unless features of the specific case made its use inappropriate. A situation in which A would be more inclined to ask B how *bad* the play was would be if A had already read a bad review of the play by a critic whom B respected. Linguists are divided on the source of our strong intuitions about markedness, which extend beyond the posing of questions to the stating of facts and the passing of judgments. Perhaps the unmarked lexeme is merely more widely distributed in discourse than its marked counterpart, or maybe markedness reflects a deeper cognitive bias built into the language, such that English speakers *presume* a peformance to be *good*, an individual to be *tall*, and so forth, until otherwise demonstrated.

In support of this latter, rather speculative hypothesis, imagine someone who consistently used *marked* lexical items in normal contexts. Such an individual would be perfectly comprehensible, in that he would not have violated the syntactic and semantic rules of English. Still, he would strike us as having a rather strange view of things, a view that presumes the bad, the short, and so forth. But unless we were exposed to this person on a regular basis, we would also probably *not* correct his anomalous utterances, invoking instead a "Tact Maxim" that presumes that, being a competent speaker, he has good (albeit mysterious) reasons for uttering as he does (Leech 1983, pp. 104-130).

Now consider a variation on the above theme. Instead of marking members of lexical oppositions, we shall mark members of *propositional* oppositions. Let us see how this would work. An alien anthropologist has decided to study modern English culture. His preparation for the task has been so comprehensive that he can easily pass as a fluent English speaker. He then mingles among various professionals, most notably philosophers and engineers. In the course of conversing with members of the two professions, he asks each the same question: Do you believe that chairs exist? Not surprisingly, both philosophers and engineers say yes. However, their reaction to such a question being posed is quite different, though this difference is unlikely ever to reach the anthropologist's ears, largely due to their observance of the Tact Maxim. The philosophers treat the question as quite natural, since most philosophers as a rule treat every denial of a proposition as unmarked. In other words, the skeptic is presumed correct, and it is up to the constructive philosopher to shoulder the burden of proof in refuting him. And from the standpoint of pragmatics, to pose a question such as the one posed by the anthropologist, is to grant the audience the license to doubt that proposition. Thus, the philosophers may well be fooled into thinking that the anthropologist is one of their own. However, the engineers are not so easily fooled. As with most commonsensical folks, there is normally no reason to grant one's audience the license to doubt propositions concerning "medium-sized dry goods," such as chairs. In that case, the engineers would take the assertion "Chairs exist" as unmarked, with the burden of proof shifted to those who wish to deny the assertion. And so, the anthropologist's question, while certainly comprehensible and answerable, seems unwarranted to the engineers, suggesting to them that a stranger is in their midst.

If the anthropologist now returns to his people and reports that both philosophers and engineers believe in the existence of chairs, it should be clear that he would have missed a very important—but difficult to capture—difference between *how* philosophers and engineers hold that very same belief. And, as should be expected by now, the anthropologist's failure would be due to a conspiracy of *silence*. But in his case, we have double inscrutability. First, the anthropologist did not know how the philosophers marked their propositions because he did not have the pragmatic intuitions of the professional speakers. But second, and more interesting, the anthropologist's virtually successful attempt at "going native" proved to be his main *obstacle* in trying to discover the two marking systems. Since the anthropologist appeared to be a rather competent English speaker, the engineers applied the Tact Maxim and presumed that he had some reason for asking his peculiar questions. From the anthropologist's standpoint, however, it would have been better if the engineers had not been so charitable in their attributions.

Finally, consider a more realistic version of this thought experiment. It may well be true that the same percentage of English speakers would assent to a belief in God now as three hundred years ago. Still, we would want to say that the 1988 speakers do not hold their belief in the same way as the 1688 speakers did. For example, whereas the question "Do you believe in God?" would strike the 1688 speakers as strange because it licenses doubt where doubt is not normally licensed, the same question would strike the 1988 speakers as reasonably posed because "God exists" is precisely the sort of proposition about which one normally licenses doubt. Notice that this difference cannot be readily cast as a three-hundred-year shift in the "degree of belief" with which one asserts *his own* belief in God. On the contrary, the difference in markedness is primarily a shift in the degree to which the speaker would deem reasonable *others* who dissented from his belief, which he may still hold as fervently as ever.

If nothing else, this point should make us wary of texts collected from diverse cultures and periods that seem to testify to the same beliefs. For beyond this superficial similarity, the humanist needs to determine how tolerant of dissent in their respective audiences would the authors of those texts be. One clue is how explicit the interpreter finds an author's justification of his belief. Outside pedagogical contexts, a more explicitly justified belief is probably one that the author would not necessarily expect his audience to hold, and so he realizes that he must shoulder the burden of proof himself (see ch. 4). In that case, once the humanist gauges the degree of explicitness with which a belief is justified (not an easy task, admittedly, since one's sense of explicitness is relative to one's sense of expressive economy), he can then begin to reconstruct the author's intended audience, whose identity establishes the communicative context that will finally permit the humanist to decide whether the silences in the author's text should be taken as marks of the familiar or the alien.

4. Postscript: A Diagnosis of Davidsonism

In this chapter, I have used variants of Donald Davidson's name as an adjective ("Davidsonian") and a verb ("Davidsonize"). Now we shall use it as a name of a sensibility, *Davidsonism*, which is oblivious to the inscrutability of silence. In the first section, we discussed Davidson's approach to translation, which aims to render the beliefs expressed in an alien discourse as close to our own as possible. Indeed, Davidson believes that if we did not render the alien beliefs in as familiar a manner as possible, it would not be clear that we had actually performed a translation. Given the importance of this position in contemporary analytic (and, increasingly, continental) philosophy, it would be worthwhile to study the details of Davidson's argument:

> Why must our language—any language—incorporate or depend upon a largely correct, shared, view of how things are? First consider why those who can understand one another's speech must share a view of the world, whether or not that view is correct. The reason is that we damage the intelligibility of our readings of the utterances of others when our method of reading puts others into what we take to be broad error. We can make sense of differences all right, but only against a background of shared belief. What is shared does not in general call for comment; it is too dull, trite, or familiar to stand notice. But without a vast common ground, there is no place for disputants to have their   quarrel. Of course, we can no more agree than disagree with someone else without much mutuality; but perhaps this is obvious. [Davidson 1984, pp. 199-200]

The self-effacing modesty of this passage should not distract us from the chain of necessitation forged by its sentences. The appearance of such words as "must" and "only," as well as the expression "without...there is no..." are the signs that Davidson is engaged in a transcendental argument. The basic structure of such an argument is as follows:

(P1) If X were false, then Y could not be true.

(P2) But Y is clearly true.

(C) Therefore X must be true.

Now, in light of what Davidson says above, we can substitute the following propositions for X and Y:

(X) We share most of the beliefs of the people we interpret.

(Y) Our interpretations are correct most of the time.

And so we have Davidson's argument.

Generally speaking, a transcendental argument will be successful only if the truth of Y is much better established than the truth of X, perhaps even to the point of commanding universal assent. But the truth of Davidson's Y seems no more certain than the truth of his X, especially given the considerations that I have raised in this chapter. Carried to an extreme, the difficulties involved in deciding whether to interpret the unsaid as indicative of familiarity or strangeness are reflected in the fact that a completely correct and a systematically distorted understanding of a text could well be indistinguishable, for all practical purposes. Davidson seems to be capitalizing on the fact that the most easily detected cases of interpretive error are fairly local in nature. But there is no reason to think that ease of detection is a reliable indicator of either the frequency or seriousness of interpretive errors in general, which is what Davidson needs to make his point stick. Indeed, the alarming regularity with which "revisionist" interpretations of history gain scholarly credibility suggests that many large-scale misunderstandings have been perpetrated over the years.

So much for Y. As for X, its status is even more controversial, for there is a basic problem with the intelligibility of Davidson's claim. How exactly does one count "beliefs" so as to be able to tell that we and the alien agree on more than we disagree? However, Davidson may argue that we are allowing a "technical point" to obscure the general intuition at work here. After all, even if we have the greatest of difficulty in making sense of what an alien has said, we have still already made sense of the fact that he has said something that was intended to be understood, which means that he regards us, at least in principle, as interpreters of his discourse. Those brute facts about the interpretive situation alone presuppose that we and the alien share fairly extensive beliefs about the coordination of bodies in space and time, the distinction between persons and ordinary physical objects, and so forth. Put in this way, Davidson's claim seems rather persuasive. But how exactly does one characterize those common beliefs? More to the point, can they be characterized so that both the alien and we would assent to them? Like the first "technical" question that I asked, these last two require that the Davidsonian come up with a way of individuating beliefs so that both the alien and we would agree that those beliefs can be expressed in their respective languages. As we shall now see, this is a task that is easier said than done.

Any metalanguage that is proposed as expressing the beliefs that we supposedly share with the alien will beg the question unless the alien can assent to the translation scheme proposed in the metalanguage. The following case, abstracted from various color perception experiments done by anthropologists on natives, illustrates how easily the question may be begged (Cole and Scribner 1974, chs. 3-4; Rosch 1973; Anderson 1980, ch. 12). A common way of operationalizing the Sapir-Whorf Hypothesis of Linguistic Relativity is to say that if a language does not have the word, then the culture does not have the concept. Color perception is a particularly good test case, since it involves a thought process that is both closely tied to well-defined bits of evidence and, in most languages, a well-defined set of words. In the experiments, the anthropologist presents the native with a rich array of colors, representing many subtler distinctions than the language of either party can easily express. As it turns out, the native has little problem performing various identification tasks, some of which require that he remembers the presented color for various lengths of time. The anthropologist then concludes that the Sapir-Whorf Hypothesis has been falsified, at least for color perception. Now what could be wrong with this interpretation?

Experiments of the above kind typically overlook the obvious fact that the native uses the protocols for identifying colors *only* because the anthropologist requires this of him for purposes of the experiment. The "only" here is important because, as was suggested earlier in the Aristotle/Galileo thought experiment, the interesting question is not whether the native could ever learn to identify colors not normally expressed in his language (the answer is obviously yes), but whether he would ever be likely to identify those colors without the intervention of an anthropologist. After all, linguistic relativists should have no trouble explaining the results of the color perception experiments, namely, that the natives were able to identify a vast array of colors because they were forced to speak to the anthropologist in the language of the experimental protocols. Indeed, often the ultimate reason why experiments of this kind are thought to refute the Sapir-Whorf Hypothesis is that linguistic relativists are portrayed as believing not only that language determines thought but that each person's thought can be determined by *only one* language. On this interpretation, then, the native would be expected to continue thinking in terms of his first language even during the experiments. However, the linguistic relativist normally holds the more plausible view that there is, as it were, a *default language,* in terms of which the native will naturally think, unless he is forced to do otherwise (De Mey 1982, ch. 11). A test for this view would involve, among other things, seeing whether the native continues to incorporate the protocols in his natural language after the experiment. Evidence from a variety of cognitive domains suggests that subjects generally do not carry over the skills they learn in one situation to make sense of another, rather different one, especially if the subject found the original learning situation artificial or forced, as would likely be the case in the color perception tests (Newell & Simon 1972).

And so, we see that the real problem of linguistic relativity is not whether people have the *ability* to conceive of things not normally expressed in their native languages but whether they have the *need* to do so. Moreover, if people do not want to change the way they think about things, can the anthropologist or philosopher cause them to do so by working solely *within* their native modes of thinking?   Or, is it always necessary to constrain the native's response patterns in the manner of experimental protocols?   These questions implicitly challenge a fundamental tenet of Davidsonism, namely, that a person's beliefs, desires, and other intentional states constitute a conceptual system, a framework integrated by the inference rules of deduction and induction. This tenet, generally known as *holism*, presumes that the native's ability to use protocols for identifying the otherwise inexpressible colors was rooted either in knowledge already present in his conceptual system which had never been articulated or in knowledge recently integrated into his system as a result of his contact with the anthropologist. In both cases, the holist expects that, unless there was a problem in how this knowledge was learned or stored by the native, he should be able to use it again in a wide range of circumstances (Hallpike 1979).

The opposing view suggested by our questions, sometimes called *molecularism* (Dummett 1976, ch. 17) or *modularism* (Fodor 1983), denies that a person possesses such an integrated conceptual scheme. Rather, the modularist believes that knowledge is naturally compartmentalized or "indexed" (Knorr-Cetina 1982) to particular activities or situations. For example, Aristotle may grant that Galileo's terrestrial mechanics is operative in the controlled circumstances of his experiments, but would deny that the Galilean principles can be generalized to a wider body of phenomena. Likewise, a native who does not have a word in his own language corresponding to "blue" in English may easily learn how to use the blue-protocol during an experiment but continue to regard "blue" as a technical term with no wider applicability than the laboratory.

One of the most interesting features of the modularist view is that it dissolves a famous diagnostic problem first introduced by Donald Campbell (1964). On the basis of experiments on optical illusions that psychologists and anthropologists conducted on members of a wide range of cultures, Campbell concluded that, unless careful follow-up studies are done, there was no principled way of diagnosing radical cross-cultural differences in perceptual responses: they could be due either to genuine differences in perception (perhaps due to linguistic relativity) or simply to the experimenter's failure to convey the point of the experiment to the subject. (To his credit, Campbell realized that the problem could also arise in cases of *convergent* cross-cultural responses: for discussion, see Segall 1979, ch. 3.)   On the modularist view, this choice is dissolved, since *communication failures of one sort of another are taken to be the primary cause of radical conceptual differences.* Campbell sees a diagnostic problem here probably because he believes that communication failures can be easily remedied by the experimenter making his point clearer to the subjects, in which case the subjects will act appropriately and more (or "genuine") convergence in the data will result. But once again, this is to suppose that the experimenter is merely getting the subjects to do something that they would do naturally under normal circumstances and not, as we have argued, persuading (or, in some other way, constraining) the subjects to behave in a special way for purposes of the experiment.

Precedents for our version of modularism may be found in the social phenomenologist Alfred Schutz's (1962, pp. 207-259) thesis that the lifeworld is composed of discrete "spheres of relevance," a notion derived from William James' idea that we live in "multiple realities." Indeed, when questioned on the motivation for introducing the incommensurability thesis, Kuhn (1970b, p. 207) himself pointed to the fact that a bilingual speaker has an easier time switching from one language to another than actually translating between them—a clear case of compartmentalization of especially large bodies of knowledge, namely, entire languages. Kuhn's remarks are particularly instructive, since commentators (even supportive ones) have all too often been willing to assimilate his view that the units of compartmentalization are quite large (whole languages) with the Quine-Davidson view that every part of our knowledge is integrated into *one* whole.

In conclusion, then, how are we to assess Davidson's transcendental argument? Its premises are hardly incontrovertible, and, as we have argued, may well be false. But this much may be said on the argument's behalf: it does express certain presumptions that interpreters make about the strategies that are likely to lead to successful interpretations. Of course, the fact that these presumptions are made frequently and unreflectively does not imply that they actually lead to successful interpretations. More likely, acting on the presumptions has consequences whose undesirability is very difficult to detect, precisely because they are not expected. A situation of this sort probably lurks behind Davidson's presumptions about interpretation; hence the *inscrutability* of silence.

HOW TO DO SUBTLE THINGS WITH WORDS—
THE INS AND OUTS OF CONCEPTUAL SCHEMING

"Give me a place on which to stand, and I will move the world"
—*Archimedes*

Indeed, a *place*. In this appendix I propose to grant Archimedes his wish by introducing a *place logic* for conceptual change. The tradition of place logics—extending from Aristotle's *Topics* to Chaim Perelman's "loci" and epitomized by the "methods of invention" devised by the Renaissance rhetorician Peter Ramus—has been guided by the idea that certain kinds of arguments will be more persuasive than others insofar as they appeal to norms shared by the speaker (presumably) and his audience (Perelman & Olbrechts-Tyteca 1969, chs. 21-25; Ong 1963). These arguments are valuable for a speaker to know, since, by invoking them, he may be able to break down the audience's resistance to whatever controversial or perhaps even novel proposal that he is bringing to their attention. For example, a locus commonly invoked by politicians in order to prod their citizenry into war is "the extraordinary circumstance." Both the speaker and audience know that if the label is accepted, an appropriate course of action is prescribed. Meanwhile, spokesmen for pacifism or appeasement might appeal to the locus of "temporary strain in relations" and try to explain the apparently hostile activities of the foreign state as really the product of misspeakings and misunderstandings.

This example highlights the role that loci play in *dialectical* arguments: a role analogous to that played by natural kind categories in *demonstrative* arguments. Following Aristotelian usage, conclusion "demonstrated" from its premises is fully determined by them, and thus incontrovertible. It follows that the terms in such an argument are used univocally to refer to objects that fall under determinate categories. In contrast, the conclusion of a dialectical argument is underdetermined by its premises, and thus controversy ensues. Likewise, the identity of a state of affairs referred to in such an argument is underdetermined, and so, as the example shows, the "hawk" can interpret it one way and the "dove" another.

For the relevance of place logic to conceptual change, we need only reflect on Kuhn's (1970a, ch. 7) claim that the key sign of "crisis" in a scientific paradigm, and hence of the paradigm undergoing change, is that scientists are less concerned with adding to the body of data than with questioning the principles on which the currently available data have been interpreted. As we saw in chapter five, Kuhn's preferred metaphor is the "duckrabbit" Gestalt figure, with the figure itself constituting the data which may be interpreted as either a duck or a rabbit. A shift in paradigms is likened to a Gestalt switch, whereby the viewer fixates on one interpretation, biasing the ambiguity of the actual figure toward that interpretation.

For all its appropriateness, a place logic for conceptual change has been long in the waiting, and—if Popper (1970) is to be believed—Kuhn himself is largely to blame. One obstacle has been what Popper has dubbed "The Myth of the Framework," which presumes that an individual is normally so constrained by his own worldview that only by a radical shift in consciousness (which, by definition, is inconceivable *within* a worldview) can effect any significant conceptual change. Admittedly, Kuhn's talk of "conversion" as the means by which a new paradigm replaces an old one conveys an irrational image of such change, as does Michel Foucault's (1975) talk of "ruptures" between epistemes (which, on his own account, cannot even be explained). I think, however, that one feature of this myth is largely correct: to wit, that one does not intentionally bring about a conceptual change, but rather a conceptual change is something that is shown (in histories and textbooks) to have happened, usually as the long-term consequence of a collection of shorter-range activities. Most scientists who were persuaded by Einstein's over Lorentz's interpretation of the Michelson-Morley experiment did not realize that they were witnessing the birth of a new paradigm in physics. Indeed, even a generation after Einstein's 1905 Special Relativity papers, the distinguished historian of physics Edmund Whittaker (1929) referred to his own time as "The Age of Poincare and Lorentz."

Yet Kuhn, like theologians before him, takes the wide-ranging, yet unanticipated, consequences of a particular conversion episode to imply that, in principle, the cause of the conversion must exceed the grasp of (at least) the converted's intellect. The narrative flow of histories of science have all too often followed the model of biblical tales, in which an event with major consequences, such as Saul's conversion to Christianity, is itself portrayed as having been experienced in a major way, say as Saul did, by being knocked off one's horse. Furthermore, narrative demands seem to dictate that the unexpected nature of the consequences following from the conversion episode be prefigured in the highly improbable, or "miraculous," nature of the episode itself. Thus, Saul is not merely knocked off his horse— an event of some probability—but he is confronted by a messenger from God. Likewise, histories of science have left too much of the explanatory burden to be shouldered by the personal revelations of great scientists, whose insights are soon recognized for what they are by a waiting public. Although Kuhn and Foucault have successfully abandoned such naively teleological accounts of conceptual change, they have yet to fully recognize that, whether it be in science or religion, a conversion is ultimately an exercise in a rather subtle form of persuasion, and should be thus be amenable to the kind of rhetorical analysis offered by a place logic. And so, rather than concluding that major conceptual change occurs *supernaturally*, I would say that it occurs *subliminally* in the act of licensing a few seemingly innocuous inferences.

Marc De Mey (1982, ch. 10) has done much of the spade work necessary for understanding the dynamics of subliminal conceptual change. For instance, he has shown that Harvey's discovery of the blood's circulation was the result of a Gestalt switch performed on Galen's picture of the heart. De Mey makes sense of what happened by drawing a distinction between the extent to which Harvey's cognitive processing was driven by *concept* or *data* and the extent to which it was *top-down* or *bottom-up*. The original Gestalt psychologists, as well as the historians of science who have appropriated their work, have generally collapsed these two dimensions, so as to produce two seemingly irreconcilable views of the scientist's epistemic encounter with the world: the *empiricist* view, which equates data-driven with bottom-up processing, thus presenting the scientist as a passive receptacle whose theory automatically changes as his experience changes; the *rationalist* view, which equates concept-driven with top-down processing, thus presenting the scientist as a conceptual schemer who molds experience to meet his cognitive ends. Whereas the positivists exemplified the empiricist view, Kuhn is a clear case of the rationalist view. De Mey notes, however, that the empiricist view makes resistance to conceptual change unmotivated, while the rationalist view makes openness to such change equally unmotivated. This would seem to leave the sort of radical conceptual change associated with scientific revolutions without any general explanation, largely because neither view permits a clear articulation of the phenomenon.

De Mey's own strategy is to treat concept- versus data-driven processing as concerning *the direction of scientific discovery* and top-down versus bottom-up processing as concerning *the direction of scientific pursuit* (Laudan 1977, ch. 3). Consequently, discovery is concept-driven when the scientist's model of the object under study (which may perhaps be nothing more than an extended analogy: see Hesse 1963, Harre 1970) prompts him to reinterpret the object, while it is data-driven when the object (usually an anomalous observation) prompts him to alter his model in some way. In both cases, nothing is implied about whether the whole or only part of the model/object is affected by the discovery process. For example, the fact that Harvey was led to his discovery by studying the *overall* movement of the blood around the heart does not necessarily mean that it was concept-driven. After all, as art historian Ernst Gombrich (1979) has noted, if one's visual angle is wide enough, it is possible to register the unity of an object as a single datum, while its parts remain perceptually undifferentiated. Now, whether one then proceeds to situate the object in an even more comprehensive whole or instead analyzes the object into its parts is a matter of cognitive pursuit, the former being bottom-up and the latter top-down. Thus, it is entirely conceivable that Harvey's achievement was due to a combination of data-driven and top-down processing, one of the possibilities excluded by the standard empiricist and rationalist conflation of cognitive processes.

Given the rationalist and empiricist views just sketched, we can see how radical conceptual change could be taken as happening in an unmotivated, and hence "supernatural," fashion. Another source of the supernatural theory's persuasiveness is a residue of the Aristotelian view that like causes bring about like effects, which means that big changes must happen in a big way. This is perhaps not a surprising diagnosis to make of the scholastic discourse of theologians, but more surprising to make of the discourse of historians of science. A case in point, though, is the origin of the so-called Scientific Revolution of the High Renaissance (for a survey of the relevant theories, see Bullough [1970]). At the turn of this century, Pierre Duhem (1954) proposed that the key concepts of modern physics, including "acceleration" and "inertia," were already available to fourteenth-century commentators on Aristotle—that is to say, nearly three centuries before Galileo had been normally credited with making the "major break" with Aristotelian physics. More recently, Alistair Crombie (1967) has supplemented Duhem's thesis by showing that the medievals also had Mill's canons of inductive proof and even conducted some primitive experiments.

Nevertheless, the prevailing view has remained that Galileo's work constituted a major change in the Western worldview that could only have arisen by deliberately renouncing major medieval conceptual commitments, as dramatized in Galileo's encounter with the Papal Inquisition. In other words, as a latter-day scholastic might have told Galileo, the cause must be in proportion to the effect: if Galileo's work has had significant consequences, then its cause must be at least as significant; hence, his need to break with the past. In trying to counter this line of reasoning, Crombie has argued that what made the difference between Galileo and his medieval precursors was simply that Galileo, unlike the medievals, had access to some rather highly developed examples of Greek experimental and mathematical science, once Tartaglia translated Archimedes into Italian in 1543. As it turned out, Archimedes had been translated into Latin as early as 1269, but the translations were generally available only in Italy, and not in Oxford and Paris, where Galileo's medieval precursors were working (Grant 1977, ch. 2). Lacking such examples, medieval scientific method remained at a level of generality that was not conducive to the kinds of complex experiments that had to be performed in order to see the revolutionary implications of the medieval concepts.

The import of Crombie's argument then is that the difference between the medieval and modern mind is less a matter of "temperaments" or "mentalities" and more one of such subtleties as cues in the conceptual environment: if the medievals had read Archimedes, the Scientific Revolution would have happened three centuries earlier. This talk of "subtle cues" returns us to Kuhn's original duckrabbit Gestalt, the model of radical conceptual change. For while Kuhn is right that the incommensurability of the duck and rabbit images of the figure demands a radical switch between perpsectives, he fails to mention that the psychologist is able to manipulate which image the subject sees by *slightly* altering the contextual cues grounding the figure. In presenting the rudiments of a place logic for conceptual change, we are attempting to capture just how those subtle cues may work.

Instead of "loci," a place logic for conceptual change would study *fulcra* (plural of *fulcrum*), dialectical supports upon which a would-be Archimedes can set his lever so as to propel his audience out of one conceptual space and into another. As with loci, fulcra are identified primarily in the texts of arguments. This point needs to be emphasized, if we are to take seriously the idea that conceptual change is largely subliminal. Just as the persuaded scientists did not realize the ultimate import of Einstein's interpretation, it is equally unlikely that Einstein himself realized it. Large scale conceptual change occurs not because of what the author intends to put into his text but because of what a series of readers get out of it. Of course, the entire story does not rest on the one text alone, since, for various reasons, many "potentially revolutionary" texts never become persuasive. This part of the story belongs to the sociology of knowledge. However, a place logic should be able to specify the fulcra present in a text that *would be* responsible for a given change, *were* a given audience present. And like the more traditional place logics, ours would have practical import, since knowledge of the fulcra makes for more provocative arguments. We shall present here only two of the broadest distinctions among fulcra: (i) fulcra concerning the speaker's sense of how a conceptual change occurs; (ii) fulcra concerning whether distinctions should be drawn or blurred.

The most basic fulcra address the speaker's sense of what it means to effect a conceptual change, and so, not surprisingly, they involve positing some relation between three metaphysical elements:

(a) *experience*—what the speaker and audience take as the natural attitude toward the world;

(b) *theory*—a conceptual scheme, that is, the articulation of the concepts that ground one's natural attitude toward the world;

(c) *world*—what experience and theory are "about" in some ultimate sense.

Among these elements two metaphysical relations may be derived, as captured by the following theses:

(M1) Experience is the theory about the world that we currently accept.

(M2) Theory is the organization of experience that constitutes our world.

Notice that in each thesis, the three pivotal terms are used somewhat differently: (M1) implies that "theory" is a representation of the world used by human beings who cognitively stand outside the world as spectators. (M2) implies that "theory" is the method by which human agents move within the world, as in the rules to a language game. In the history of philosophy, (M1) has been associated with various attempts to maintain the appearance-reality distinction, while (M2) has been associated with antirealist attempts to blur the distinction, such as idealism, pragmatism, and phenomenology. (M1) and (M2) are conveniently contrasted in their respective attitudes toward the mind-body problem, an issue where much of contemporary discussion has centered on whether findings in the neurosciences would provide adequate grounds for changing how we conceive of our mental life. Following the contrast, we will be able to derive the fulcra on which the arguments of (M1) and (M2) rely.

An (M1) metaphysician would argue that our ordinary mental concepts, such as "beliefs," "intentions," "desires," and "pains," do not offer a unique access to our mental life; instead, they constitute a theory for predicting mental behavior (as measured, say, by verbal reports) that must be tested against whatever rival may be offered by the neurosciences. If the neuroscientific theory proves to be a better predictor, then we should relinquish our ordinary mental concepts and conclude that, say, what we used to regard as "pain" is more accurately represented in terms of a specific firing of neurons. In contrast, an (M2) metaphysician would argue that it is not so much that the ordinary and scientific theories are competing to explain the same "fact of the matter," but rather, they are descriptions of what is experienced at different, yet compatible, levels of reality. The difference between these levels can be demonstrated in the means by which one comes to know that he is experiencing a pain (through self-consciousness) vis-a-vis how he comes to know that he is experiencing a certain neural arrangement (through an electroencephalogram). And so, while no "crucial experiment" can be performed to show whether the ordinary or the scientific account of the mind is correct, there may be various sociological reasons (having to do with which account holds cognitive authority) for claiming, say, that the EEG is a more "proper" approach to the mind than the deliveries of introspection, and so should supersede introspection in practice. But such reasons would obviously involve appeals to how the world *ought to be* rather than to how it *is*.

As we search for the fulcra tacitly employed by (M1) and (M2), first notice that the (M1) metaphysician marks off a conceptual change by moving from the assertion that pains exist to an assertion that something happens to people which get called "pains." The mere mention of the word in the latter case implies that pains as such do not really exist, although the word "pains" may be a useful, albeit oblique, way of referring to what really does exist, namely, a specific firing of neurons. Oblique reference also occurs in metaphorical utterance, where the metaphor is a tentative characterization of some aspect of reality that awaits more literal description. And so, we can now state the fulcrum implicit in (M1) as follows:

(F1) Conceptual change occurs when an utterance passes between mere mention and actual use.

For his part, the (M2) metaphysician marks off a conceptual change by noting how the license for making certain inferences gets extended or retracted. A claim becomes unassertible either when no circumstances are prescribed for asserting it, or when circumstances are prescribed for not asserting it. Much of Foucault's work deals with how social institutions blur the distinction between these two possibilities: roughly, *the unwarranted* versus *the irrational*. And so, a time may indeed come when introspection falls into disuse because people become more interested solely in predicting behavior, at which the neurosciences are admittedly more reliable. But unlike (M1), (M2) would not thereby be conceding the falsity of introspection and the truth of the neurosciences, but rather it would be recognizing that the kind of world in which introspection served a purpose (and was thus employable under specifiable circumstances) would have disappeared. Introspection would then be unassertible in the sense of "unwarranted," but not necessarily in the sense of "irrational," though sociologically it may be just a short step from one to the other. Thus, we may characterize (M2)'s fulcrum as follows:

> (F2) Conceptual change occurs when the assertibility conditions of an utterance is altered.

A fulcrum may also be identified as either an *acuteness* or an *obtuseness* strategy. An acuteness strategy draws distinctions, while an obtuseness strategy eliminates them. Since Socrates started to define his terms by division, philosophers have perennially supposed that clarity of thought is attained through the analysis of terms. It is in this spirit that Hartry Field (1973) has proposed a theory of scientific progress based on the idea of "denotational refinement," which attempts to account for the often radical difference in term use between paradigms without having to embrace Kuhn's relativism. For example, after special relativity showed that an object's mass is affected by its speed, the post-Einstein physicist found himself unable to evaluate Newtonian assertions using the term "mass" without further clarifying the how term was used in each case, so as to match his own finer-grained understanding (namely, by specifying the speed of the object). Depending on how each assertion is clarified (sometimes the context of the original utterance will be sufficient, sometimes not), it may turn out to be true or false. Progress is thus measured in terms of the number of distinctions a modern can draw that his precursor could not. The general acuteness strategy should then be clear:

> (AS) For any set of objects that are said to be "essentially" the same (that is, fall under the same concept), there will always be some property that only some members of this set will have. From there argue that the difference between objects having and lacking this property is more significant than the "superficial" resemblance they

bear to one another, regardless how "essential" this resemblance was initially said to be.

Although acuteness strategies are especially prized by pedagogues, obtuseness strategies are arguably the more persuasive fulcra. Major conceptual change requires a subversion of "presuppositions," which may be defined as those propositions whose truth must be presumed in order to either assert or deny certain other propositions (van Fraassen 1968). In a more rhetorical vein, presuppositions are the tacit agreements that make overt disagreement possible. And so, a sure means for subverting a presupposition is to deny the sense of the dispute or distinction that it allegedly grounds. Quine's (1953, ch. 2) "Two Dogmas of Empiricism," generally regarded as the most influential philosophy journal article of this century, adopts a strategy of sheer obtuseness. In particular, Quine cannot see the point of sharply distinguishing truths about language from truths about the world, since the current state of empirical knowledge had by a linguistic community will bear on which terms are introduced into usage and how susceptible the terms are likely to be to changes in the community's knowledge base. Thus, the only difference that Quine can see between the two kinds of "truth" is that the "truths of language," which constitute the core logical concepts of the community, do not admit of easy empirical refutation. However, this difference is itself only one of degree, for Quine can envisage a situation where the applicability of quantum mechanics, say, is sufficiently pervasive to warrant a change in the rules of deductive logic. Thus, the obtuseness strategy may be defined as follows:

> (OS) For any "difference" that is said to exist between two sets of objects, the prima facie reason for thinking that such a difference is real is probably some corresponding verbal distinction. From there argue that the difference goes not deeper than that, and that proponents of the distinction have confused what Carnap (1934) called the formal and material modes of speech: there may be a formal distinction, but no material difference is made by it.

If successful, an obtuseness strategy can leave one wondering how one's predecessors could have put so much stock in such pointless distinctions. This is often a sign that the distinction was indeed *very* entrenched, such that, once adopted, no one ever had need to defend it again. But over the course of generations, people came to forget why the distinction was initially drawn and to substitute reasons suitable to their own local cognitive tasks. In that case, an appeal to obtuseness may ironically work by taking the tacit quality of deep-seated presuppositions as a sign that they could not be defended, were they explicitly challenged.

The ironic twist, however, is that the presupposition may turn out to be indefensible *only* because discrepancies (and hence incommensurabilities) have developed over its exact meaning. And so, whereas Hume's and Kant's original motivation for drawing a distinction between truths of language ("analytic") and truths of the world ("synthetic") may have presupposed a rather eighteenth-century division of the cognitive faculties into the "rational" and the "sensory," this was certainly not the main reason for retaining the distinction by the time Quine wrote "Two Dogmas." In fact, there were many, rather incompatible reasons, spanning the entire gamut of positions in the philosophy of language. This alone suggested that the real problem lay in getting agreement on a statement of the distinction that had to be defended rather than in actually providing the defense. But since an agreement on the distinction was not forthcoming, Quine refused to divide and thereby conquered.

PART THREE

ISSUES IN THE SOCIAL ORGANIZATION OF KNOWLEDGE

CHAPTER SEVEN

THE DEMARCATION OF SCIENCE:
A PROBLEM WHOSE DEMISE HAS BEEN GREATLY
EXAGGERATED

Larry Laudan has recently argued that the demarcation of science from non-science is a pseudoproblem which should be replaced by the more modest task of determining whether and why particular beliefs are epistemically warranted or heuristically fertile. In response, Thomas Gieryn has rejected this exercise in philosophical self-restraint, arguing that the scientific community itself takes measures to distinguish itself from others who compete for cognitive authority and its attendant political and economic benefits. As a result, rhetorical strategies develop—"boundary work" Gieryn calls them—which are proper objects of sociological study. In this chapter, I shall argue that Laudan is wrong to think that there is nothing at stake in demarcating science from nonscience, but I shall also argue that the importance of the demarcation problem has not been fully appreciated by Gieryn. My critique will reveal a basic confusion that needs to be dispelled before the full significance of demarcating science from nonscience can be seen: namely, the failure to distinguish the relatively constant social role played by whatever has been called "science" from the historically variable social practices that have played the role of science. In addition, I shall claim that this confusion is itself one of the key ways in which a social practice retains its status as science.

1. Laudan and Gieryn on the Demarcation Problem

Laudan's (1983) history of abortive efforts at solving the demarcation problem may be reconstructed as two general arguments for rejecting the project altogether. First, he attempts to discredit the motives of the philosophers who have proposed criteria for demarcating science from nonscience. Aristotle, Carnap, and Popper did not merely try to arrive at a procedure for deciding which beliefs and practices warrant our assent; more tellingly, each philosopher designed his procedure with an eye toward excluding specific beliefs and practices which he found at the time to command more cognitive authority than were their due. Thus, Aristotle's criteria ruled out Hippocratic medicine, Carnap's ruled out Bergsonian metaphysics, and Popper's excluded Marxism and Freudianism. In fact, the criteria proposed by these philosophers do little more than exclude the undesirable cases, since, as Laudan shows, they would also allow clear cases of nonscience to pass as science. However, this logical deficiency did not concern the demarcators at the time because no one had been claiming a scientific status for the clear nonsciences. And so, given the makeshift character that the criteria have had, Laudan concludes that, rather than claiming to know the universally defining features of science, it would be more honest of philosophers to attack particular pretenders to cognitive authority on the basis of their specific conceptual and empirical inadequacies. Laudan sees Adolf Grunbaum's (1984) much publicized critique of psychoanalysis as an exemplar of this kind of activity.

Laudan's second argument against the legitimacy of the demarcation problem turns on the results of philosophical attempts at proposing criteria sensitive to the history of science. The main problem facing all such attempts is accounting for how certain disciplines seem to have achieved and lost (and sometimes later regained) the status of science over time. As an example (whose historical validity will simply be presumed here), Laudan contrasts the scientific status of astrology with the unscientific status of astronomy during the Middle Ages, roles which were finally reversed in the seventeenth century. Admittedly, prior to selecting demarcation criteria, contrasts of this kind are somewhat impressionistic, but the point is clear enough: even a set of criteria which managed to pick out every current science and to leave out every current nonscience would have difficulty maintaining this track record for the entire history of science. Laudan is crucially silent on whether this is due to the nature of science itself changing over time or simply to the practice of, say, astronomy and astrology changing. Nevertheless, when philosophers have tried to incorporate both contemporary and historical considerations into their criteria, the results have been like Popper's falsifiability criterion—more aimed at making any discipline in the long run yield reliable knowledge claims than at identifying current disciplines whose knowledge claims command our assent now. And so, given their demonstrated uselessness, Laudan dubs demarcation criteria "toothless wonders."

For our purposes, Laudan's position is open to one central objection. It fails to recognize that demarcation criteria respond to a problem that runs deeper than political expedience or even historical understanding—in fact, it is the very problem that Laudan would see replace the one of demarcation: namely, how to determine which beliefs are epistemically warranted. Since, at any given moment, there are more claims vying for our assent than could possibly be tested, we need a way of presorting the claims into the "plausible" and the "implausible," so that the limited resources allotted for testing can then be focused on just the plausible claims, the ones with the highest prior probability (however that is measured) of finally earning our assent. The signs of plausibility are readily detected from the language of the claims (its competent use of jargon), the credentials of the claimant, and so forth. They are issued by the practices which function as science in the society. In short, demarcation criteria provide an institutional means for achieving cognitive economy, which is, in turn, a necessary—albeit fallible—condition for granting epistemic warrant (for more on this general strategy, see Simon [1981], ch. 6). However, this function is bound to be lost on someone like Laudan who assumes that the social role of science is nothing more than the sum of its historical players. In that case, the diversity of the players obscures their common stake in passing the demarcation criterion. But for more on the stakes, we need now to turn to Gieryn.

In some recent articles Gieryn (1983a, 1983b) has traced the moves made by the scientific community in Victorian England, especially by John Tyndall, to demarcate itself from theological, philosophical, and technological rivals. Tyndall's boundary work happens to be of more than historical interest since we still rely on it, at least intuitively, when trying to define science. For example, his exemplar of the scientist is the "experimental physicist," whose virtues were epitomized in Tyndall's day by Michael Faraday. Tyndall also brought together, probably for the first time, three now familiar arguments for the cognitive authority of science: (i) scientific knowledge is necessary for technological progress; (ii) science is unemotional, unbiased, and unpersuaded by appeals to the authority of tradition; (iii) science pursues knowledge for its own sake.

Gieryn has a clear sense of the beneficial social consequences—call them the *Baconian Virtues*—for a discipline which passes the demarcation criterion and earns the title of "science": it acquires the authority to promulgate truthful and reliable knowledge, control over education and credentials, access to money and manpower, and the kind of political clout that comes from possessing knowledge that is essential yet esoteric. Following the "socio-logic" of functionalism, as Gieryn seems to do, the role of science would then simply be defined as the maintenance of these consequences. In that case, the social benefits gained by passing the demarcation criterion may remain relatively constant over time, while what it takes to pass the criterion may vary, as do the cast of would-be scientists and their respective publics vary. Thus, aspirants to the role of scientist are continually negotiating "the rites of passage," which will indirectly bias the odds in favor of certain actors occupying cognitive center stage at a given time. But prior to an actual negotiation, no one knows for sure whether theologians, philosophers, engineers, and/or experimental physicists will get the chance to play scientist.

I have just presented a "purified" version of Gieryn's thesis, one in which the distinction between the science role and the would-be role players is clearly made. However, Gieryn himself vacillates between this formulation and a fuzzier one, which are below summarized, respectively, as (A) and (B):

(A) Tyndall managed to secure for experimental physics exclusive rights to play the role of science, which had been contested by ideologues for philosophy, theology, and technology.

(B) Tyndall managed to secure cognitive authority for science by cutting into the authority previously held by philosophy, theology, and technology.

The main difference between (A) and (B) is that in (B) the role of science has been conflated with a current role player, experimental physics. This difference has important consequences for how one writes the history of science—especially for how one identifies its subject matter. But before identifying those consequences, a few words should be said about the considerations from recent analytic philosophy of language that inform the above distinction. The referent of "science" can be identified in two ways, corresponding to (A) and (B):

(a) in terms of the social practices that satisfy the definition of "science" (namely, practices possessing the Baconian Virtues), regardless of whether a particular individual would call those practices "science";

(b) in terms of the social practices that a particular individual would identify as satisfying the definition of "science."

In (a) "science" refers to all the disciplines that have played the social role entitled to the Baconian Virtues, while in (b) "science" refers to only the disciplines that a particular historian or historical agent would take as playing that role. The distinction drawn between (a) and (b) allows us to articulate the very real possibility that Tyndall, say, would be correct in using "science" to refer, in sense (b), to experimental physics but incorrect in using the word to refer, in sense (a), to experimental physics (since before Newton "science" would not have primarily referred to experimental physics). In short, Tyndall's (a)-usage would mark him as a competent Victorian speaker, but his (b)-usage would equally mark him as having a presentist bias toward history. This distinction is central to "realist" approaches to the theory of reference, championed by Keith Donnellan, Saul Kripke, and Hilary Putnam (Schwartz 1977). Following Kripke's (1977) coinage, we would say that (a) involves *semantic reference*, while (b) involves *speaker's reference*.

2.   The Two Histories of Science: Of Role and Player

Let us now turn to the implications that these two readings of Gieryn's thesis has for the historiography of science. On the one hand, it is possible to do what virtually all histories of science have done, namely, to identify the object of the history in terms of the current players and then project backward. This is the semantic strategy behind the wording of (B). In that case, former players of the science role, such as theology, enter into the history only when their activities can be shown to have contributed to the ascendency of the current role players. Thus, included in this category are not only the Whig histories which take brief negative side glances at theology (as well as philosophy and technology), but also the histories which have followed Pierre Duhem's lead in rehabilitating the scientific image of the High Middle Ages, since they typically stress only the features of scholastic discourse which issued in the prototypes of such modern physical concepts as inertia. And so, from reading Crombie's (1967) monumental account of "medieval and early modern science," one could easily conclude that the Oxford and Paris theologians were concerned more with demonstrating the existence of induction than the existence of God.

A historiography that identifies the science role with the current role players tends to have a curious narrative structure; for the farther back in time that the historian reaches for anticipations of the claims and practices made by current players, the more elusive the trail becomes and the more likely he will be forced to conclude that the roots of modern science are to be found in such disparate "nonsciences" as theology, astrology, alchemy, technology, philosophy, and politics. Of these disciplines the historian is then inclined to ask, "How were they able to get as far as they did, yet fall far short in so many other respects?" Answers to this question, even when intended as sympathetic criticism of the nonsciences, serve indirectly to heighten the heroic efforts of someone like Newton, who "finally" pulled together these insights from their original seats of "cognitive authority" into a real "science."

While my account of this historiography may seem to caricature its Whiggish element, nevertheless it cannot be denied that even the most circumspect historians tend to portray the practitioners of the nonsciences as forming relatively self-contained traditions, while the individuals designated as "scientists" appear to be unconfined by such institutional distinctions, "open" (as Popper would say) to the ideas and techniques of any tradition, just as long as they advance the cause of knowledge growth (Horton 1970). Indeed, the only place that a study of institutions would have in a history of science featuring (B)-like sentences would be in accounting for the delay that the current science players experienced in acceding to the science role. Thus, one way of reading Gieryn's boundary-work thesis is as recounting one of the last episodes of institutional resistance to science's claim to supreme cognitive authority.

However, an alternative and more interesting historiography is suggested by the (A) reading of Gieryn's thesis. Here the science role is clearly distinguished from the rival players, the implied history being of the role rather than of its players. No one has yet written this history, which would effectively trace the battles that have been waged over rights to the title of "science" and such cognates as *episteme*, *scientia*, and *Wissenschaft*. Such a history would have a constant focus, namely, the social benefits that Gieryn has identified as following from playing the science role. It would also have two main historical variables, which jointly trace the career of the demarcation criterion:

(c) the strategies that the rival disciplines have had to deploy in their attempts at earning the title of science;

(d) the strategies that the successful disciplines have had to deploy in order to maintain their title of science.

Although we shall later discuss these historiographical variables, for now we shall examine the constant focus of this enterprise more closely.

One way of explicating the "constant focus," which recalls the preceding analysis of the referent of "science," is by observing that while historical figures (both scientists and their historians) have intended a wide variety of disciplines when using "science" or one of its cognates, they have attributed roughly the same properties of those disciplines, namely, possession of the Baconian Virtues. In Kripke's terms, the speaker reference of "science" has changed, while its semantic reference has remained the same. Moreover, it should be noted that the variety in the speaker reference tends to go undetected because "science" and its cognates attach directly to the role and only indirectly to the role players. For example, if we could not identify what speakers had in mind when they said "science," it would be easy to conclude that when a thirteenth-century scholastic described *scientia*, a nineteenth-century Prussian characterized *Wissenschaft*, and a twentieth-century logical positivist spoke of "science," they had roughly the same disciplines in mind. In fact, of course, despite a certain amount of overlap, each speaker would identify a different discipline as paradigmatic of the science role: theology, philology, and mechanics, respectively. Yet, all would agree that whatever played the science role was entitled to the socio-cognitive benefits of the Baconian Virtues.

Now, it might be thought that I have overstated the case for there being a continuous history of the science role, insofar as, say, the positivist could argue that prediction and control are intrinsic to what he calls "science," while the medieval scholastic or the Prussian philologist always had to rely on politics to enforce the "laws" of what they called "science." Two responses are possible to this objection. First, in their heyday as players of the science role, such humanistic disciplines as theology and philology had, in the art of *rhetoric*, an analogue to the prediction-and-control features of today's natural sciences. Indeed, for all of rhetoric's many philosophical detractors over the centuries, none of them has ever complained that rhetorical techniques for manipulating belief and action do not *work*, but rather that the techniques work only if the audience is not aware that it is being so manipulated. The reason, of course, is that the efficacy of rhetoric rests largely on the fact that logically unskilled people are susceptible to endorsing fallacious arguments. Starting in the seventeenth century, it became common to contrast the deceptive nature of rhetoric's efficacy with the more explicit, and hence philosophically more acceptable, nature of experimental efficacy. Not surprisingly, then, rhetoric declined as rapidly as experimental natural philosophy gained credibility (Ong 1963). But even if we confine ourselves to the experimentally based sciences, there is a second reason why the distinctiveness of their prediction and control features should not be exaggerated: namely, because a discipline's ability to demonstrate control over a range of phenomena depends on its having socially protected spaces, such as laboratories, where practitioners of the discipline can freely implement *ceteris paribus* clauses, which exclude factors that could interfere with the demonstration of a proposed "law" (Rip 1982, Apel 1984).

One striking consequence of focusing on the history of the science role is that protagonists other than the likes of Newton would be featured. For example, two individuals who would figure prominently in the new history but do not in the old are Albertus Magnus, who set the precedent for medieval theologians incorporating remarks on natural history in their biblical commentaries (Weisheipl 1978), and Denis Diderot, who first fully realized that accepting Newtonian mechanics as "queen of the sciences" would probably undermine once and for all the possibility of unified knowledge on the model of Aristotle (Prigogine & Stengers 1984). The careers of Albert and Diderot help mark the shifting boundary between science and nonscience: Albert's career marked the expansion of the boundary, thereby laying the institutional groundwork for the "scientific" interest in mechanics that the Oxford and Paris clerics showed during the fourteenth century; on the other hand, Diderot's career marked a contraction of the terrain covered by science, a formal recognition that a key contingent of Aristotelians—the students of "life" and "mind" who by the nineteenth century were readily identified as "vitalists"—had become disinherited once Newtonian mechanics gained exclusive rights to the science role.

Of course, none of the above is to say that the seventeenth century, the height of the Scientific Revolution, would entirely lose interest. But even here the relative significance of the characters would change. An interesting study in contrast, from our standpoint of the changing players of the science role, would be Pierre Gassendi and Christiaan Huygens. Gassendi defended the mechanical and atomistic worldview almost entirely within the model of scholastic disputation, explicating the texts of Lucretius and other ancient Epicureans and avoiding, for the most part, any reference to concrete experiments. Huygens, on the other hand, despite his Cartesian sympathies, eschewed metaphysical arguments in his studies of luminous and pendular motions, referring only to the performance and interpretation of experiments. Typical histories of science cast Gassendi and Huygens as co-protagonists in the Scientific Revolution, but fail to explain their rather distinct fates: Gassendi has become a "minor philosopher," while Huygens has turned out to be a "major scientist." It would seem that if there is a "cunning of reason" to the movement of history, then seventeenth-century natural philosophers were transformed into either "scientists" or "philosophers," depending on where they stood on the cognitive value of experimentation. Thus, antiexperimentalists like Hobbes and Descartes, who chastise Galileo for failing to derive the law of falling bodies exclusively from first principles, are nowadays "philosophers," while experimentalists like Robert Boyle and Isaac Newton are "scientists" (Shapin & Schaffer 1985).

3. Science and Its Kindred Roles

Since a role is defined in terms of its functional interdependence with other roles, a history of the science role would need to consider the relation of science to other roles. Ideally, one would want to map out all the role relations for an entire society over long expanses of time. However, in the short term, there are a small cluster of roles, whose relation to the science role is intimate enough to satisfy even the staunchest "internalist" historian of science. To get at these roles (which, recall, remain relatively constant as their players change), we may start by presuming that at most times there is one discipline which has an "exemplary" status as science. It may not be the only player of the science role at the time, but the other players are normally considered imitators of this exemplar. For example, Tyndall's more famous boundary coworker, Thomas Henry Huxley ("Darwin's Bulldog"), argued for the scientific status of his own discipline, physiology, on account of its methodological resemblance to experimental physics. Such attempts by other disciplines to model the exemplar we will call *reductionist*, a term that is normally (but need not be) reserved for when the exemplar is physics. This is to be distinguished from attempts by the exemplar itself (or one of its successful imitators) to bring other disciplines into conformity with its image, as in the recent forays of ethologists and sociobiologists into anthropology (Rosenberg 1980). These attempts may be called *eliminationist* in that their ultimate purpose is to eliminate the need for the less scientific discipline (for a sophisticated discussion, see McCauley [1986]).

Moreover, there are disciplines which try unsuccessfully to imitate the scientific exemplar; these are covered by the role of *pseudoscience,* which nowadays constitute a familiar litany: Creationism, psychokinesis, extrasensory perception, UFO-logy, astrology, etc. These disciplines claim to abide by the methods most emblematic of the current holder of the science role, only to be unmasked by a muckraking science popularizer like Martin Gardner or (when subtlety is in order) Stephen Gould. Then, there are the disciplines which make no claims on the science role, and in fact define themselves explicitly against the current science players. Such is the role of *antiscience,* whose current players tend to be past players of the science role or their descendants—the so-called "disinherited" alluded to earlier. Thus, we find theologians, humanists, and vitalists often joining forces against the socio-cognitive authority of natural science and its allies on such issues as vivisection and nuclear energy. As testimony to their historically backward-looking perspective on the history of science, antiscientists are often seen as "romantic" (Nowotny 1979). Moreover, some pseudosciences may be illuminatingly cast as antisciences. A case in point is the leading populist movement against Darwinian evolution, Creationist science, being a throwback to catastrophist biology and geology, whose cognitive authority had peaked by 1830.

The cast of characters in the history of the science role would not be complete without *cryptoscience,* that is, a discipline whose activities are—by the practitioners' own accounts—not scientific, but which nevertheless seem to outsiders as conforming to a current model of science. Cryptoscience is a role that perhaps all disciplines play at some point in order to defend their boundaries from outside attack and to enhance their mystique as cultivators of esoteric knowledge. The history of magic is an instructive case. When theologians played the part of scientists in the Middle Ages, many magicians tried to preserve their discipline by claiming not to be involved in divination, a topic about which only theologians could speak with authority; however, this did not stop Thomas Aquinas from scrutinizing magical practices and concluding that the magicians indeed had profane knowledge of divination since they needed to influence divine sources in order to intervene in nature (Hansen 1978). Even today, though it plays the role of pseudoscience with respect to the natural sciences, magic retains its cryptoscientific status. Reflecting the shift in exemplars of the science role and the continual need to distance themselves from it, magicians now tend to emphasize the inexplicability of their feats when regarded in exclusively naturalistic terms. But scientific critics then observe that these feats are just the result of magicians covertly relying on basic psychological principles to manipulate the perception of their audiences—cryptoscience exposed yet again.

Another case of cryptoscience lurks behind the sharply negative reaction of natural science ideologues to, say, Derek Price's (1964) call for a "science of science" or David Bloor's (1976) reflexivity principle which undergirds "The Strong Program in the Sociology of Knowledge." Both proposals are based on the idea that the scientists' very own behavior is subject to the same kind of lawlike regularities which they find exhibited in the behavior of natural objects. Among the strongest opponents of this idea have been Popper (1957) and Friedrich von Hayek (1973), who trace the cognitive success of the natural sciences to their (allegedly) near-perfect approximation of a free enterprise system. As in the economic sphere, these neoclassicists argue that to regulate such a spontaneously occurring system would be to ruin its fertility and routinize is creativity. Indeed, Popper and von Hayek have documented in great detail the disastrous consequences of policymakers—usually socialists of some sort—thinking that they have a scientific understanding of how science develops.

However, this defense of laissez-faire scientific capitalism has been met with charges of cryptoscience by a team of historians and philosophers of science associated with Juergen Habermas during his directorship of the Max Planck Institute at Starnberg in the 1970s. The team, who go under the name of "Finalizationists," point out that to claim that science works best when socially unconstrained is to obscure the fact that this "lack of constraint" is itself a product of social constraint, albeit one whose power source is carefully hidden from public view (Schaefer 1984). For example, a key stipulation in the charter granted to the founders of the first modern autonomous scientific body, the Royal Society of Great Britain, was that they scale down Francis Bacon's vision of a "New Atlantis" by refusing to extend their experimental studies to "religion, morals, and politics," the results of which could easily have subversive implications for the status quo. The Finalizationists believe that political circumspection of this kind, rather than any metaphysical distinction between *Natur* and *Geist*, has usually motivated the widespread view that human beings—including scientists—are not proper objects of natural scientific inquiry.

Interestingly, cryptoscience may also be found among ideologues for the *social* sciences, especially such positivistic followers of Robert Merton as Bernard Barber (1952), who wish to undermine the critical function that a sociology of knowledge could perform as a result of identifying the social interests that benefit from the acceptance of claims to social scientific knowledge. It should be noted that in both the natural and social scientific cases, cryptoscience emerges as a prohibition on any reflexive application of the scientific method, largely for fear that reflexivity would destroy the legitimacy of the science in question. As we have suggested, the natural science ideologue also has the more specific worry that if a scientist could indeed be studied as another regularly occurring natural phenomenon, then the determinism implicit in this viewpoint would destroy the free spirit of inquiry, not only in terms of how the scientist would start to regard himself but also in terms of how policymakers are likely to treat the scientist. In contrast, while the social science ideologue does not worry that all societies might be determined by the same set of laws, he is still concerned that if each society is subject to *its own* laws—especially ones which correlate accepted knowledge claims with the social interests benefitting from their acceptance—then the universal validity of social scientific claims would be subverted. In short, then, reflexivity would seem to threaten the natural scientist's motivation for doing anything and the cross-cultural efficacy of whatever the social scientist did.

However, the fears expressed by both ideologues are largely ungrounded. On the one hand, the evidence of quantum mechanics, statistical thermodynamics, and evolutionary biology suggests that universal determinism is false. And even if it were true, it is unlikely that we could ever have as exact an understanding of the laws governing the behavior of natural scientists as the laws of classical mechanics, if only because of interaction effects between the inquirer and the inquired (von Wright 1971). At the very least, then, residual ignorance of the deterministic processes would always give us the illusion of freedom, without compelling the conclusion that human beings, even natural scientists, are entirely unpredictable (Dennett 1984). On the other hand, both natural and social scientific knowledge claims clearly have specific social origins, and yet we do not see such origins as undermining the validity of the natural scientific claims. So, why should the validity of social scientific claims be especially vulnerable? Moreover, we can even countenance a possibility that would normally be raised only by sociologists espousing a radical relativism: namely, that there must be some underlying cultural unity among societies that accept a given knowledge claim as valid, a unity that was particularly well exhibited by the society originating the claim. For in this radical case, we can still wonder whether anything more than an accident of history was behind one culture rather than some other originating the claim in question.

As the previous remarks suggest, the epistemological deep structure of cryptoscience is informed by a certain kind of *relativism*, namely, a relativism that respects the local sovereignty of cultures and disciplines in adjudicating knowledge claims, and that recognizes "natural" limits to the applicability of certain concepts and methods beyond their original disciplinary and cultural contexts. Indeed, the connection between cryptoscience and relativism has been made most explicit by Harry Collins (1985) who argues, against Steve Woolgar (1983) and the more radical social constructivists, that the sociology of science would lose its disciplinary focus if it included itself as one of the sciences under investigation. In large part, Collins is moved to this position because of his own research findings, namely, that "empirical generalizations" in the natural sciences are more textual rhetoric than experimental replication. If the sociology of science is likewise a science, then its generalizations should also have the same rhetorical status. But of course, confirmation of this prediction would only serve to undermine Collins' original thesis. And so, presumably, Collins would be cryptoscientific only about his home discipline, but not about the other disciplines to which he wants to apply the sociological method (Mulkay 1984).

4. Conflating Role and Player as an Historiographical Strategy

In terms of the two historical variables identified earlier, it is not clear whether Gieryn intends his work as a contribution to the study of (c) or (d), since that depends on whether he thinks that Tyndall's rhetorical victories marked the origin (c) or simply the continuation (d) of experimental physics' exclusive rights (at least vis-a-vis technology, philosophy, and theology) to the science role. In any case, (d) deserves closer attention than it has yet received. We shall conclude by making a contribution to (d) that takes into account what has been said so far about the conflation of the science role with the role players; for a subtle but crucial way by which a discipline maintains its hold over the science role is by inducing such a conflation in the process of "managing its past." By this last expression, I am referring to the inevitable problem of deciding what to record of what is observed, and then what to preserve of what is recorded. If one simply tried to record and preserve everything, there would never be time for anything else. Because of its greater significance and longer duration, an institution faces the problem more acutely than an individual; but it also has strategies for managing its past which are ready-made to extend its life. If the institution is a discipline and its interest is in maintaining the science role, then it engages in what Marxists call a *reification* of its history.

As Marx first observed, perhaps the most deceptive (and therefore, in a key sense, "ideological") feature of classical political economy was its claim to being a science of human nature. The political economists supported this claim by portraying capitalism as man's innate egoism brought to self-consciousness. For example, an unreflective grasp of David Ricardo's "iron law of wages"—which placed the "natural wage" of a laborer at the subsistence level (that is, just enough to make it in his interest to return to work the next day)—was taken to have been responsible for whatever success precapitalist economies had at resource management. However, Ricardo's law also had the effect of licensing and even promoting, in the name of "scientific management," the view that the currently prevailing horrors of the workplace were permanent fixtures of the human condition. Still, political economy had tremendous clout in nineteenth-century Europe, largely because it was able to portray all previous economies as either potentially capitalistic (insofar as past economic agents were motivated primarily by self-interest) or simply abortive.

Moreover, since the political economists had, in effect, *invented* economic history as a field of inquiry, they had presumptive authority over all the evidence and tools of analysis; hence, the laborious efforts—issuing in an unfinished, three volume *Das Kapital*—that Marx had to undergo in order to contest their historiography. And so, aside from manifestly explaining (and latently justifying) capitalist practices, the political economists also tried to show that insofar as Aristotle, the medievals, and others who spoke of "economy" were correct, they anticipated the political economists; otherwise, the earlier thinkers were simply wrong or irrelevant. Marx called this kind of past-management "reification" because the political economists had rendered history static, "thing-like," by removing all the elements which made the nineteenth-century economic situation fundamentally different from the earlier situations with which continuity was now being claimed.

One way of looking at the Marxist critique of political economy is as finally distinguishing the science role from the role player, whose conflation had allowed political economists to lay claim to being the scientific culmination of two thousand years of economic theory and practice. Within the Marxist tradition, the study of this conflation, or reification, has since moved in two directions—though still not far beyond the scope of Marx's original critique.

On the one hand, those following Georg Lukacs (1971, pp. 83-222) have stressed the Whiggish elements of reification, whereby the significance of the actions of earlier economists or economic agents is identified solely in terms of their consequences for contemporary theorists and practitioners. Indeed, Lukacs observed that this process begins in the present, as the bourgeois consumer tends to evaluate producers exclusively in terms of the desirability of the goods they produce—whether they be industrial or cultural in nature. As a result, it becomes difficult for the consumer to think of the producer except as someone who works for him. Likewise, the historian may not be able to make sense of an historical figure unless he attributes to him goals which could only be fully realized in the historian's time. For example, potted histories of capitalist economics often cite Aristotle's discussion of *oikonomia* in the *Politics* as the origin of the field. The historians then downplay Aristotle's almost exclusive concern with managing the resources of a household by pointing to the technologically limited horizons of the Greeks—the idea being that if they had our means of production, transportation, and communication, they too would have focused on market economics.

On the other hand, those following Theodor Adorno (1973) have studied the systematic cancellation of differences between particular historical situation which, if fully recorded, would remove the illusion of long-term continuity that props up the political economists' claim to codifying a persistent feature of human existence. Adorno appropriately called his critical stance "nonidentity thinking," in contradistinction to the "identity thinking" of Hegel, who suggested that history's special "cunning" lies in its selecting out the essential from nonessential features of actions so as to make the essential parts available to future agents for their own use (perhaps in ways against the designs of the original agent) and to condemn the nonessential parts to oblivion. And so, to return to our example, in order to turn Aristotle into an unwitting legitimator of capitalist economics, historians—either out of design or ignorance—neglect Aristotle's own references to the primitiveness of the marketplace and the Greek metaphysical preference for self-sustaining form (like a household) over endless growth and instability (like a market). It would, then, be the task of Adorno's nonidentity thinker to overcome reification by articulating these neglected differences.

The argument in this chapter may be summarized as posing a philosophical problem, employing an historical method, and reaching a sociological solution. The philosophical problem is the familiar one of what are the invariant features of science: Are there any universally applicable ways of demarcating science from nonscience? Recently, philosophers of science such as Laudan have despaired of finding an answer to this question. Yet if Laudan's positive suggestions were taken seriously, the autonomy of "the philosophy of science" would be thrown into doubt, since the task of judging epistemic merits on a belief-by-belief, rather than a discipline-by-discipline, basis is nothing short of a retreat to classical epistemology. What Laudan has forgotten, however, is that "science" primarily picks out the institutional character of some of our epistemic pursuits. But here too we must be careful. The institutional features of science we found in this chapter to be historically invariant, the so-called Baconian Virtues, are the social benefits enjoyed by a discipline deemed scientific. How one manages to become and remain such a discipline—the usual topics of methodological discussions in the philosophy of science—*do* change over time, thereby partially justifying Laudan's despair. Still, there is a kind of constancy even amidst these changes, as the current players of the science-role "reify" their histories by fusing the image of their discipline with that of science, namely, to extend the Marxist critique of political economy to any discipline that would lay claim to the science role.

5. New Demarcation Criteria for Science

The most natural way of ending this chapter is by showing how the foregoing considerations contribute to a set of demarcation criteria for science. With that in mind, consider the following:

Disciplines that function as "science" for a given social order typically have these characteristics:

(1) They exhibit *the duality of objectivity.*

(1a) The scientist is a nonreflexive subject, that is, he does not apply his methods to himself under normal circumstances (physicists making observations above the quantum level do not measure the mass and velocity of their eyeball motions; psychologists do not monitor their own attitudes toward their subjects; historians do not treat themselves as historical agents). This permits objectivity in the sense of "personal detachment."

(1b) The scientist's data are themselves objectively detached from the scientist, that is, the scientist must admit that predictions are occasionally thwarted to convey the sense that he is not simply conjuring up the data at will. Whereas (1a) ensures that the science's domain of inquiry is bounded and controllable, not generating endless interference from the scientist himself, (1b) ensures that the domain has not yet been exhausted.

(2) *Scientists exercise power without force,* that is, the scientist's power arises from persuading others that he knows about ways of controlling them that they themselves do not know.

(2a) This applies to the scientist's *external* relations, as in his ability to persuade politicians and members of subordinate disciplines.

(2b) This also applies to his *internal* relations, as in his ability to persuade his experimental subjects of the rightness of his account of their behavior.

(3) *Sciences control the recording of their past, which tends toward the perfection of reification.*

(3a) *L-Reification* (for Lukacs) applies to the history of the science's external relations. It enables the Whig historian to objectify the subjectivity of earlier inquirers by identifying their actions solely by their consequences for the dominant science.

(3b) *A-Reification* (for Adorno) applies to the history of the science's internal relations. It enables the historian of laboratory life to ignore the differences in context between cases taken at various times in order to arrive at the appropriate generalization.

CHAPTER EIGHT

DISCIPLINARY BOUNDARIES:
A CONCEPTUAL MAP OF THE FIELD

1. The Boundedness, Autonomy, and Purity of Disciplines

For our purposes, a discipline is "bounded" by its procedure for adjudicating knowledge claims. This procedure consists of an *argumentation format* that restricts (i) word usage, (ii) borrowings permitted from other disciplines, and (iii) appropriate contexts of justification/discovery (for example, some claims may be grounded on "reason alone," some on unaided perception, some on technically aided perception). A discipline that is fully bounded is *autonomous*: it controls its own academic department, program of research, historical lineage, and so forth. T.S. Eliot (1948) coined the term *autotelic* to express a rather strong sense of autonomy, namely, when a discipline not only controls its own affairs but sees those affairs as worth pursuing for their own sake.

Although Eliot was specifically interested in distinguishing art from art criticism (only art is autotelic), his concept applies equally to the humanities and the sciences. For example, we may distinguish degrees of disciplinary purity according to how one understands the idea of a discipline being practiced "for its own sake" or "an end in itself":

(a) *Holier Than Thou:* The discipline's internal justification of its own practice (such as its exclusive rights over some "natural kind" or other well-defined domain of objects) is sufficient for continuing that practice. There is no need for external justification, such as the social benefits promised by the discipline's practice.

(b) *Holiest Than Thou:* The discipline's very performance of its practice is self-justifying without have recourse to either internal or external forms of justification.

Here are some examples of each from the natural sciences:

(a1) It is enough of a reason for doing experimental science that it is designed to get at the truth; hence, it needs no further justification, say, in terms of its technological byproducts.

(b1) The very doing of science—the experience of experimenting and calculating—is its own justification. Polanyi (1957) describes this sort of scientist, who treats his work aesthetically and hence does not care whether he ultimately gets the right results.

191

Now, here are some analogous examples from literary criticism:

(a2) It is enough of a reason for doing criticism that it is designed to identify good works of art, regardless of whether the criticism has any practical impact in changing art or even tastes.

(b2) The very doing of criticism—the experience of creatively misreading texts and constructing conceits and puns that only the erudite can decipher—is its own justification. This attitude is associated with the more "playful" followers of Derrida (1976).

Matthew Arnold (1972) is to be credited with the insight that disciplines can remain bounded without being fully autotelic. Arnold justified the pursuit of criticism as necessary for a proper appreciation of art. In the nineteenth century and earlier, art was generally seen as a source of highly refined forms of sensory gratification. Thus, Arnold argued that the public had to be taught how to regard art "distinterestedly," or for its own sake. Consequently, criticism occupied the unique position of being the *means* by which something else, art, can be treated as an *end in itself*. However, as Davidhazi (1986) has pointed out, criticism has largely failed in its public mission, yet this dysfunctionality has coincided with the rise of criticism as an academic discipline pursued for *its* own sake. This suggests that by the time it became clear, in the early twentieth century, that criticism had failed on Arnoldian terms, it had accumulated a large enough body of its own literature to justify its continuation. Another case in which dysfunctionality made a discipline more autotelic may well be natural history, which first gained epistemic legitimacy as being the record of divine messages to man. However, by the Scientific Revolution, it was no longer believed that natural history functioned in such a communicative capacity. But by then a body of knowledge had already developed that was worthy of pursuit in its own right (Foucault 1970, ch. 2).

An interesting picture of disciplinary formation is implied by the above account that goes against the more orthodox account offered in Kuhn (1970a). On Kuhn's view, fields of study become disciplines (or "paradigms") once a wide range of previously unrelated phenomena are gathered together under a set of unifying principles, which can be verified through different but converging methods. In addition, once a paradigm is formed, the direction in which research should proceed is clear. Newton's synthesis of terrestrial and celestial mechanics under one set of laws is the typical example. In contrast, the view implied in the preceding account of the history of criticism is that disciplines form *not* by staking out a clear domain for itself, but rather by successively failing to control some *other* body of knowledge. We can imagine the successive instrumental failures of criticism—*The Retreat to Purity*—running as follows (each stage probably corresponds to a position actually taken in the history of criticism; see Hirsch [1976], chs. 7-8):

(c) Criticism aims to prepare the audience to receive great artworks once they are made (and hence prevents bad taste from ever arising).

(d) Failing that (because bad taste arises), criticism aims to change bad taste to good.

(e) Failing that (because it has no real influence), criticism aims simply to identify good and bad taste in artworks.

(f) Failing that (because critics cannot agree on what is good taste), criticism aims to record the history of attempts at identifying good and bad taste, and show how the attempts have neglected to see the essentially contested nature of "good taste." (At this point, critics spend more time talking about each other than about artists.)

(g) Failing that (because critics cannot agree on what their disputes are about), criticism takes on a poetic quality, done primarily because of the experience one gets from doing it.

2. Three Techniques for Detecting Disciplinary Boundaries

First, examine disciplines that adjudicate "ostensively similar" knowledge claims (Jones 1983, p. 132). For example, philosophers (especially epistemologists) appear to argue about claims that are also contested by linguists, psychologists, sociologists, and sometimes even physicists. Yet philosophy's argumentation format is quite different from the formats of these other disciplines. Failure to note this fact has led to premature reports of philosophy's obsolescence. In honor of a famous recent case (Rorty 1979), we shall dub this oversight *The Rorty Fallacy*. It is remedied by using a discipline's argumentation format to infer the attitude that one is supposed to adopt to a given proposition (Fuller 1982). Another way of distinguishing disciplines under these circumstances is to determine the background knowledge implicit in the *ceteris paribus* clause presupposed in a fair test of the claim. For example, many of the social sciences seem to test the same claims, yet have great difficulty in pooling their results, largely because their *ceteris paribus* clauses contain radically different conceptions of the human being, which are simply presupposed but never directly put to any "crucial experiment." Indeed, as we shall later see, it is only a short step from rival theories that cover roughly the same domain, but presuppose incommensurable *ceteris paribus* clauses, to entirely discrete disciplines.

Second, examine the metascience implicit in a discipline's argumentation format. When the claims of one discipline conflict with those of another, which discipline yields to the other's cognitive authority? The answer, which reveals the balance of cognitive power between the two disciplines, should be expected to change over time, as in the case of natural theology vis-a-vis natural philosophy from the Middle Ages to the nineteenth century. When the cognitive resources of one discipline are insufficient to solve one of its own problems, which other discipline "just outside" its boundary is invoked for help? When the validity of claims in one discipline is challenged, the validity of claims in which other disciplines is most threatened? Not only should the answers to these questions be expected to change over time, but they are also likely to be asymmetrical.

For example, classical political economy's model reasoner was originally drawn from the rational egoist psychology then current in the eighteenth century; yet once psychology surrendered the model (in the early twentieth century) economics also did *not* immediately follow suit. Whereas the model was completely undermined in psychology once the significance of unconscious irrational factors on behavior was appreciated, economists have so far attacked the model largely on practical grounds, especially in terms of the economist's inability to predict real economic behavior (Simon 1976). And while granting that criticism, neoclassical economists still believe that even in practical situations, the only problems with the model are due to "interference" effects. An effort has been made to draw attention to (and perhaps criticize) the fact that economics benefitted from a particular psychological model when it was warranted without suffering the consequences after the model lost its warrant. Thus, Willard (1983, p. 269) has argued that interdisciplinary borrowing should be treated like any other case of borrowing, namely, that it "incurs obligations." Thus, economics *should have* given up the rational egoist model immediately after psychology did or suffer the consequences.

Third, examine the strategies used to synthesize the research of two or more disciplines. Often a metalanguage is constructed for reducing the claims of the two disciplines to some "common ground" that mainly takes into account the synthesizer's intended audience. If the synthesizer relies on the lexicons of the original disciplines at all, it will be often by metaphorically extending word usage, perhaps so much so that the extensions would be deemed too ambiguous by *intra*disciplinary standards. And so, unless the synthesis itself spawns a new discipline, it is unlikely to affect day-to-day workings of the original two. There is, however, one "intrinsically synthetic" discipline, *pedagogy*, whose recent British theorists have come to realize that while discliplinary boundaries may be the "grown-up" solution to the problem of knowledge, the idea of education presupposes that children can be taught the distinctive methods of *all* the disciplines (Degenhardt 1982). Nevertheless, more typical of the fate of syntheses are the checkered attempts at fusing cognitive psychology and neurophysiology via artificial intelligence into "cognitive science," which is arguably a branch of *philosophy* (Haugeland 1981, Churchland 1984).

The example of cognitive science also suggests that two disciplines separated by a boundary need not be limited to mutually exclusive domains of inquiry (Darden & Maull 1977). Instead, they may cross-classify the same general subject matter. We shall follow Jerry Fodor (1981, ch. 5) in calling this phenomenon *orthogonality*. For example, cognitive psychology and neurophysiology are orthogonal disciplines: reports of a particular type of mental state do not always correspond to reports of the *same* type of brain state, yet each report of a mental state corresponds to a report of *some* type of brain state. And so, despite the fact that both disciplines study the thought processes of the human organism, laws interrelating types of mental states do not appear as laws when translated into the neurophysiologist's discourse. This is a key reason why the two disciplines cannot simply "build on" each other's work.

Interestingly, the same situation holds for such *incommensurable* domains as phlogiston chemistry and oxygen chemistry. In that case, though not all reports of phlogiston correspond to reports of the *same* substance in oxygen chemistry, each report of phlogiston corresponds to a report of *some* substance in oxygen chemistry (Kitcher 1978). Indeed, orthogonality simply *is* incommensurability, but without the connotation that only one of the two disciplines can survive in the long run. But even here the difference may boil down to one of historical perspective: two disciplines that appear merely orthogonal now may later be shown to have been incommensurable. It should come as no surprise, then, a recent school of metapsychologists, *eliminative materialists* have preempted history by arguing that only the familiarity of cognitive psychology's theoretical discourse (which refers to beliefs, desires, and other intentional entities) keeps it from being replaced by the scientifically more promising neurophysiology (Churchland 1979). If such claims are generally correct, then disciplinary boundaries many be seen as fault lines that conceal future scientific revolutions (McCauley 1986).

3. Are Disciplinary Boundaries Necessary for the Growth of Knowledge?

Here is a thought experiment to test your intuitions on this issue. Suppose you were given our current corpus of knowledge and were asked to design the most efficient division of cognitive labor that would have produced the corpus. How different would your design be from the disciplinary boundaries drawn in the actual course of history? Start by treating this as a problem in bureaucratic management. You would then want to eliminate task redundancy by having each department of knowledge work on a discrete domain, with the research of several such departments coordinated at a higher level in the organization. Moreover, you would want perfect communication flow, with the work of the lower departments informed by, yet corrective of, the work of the higher ones. If you find this *systematic* strategy attractive, then you probably think that disciplinary boundaries are in principle dispensable, for, as we have seen, disciplines often cross-classify the same subject matter and impede any mutually useful synthesis. (Whitley [1986] is an entire theory of disciplines based on this thought experiment.)

However, history tells against the systematic approach. Its ideal hierarchy of domains—social groups that are successively decomposed into multicellular organisms, cells, molecules, atoms, elementary particles— overlooks that many key objects of knowledge have been products of orthogonality, including that emergent entity "man" (contra Oppenheim & Putnam 1958). Indeed, anthropology is not merely a *part* of primatology, but the linguistic and technical reorganization of *all* bioevolutionary phenomena. Evidence of this reorganization may be seen in that while man's genetic similarity to *apes* seems to best explain our intelligence, man's ecological similarity to *wolves* must be invoked to account for our sociability (Graham 1981, chs. 6-7). Thus, two features traditionally thought by anthropologists to develop concommitantly, cognitive and social structures, appear unrelated from a bioevolutionary standpoint. This point is made more generally by the tendency of sociobiologists to drawn on an assortment of species from various branches of the evolutionary tree—ants to apes—in order to model the full range of human phenomena (Rosenberg 1980).

Still, the systematist need not be deterred at this point. He can simply argue that these "products" of orthogonality are really *problems* that have arisen due to failures of communication and coordination; hence, anthropologists continue to practice their trade only from ignorance of sociobiology. We shall call an extreme version of this response *Boundary Berkeleyism*, after Bishop George Berkeley, the eighteenth-century radical empiricist. It holds that boundaries arise solely because a discipline's activity is typically not monitored by other disciplines or the public, which allows a hermetic "insider's" discourse to develop. However, once "outsiders" enter this discourse—say, when a biology lab is invaded by sociologists—the boundaries dissolve as the insiders account for their work in terms quite familiar to the outsiders (Latour 1981).

Admittedly, failures to meet the systematist's ideal may be by design, since disciplines actively set up boundaries to expand, protect, and monopolize their cognitive authority (Gieryn 1983b). And even if not by design, there may be more of such failures now than ever before, as the expertise of the average researcher decreases and his need to rely on the unquestioned authority of other experts increases (Friedson 1984). Yet the systematist may generally agree with the eliminative materialist that these sociopolitical obstacles will be overcome in the long run. Indeed, he may facilitate matters by pursuing a policy of *reductionism* (Neurath 1983), which calls for the construction of, so to speak, an interdisciplinary Esperanto. But on what shall this Esperanto be based? The logical positivists were torn between an authoritarian and a democratic solution: the former solution, *physicalism*, would have the lower disciplines recast their claims in terms of the cognitive authority delegated to them by the executive discipline, physics; the latter solution, *phenomenalism*, would force all the disciplines to recast their claims in terms of a neutral medium of cognitive exchange (as in "sense data"), which the positivists would provide in the form of a *theory of evidence.*

4. When Disciplines Collide: The Bernard Principle

In either case, would the result look anything like the deep structure of knowledge growth? There is reason to think not (Feyerabend 1981a, ch. 4), which may mean that disciplinary boundaries are, after all, necessary for the growth of knowledge. A strategy that recognizes this possibilty is *encyclopedic*, so named for the very embodiment of cross-classified knowledge, first proposed in 1751 by Diderot and d'Alembert with many of the above concerns in mind (Darnton 1984, ch. 5). In particular, the Encyclopedists held that the orthogonality of disciplinary domains fostered the growth of knowledge by permitting one discipline to problematize the research of another discipline, thereby ensuring that the highest critical standards were maintained by everyone, a situation that did not obtain when theology was "queen of the sciences." In fact, Diderot was so averse to the systematist's ideal that he suspected Newton's mathematical physics of trying to replace theology in the role of cognitive despot (Prigogine & Stengers 1984, ch. 3).

Once a discipline's domain of inquiry has been "staked out" (Cambrosio & Keating 1983), its practitioners must define and maintain the "normal" state of objects in the domain. This involves experimental and textual techniques for foregrounding the problematic claims under study against a background of claims that are stipulated to be unproblematic. The need for a vacuum in which to demonstrate the laws of motion is perhaps the most famous of these normal states. Philosophers have referred to this activity as "filling in the *ceteris paribus* clause," whose recognized function is to protect the claims that are problematized by a discipline from being too easily falsified by extradisciplinary considerations (Lakatos 1970). However, philosophers have generally overlooked the fact that in order to fill in such a clause, objects and processes may need to be obscured that might have otherwise been the concern of other disciplines. The term *ontological gerrymandering* (Woolgar & Pawluch 1984) nicely captures this phenomenon.

Consider Claude Bernard's demarcation of experimental medicine from the rest of biology. Bernard defined the normal state of an organism in terms of its *milieu interieur*, the equilibration of the organism's blood and lymph flow. For example, a rise in temperature in a mammal's *milieu exterieur* leads to vasodilation, which allows some heat to escape from its body, thereby restoring normal body temperature. Disease is simply the failure to make such homeostatic adjustments, as judged by a physician upon seeing the organism function in the new milieu exterieur (Canguilhem 1978, pp. 29-45). It would seem that Bernard had drawn the boundary around his discipline very tightly—perhaps too tightly. Nineteenth-century France was slow to accept microbiology and evolutionary biology, and the autonomy of Bernard's discipline may be partly to blame (Mendelsohn 1964). First, Bernard defined disease from the patient's standpoint, organic disequilibrium, rather than from the standpoint of a pathogenic agent. Second, experimental medicine had no conceptual place for a disequilibrium that could not in principle be medically corrected, such as an organism's inability to adapt to a radically new milieu exterieur. Thus, microbes and natural selection, respectively, were disallowed. It is, therefore, fitting that we label the thesis that a disciplinary boundary can be drawn only at the risk of excluding other possible disciplines *the Bernard Principle.*

The Bernard Principle assumes many forms, which are particularly well illustrated in the various attempts to stake out the foundational discipline of the human sciences. Consider these seven easily overlooked cases:

(1) Descartes foreclosed the possibility of a *sociology* of knowledge when he declared at the start of the *Meditations* that one must entirely withdraw from daily life in order to consider the nature of things. Virtually all previous philosophers had recommended a restricted institutional setting, such as a school.

(2) Classical political economy, in search of a unified theory of value, followed the Newtonian strategy of reducing the different kinds of value in objects to their lowest common denominator, namely, commodity value. As a result, the discipline could not in principle distinguish between the value of human labor and the value of a product of human labor, which implied that political economy had taken the "human" out of the human sciences. Moreover, as Marx saw, the alienation of labor under capitalism threatened to remove all reminders that such a distinction needed to be made (Althusser 1970).

(3) John Stuart Mill's *A System of Logic* was intended to lay the groundwork for the "moral sciences" (R. Brown 1984, ch. 8). That the book did, especially after it was translated into German in 1849 and read by Wilhelm Wundt, who founded experimental psychology as a discipline. Mill's *Logic* also unintentionally rendered the discipline of history, and later all the humanities, problematic. History, as practiced by Ranke and Niebuhr, claimed to study the past in its specificity. However, Mill's empiricist epistemology did not permit this possibility: either one knows the past in its generality (by induction, the psychologist's way) or one knows the present in its specificity (by direct acquaintance, the ordinary way). *Verstehen* was Wilhelm Dilthey's attempt at bridging this difficulty. But notice that the *Geisteswissenschaften* (the German translation of "moral sciences") would not have appeared problematic, had Mill's radical empiricism not been presumed unproblematic by late nineteenth-century German methodologists (Fuller 1983b).

(4) In order to draw a clear boundary between psychology and physics, Wundt trained subjects to report only their "sensations" and not the physical objects "inferred" from them, which figure in ordinary accounts of experience; hence, in a vision experiment, one would report a "red-round-shiny-presence" instead of an "apple." This stricture also served to prevent psychology from studying higher mental processes. Wundt justified the move on the grounds that reliable results could not be ensured for the higher processes. Nevertheless, the Wuerzburg School performed the forbidden experiments and were promptly accused of committing "stimulus error" and practicing (mere) philosophical introspection (Boring 1950, ch. 18). In a 1913 review of the curious difficulties encountered by Wundt in training subjects to issue proper reports, Wolfgang Koehler (1971, ch. 1) concluded that Wundt was so concerned with protecting the scientific autonomy of psychology that he missed the point of all his difficulties, which was that the distinction between raw sensations and cognitive meaning is an empiricist *philosophical* myth whose survival was due entirely to the "artificiality" of Wundt's own technique. Soon thereafter Koehler and Max Wertheimer spearheaded the Gestalt movement.

(5) Although behaviorist accounts are notorious for avoiding any reference to mental processes not accessible to the experimenter, it has gone relatively unnoticed that behaviorist experiments are typically designed to minimize the appearance of traditional "outward signs" of mental process. For example, Edward Thorndike operationalized animal intelligence as a function of learning rate, the aim being to lower the time taken by an animal to solve the "puzzle box," a prototype of the Skinner Box. He supposed that once placed in the box, the animal would know what was expected of it. Consequently, any of its behaviors that did not immediately contribute to a solution were counted as errors. However, in Thorndike's day, the two main powers of the active mind were taken to be creativity and deliberation, whose outward signs were, respectively, spontaneity and hesitation. Both were associated with, as William James put it, a "facility of nervous discharge from sense organs to motor response" (Boring 1950, ch. 21). In short, the truly intelligent animal could not be set in its ways, as Thorndike's laws of automatic response would surely make it. The postulation of an active mind rested on a view of the animal as always being in a situation that may be rendered intelligible in many different ways. In fact, this view especially suited *nonhuman* animals, which were never expected to have understood what the experimenter had planned for them. Thus, an animal's initial fumblings in the puzzle box should be regarded as attempts at defining the problem rather than as failures at providing a solution. Interestingly, Koehler (1971, chs. 10-11) was also behind this critique of behaviorism, from

which he concluded that psychology could not continue to be the "science of mind," unless it relinquishes the efficiency aims of instrumental conditioning.

Yet behaviorism remained the paradigm of academic psychology in the U.S. for forty years, precisely because J.B. Watson was originally able to convince his colleagues that the discipline could exhibit cumulative growth if it conducted research whose results would be unaffected by whichever theory of introspection or neurophysiology turned out to be correct. Indeed, Watson argued that, if nothing else, the range of mental contents that had been reported by introspectionists proved that subjects could be verbally conditioned in any number of ways (Fuller 1986). And with that began the era of "black box" thinking in psychology.

(6) Freud's avowed aim in declaring sanity to be the limiting case of neurosis was to make all psychological phenomena—not merely pathologies—fair game for the psychoanalyst. More interestingly, since all sane people are virtual neurotics, the self-reports made during Wundt's controlled introspection cannot be presumed unproblematic, but must first be decoded for repressed messages from the unconscious. This line of reasoning justified Freud's dismissal of experimental psychology as pseudo-scientific. And although a similar charge would later be levied against psychoanalysis, at the turn of the century it contributed to the fall of the introspective paradigm. However, Freud also refashioned certain introspection techniques for his own ends, largely through the influence of Carl Jung, a student of the Wundtian psychopathologist Emil Kraepelin. For example, Jung introduced free association, which Kraepelin had used as a diagnostic tool for identifying fixations by counting how often the same word appeared in a subject's set of responses. Psychoanalysis supplemented the method, against Wundtian strictures, by drawing inferences about the *significance* of the repeated words (Maher & Maher 1979, pp. 566-573).

(7) Sensitive to the attempts by Sechenov, Pavlov, and Bechterev to "naturalize" the study of man, the school of critics known as "the Russian Formalists" sought to ground "literary science" on a methodology designed to break the laws of classical conditioning of linguistic reflexes and to extinguish such reflexes once they had been conditioned. The exemplar of this process of "defamiliarization" was difficult Symbolist poetry, whose syntactic ambiguity forced one to reconsider his normal reading habits. The Formalists were philosophically influenced by Ernst Mach (and hence roundly condemned by Lenin in *Materialism and Empirio-Criticism*), which led them to regard the literary scientist as a technician much in the same

way as the "reflexologist" regarded himself—the difference being, of course, that the literary scientist develops techniques for *systematically undermining* the effects of reflexology (Lemon & Reis 1965). This unabashedly "neopositivist aesthetic" legitimated several modern art trends, most notably Surrealism's subversion of perspective. After the Bolshevik Revolution, the formalists emigrated to Prague, and eventually to Paris, where one of their number, Roman Jakobson, started the Structuralist movement in linguistics and literary criticism (Merquior 1986).

5. Disciplinary Ambivalence: Popperian and Foucauldian Versions

Robert Merton (1976) introduced the concept of *sociological ambivalence* to capture the fact that social roles often serve multiple functions whose performance cannot be jointly maximized. Moreover, society does not usually offer any ready-made rules for making the necessary tradeoffs, which leaves the role occupant in a state of tension. For example, the scientist is supposed to *both* expedite the flow of knowledge *and* not rush into print. But how can he "expedite" without also "rushing"? While Merton tends to suppose that all scientists experience the same kinds of ambivalence, a finer-grained analysis of the concept might reveal that each discipline has a characteristic way of resolving its ambivalences, which, in turn, become the basis on which its cognitive status is evaluated by other disciplines and the public at large. This thesis of *Disciplinary Ambivalence* may be illustrated by considering the multiple *linguistic* functions performed by the discourses of disciplines. Our model, adapted from Popper (1972, pp. 119-121), specifies four such functions, each associated with a virtue of disciplinary discourse:

> (j) The virtue of *signalling* is efficiency. A discipline aims to convey the most (new) information per unit of discourse expended.

> (k) The virtue of *expressing* is surveyability (Wright 1980). A discipline aims to make each step of its reasoning evident in its discourse.

> (l) The virtue of *describing* is accuracy. A discipline aims to maximize the total amount of truth conveyed in its discourse.

> (m) The virtue of *criticizing* is precision. A discipline aims to maximize the total amount error eliminated from its discourse.

We shall call the ambivalence that arises between (j) and (k) *Foucauldian*, after the most famous recent student of disciplines as the means by which knowledge is used to control nature and culture (Smart 1983). Foucauldian ambivalence has little interested analytic philosophers of science, with the exception of Stephen Toulmin (1972) and the Lakatosian Yehuda Elkana (1982). In contrast, the ambivalence that arises between (l) and (m) has been virtually the sole concern of analytic philosophers. We shall call it *Popperian* after the philosopher who took a particular resolution of this ambivalence—namely, maximizing the precision of hypotheses at the risk of their accuracy—as the criterion for demarcating "science" from other disciplines (Popper 1972, pp. 193). As we shall now see, both the Foucauldian and Popperian species are needed for providing a framework capable of charting the history of Disciplinary Ambivalence. But first let us explore the considerations involved in each ambivalence.

Foucauldian Ambivalence. Paul Grice's rules of conversational implicature, especially the Quantity Maxim, force a trade-off between efficiency and surveyability (Leech 1983, pp. 84-89). For any given discipline, the most efficient discourse would convey only new information supplied by the intended audience. However, this move would also minimize surveyability by making the discipline's discourse accessible only to insiders. Still, the discipline might not at first regard this hermeticism as such a loss, for if its discourse also exhibits a measure of accuracy and precision, then insiders will, in effect, have knowledge over some domain, the source of which would remain a mystery to outsiders unable to survey the discipline's reasoning. This is the cult of expertise, associated with the professionalization of knowledge (Collins 1975, ch. 9). Furthermore, if the insiders are experts on something that affects the behavior of the outsiders, then the formal definition of institutional power has been satisfied (Crozier 1964).

Yet the promise of power is not enough to dispel the ambivalence. Some degree of surveyability is necessary for introducing novices into a discipline. In fact, another such pedagogical function is also relevant to mature practitioners. For if each step in one's reasoning is made explicit, then errors, misunderstandings, and disagreements can be localized and treated as they occur. But this depends on complete surveyability, which is impracticable, since members of the same discipline generally work in disparate communities with only the elusive medium of print connecting them (Collins 1974). If unchecked for too long, incomplete surveyability may lead to deep misunderstandings between such communities, engendering "schools" and perhaps even Kuhnian incommensurability, which is often followed by the formation of new disciplines (Mulkay, Gilbert & Woolgar 1975, p. 198). Thus, while a strategy of maximizing efficiency promises power outside a discipline, a strategy of minimizing of surveyability adumbrates instability within that discipline.

Popperian Ambivalence. There is something paradoxical about Popper's falsifiability thesis that instills the ambivalence bearing his name. The thesis implies that a discipline becomes scientific once its members realize that eliminating errors is, in the long run, the most effective means of accumulating truths—indeed, more effective than simply trying to accumulate truths in the short run. Furthermore, the short-and long-run pursuits of truth are incompatible—the short run being guided by accuracy and the long run by precision. Accuracy demands that a discipline issue claims that are highly probable given the current knowledge base, while precision demands that it issue highly improbable (high risk) claims that ultimately turn out to be true.

Consider a claim that has just been shown false. How does the discipline correct the error? The easiest way of increasing the claim's probability is by specifically excluding the falsifying case—say, by appending an ad hoc hypothesis or by nimbly rewording the original claim. In both cases, the discipline has adjusted its discourse, more to describe past encounters with the world than to anticipate future ones. While some (Skorupski 1976, pp. 205-223) have taken this dogged pursuit of accuracy as emblematic of the subrational mind, others (Bloor 1979) have pointed out that not even mathematicians are immune to its charms. In contrast, Popper would have the discipline replace the original false claim with one equally vulnerable to falsification. And if that claim turns out to be corroborated, then the discipline would be advised to make it even more vulnerable by placing further constraints on the possible situations that will subsequently count as corroborations. Thus, whereas the pursuit of accuracy encourages consensus (and perhaps even stagnation) in a discipline, the pursuit of precision promotes divisiveness as its members undermine each other's claims in the course of circumscribing their truth content. But contra Popper, the dogged pursuit of precision is more a gamble than a guarantee for ultimate truth. What precision does guarantee is a quick turnover in claims, which may lead to the discipline's demise, if some fairly uncontested truths are not collected along the way (Mulkay, Gilbert & Woolgar 1975, p. 195).

Can an historical trend be discerned in the resolution of Disciplinary Ambivalence? If we look at the full panoramic sweep of organized knowledge in the West (say, from the pre-Socratics to the present), the trend has been to accord high cognitive status to disciplines whose discourses maximize efficiency and precision at the expense of surveyability and accuracy. Moreover, this cognitive status has been "accorded" not only through the plaudits dispensed by philosophical kibitzers but also through the allocation of economic and political resources. The facts surrounding this trend are by now familiar to sociologists: the increased division of cognitive labor, the increased frequency with which disciplines come and go, the increased technical control over well-defined domains, the increased store of undigestible information.

Of course, even to the most Whiggish eyes, the panoramic sweep of our cognitive development presents several slowdowns and setbacks along the way. One of these seems to have a permanent place in the social structure of knowledge—namely, *folk wisdom*—which, regardless of content, resolves Disciplinary Ambivalence in a manner diametrically opposed to the trend, by maximizing surveyability and accuracy. A discipline (or its wayward practitioners) whose discourse heads in this direction is thus engaged in "popularization."

A more interesting deviant resolution of Disciplinary Ambivalence is to maximize surveyability and precision in one's disciplinary discourse. This is the image of science as "conjectures and refutations" on which Popper and most analytic philosophers have fixated. Whatever may be its normative status, as a sociological phenomenon this image has been limited to the Athenian polity and scholastic disputation. Although it is well known that the Athenian citizenry were entertained by public debate, less known is the fact that scholastics were similarly amused by disputation. In fact, there is reason to believe that, at least for Thomas Aquinas, the primary concern in composing a disputation as a series of objections followed by responses was to heighten the suspense of the lecturer's dialectical fate. Moreover, in order to make the lecturer's task seem as formidable as possible, trivial and important arguments were thrown together indiscriminately so as to pad the number of opening objections (McInerny 1983, p. 261). The net result was high drama, indeed, but also a rather ineffective way of gauging cognitive progress, as was observed by those otherwise opposed ideologues of the Scientific Revolution, Bacon and Descartes (Fuller 1985b).

No doubt such unmitigated enthusiasm for dialectics has also contributed to scholasticism's confusing legacy. But most importantly, since scholasticism has more closely approximated, on a large scale, the "up-against-all-odds" attitude to inquiry than any other discipline, its fate suggests that a proviso needs to be added to the Popperian imperative: namely, that a discipline's practitioners should not get so caught up in the *activity* of falsification that they lose sight of falsification's long term *goal* of truth, or, in an anti-Kantian spirit, falsification should always be a means and never an end in itself.

The last possible deviant resolution of Disciplinary Ambivalence remains the subject of much controversy, as documented in Adorno (1976). Maximize efficiency and accuracy in one's discourse: so goes the imperative of the hermeneutical disciplines—theology, jurisprudence, comparative literature, as well as several continental European schools of history, philosophy, and even sociology (Baldamus 1976, pp. 18-29). Since our terms for the linguistic virtues seem to obscure more than illuminate in this case, let us consider a piece of hermeneutical discourse, the *brocard* (Tourtoulon 1922, pp. 310).

A brocard is an aphorism that often introduces a judge's decision in civil law countries. The decision itself takes the form of a commentary on the brocard, during which the case under consideration is shown to exemplify the judge's interpretation. Brocards are designed to be used repeatedly for various cases by various judges, the overall effect being to lend continuity to the legal tradition. They are thus short and memorable, but also somewhat oracular, since their intended range of application is wide. Indeed, brocards are generally worded so that contradictory propositions can be read off them. And so, since a given brocard is applicable on virtually any occasion—

under different interpretations—it is quite literally never wrong (hence, brocards maximize accuracy). Furthermore, a brocard does not become less informative with repeated use, since it is always difficult to predict how the judge will use his discretion to interpret a given brocard in a given case (hence, brocards maximize efficiency). Take, for instance, *The end never justifies the means.* There is, of course, the standard Kantian reading of this brocard, but a clever judge can also divine an ultra-Machiavellian reading from it: to wit, the end *alone* never justifies the means used for achieving it, since the means should *also* have some desirable byproducts.

However, the cost of hermeneutical discourse is high. Like the discourse of the natural sciences, hermeneutics is hardly surveyable on a systematic basis; but unlike natural scientific discourse, it systematically avoids confronting error by trying to accommodate all interpretations. As a result, hermeneutical discourse is incapable of registering cognitive change. This feature has clear reactionary methodological and ideological consequences, as Popper (1972, pp. 183) and Habermas (McCarthy 1978, pp. 169-187), respectively, have noted. Curiously, theology has been the one hermeneutical discipline most sensitive to the problem of making progress in its inquiries. In the field of *redaction criticism,* liberal Protestant theologians have suggested criteria for our coming to a greater understanding of Christ's message. In the late nineteenth century, Adolf von Harnack proposed that Christ's message is whatever is distinctive about the Gospels, once its similarities with other texts of the period have been discounted (Pauck 1965). Fifty years later, Rudolf Bultmann proposed that Christ's message is whatever the Gospels have in common with the canonical texts of the other major religious traditions (Macquarrie 1965). Thus, theological progress is tied, in Harnack's case, to findings in literary archaeology, while, in Bultmann's case, it is tied to findings in comparative religion.

Nevertheless, the cognitive degradation of hermeneutics has been long in the making. Perhaps because many hermeneuticians today define their own activity as having emotive or pragmatic import *instead of* cognitive import, it is often forgotten that the revival of classical learning known as the Renaissance was largely a "Hermeneutical Revolution" (Yates 1968). Cognitive "progress" then consisted of clarifying one's understanding of the wisdom contained in ancient texts. These texts were thought to be wise precisely because of their authors' temporal proximity to the Creation. Indeed, Nature itself was regarded as a book that could be "cross-referenced" with the canonical texts (Gadamer 1975, p. 160). Moreover, this was the attitude taken by the seventeenth century's greatest natural historian, Robert Hooke, and it was prevalent well into the nineteenth century in the work of the *Naturphilosophen.* The point here is that while "hermeneutics" is nowadays used exclusively to characterize the methodology of the humanities, the term primarily identifies one general way of disciplinizing the discourse of one's inquiry, which has applied to what we now call "sciences" as to the humanities.

Interestingly, the hermeneutical sense of cognitive progress also legitimated the Ciceronian theory of translation, which we still accept today, albeit rather uncritically: that a translation should preserve the *content* of the original text. (Why not aim, instead, to preserve the *response* that the text elicited from its original audience? This question was treated in chapter five.) Even during the Scientific Revolution, no less than Isaac Newton can be found to justify his harmonious world-system as an explication of the *prisca sapientia* of the early Greeks and Hebrews (McGuire & Rattansi 1966). However, the precedent for regarding hermeneutical knowledge as both old and *obsolete* had already been set. In an attempt to integrate the recently recovered Aristotelian corpus into the scholastic curriculum, Aquinas argued that Aristotle's natural scientific method fully articulated reliable routes to knowledge that had only been inchoately expressed by the more hermeneutical liberal arts (McInerny 1983, pp. 258).

When and why did the balance of cognitive power weigh decisively against hermeneutics? The answers to these little examined questions are far from clear. But an important key lies in an interdisciplinary history of the theory and practice of translation, which has so far been subject to purely "internalist" treatments (Bassnett-McGuire 1980). In particular, one would want to see under what conditions translators started to challenge the intuition that maximum understanding is necessary for making maximum use of a text. For what probably separates practitioners of the "sciences" from those of the "arts" is the scientist's sense that the time and effort spent in interpreting his precursors is time and effort *taken away* from contributing to the growth of knowledge.

CHAPTER NINE

THE ELUSIVENESS OF CONSENSUS IN SCIENCE

Consider Larry Laudan's (1984) recent statement of the role that consensus plays in scientific validation:

> What makes the broad degree of agreement in science even more perplexing is the fact that the theories around which consensus forms do themselves rapidly come and go. The high degree of agreement, which characterizes science might be surprising if science, like some monastic religions, had settled upon a body of doctrine which was to be its permanent dogma. Consensus, once reached in those circumstances, could well be expected to sustain itself for a long period of time. But science offers us the remarkable spectre of a discipline in which older views on many central issues are quite rapidly and frequently displaced by newer ones, and where nonetheless most members of the scientific community will unhesitatingly change horses in midstream to embrace a point of view which may even have been mooted a decade earlier. [p. 4]

Laudan then goes on to show that Kuhn had noted the above phenomenon, but lost his train of thought along the way to an explanation. In particular, Kuhn offered reasons for thinking that a stable consensus could never form in science, reasons which all turned on the self-reinforcing character of one's own paradigm (for example, one's own theories meet one's own criteria of theory choice, while no one else's theories do; hence, incommensurability). In that case, the standard positivist (the most well-confirmed theory survives) and Popperian (the least falsified yet most falsifiable theory survives) accounts of theory choice, which rely on rational standards mutually acceptable to all scientists, will not apply. As Laudan points out, this leaves Kuhn few options for explaining consensus formation, which results in what Laudan takes to be an unsatisfactory state of affairs:

> We have to wait, [Kuhn] says, for the older generation to die off before the new paradigm establishes hegemony (the so-called Planck Principle). But, even if true, this provides no answer to the central question, for it fails to explain (if it be so) why the younger scientists are able to agree that one particular rival to the orthodoxy is preferable to others. After all, transitional periods of crisis are, for Kuhn, typified by the existence of a multitude of new paradigms, each vying for the allegiance of the relevant scientific practitioners. Even if we assume (with Kuhn) that younger scientists are more open to novelty than their elders, we still have no explanation for the fact that the "young Turks" are so often able to agree about which dark horse to back. Young advocates of rival paradigms should, if Kuhn is right about incommensurability of beliefs and incompatibility of standards, have all the same difficulties their elders do in reaching agreement about the respective merits of competing paradigms. [p. 18]

Like Popper, Laudan is struck by the "fact" that science manages to steer the middle course between permanent dissensus (as in philosophy) and permanent consensus (as in religion) and, in so doing, allows a genuine growth of knowledge to occur. Also like Popper, Laudan believes that we should treat this alleged historical fact about science as being the result of the way in which the scientific enterprise maintains itself over time. In that case, we are to presume that our historical inquiry into the nature of science's cognitive success will deliver an answer that can be extrapolated beyond the historical cases considered in order to serve as a procedure—or "method"—both for maintaining science's cognitive success and for making the cognitively less successful disciplines more successful. Popper and the positivists failed at this task because the methods they suggested (inductive logics of one sort or another) were sufficiently removed—or "abstracted"—from the practices of specific scientific disciplines to make it all too easy for scientists to come to agreement on the relative acceptability of any set of theories. Kuhn, on the other hand, failed because, as Laudan notes, he proposed that the relevant procedures were so specific to particular disciplines that consensus would be virtually unachievable on the global level which typically interests philosophers.

Given Laudan's aims, the last thing he would want to learn is that consensus formation is largely an *accidental* phenomenon, the result of a statistical drift in allegiances, in which the reasons invoked by the individual scientists may have little to do with each other. A discovery of this kind, which would amount to an "invisible hand explanation" (Ullmann-Margalit 1978) of science's cognitive success, would obviously be difficult to implement *deliberately* as a piece of rational science policy. It should come as no surprise then that Laudan never actually says why an appeal to the Planck Principle would be insufficient to explain consensus formation—except to stigmatize it as an "external" factor, which is to say, outside of what he implicitly takes to be the design features of science. We shall now argue that there is nothing intrinsically inadequate about the kind of statistical drift explanation that Kuhn gives for consensus formation in science. Moreover, if Laudan's conception of consensus in science is as different from Kuhn's as he claims it to be, then, historically at least, the burden of proof would seem to rest on Laudan, *and not Kuhn*, to show that an interesting problem has failed to be solved.

1. Two Pure Types of Consensus and Four Mixed Ones

We can imagine two groups of individuals, A and B, who come to agreement in the following manner:

(a) A comes to agreement by each individual deciding by himself to do the same thing.

(b) B comes to agreement by a collective decision to do the same thing.

Let us say that the agreement concerns the acceptability (or "assertibility," if you will) of the sentences which constitute a particular scientific theory. In group A, each individual assents to the sentences for his own reasons, perhaps similar to those invoked by other individuals, but perhaps not. Since in group A the presence of the other individuals does not bind a given deliberator in any way, the reasons privately invoked by the deliberator may be considered totally unreasonable by all the rest. And it may be that upon closer examination (so as to save Donald Davidson's maxim that seeming irrationalities are the product of faulty contextualizations by the interpreter), the deliberator's strange reasonings can be explained as an eccentric reading of the agreed upon sentences. Since the deliberator need not make his reasons public to the other members of the group, he may be expected in the short run, at least, to suffer no recriminations. However, should he decide to use the sentences which he has so eccentrically interpreted as part of the justification of some equally eccentric viewpoint, then debate is bound to break out, and some measure of dissensus will ensue. Whether the eccentric manages to sway the others to his viewpoint is an open question, since nothing in the way in which group A formed binds its members indefinitely to the sentences originally agreed upon. They may drift away from endorsing the sentences for different reasons at different times. And so, from the standpoint of an outsider who only knows the sentences which group A had agreed upon but not any of the reasons, dissensus would thus appear unpredictable.

In contrast, group B is not nearly so open to this sort of instability, since its members thrash out their reasons in the presence of one another before reaching agreement. The need to present one's reasons as being of the kind that all the members would find reasonable encourages each deliberator to aim for commonly accepted usage, standards of evidence, and sense of relevance. And so, once group B reaches consensus, it is presumed that they have done so for the same reasons, which means that a competent disturbance the consensus could arise only under circumstances that, at least in principle, could be agreed upon by all. And even if its members fail to anticipate an anomaly, they will unanimously agree to the fact that it warrants a dissolution of the consensus and a resumption of the debate. And so, for group B, both consensus and dissensus are well defined and binding.

Let us call group A an *accidental consensus,* since the fact that everyone in the group assents to the same set of sentences is accidental to the fact that each individual has. For example, the reasons why most of my colleagues have endorsed a particular theory may be unrelated to the reasons why I have as well. These reasons may be "unrelated" either in the sense of being different from one another or in the sense of being reached through independent means. Group B is an *essential consensus,* since the fact that the entire group has assented to this set of sentences is essential to the fact that each individual has. Another way of putting the distinction is that, in an essential consensus, one can, in principle, specify a network of persuasion among all the individuals in the group that issues in their collective decision, while no such network can be specified in an accidental consensus.

The paradigm of an accidental consensus is the kind of agreement that pollsters find in the course of surveying public opinion. Although the pollster presumes that everyone surveyed understands the question in the same way, he usually does not check. And indeed, studies show that by paraphrasing a question one way instead of another, the extent of consensus may be manipulated. This suggests that the degree of agreement on what the question means is never particularly deep (Deutscher 1968). Why? One reason is that the individuals surveyed do not generally interact with each other or even the pollster beforehand in order to negotiate the exact meaning of the question. And when the question concerns an issue on which the individuals will eventually have to make a binding choice, such as a presidential election, this polling procedure is deliberately used, since pollsters are interested in the varying "perceptions" of a candidate that may be the source of many unrelated and even incompatible reasons for a collection of interest groups either supporting or opposing him. Needless to say, the mass media, which present issues to individuals in relative isolation from each other (for example, through an individual newspaper or television), foster this phenomenon of accidental consensus.

Before jumping to the conclusion that consensus is the mark of something like "objectivity" in science, we must make sure that the consensus in question is not merely accidental in the above sense. Just as public opinion pollsters can fabricate consensus by phrasing their questions sufficiently vaguely or abstractly, or by preselecting the group of eligible respondents (even if they randomize the individuals selected *within* that group), so too historians of science can construct a convergence of opinions on a particular point. In both cases, once a finer-grained question is asked, disagreement arises. We shall soon delve into this matter at greater length, but for now let us suggest one phenomenon, much discussed by historians and sociologists of science, which may well be the product of an accidental consensus formation: namely, *multiple* (or *simultaneous*) *discoveries*. (Lamb [1984] is the first extended philosophical study of this phenomenon.)

A multiple discovery occurs when several scientists, who otherwise have little or nothing to do with each other's research, seem to arrive at roughly the same discovery at roughly the same time. Since the scientists were clearly not in collusion with one another, and in fact may be from national or disciplinary traditions of quite opposing makeups, it is argued that this phenomenon points to the objectivity of the knowledge claim involved in the discovery. The energy conservation principle is usually taken to be the paradigm case of a discovery of this kind, as it had been proposed independently by Carnot, Joule, Helmholtz, Mayer, and Rumford around the late 1830s. These scientists represent several national traditions— British, French, German—as well as several contexts in which scientific research was done—metaphysical, interdisciplinary, experimental, technological. But the "multiplicity" of this discovery may simply be—as

Kuhn (1977a, ch. 4) has suggested—the result of historians, following the pollster, finding consensus by stating the principle abstractly enough. This is, after all, how the conservation principle is normally stated: "work and heat are mutually convertible" or "the net energy added to a system equals the net change of energy within the system." The historian would have a stake in proceeding this way, since the principle is the foundation of contemporary thermodynamic theory.

In contrast, since we no longer believe that light travels through an aether medium, the consensus over the existence of an aether in the nineteenth century is portrayed as the product of divergent conceptions traveling under the same confusing term. Moreover, in the social sciences, multiple discovery is quite frequent (examples include the origin of the following concepts by psychologists and sociologists around 1900: the division of labor, the unconscious, the distinction between "community" and "society"), but there it is normally attributed to the failure of communication between research programs whose members have had largely the same training and background information. However, rather than pooling their collective cognitive resources, and thereby minimizing the redundancy of effort implied by multiple discovery, social scientists are typically overcome by ideological differences which prevent them from taking an active interest in (or perhaps even generating hostility toward) each other's research. The failure of Emile Durkheim and Max Weber to appreciate each other's work is a striking case in point. This sort of multiple discovery is then used to explain *the lack of progress* in the social sciences? Why couldn't the same be said about the status of the energy conservation principle as a multiple discovery?

To make matters even more complicated, consider that multiple discovery is more likely than ever to be seen as a mark of *objectivity*, insofar as natural scientists see themselves as having good communication links with each other. Consequently, a failure in communication would not strike *them* as a viable explanation of the multiple discovery. However, even though scientists are able to access more information than ever before, there is also more information to be accessed, which means that scientists can easily have a false impression of just how well informed they really are.

Turning now to the essential consensus, its paradigm case is Peirce's ideal scientific community, which anticipates the Popperian vision of the environment in which the method of conjectures and refutations is ideally deployed. (As Haskell [1984] points out, Peirce, like Popper after him, drew his model of the ideal scientific community from the capitalist marketplace.) Although Peirce's scientists are very ego-involved in their conjecturing (Peirce imagines each of them to be competing for having his name attached to the ultimate explanation of the universe), and hence prone to divisiveness, nevertheless they also realize that their egos cannot be gratified unless they have persuaded their fellows in terms that have communal clout. This leads to both intense competition *and* intense communication among the scientists, which ensures that whatever agreement is finally reached will be for reasons that are understood and accepted by all.

As the title of this section suggests, "accidental" and "essential" are two pure types of consensus. They are "pure" in the sense that they make no assumptions about the cognitive state of the individuals involved, aside from their having a belief about the pattern of social interaction that is necessary for justifying their beliefs. In an accidental consensus, the individuals believe that no social interaction is necessary, which explains why once individuals are shown that they have interpreted, say, a survey question in different ways, they feel no need to converge on a single reading or response; hence, public opinion fragments just as easily as it solidifies. In contrast, each member of an essential consensus recognizes that he needs to defend his belief to the rest of the group before he is accepted as justified in his belief; the need for total social interaction thus motivates the convergence of opinion in the long run, as Peirce observed. However, we can imagine somewhat more complicated situations, which impute richer cognitive states to the individuals, thereby creating "mixed" types of consensus.

Near-Essential Consensus: There may a group of individuals, each of whom recognizes that he must convince the other members in order to be accepted as having a justified belief; but also some of the members believe that the relevant context of justification extends to other individuals outside this group. (Indeed, there may be little agreement among the members as to the identity of these "other individuals.") A hypothetical case of such a near-essential consensus would be a group of English biologists, circa 1870, each of whom recognizes that he must justify his belief about "the origin of species" to the rest of the biologists; but, in addition, some of these biologists think that their belief must also pass muster by the justificatory standards of natural theology. In that case, the following dialectical impasse may arise within the group that breaks down the consensus. Everyone agrees that *if* the design features of divine creation need not be explained by an acceptable account of the origin of species, then Darwin's theory is clearly the most justifiably believed. However, some of the biologists—the theologically sensitive ones—believe that such features do indeed need to be explained, which makes them unable to accept Darwinism (for the relevant history, see Young 1985).

Near-Accidental Consensus: As in the case of the accidental consensus, the members of this sort of group do not believe that a certain pattern of social interaction is necessary for their beliefs to be justified. However, unlike an accidental consensus, the overall coherence of the group's activities would not be jeopardized by the members learning that they in fact disagree more than they thought. There may be two reasons for this situation arising:

(c) The mechanism by which a group's beliefs are selected, at least in the long term, lies outside any context of justification that members of the group are likely to recognize. An example of such a selection mechanism would be the the the Planck Principle in its most extreme (and least plausible) form: no matter how contested a particular belief may currently be, it will nevertheless triumph in the end if the majority of younger group members support it; yet, the fact that this belief tends to attract the younger members would not be recognized by anyone in the group as being a good reason for supporting it.

(d) There is a "functional differentiation" of group dissensus that serves to promote the group's overall goals. In other words, a group may consist of subgroups that cannot agree on issues as basic as the relative importance of the other subgroups' activities for the group's overall goals; still, there may be discernible "progress" toward the group's goals, if the subgroups do not draw from the same pool of material resources and hence do not need to compete. An example of this situation would be a rather idealized division of cognitive labor into academic disciplines, especially between the "sciences" and "humanities." Scientists may be skeptical of the value of the work done by the humanists, but as long as they do not draw from the same pool of funds, these irreconcilable differences do not affect the overall gain in knowledge produced by the collective activities of the two camps.

With respect to (d), Michael Polanyi (1957, pp. 7-9) has suggested that the functional differentiation of group dissensus began when mathematics and physics started to have separate histories, reflecting the different directions in which developments from Newton's *Principia Mathematica* went. Physicists soon took a realist attitude toward their own pursuits and an instrumentalist attitude toward mathematics, while mathematicians tended to be realists about their own activities and instrumentalists about those of the physicist. Thus, physicists and mathematicians did not regard each other as making claims to knowledge of reality: physicists saw mathematicians as conceptual and computational facilitators (Lagrange and Laplace's elegant reformulation of Newtonian mechanics is an example), while mathematicians saw physicists as applied mathematicians and makers of concrete models of mathematical truths (Einstein's appropriation of Riemannian geometry as the model of general relativity is an example). This trend continued as the knowledge system gradually became divided into still more specialized disciplines, which accounts for the rise of instrumentalism as a general philosophy of science (namely, to account for everyone's research but one's own). The lesson to learn here, once again, is that disciplines can have mutually *debunking* attitudes toward one another which nevertheless turn out to be mutually *supporting* at the level of daily practice.

Procedurally Enforced Consensus: This situation obtains in any group activity where the means of social interaction is highly constrained, say, by a technical language in which all claims must be expressed. These constraints serve to prevent any potentially debilitating disagreements from arising. For example, a "well-constructed" discipline (institutionally speaking) will minimize the opportunities for disputes over worldview (Whitley 1986). And insofar as historians of science rely on the linguistic behavior of scientists as their primary source of evidence, they contribute to essentializing what may just be an accidental consensus, since the discourse of scientists reveals many common idioms, which at face value indicate many common beliefs. However, in discussing the multifarious reception of Newton below, we suggest that procedurally enforced consensus may foster incommensurability (in the sense of systematic miscommunication), on the grounds that even if the practitioners of a discipline cannot express their personal ideologies and interests within the official idiom, they draw on those extradisciplinary factors as background context to (mis)interpret the utterances of their colleagues. However, the incommensurability becomes evident only once the disciplinary matrix breaks down and the procedurally enforced consensus is no longer in effect.

Suboptimal Essential Consensus: A suboptimally functioning essential consensus produces what social psychologist Elisabeth Noelle-Neumann (1982) calls, after Alexis De Tocqueville, *the spiral of silence.* An essential consensus functions optimally when each member of a group knows the justificatory standards and current beliefs of all the other members, especially as changes come about as the result of social interaction. However, even in the best designed essential consensus, perfect information of this kind is unlikely to be readily available, if only because not everyone is constantly making his views heard. What more often happens is that those who arrive at a belief which they take to be justifiable engage the other members in a public defense; those who either agree with a standing belief or have no strong views simply remain silent. However, if the public forum is presumed to be a democratic one (that is, equally accessible to all), as Peirce's ideal scientific community is, then there is a strong temptation to take the more highly visible (or audible) positions as the ones most representative of group opinion. For example, if a particular belief is either defended or attacked frequently, members tend to presume (so Noelle-Neumann's research suggests) that the belief has a relatively large following, when, of course, it may just have a few very articulate spokesmen.

A democratic setup is especially prone to a faulty inference of this kind because its members have no prima facie reason for thinking that anyone is holding back on what they really believe. As a result, the silent members of the group, who might otherwise be noncommittal, start to move toward what they take to be the trend of the rest. Tocqueville (1955) first drew attention to this phenomenon, which he took to be the source of the "sixth sense" that people have been traditionally thought to have about the opinions of others. He uses the spiral of silence to explain the rapid decline of the clergy in France after the Revolution of 1789. The reason was *not* that most people had been convinced by the secular ideals of the revolution, but rather, that the revolutionaries had been so vocal in their attacks of the Church, and the Church itself so silent (since it believed, quite correctly but inexpediently, that its supporters vastly outnumbered its attackers), that citizens began to think that most of their fellows had strayed from the faith, and thus began to see such an attitude as publicly licensed.

In trying to identify the sources and extent of consensus and dissensus among scientists, the historian is an easy target for the spiral of silence, since the only views on which he typically feels safe to comment are the ones that are actually expressed. But if indeed all the beliefs expressed are not necessarily all, or even most, of the beliefs held, then some embarrassing interpretive problems arise. For example, much philosophical argument throughout the centuries has been addressed to silencing "the skeptic," as if he had many followers (or even just many individuals who found his arguments persuasive). However, tracking down actual skeptics turns out to be very elusive. The effects of this particular spiral of silence can be seen in the behavior of contemporary epistemologists, most of whom admit that *their field* takes the skeptic's challenge to be important, though *they personally* do not find it nearly so formidable. An even more telling case may be the origins of the most recent revolution in the human sciences, the so-called Cognitive Revolution associated with the importation of Noam Chomsky's generative linguistics into experimental psychology. We can do little more here than observe that what turned out to be the decisive event in the revolution, Chomsky's devastating 1959 review of B. F. Skinner's *Verbal Behavior,* was met by no response from the behaviorist camp. Although Skinner later explained that since Chomsky had clearly not kept up with the latest developments in behavioral linguistics and that Chomsky's own theory was an extension of the work of Zellig Harris, a leading behavioral linguist, Skinner saw no need to reply. However, those on the dialectical sidelines saw the matter much differently, namely that Skinner *could not* answer Chomsky's critique, which permitted the Cognitive Revolution to proceed in silence (Zuriff 1985, ch. 7).

In concluding this examination of the types of consensus, we shall briefly reconsider the thesis proposed at the start of this paper about the difference between Laudan and Kuhn on the role of consensus formation in science. This will give us a taste of the elusiveness of this role, which will be studied in greater detail in the next section. Our reconsideration is framed by the following question: Does Laudan overplay the extent to which Kuhn's account of scientific progress is merely result of an "invisible hand" mechanism, a rationality that is displayed only on the macro, but not the micro level, of the history of science?

Kuhn (1970a) makes a point of stressing the variety of arguments that tend to move members of the scientific community in what, from the historian's standpoint, appears to be the same direction:

> Because scientists are reasonable men, one or another argument will ultimately persuade many of them. But there is no single argument that can or should persuade them all. Rather than a single group conversion, what occurs is an increasing shift in the distribution of professional allegiances. [p. 158]

Kuhn is here describing the formation of what we have called an accidental consensus. Laudan (1984) wishes to mask over this brute fact with a self-styled "reticulated" theory of scientific justification, whereby scientists are able to resolve their disputes over factual, methodological, or axiological points because, at any given moment, only one of these points is contended, while agreement is presumed on the other two. Laudan's approach here, reminiscent of debate forums, is one of essential consensus formation. And this approach *would* work, if all the scientists Laudan wished to include as part of the "debate" on a given point actually constituted themselves (through, say, a communication network) as a common audience, which was, in turn, recognized as the final arbiter of an argument's validity. But the question, of course, is whether the approach *does* work.

Perhaps the best way of addressing this question, in brief compass, is by indicating the controversial nature of Laudan's historical interpretations. For example (Laudan, pp. 56-59), in the mid-eighteenth century, scientists took Newton's "hypotheses non fingo" to heart and attacked the following heretical theories for postulating unobserved entities: Hartley's neurophysiology of aethereal fluids, Lesage's ultramundane particle explanation of gravity, and Boscovitch's alternately charged mass-points. However, Laudan claims that since these heretics agreed with the scientific establishment on what counted as a good theory, namely, Newtonian mechanics, they were able to resolve their methdological and axiological disagreements. In fact, the heretics managed to show that while Newton was explicitly an inductivist, implicitly (that is, in practice) he was a hypothetico-deductivist. So says Laudan.

From the standpoint of the next section, the interesting feature of Laudan's account is that he supports it exclusively by citing the heretics' appeals to Newton's authority and their reinterpretation of the Newtonian corpus to legitimate their own scientific practice. But does Laudan's evidence really imply that consensus had been reached on something as substantive as the exemplar of a good scientific theory; or does it warrant, rather, the weaker claim that consensus had been reached on the canonical language in terms of which all claims to scientific legitimacy had to be negotiated? As will become clear, I argue for the latter option.

2. The Elusive Object of Consensus in Science

Let us assume that group A and group B (as defined above) represent fundamentally different situations in science. Each group B should be regarded as composed of actual human beings who have regular interaction about scientific matters, in virtue of being part of the same university department, school of thought, research facility, or "invisible college" (Crane 1972). The various units, the various group Bs, are, in turn, the members of a group A. Thus, we are envisaging a situation in which an accidental consensus is composed of a collection of essential consensuses. In thinking that there is more to consensus formation in science than Kuhn makes out, Laudan—so I shall argue—mistakenly assumes that the global group A situations just described operate like the more local group B situations. We shall take as our example the agreement from diverse quarters on the acceptance of Newtonian mechanics, a "pre-analytic intuition" which Laudan (1977, pp. 158-163) claims that the historian has about the state of science in 1800.

The first problem facing any attempt to explain consensus in science is to specify exactly what the parties are supposed to have agreed to. Laudan exacerbates an unfortunate tendency among philosophers of science to identify the objects of consensus as "theories," "methods," and sometimes even "metaphysics." Within the discipline of philosophy, these terms can be made more or less precise. For example, someone may want to axiomatize a specific scientific theory. While he will, of course, take some care to ensure that the axioms and propositions derivable from them bear some resemblance to what has, at some point, gone under the name of, say, "Newtonian mechanics," the axiomatizer will not be too concerned about whether particular scientists would have ever assented to all the axioms and propositions of which his theory is constructed. Such is the nature of rational reconstruction. Once the axiomatization is complete, he and his fellow axiomatizers can unambiguously refer to it whenever they want to say something about Newtonian mechanics, without ever having to open a history book (or a physics book, for that matter). And the contexts in which they would likely refer to Newtonian mechanics would ensure that they are not missing anything by not knowing the history *or* the physics: for example, "Does Newtonian mechanics logically subsume Galileo's Law?" However, once the axiomatizer ventures beyond this precise and formal sense of "theory" and claims that it was rational at a particular time for a particular group of scientists to accept Newtonian mechanics, he only begs the question in presuming that there was *exactly one* Newtonian mechanics which all of them decided to accept. For how would the philosopher of science identify this one theory?

Admittedly, historians of science often mention the names of such theories as "Newtonian mechanics," "Darwinian biology," and "phlogiston chemistry." However, they tend to use the names as a convenient way of individuating camps of scientists, often simply on the basis of the fact that these scientists either have appropriated the labels for themselves or—more likely—have had the labels foisted upon them by their rivals. And perhaps every scientist would presume that the other scientists in his camp adhered to the same core tenets. The commonality of labels has normally been enough to dissuade the scientists from delving into the matter, united as they seemed to be against a common foe. Consequently, it is not unusual for a historian to examine the microstructure of a scientific camp only to find that the scientists must have been presuming of each other quite different core tenets—a fact that may surface only much later in internal disagreements (Gilbert & Mulkay 1984, ch. 6).

An astute scientist, such as Heinrich Hertz (1899), may be aware of this tendency. At the turn of the century, Hertz identified three versions of Newtonian mechanics, each grounded on a slightly different set of principles but with major differences in research orientation. All three identified space, time, and matter as primitives, but two versions proposed a fourth primitive. While the classical "textbook" account added *force*, the then fashionable energeticist account added *energy*. Hertz observed that both force and energy were unnecessary additions: on the one hand, (centrifugal) force, being nothing more than inertia, is derivable from space, time, and matter alone; on the other hand, treating (potential) energy as a substance is a contradiction in terms. But if this diagnosis is correct, how was it possible for theoretical debate in late nineteenth-century physics to center on the search for the fourth primitive? Hertz suggests that the entire debate was orchestrated by philosophically minded physicists, such as Helmholtz, who wanted to show that their own particular worldview was implied by a body of knowledge, "Newtonian mechanics," which ostensibly had universal assent.

In short, the names of theories function for the historian of science much as the names of ideologies do for the historian of politics. Of course, many historians study particular classical texts, such as *Principia Mathematica* and *On the Origin of Species,* and they may use the terms "Newtonian mechanics" and "Darwinian biology" to refer to them. However, philosophers of science do not mean the terms in that sense either—that is, when Laudan wonders whether it was rational to accept Newtonian mechanics in 1800, he is presumably not wondering whether it was rational for scientists to have assented to the sentences composing *Principia Mathematica* as Newton intended them. What, then, is the nature of Laudan's query?

There is one way of interpreting Laudan's query that is not intrinsically problematic, but which Laudan himself would probably not find attractive. Perhaps by "Newtonian mechanics," Laudan means the object inhabiting Popper's (1972) World Three that is imperfectly represented by *Principia Mathematica* and Laplace's *Celestial Mechanics,* which were themselves originally products of World Two (minds) that were then embodied in World One (as books). It is the object that Koyre (1969) and other historians have identified as "the Newtonian worldview." In other words, the scientists in 1800 are purported to have (rationally) agreed to the "essence" of Newtonian mechanics, which can be identified, via a "causal theory of reference" (Putnam 1984) linking Newton's 1687 text with Laplace's 1799 text (and other texts as well).

Notice that such an agreement is different from agreeing to the essence of what Newtonian mechanics purports to be a representation of—the real physical structure of the universe. This latter sort of consensus is the one that Hilary Putnam identifies as necessary for ensuring that the scientists are on a joint inquiry toward the Truth. However, Laudan the instrumentalist is unlikely to embrace the idea that theories themselves have essences quite apart from the essences of their objects. For to accept this Meinongian proposition would be to countenance the following question: Does coming to more adequate representations of Newtonian mechanics (however, we might come to do that) necessarily involve also coming to more adequate representations of what Newtonian mechanics represents (namely, physical reality)? We do not mean to cast aspersions on the validity of the question. Indeed, social historians, who often want to portray a group of scientists as pursuing a theory on ideological grounds, regardless of its representational adequacy, would find our metaphysical distinction helpful. In that context, we would suggest that our question may be answered as follows: The essence of Newtonian mechanics is a Lakatosian contraption, replete in heuristics and belts, that renders Newtonian mechanics invulnerable to all possible falsifications. Thus, the answer to our question is "no." A better representation of Newtonian mechanics—one that captures the Newtonian worldview more exactly—is not necessarily a better representation of what Newtonian mechanics represents, physical reality. This is a lesson that Lakatos (Hacking 1981b) learned from Henri Poincare (1965, pp. 98-100). In the end, though, despite their intrinsic interest, these metaphysical issues are exactly the sort that most philosophers of science have avoided since the advent of positivism.

One deceptively simple way of identifying the object of consensus that Laudan and others call "Newtonian mechanics" is by listing exactly those sentences in *Principia Mathematica* (and other related works) that all the relevant scientists would have agreed to. As Kuhn (1977b) has pointed out, the most likely candidate sentences would be mathematical ones—which he calls "symbolic generalizations"—since computational virtues can be less ambiguously shown to scientists who would readily disagree on the interpretation of sentences in a natural language. However, to establish that the scientists have agreed upon a certain mathematical formalism in which to do celestial mechanics is hardly enough to show that they have decided to pursue something in common. There must be some significant uniformity of interpretation as well. But this is where the scientists are most likely to turn philosophical and, hence, divisive. Should Newton's Laws be interpreted as self-evident truths, empirically falsifiable hypotheses, definitions adopted solely for computational convenience, partial instructions for constructing a mechanical model of the universe, or representations of how things really are? (Buchdahl [1951] reviews the merits of these options.) Although most eighteenth-century scientists—at least in continental Europe—interpreted Newtonian mechanics instrumentally, contrary to Newton's own realist tendencies, philosophers of science generally (and Laudan in particular) would want to distinguish a consensus over a theory from a consensus over a methodology, however mutually supporting the deliberations on these two matters may have been historically.

Perhaps this situation may be salvaged for Laudan by treating the various interpretations as the bases of different reasons for accepting Newtonian mechanics. For example, someone who believed that Newton's Laws were empirically falsifiable hypotheses would now be taken to have endorsed those Laws because they best survived the stiffest experimental tests. In that case, the agreement on the acceptability of Newtonian mechanics could occur for several reasons, each one bringing out a strength that the scientist saw in the theory as he interpreted it. Thus, as long as each scientist could cite grounds that were good by the methodology through which he understood the theory, the agreement would be rational. In this way, theoretical consensus could be sustained in spite of methodological pluralism.

However, one may wonder whether this technique does too much violence to the historical record to be regarded as paying anything more than lip service to what actually happened. It would probably be quite easy to show that each of the relevant scientists had at least one good reason relative to his methodology for deciding to accept Newtonian mechanics. In fact, let us imagine the extreme case—which caricatures the actual situation in the late eighteenth century—of all the scientists endorsing at least the computational interpretation of Newtonian mechanics. Unfortunately, each of these scientists probably had other, perhaps idiosyncratic and certainly not universally invoked, reasons for accepting the theory. Divergent conceptions of nature and God would be a good starting point. (And for the sake of argument, let us confine our search for reasons to those that would have been introspectively available to the reasoning scientist.) But while each scientist is likely to have conceived of his particular set of reasons as one package (that is, a logical *conjunction*), the philosopher of science picks out only the reasons that suits his interests (namely, the ones that they all share in common). In other words, the philosopher treats each scientist's set of reasons as a logical *disjunction*.

In claiming that the logical structure of the scientists' reasons is conjunctive rather than disjunctive, we are appealing to a general principle of pragmatics, along the lines of Grice's maxims of conversational implicature: namely, that a conjunctive structure is presumed to be the norm unless the speaker indicates otherwise. For example, when an individual offers some reasons for asserting a claim, he may intend that his audience accept whichever reasons they wish (that is, a logical disjunction), just as long as they agree with his claim. Such situations are in fact common when the individual thinks that speaking his mind and persuading his audience are two radically distinct activities, and he needs to persuade an audience with widely divergent beliefs. Under these circumstances we would be inclined to say that the speaker is insincere, though perhaps rhetorically astute. Still, if the individual *does* succeed in convincing his audience, it will probably be precisely because the audience *understood him* as adhering to the conversational norm, and thus speaking his mind. In that case, the members of the audience would have read his "apparently" divergent lines of reasoning charitably as reinforcing the particular arguments that each member happened to have found especially persuasive.

Does the philosopher's subtle shift in the logical structure of the scientist's reasons, from conjunction to disjunction, count as doing violence to the historical record? In particular, does the shift obscure the answer to whether the scientists had rationally decided to accept Newtonian mechanics? Consider an analogous situation, one in which a high school science teacher evaluates the lab reports of a group of students, all of whom have reached the same conclusion as a result of performing an experiment. The teacher expects the students to have defended their conclusions by at least citing some standard observations and principles. Let us say that they have all done at least that, since it was a relatively simple experiment. However, the teacher normally looks for more than a mere coincidence of inscriptions before determining who will and will not pass the lab (and by how much). The extra sentences appearing on each student's page will be the final arbiter here, for the teacher can then use those sentences to judge whether a given student has understood (that is, correctly interpreted) what he and the other students have written in common. In other words, the teacher treats each student's reasons as a logical conjunction, and thus they stand or fall together. In that case, to award full marks to a student who has reproduced the desired sentences along with some apparently irrelevant or erroneous material would be unduly charitable, since it would involve misinterpreting the student as having specifically intended the teacher's answer, when in fact he intended something much more diffuse and perhaps even incoherent.

If the above analogy is apt, then the philosopher of science, in his persona of the high school teacher, would be practicing bad pedagogy to pass all the scientists who agreed to Newtonian mechanics as "rational" simply because they can be found to mouth the same words at some point which we now can readily interpret as appropriate to have uttered. Of course, it may happen that a particular group of scientists did more than just mouth the minimum number of words necessary for a "rational" decision. These scientists would be like the students who worked on their lab reports together, and thus had to justify most of the moves in their reasoning to one another. One such group would obviously form an essential consensus, though probably only an accidental consensus when taken with the rest of the scientists.

3. Consensus Rigging by Disciplinary Realignment

Where does this leave us? One reason why Kuhn may not have felt compelled to pose Laudan's question about consensus formation in science is that, unlike Laudan, Kuhn wants the philosopher to have a relatively clear sense of how he would identify "theories" and "methods" when reading the history of science. Most often, Kuhn (1977b) seems to mean by "theory" a set of scientifically uninterpreted strings syntactically well formed by some grammar, so-called symbolic generalizations. Usually, these strings are mathematical (not surprisingly, given his heavy reliance on the history of physics), but in the less formalistic life and human sciences, the strings may be entirely linguistic. In the linguistic cases, the words would receive some rather ordinary interpretation, which would be insufficient for pursuing research. Since very few linguistically expressed theories are "systematic" in the sense that mathematically expressed ones are (that is, explicitly deductive in structure), it is perhaps better to regard the linguistic strings as a "canonical text," the suggestion being that there may be several different reading canons, depending on one's research program (Masterman 1970).

In the disciplines where theories tend to be expressed solely in natural languages, two scientists would share the same theory if they recognize each other as engaged in the same disciplinary discourse (regardless of what each might mean by what he said). For example, the sentence, "The unconscious causes the repression of infantile desires," uttered by members of many different schools of psychology (for example, Freudian psychoanalysis and the Miller-Dollard behaviorist reformulation of Freud), may be derived from other related sentences and may be used to derive still other sentences. Moreover, all the psychologists uttering this sentence would make sure that appropriate terms are on either side of the "causes." However, disagreement arises once we wish to say anything more about this sentence, namely, its interpretation. The schools of interpretation generally focus on the "linguistic function" (Popper 1972, pp. 119-122) that the sentence performs in their respective research programs, and this would be the source of the kinds of debates that philosophers of science are most likely to call "methodological."

We earlier noted some possible interpretations of the formalism of Newtonian mechanics, and, likewise, the Freudian sentence may be subjected to various instrumentalist and realist readings. Whereas Freud and his immediate disciples seem to have thought that the terms in "The unconscious causes the repression of infantile desires" have real referents in human beings, Miller and Dollard tied each of the terms to specific experimental operations that could be performed on rats. These Yale behaviorists adopted Freudian "theory" (that is, in the Kuhnian sense of the Freudian way of talking about things) simply because its lexical richness captured (at least in name) many of the aspects of an organism's affective life that could not be adequately expressed in Clark Hull's drive-reduction theory, inspite of the latter's explicitly hypothetico-deductive formulation. Although it is true that during the 1950s the psychoanalysts and the Yale behaviorists (as well as Neo-Freudian anthropologists) had all agreed to a Kuhnian sense of "Freudian theory," it would be seriously misleading to conclude that this involved a "rational consensus." Rather, Freudian theory is better seen as a versatile linguistic tool that happened to be available to serve diverse research interests at the time. The best way to see this point is to consider the conditions under which each of the programs would relinquish Freudian theory: the die-hard realists in psychoanalysis would probably never (which, for Popper and the positivists, would count them as holding the theory "metaphysically"), the behaviorists would do so as soon as a richer and/or more easily operationalized technical language had developed, and so forth (Miller 1959). In short, since a theory is a multifunctional tool, it may also be multidysfunctional. But can the same be same be said of Newtonian mechanics, which, after all, is Laudan's own example—and certainly a theory around which philosophers are more likely to find a consensus "rational"?

The case of Newtonian mechanics is more difficult to establish, if only because we must contend with over two centuries of Whig history. However, a good place to start would be with the eighteenth-century French scientific and philosophical community, the largest and most prestigious in Europe, which endorsed Newtonian mechanics with only the greatest reluctance. Usually this reluctance is attributed to the mathematical inelegance with which Newton originally formulated his mechanics, which made astronomical computations difficult. As the history is normally told, once Laplace's *Celestial Mechanics* started to appear in 1799, dissent was silenced, and so, not surprisingly, Laudan chooses 1800 as the year by which rational consensus had emerged over Newtonian mechanics.

But recently Ilya Prigogine has attempted to tell the history somewhat differently, in a book that has been especially influential among French philosophers of science (Prigogine & Stengers 1984). As he sees it, the concern over the computational adequacy of Newtonian mechanics was merely a pretext for deeper problems that the French had with the theory. In particular, the Encyclopedists Diderot and d'Alembert were troubled by what the Lakatosians call the "Kuhn Loss" involved in the Newtonian synthesis. Kuhn Loss describes the feature of paradigm change that prevents it from being unequivocally progressive, namely, a retraction of part of the old knowledge base. A crucial difference between Galileo and the fourteenth-century Parisian natural philosophers Nicholas of Oresme and John Buridan was that Galileo aspired to account for only what the Aristotelians called "local motion," one of Aristotle's four types of motion. The Newtonian synthesis made Galileo's break historically irreversible, since the mathematical power of Newton's theory far outweighed its rather metaphysically limited treatment of motion as the change of bodies in time and space. However, the Encyclopedists remained disturbed by this Kuhn Loss, especially the difficulties it spelled for accommodating the "generation and corruption" aspect of the old Aristotelian theory of motion to Newton's static picture of the universe (for example, Newton's Laws of Motion are reversible in time).

As largely earth-bound and historically oriented theorists, the Encyclopedists took the explanation of such thermodynamic phenomena as heat and life as the cornerstone of any adequate physical theory. Since Newtonian mechanics seemed to make such phenomena more mysterious than they already were, it was only a marriage of computational convenience that wedded the French to the theory. Indeed, Prigogine (1984, pp. 62-68) suggests that the extensive refinement and testing of Newtonian mechanics in which the French dominated throughout the eighteenth century was born from the intent to falsify it. A crucial year here is 1747, when d'Alembert, Euler, and Clairault all thought they had shown that Newton's formula for gravitational attraction could not account for the moon's orbit. Since this looked like a definitive refutation, d'Alembert—in typical Enlightenment fashion—advertised for a successor to Newtonian mechanics. However, two years later their calculations were shown to be in error.

It is easy to conclude that since no more refutations were forthcoming, and the next generation of scientists—led by Lagrange and Laplace—cleared up any doubts that remained about the computational adequacy of Newtonian mechanics, rational consensus had been achieved. Moreover, as Prigogine points out, by the end of the eighteenth century, claims that Newton had discovered the real structure of the universe were as numerous in France as in Newton's native England. Discounting, for the sake of argument, our earlier objection that each of the relevant intellectuals probably backed their claim by a combination of reasons that would not have been mutually acceptable (or acceptable to us, for that matter), would this joint profession of realism constitute a rational consensus over Newtonian mechanics? No, for Prigogine's account of the gradual emergence of thermodynamics suggests still another reason for questioning the consensus, though admittedly it is one that must be teased out of Prigogine's own ambivalence to the success of Newtonian mechanics (since, after all, Prigogine maintains that its overwhelming success—at least in Whiggish retrospect—impeded the rise of his own discipline, thermodynamics).

To get at this new objection, let us start by asking which groups of individuals would and would not be relevant for determining whether a rational consensus existed over Newtonian mechanics in 1800. The obvious place to turn would be to the disciplinary boundaries of the time: Who were the physicists and who were not? Unfortunately, the rigid disciplinary boundaries that we today associate with academic departments did not emerge until well into nineteenth century. Philosophers of science often forget this crucial fact, which contributes to the ease with which they are able to detach the "scientific" from the "philosophical," "theological," and "political" reasons that a "natural philosopher" gives for endorsing a particular theory. While this distinction may be clear to us, it was not so clear to them. Indeed, it may have been the subject of controversy. Here we are specifically interested in whether chemistry and biology were so easily detachable from physics in the late eighteenth century.

Prigogine (1984, pp. 79-85) notes that Diderot cited Georg Stahl's phlogiston chemistry and vitalist biology as promising lines of inquiry that could well overturn Newtonian mechanics in the long run. Although philosophers of science Whiggishly focus on Stahl's ill-fated phlogiston as the precursor of scientific chemistry, he conceived of his research program as one anti-Newtonian package. Among Stahl's lasting contributions was to stress the role of "organization" in chemical and biological phenomena, which came to be the basis of nineteenth-century arguments for the "emergent" and "organic" character of life forms. Given the hindsight of today's disciplinary boundaries, it would be easy to place Stahl's program on the losing side of several major theoretical debates in chemistry and biology and to exclude the program from debates over Newtonian mechanics. Indeed, in 1800, a vocal community of anti-Newtonians influenced by Stahl was present in Germany—the *Naturphilosophen* (including Schelling, Hegel, and Goethe)—whom, for presumably these Whiggish reasons, Laudan does not consider relevant for determining whether there was a rational consensus over Newtonian mechanics.

But perhaps we have not been sufficiently charitable in presenting Laudan's reasons. One traditional reason why Laudan may not have wanted to treat the *Naturphilosophen* as a serious group of anti-Newtonians is that their substantive contributions to science amounted to little more than criticism of, admittedly, glaring holes in Newton's world-system. And most of the criticism was itself on a priori metaphysical considerations about the organic nature of reality. In this regard, the *Naturphilosophen* are perhaps better compared to contemporary Creationist biologists, whose real stock-in-trade is to highlight the inadequacies of the Neo-Darwinian synthesis, despite the idle gestures toward a divine explanation grounded on biblical exegesis. In other words, was the research tradition of *Naturphilosophie* articulated in a way that could positively direct empirical scientific research?

According to L. Pearce Williams (1967), the answer is yes, especially in the development of electromagnetic field theory. After reading Schelling, Hans Christiaan Oersted was converted to the idea that electricity was a force and not a special form of matter, as the Newtonians had maintained. Oersted concluded that it should be possible to electrically induce magnetism, since all that would be involved would be a conversion of forces. He eventually demonstrated this effect by the simple experiment of bringing a compass near an electrically charged wire and noting the movement of the needle. Soon afterward, the Newtonian Ampere observed that no one had thought of performing such a simple experiment earlier because scientists had been convinced that Coulomb had proven that electricity and magnetism were two separate fluids, similar only in being governed by Newton's inverse square law.

We may suggest one final reason why Laudan may not want to include the *Naturphilosophen*. A general feature of Laudan's conception of scientific rationality is that consensus forms over a theory which solves more empirical problems than it generates conceptual problems. In that case, the guiding assumption of both the Encyclopedists and the *Naturphilosophen* was that Newtonian mechanics had failed by Laudan's criteria, since it lost the cosmic unity epitomized by Aristotle's theory of motion and gained "mere" computational efficiency in its stead. Regardless of how he evaluates the contributions that Stahl's followers made to solving the conceptual problem of cosmic unity, Laudan never explains why such a major Kuhn Loss should not weigh heavily (and negatively) in our cost-benefit analysis of Newtonian mechanics' problem-solving effectiveness. It is in this critical spirit that we should thus take Feyerabend's (1975, ch. 12) occasional pronouncements that modern science has *devolved* from the science of the classical Greeks.

4. Implications for the Historiography of Science

Now where do we stand? We started with the observation, frequently made by philosophers and sociologists but especially highlighted by Laudan, that science is distinguished by its rapid consensus formation and dissolution. Unlike Kuhn, Laudan suggests a "rational" explanation for how disputes are managed in science. We have called into question whether any such "design" account of science is in fact needed. As we have seen, what Laudan would call a rational consensus reveals itself historically to be a much more superficial phenomenon than he suggests—perhaps merely an agreement to talk in a certain way or to use certain equations in one's calculations. And if the consensus is relatively superficial, then it is fundamentally unstable, and for that reason alone it would tend to form and dissolve quickly, much like the consensuses that pollsters find in the electorate. Thus, Laudan's "rational consensus" ought to be an essential consensus, whereby the actual interaction of all the relevant parties would lead to a mutual understanding not only about the physical object(s) of agreement (one sort of text rather than another: the "theory"), but also about the aspect(s) under which that object is to be regarded (the linguistic function performed by the text: the interpretation or "method"). This latter feature would include, among other things, an agreement over the conditions for relinquishing a given text-plus-interpretation, and thereby explain rapid consensus dissolution.

And while the kind of essential consensus just described exists in localized pockets (for example, a research team at a university), it is unlikely to exist as the impressive global phenomenon that Laudan suggests. On the global level, there is less mutual monitoring and hence more opportunity for differences in interpretation of the same text to arise. This becomes the basis of the unjustly maligned *incommensurability thesis*. But notice here that we have shifted the basis of the thesis. Normally, incommensurability is alleged between two fully interpreted theories that seem to divide the world differently, such that tokens of the same type identified in one theory do not appear in translation as tokens of the same type identified in the other theory. In that case, as Philip Kitcher (1978) has pointed out, the obvious solution is to claim that there is only token-token correspondence between the two theories. For example, although instances of "phlogiston" do not always refer to instances of the same substance identified in modern chemical theory, they do refer to instances of some substance that can be identified in modern chemical theory.

However, to resolve the incommensurability between the two chemistries in this manner is to muddle "theoretical" and "methodological" considerations (in our Kuhnian sense of this distinction) by supposing that the linguistic function common to all scientific theories is something like "representation" or "reference." And while it is easy for the philosopher to retrospectively regard all theories as attempts at revealing the structure of the universe or some part of it, this would be to commit them all what Laudan (1984, ch. 5) has called "intentional realism." This commitment would, of course, involve a gross distortion of the history of science, since the methodological disputes therein show that the text of a theory may be put to many uses aside from, or instead of, representing reality. And so, the appropriate object about which incommensurable interpretations arise is a canonical text, not "the world," whatever that might be. The incommensurable interpretations are different linguistic functions that the same text may perform—representational, instrumental, hypothetical, and so forth.

Incommensurability, in our sense, may be detected among the various interpretations of Newtonian mechanics offered in the eighteenth century. As we have seen, even the consensus on the computational adequacy of the theory, which allegedly united Newton's English supporters and Stahl's French supporters, turned out to be more superficial than it first seemed: the latter group saw the computational adequacy of Newton's theory as an obstacle to be overcome rather than to be built on. As we shall now see, the controversy over the existence of chemical forces makes this point more vividly, for here incommensurability can be seen to fluorish between scientific communities who had defined themselves as wholeheartedly pro-Newtonian (Guerlac 1965).

First recall that among the most striking features of Newton's methodology was its admittedly uneasy acceptance of both mathematization and experimentation as routes to knowledge. This distinguished it from, on the one hand, the mathematical but antiexperimental Cartesian method and, on the other hand, the experimental but antimathematical Baconian method. Although I.B. Cohen (1981) is correct that this alliance has at least been strong enough as a "style" to color the last three hundred years of scientific practice, interpretations of this practice have often tended toward either the Cartesian or the Baconian extreme.

For example, a professed French defender of the Newtonian cause, Maupertuis, did both mathematics and experiments, most notably in the case of calculating the earth's shape on the basis of Newton's hypothesis that the force of gravity was weaker at the equator than at the poles, and then traveling to Peru and Lapland to check the results. However, like the other French Newtonians, the results of the experiments were always treated as measurements to be checked against the original mathematical computations, never as evidence for the existence of particular entities, as the Baconian side of Newton would have it. Thus, as formulated by the French Newtonians, the problem of chemical forces would be solved by the discovery of inverse square laws at the various levels of nature, with the metaphysical status of these forces left open and, in any case, not experimentally decidable. This "proto-positivism" of the French Newtonians explains how they were able to work so well with the anti-Newtonian Diderot in constructing the Encyclopedia.

On the other hand, Newton's followers in medicine, many of whom were trained by Hermann Boerhaave (or through one of his textbooks), stressed the appropriateness of drawing metaphysical inferences from experimental results, which led them to develop accounts of chemical forces in terms of aether-like fluids of subtle particles having varying densities which repelled each other and larger bodies as well. Boerhaave had called the ultimate aether "fire," and it turned out be especially influential on the Scottish physician Joseph Black, who understood his theory of specific and latent heats as an elaboration of Boerhaave's speculations. This, in turn, was taken to support a generally Stahlian view of chemical forces.

Indeed, after examining the instability of the Newtonian consensus on the issue of chemical forces, Arnold Thackray (1970; compare Schofield 1970) has argued that the supposedly united pursuit of the Newtonian research program in the eighteenth century actually had long term anti-Newtonian implications for the development of chemistry in the nineteenth century. Having said this, however, it must be admitted that the eighteenth century has been traditionally portrayed as a gradual convergence of opinion on the acceptability of Newtonian mechanics. On the basis of our earlier discussion, even before looking closely at the history, there are three reasons why this picture is bound to be misleading.

The Latency of Imcommensurability: Until philosophers, or scientists in the guise of philosophers, get into the act of trying to legislate methodological rules for every research community, methodological differences—the source of incommensurability—can remain hidden as different communities perform linguistic functions appropriate to their respective research programs on the same theory. Moreover, this latency effect is likely to have been common through the entire history of science, during which, for different reasons, major research has usually been conducted in secrecy. Before the Scientific Revolution, scholars saw themselves primarily as preserving and transmitting a body of knowledge that could be appreciated by a small group of similarly learned individuals. Thus, Copernicus was hardly unique in thinking that the heliocentric theory of the universe should not be publicized, for the fear of disrupting the masses. After the Scientific Revolution, despite an official ideology of openness, research likely to have an impact on the general public has usually been suppressed in the name of public stability, while the possibility of discovering "new" knowledge has led to much secret research punctuated by priority disputes (Boorstin 1983, pp. 408-418). With all these opportunities for miscommunication, intentional or otherwise, we should expect a widespread incidence of incommensurability.

Let us look at an example of this phenomenon drawn from our earlier discussion. Eighteenth-century English and French scientists, say, can communicate without any trouble about the latest refinement made on the mathematical features of Newtonian mechanics—just as long as they do not inquire of one another into the deeper question of why each would be interested in such information. For in that case, the Englishman would confess his interest in fine-tuning the world system so as to more adequately represent the way things really are, while the Frenchman would admit his stake in seeing the only redeeming feature of the world system, its computational adequacy, subverted as quickly as possible. Against this point, a glib logician may argue that in fact the Englishman's and Frenchman's uses of Newtonian mechanics are "commensurable" in a very ordinary sense: namely, the Englishman aims to verify what the Frenchman aims to falsify. To keep such facile remarks at bay, we must note that many of the French scientists regarded Newtonian mechanics as the Aristotelians regarded Ptolemaic astronomy—as a purely predictive instrument, which may work well or not, but which could not be "true" or "false." Again, the difference in linguistic functions has not been observed by the logician.

Disjoining the Reasons: Each scientist probably endorsed Newtonian mechanics for a combination of reasons that are misleadingly regarded as a set of alternatives from which the philosopher may choose the ones he finds retrospectively rational. This shift in the logical structure of the scientist's reasoning is misleading *not* because there would be no overlap among the reasons offered by all the scientisits (for there would be, especially among those in regular interaction with one another); but because the overlapping reasons, while perhaps necessary, would certainly not have been sufficient to motivate all the scientists that are said to have formed a rational consensus.

Deciding Who is Eligible: It is much too easy for the philosopher to circumscribe which individuals were in retrospect relevant for achieving a rational consensus, so that persistent disagreements—such as the one we noted between the Stahlians and the Newtonians—can be eliminated. To prevent this Whiggish maneuver, the philosopher should be restricted to circumscribing the relevant individuals within the disciplinary boundaries in effect at the time of the alleged consensus.

At this point, let us dispose one possible objection to the way in which we have criticized consensualism in the philosophy of science. A radical retrospective rationalist, such as Lakatos, might argue that the history of science is really little more than a Rorschach inkblot test for the philosopher's sense of scientific rationality. In that case, the philosopher simply reads the history for episodes that intuitively strike him as paradigm cases of rational theory choice, and then analyzes these episodes to attain a more precise sense of the basis for his intuitive response. Indeed, upon analyzing his intuitions, Lakatos decided that even the better episodes needed to be tidied up before appearing fully rational. Thus, it should come as no surprise that philosophers misrepresent the history of science in all kinds of ways, including the ones we have cited. Unless we were to argue the difficult—and rather Hegelian—case that every episode in the history of science has involved optimally rational decision making (perhaps unbeknownst to the reasoner at the time, but knowable to the philosophical historian who adopts the long term perspective of the Cunning of Reason), it would seem that a completely accurate history of science is not necessary for the philosopher's task of designing a theory of scientific rationality. In short, one cannot derive the philosopher's ought-statements about scientific decision making from the historian's is-statements about such decision making.

This objection is met by first pointing out that even though the historian's statements do not entail the philosopher's, philosophical statements about scientific decision making do seem to presuppose statements about historical possibility. Whereas the objection was formulated in terms of Hume's moral injunction, *"is" does not imply "ought,"* it may now be rebutted in terms of a naturalized version of Kant's corresponding injunction: *"ought" implies "can."* That is, a statement about how scientists ought to reach a consensus over which theory to accept implies a statement about at least one historical case in which the proposed norm was operative. If no historical case can withstand the kinds of criticism that we have just raised against the alleged consensus over Newtonian mechanics, then that is good grounds for concluding that the proposed norm is historically impossible (compare Bartley 1984, pp. 199-202). In that case, we might want then to argue that once the group of scientists relevant for a particular decision reaches a certain number and are sufficiently dispersed, it becomes impracticable to suppose that the group could reach what we have called an "essential consensus" as deep as would be necessary to support Laudan's thesis; for the intensive interaction required of the scientists simply could not occur. Thus, the naturalistic philosopher of science would be advised to study the "phenomenological geography" of scientific interactions, that is, the effects of that the spatiotemporal distances between scientists have on their ability to regulate their own activities (Collins 1981, Giddens 1984).

Less extreme but just as skeptical of the critique we have been launching is the claim—implicit in the works of virtually all philosophers of science—that the history of science may be "selectively read" without actually being misread. For example, Popperians, with their global view of the history of science, claim that they do not need an account of the actual events in as fine a detail as the professional historian is likely to provide. However, in light of our discussion of the logical structure of the reasoning of scientists, it should be clear that "selective reading" may simply involve misreading what the scientist took—and what most of us, in a similar situation, would take—for granted about the interdependency of his reasons in justifying a theory choice. Although the term "misreading" is normally reserved for interpretations that contradict something explicitly said, our critique of Laudan suggests that the term should also be extended to cover cases in which the tacit presuppositions of "conversational implicature" and other pragmatic features of the scientist's discourse are contradicted. If authors calculate what they need to say in order to convey the maximum information to their intended readership, then it follows that all texts presuppose a missing "subtext" that, were it articulated, would specify the knowledge common to the author and his intended readers. Despite its tacit status (largely in the interest of economizing expression, as discussed in ch. 6), the subtext is nevertheless just as determinate in meaning as the words which actually appear on the page.

Pending refutation, our own position is that of the deconstructionist, who holds that a selective reading is merely a subtler form of sheer misreading. The difference between the deconstructionist and, say, the Lakatosian is that the Lakatosian thinks he has a choice as to whether and to what extent he needs to rely on an historical account in order to derive his theory of scientific rationality. In contrast, the deconstructionist thinks that no choice is to be had, since misreading is inevitable, at least given the way in which history tends to be written—namely, without much concern for the pragmatics of the original utterances. However, our inevitable miswriting of history is normally concealed from view by a complex network of rationalization strategies. For a sense of how these strategies work, consider the following brief deconstruction of the Whig history on which Laudan relies for his account of scientific rationality.

In arguing that Newtonian mechanics solved more problems than it caused, Laudan is implicitly suggesting that by 1800 the Western scientific community had committed itself (that is, its socioeconomic and intellectual resources) to "local motion" as a kind of motion whose study may be pursued in its own right without any concern for the other kinds of motion identified by Aristotle. Another way of putting this is that, at that point, physics becomes the autonomous and cognitively dominant discipline we recognize today. Were we not the beneficiaries of this commitment, the trade-off implicitly required would appear somewhat less than reasonable, since computational adequacy had been bought at the cost of cosmic unity. However, measures have since been taken to ensure that this cost is not noticed: for example, the fragmentation of the sciences and the attendant rewriting of history needed to show that such a division of cognitive labor was inevitable, the unequivocal identification of the cognitively developed with the mathematized, and so forth. Once these tactics have been deployed, sour grapes (Elster 1984) about any alternative history of science easily sets in. Consider this hypothetical account:

> Of course, it paid for physics to split off from the other sciences. Just look at the evidence. Even to this day, the other forms of Aristotelian motion have not been as well quantified as physical motion. Had we waited for "The Loyal Opposition" (of Encyclopedists, *Naturphilosophen*, and other friends of Stahl) to reassert the Aristotelian synthesis, we would never be where we are today.

True enough—just as long as we do not wonder whether the standard of scientific progress might have been different had we "waited" for the Loyal

Opposition to reassert Aristotle. That we were optimally rational for not having waited can be shown, if the cost of relinquishing the Newtonian historical trajectory is made to appear high and the benefit to be derived from following through on the Aristotelian trajectory is made to appear low. One way of doing this would be by arguing that *at best* the Loyal Opposition would have had to meet the mathematical standards of our physics to be equally progressive, while *at worst* the Loyal Opposition would have fallen below the standard and thus be less progressive than our physics (Fuller 1985a, ch. 2). The possibility that a reassertion of Aristotle would yield benefits that are not particularly well exemplified in our science goes unmentioned. And so, were we even to agree with Laudan and the rest that a rational consensus in the deep, essential sense occurred over Newtonian mechanics, it would have to be seen as a risky venture, just given its implicit renunciation of the Aristotelian ideal. However, in retrospect and through historiographical rationalization, this risk has been reinterpreted as the natural course of events, since neither our cognitive ends nor the means for measuring our distance from those ends is any longer Aristotelian.

CHAPTER TEN

FROM MORAL PSYCHOLOGY TO COGNITIVE SOCIOLOGY: MAKING SENSE OF THE FORMAN THESIS

The Forman Thesis—that physicists adopted quantum indeterminism in response to the cultural milieu of Weimar Germany—is typical of many historical claims disputed by philosophers and sociologists of science in that it tends to be treated as a claim, not so much about the influence of social factors in the production of knowledge, as about the mental states of the participating scientists. Consequently, much has been said about empirically unresolvable issues concerning the "rationality" of the scientists' intentions, as if the scientists themselves had a strict sense of the distinction between intellectual and social factors. This has all been to the distinct disadvantage of social historians and their philosophical defenders, as epitomized in what I call the *Strong Objection to the Sociology of Science*. To counter this objection, the social historian needs to explain those features of a given historical context which the relevant individuals are *least likely* to regard as socio-historically variable. I propose a historiographical strategy rooted in Marx's theory of reification and approximated by Pierre Bourdieu and Michel Foucault.

1. The Social Historian in the Grip of Moral Psychology

From the first few pages of Forman (1971), it would appear that intellectualist history of science is about to be dealt a lethal blow by social history. After observing that intellectualists like Max Jammer "explain" the acceptance of quantum indeterminacy in the 1920s simply by pointing to the availability of indeterminist ideas in Europe over the previous half century, Forman remarks that such "explanations" are entirely ahistorical, for they explain neither (i) why physicists had not accepted those ideas earlier, nor (ii) why they happened to accept them when they finally did. Jammer and the rest seem to assume that the historian only needs to show that the indeterminacy thesis was reasonable in light of the evidence and theories available. But as Forman points out, this hardly explains why indeterminacy was accepted rather than some other equally reasonable alternative. Moreover, the intellectualists may be guilty of superimposing clear-cut theoretical alternatives on a situation where none existed prior to the need to make a decision. This would certainly explain why Forman and other social historians typically ignore or downplay the "evidence" that intellectualists say "test" alternative "theories"; for the social historian would take the items in scare quotes as having a clear sense only in retrospect, especially to the parties whose "theory" survived the "test" of "evidence." In short, Forman takes seriously the possibility that only the presence of "external" social pressure forced the scientists to identify distinct theories from which a choice could then be made.

Indeed, the moral of Forman's paper may be that if historians stick to the typical strategies of the intellectualist, they will remain unable to explain why scientists ever feel the need to stop debate and agree to pursue a particular theory. After all, philosophers, who are ostensibly rational inquirers, do not seem to place such a premium on consensus. But then philosophers do not need to marshal the kinds of material and social resources that scientists need for continuing their inquiries. A radical extension of this line of thinking (which unfortunately cannot be pursued here) is that the rationality of the scientist lies not in how he selects theories, but in how he selects the *occasions for selecting theories,* ideally in order to maximize the likelihood that any theory he selects on that occasion will prolong his research in fruitful directions (for evidence from actual scientific practice, see Knorr-Cetina [1982]). In contrast, intellectual historians and their philosophical backers simply presume that the moment of theory choice was rationally selected, the only questions for them being whether the right theory was chosen at that time and for the right reasons. Yet the potential to lay the empirical foundations of a normative sociology of science was somehow lost in the execution of the Forman Thesis. However, this failure is not peculiar to Forman, but indicative of deep-seated problems in how the partisans of intellectual and social history of science have argued about the significance of case studies.

For a sense of the sweeping and provocative character of the Forman Thesis and the evidence mustered in its support, let us consider the following remarks by its author:

> The possibility of the crisis of the old quantum theory was dependent upon the physicists' own craving for crises, arising from participation in, and adaptation to, the Weimar intellectual milieu. In support of this general interpretation I illustrated and emphasized the fact that the program of dispensing with causality in physics was, on the one hand, advanced quite suddenly after 1918 and, on the other hand, that it achieved a very substantial following among German physicists before it was "justified" by the advent of a fundamentally acausal quantum mechanics. I contended, moreover, that the scientific context and content...point inescapably to the conclusion that substantive problems in atomic physics played only a secondary role in the genesis of this acausal persuasion, that the most important factor was the social-intellectual pressure exerted upon the physicists as members of the German academic community. [Forman 1971, pp. 62, 110]

Notice at the outset that Forman adheres to the received distinction between "internal" (intellectual) and "external" (social) histories of science, though, significantly, he restricts the scope of internal history to physics proper, and relegates contemporary debates in other disciplines (especially philosophy) and the general intellectual culture to an undifferentiated realm of "socio-intellectual pressure." This unusual restriction on the scope of internal history justifies Forman's rather liberal use of philosophical texts (including Mach and Reichenbach) in defense of his thesis. It may also lead one to wonder whether Forman is only a pseudosocial historian, since, for the most part, he draws on the same kind of evidence as an intellectual historian of the same period would.

However, whereas the intellectualist would trace the sudden rise of talk of indeterminism to the merit of contemporary arguments made in a relatively open forum of inquiry and criticism, Forman traces it to the physicists' need to adapt to what they perceived to be the dominant current of thought at the time. And although Forman clearly believes in the authenticity of the physicists' conversion to indeterminism, it is also clear (at least to Forman) that had they not made the conversion, the future of physics as a socially organized form of inquiry would have been jeopardized. Indeed, only at this point does he introduce evidence that the intellectual historian would not normally consider, namely, the Weimar policy statements on education and research priorities (pp. 19-29). Therefore, even if Forman is only a pseudosocial historian as far as selection of evidence is concerned, he seems to be a true social historian when it comes to the sorts of purposes for which he uses that evidence.

But on closer inspection does even this turn out to be true? The Forman Thesis ostensibly is concerned with the role that social factors played in forcing an otherwise indecisive group of physicists to select a particular account of quantum phenomena. Yet much of Forman's paper (and the source of subsequent criticism of it) is devoted to making the more difficult case that the physicists themselves had a clear sense of the difference between the intellectual and social factors operating in their work, and that they also believed that social factors could "genuinely" solve problems of intellectual origin. This is a difficult case for all parties, largely because it involves penetrating not the sociology of science, but the psychology of the scientists.

For example, while Forman provides evidence that many physicists suddenly after 1918 endorsed some form of indeterminism, and even that they used some of the same Spengler-inspired anticausality rhetoric that was widespread in the general culture of the time, he provides no evidence that the physicists' talk of indeterminism was a calculated response to the popular talk. If the Forman Thesis did not depend on the presence of this evidential link, its absence would not be surprising. For as Bourdieu (1977) and Foucault (1979) have observed, the use of language is socially effective only when it serves to restrict access to a domain of objects of general interest. Thus, the esoteric languages of the professions—theology, medicine, law, and psychiatry—bestow on their speakers a credibility and legitimacy in the eyes of nonspeakers. Conversely, if the Spenglerian idiom is common to many sectors of Weimar society, then while it might be expected that physicists would also come to employ the idiom, simply the fact that they do so is unlikely add to the credibility, legitimacy, or even popularity of the physicists. However, Forman (1971, p. 103) also argues, in a Bourdieu-Foucault fashion, that one of the ways in which the physicists, especially Arnold Sommerfeld, tried to consolidate their clout was by claiming that they could provide explanations where Spengler and other popularizers could only offer metaphors.

For their part, intellectual historians would also find the pervasive Spenglerian idiom unexceptional, treating it—as they tend to do all strictly linguistic phenomena—as a bit of period "noise," eminently translatable into an idiom more conducive to evaluating its "cognitive content" in light of the theoretical and empirical knowledge of the time. We shall later consider an alternative assessment of the significance of linguistic evidence for the Forman Thesis, one stressing its key to the objective, rather than the subjective, features of Weimar physics. But for now, we see that attempts at drawing inferences about the intentions of the Weimar physicists from their use of language are inconclusive at best. Yet the debate over the Forman Thesis has been conducted on precisely this psychologistic plane. Consider that the bulk of the debate over the Forman Thesis has centered on the following two points:

(a) Would the physicists have been inclined to quantum level, had the cultural milieu not been especially conducive to such a *belief?* Did considerations raised by Spengler and other popular "philosophers of life" really cause the physicists to change their *minds* about indeterminacy?

(b) Would the physicists have espoused indeterminacy had it not served their *interests?* In other words, were they *sincere* in their accommodation to the cultural milieu?

The italicized words appear in the glosses of both friends and foes of the Forman Thesis, and, indeed, in Forman's own glosses at the beginning and end of his paper. They invite the potential critic to see whether Forman's evidence—mostly public addresses of the physicists, with some correspondence and excerpts from the prefaces of current books—licenses certain inferences about the psychology of the relevant physicists. Thus, Forman sometimes casts his own thesis as an attempt to show that the questions raised in (a) are to be answered in the affirmative. In turn, his chief critic among historians, John Hendry (1980), tries to demonstrate that in spite of their sensitivity to the cultural milieu, the physicists sincerely thought that "life-philosophical" considerations were irrelevant to scientific debates. And kibitzing from Edinburgh, Barry Barnes (1974, p. 111) and David Bloor (1982) have taken the Forman Thesis to imply that scientists, like ordinary human beings, will publicly advance beliefs that best suit their interests. Very quickly, then, the debate over the social origins of quantum indeterminacy has evaporated into a dispute over the moral psychology of the Weimar physicists.

A vivid illustration of this last point is to be found in the most sympathetic treatment to date of the Forman Thesis by a philosopher of science with strong intellectualist leanings, Andrew Lugg. Instead of either denying any role to "social factors" in the causation of scientific beliefs or relegating such factors to the causation of unjustified beliefs, Lugg has distinguished two senses in which scientific beliefs may be "caused." In evaluating the Forman Thesis, Andrew Lugg (1984) would have us separate what *determined* the Weimar physicists to believe in quantum indeterminacy (as opposed to quantum determinism, or some other theoretical possibility) from what *occasioned* them to have such a belief when they did (and not earlier or later). Lugg argues that the Forman Thesis pertains only to causation in the "occasioned" sense, a conclusion in accordance with Forman's own remarks about why he undertook the study of Weimar physics. Once this point is made, we can grant its value, says Lugg, yet see it as different from the point that intellectual historians normally try to make about the theoretical and empirical reasons that determined a theory choice.

But Lugg then advances a further claim, one that pertains not to conceptual distinctions available to the historian, but to psychological distinctions available to the historical agents. He says that social pressures may force scientists to choose a particular theory without those pressures actually being part of the reason for selecting the theory. Thus, the Forman Thesis can be seen "as suggesting that the physicists' *recognition* of the anti-mechanism and anti-determinism then being advocated resulted in *appreciating* more fully the possibility of coherently introducing indeterminism into physics" (Lugg 1984, p. 187). As my italics show, this is clearly a claim about the mental states of the Weimar physicists. But what exactly does it say? Consider three possible interpretations, each entailing a different moral appraisal of the physicists:

(c) The social milieu exerted an unconscious pressure on the scientists to decide on the nature of quantum mechanics, which was consciously done for methodologically sound reasons. Thus, the scientists appear to have been *amoral* decision makers.

(d) The scientists, fully aware of the pressure from the social milieu, nevertheless did not allow that pressure to enter their deliberations about theory choice. Thus, the scientists appear to have been *moral* decision makers.

(e) The scientists fully realized that the social milieu was pressuring them to make a decision, yet they also realized that publicly acknowledging this fact as motivating their considerations would undermine their credibility. Thus, the scientists appear to have been *immoral* decision makers.

It is unlikely that an intellectualist like Lugg would want to admit (c) as a gloss of his claim, since it portrays the scientists as laboring under false consciousness, with the "good reasons" they offer for their theory choice becoming little more than a form of self-deception, epiphenomenal on the real social sources of their behavior. As a result, an acceptance of (c) would make it difficult to make the usual attributions of "rationality" to scientists, since they would be shown not to have made a genuinely unconstrained choice.

In contrast, (d) presents the scientists in an ideally rational light from the standpoint of the intellectual historian. However, it presupposes that the scientists themselves had a clear sense of the historian's distinction between intellectual and social factors in the causation of scientific beliefs, as well as of the inappropriateness of the social factors, no matter how pervasive they might be. Even granting this Whiggish presupposition, we are left with the striking coincidence that quantum indeterminacy was accepted exactly at the moment when social pressure seemed to have been the strongest, since (d) would have predicted that this fact would play no role whatsoever in their deliberations.

Finally, (e) would have the scientists engage in what Erving Goffman (1959) has called "impression management," whereby the theory choice of the scientists is portrayed as calculated to have a specific effect on the intended audience, regardless of whether this represents the scientists' real beliefs. Thus, in order to consolidate their flagging social status, the scientists would be seen as articulating only those features of the current physics which dovetailed with the cultural milieu, and suppressing any doubts or difficulties that might be read as conflicting with that milieu. All of this is done deliberately. Yet since it is also all done by manipulating the discourse of physics, the lie is difficult to catch.

Barnes (1982) has tried to rescue (e) from making the scientists appear too unsavory by arguing that since theories are always underdetermined by the evidence anyway, we can never reasonably speak of a scientist advancing one theory in full knowledge that another is "really" better supported. Unfortunately, as in the case of (d), we are again faced with the striking coincidence of when and how the underdetermination happens to get resolved. After all, if theory choices are indeed underdetermined, why not publicize that fact once a theory is finally selected, and thereby allow debate to continue? Such openness would clearly meet Popperian standards of intellectual integrity. But as it stands, by closing their ranks, the scientists make it seem that the choice made was the only one that could have rationally been made. We see then that despite Lugg's sensitive attempt at integrating the intellectual and social historical features of science, it remains for the intellectual historian to make his version of the scientist psychologically credible and for the social historian to make his version morally appealing.

2. Toward Cognitive Sociology and the Problem of Objectivity

But ultimately, the problem with interpreting the Forman Thesis as being about the mental states of a group of physicists is that even if it is resolved in the social historian's favor, it will remain of little consequence to the kinds of claims normally advanced by philosophers of science and defended with evidence provided by intellectual historians. At best, Forman will have established that social causation operates at the subjective level: that is, particular scientists adopt particular beliefs to suit their particular interests. The significance of this conclusion can then be easily undermined by arguing that it goes no way toward explaining how subsequent scientists, including many of our own, have managed to sustain a belief in indeterminacy outside the Weimar milieu. The fact that these later scientists have been moved by quite different interests under quite different circumstances suggests that something "transsocial," so to speak, must underlie the validity of quantum indeterminacy. Indeed, the intellectualist might even go so far as to claim that the *more* socially determined the original adoption of quantum indeterminacy turns out to have been, the *less* likely that its continued acceptance can be explained in social terms. Were one still to insist on a social explanation, he would be saddled with the question of how quantum indeterminacy can be made to serve such diverse interests. Perhaps, the intellectualist would then suggest, only a theory that "really works" can be made to serve *any* social interest. If that is the case, then social interests play no role whatsoever in legitimating quantum indeterminacy. Needless to say, this response would reduce the cognitive import of the social history of science to mere epiphenomena. For future reference, let us call this argument the *Strong Objection to the Sociology of Science,* or SOSS. For though it has been underplayed in the literature (an exception is Laudan [1984a]), it is nevertheless the stiffest form of skepticism that the social historian is likely to meet from an intellectual historian.

In order to pose a serious challenge to philosophers and their intellectualist defenders, Forman must be taken as trying to show that the scientists' own sense of *objectivity* was socially generated. In other words, with all due respect to Barnes and Bloor, the case to prove is *not* that the question of determinism at the quantum level was open enough from the objective standpoint of theoretical and empirical support to permit the scientists' social interests to cast the deciding vote in favor of indeterminism. Rather, the objective standpoint itself, including the scientists' sense that it is extrasocial in origin, must be explained as the product of social practices. Clearly, the relevant social practices must have a special property, namely, that they conceal their own social nature, such that individuals engaged in those practices are led to think that they are in direct contact with an extrasocial reality—or at least a reality that requires relatively little social mediation. Once identified, these social practices should also be able to account for the intuitive strength of SOSS as an argument against the possibility of explaining the objectivity of science in exclusively sociological terms. This is a tall and tricky order to meet, but a general strategy for meeting it can be proposed.

First, something needs to be said about *the phenomenology of objectivity.* Under what circumstances does one experience something as being beyond one's conscious control? This was the problem faced by the German idealists after Kant who realized that they had to account not only for how the mind generates reality but also for how that reality appears to the mind as something *not* generated by it. In short, what accounts for the "externality" of external reality? The general idealist strategy for answering this question, especially in the hands of Fichte and Hegel, has been to distinguish the extent to which the mind determines *the world* from the extent to which the mind determines *itself.* In contrast to the first sort of "determinism," which is complete (and hence the metaphysical basis of idealism), the second sort of "determinism" is incomplete, implying that the mind cannot predict or control all of its own activity. The part of the mind that cannot be so controlled—that resists the efforts of its own will and intellect—is the metaphysical basis of matter, whose main phenomenal property is, not surprisingly, "inertness." What the mind fails to control, then, is not the world as some independent entity but the mind's own subsequent thoughts, which are, in turn, constitutive of a world that appears independent. Thus, if the mind were able to control the course of its own activity perfectly, then there would not even be an *apparent* difference between the mind and a reality external to it. Indeed, when Fichte and Hegel spoke of the history of mankind as "the progressive self-realization of reason," the end they had in mind was man's ability to freely choose his course of action, in virtue of knowing how his subsequent actions would be constrained by selecting each of the available options.

The phenomenology of objectivity has also been studied within the philosophy of science, though less centrally, by Quine and Popper. Here the issue involves reconciling a belief that science has some sort of access to ultimate reality with a belief that the scientist has virtually free rein in selecting a theory, which nevertheless is his only access to that reality. As befitting a deep metaphysical question, answers have been all too brief: Quine (1960) speaks of the scientist sensing the "recalcitrance" of data, which serves as the stimulus for revising his theory, while Popper (1963) appeals to "falsification" as a brute fact of personal experience in a way that recalls Samuel Johnson's manner of "refuting" Berkeley's idealism by kicking a stone. Moreover, post-Popperians, such as Kuhn, Lakatos, and Bloor (1979), have been just as cryptic, saying much about the scientific treatment of *anomalous results* but little about the phenomenon of *anomalousness* itself. This point is especially telling in the case of Bloor, who follows Mary Douglas in classifying cultures by their handling of anomalies. For even if Bloor (1983, ch. 7) has convincingly shown that anomalies are always "socially constructed" to satisfy the needs of a particular culture, he has yet to explain why, in the first place, did the society see itself as having to "adapt" to an anomalous situation. Notice that the phenomenon suggested by the philosophers of science as criterial of objectivity—anomalousness—is simply another expression of what the German idealists originally identified, namely, the lack of cognitive control over the world that one experiences when his intentions and/or expectations (in this case, scientific predictions) are thwarted, which then serve to constrain what one subsequently intends and expects.

In turning to the social historian of science and his philosophical backers, we may now pose an analogous problem—only here the relevant "mind" is collective rather than individual in nature. The general strategy we offer (in part borrowed from Hegel (see Schneider [1971]) involves attending to the fact that not only is an individual normally unable to anticipate all the consequences of acting on his intentions, but that this incapacity is compounded by the simultaneous activity of many individuals and, over a period of time, the activity of still other individuals who draw on the original individual's efforts. Notice that I do not deny that individuals have interests toward which their actions are oriented. Indeed, I admit that regarding individuals in this way can lead to an appreciation of the range of possible actions that the individuals saw at their disposal. However, despite Max Weber's claims for it, this approach offers little insight into why the individuals saw their possibilities for action as confined to that particular range *and nothing beyond it*, why they would consider anything outside that range as mere fancy. Yet only by addressing a question of this sort will we gain access to the features of the individual's experience that they took to be objective, and hence limiting on their possibilities for action. Then we can search for the socially generated source of this experience. As a point of departure for this inquiry, consider the following "brute facts" of social action:

> (f) Although an individual must engage in a given practice as a means to his own end, whether this end is actually brought about will depend, in large part, on how his actions (that is, the means he uses) are received by other individuals whose (at least implicit) cooperation he needs to insure his success. Their cooperation, in turn, hinges on whether the individual's actions display the appropriate competence, which may itself be quite incidental to the individual's original aim.

> (g) Although the individual engages in the practice as a means to his own ends, he is rarely able to gauge the full range of effects that his actions has in the long run, largely because his actions leave a material residue that becomes available for the use of other individuals, who may pursue ends which entail subverting the outcome intended by the original individual.

Arguably, all social practices, especially when regarded from an historical standpoint, exhibit these two characteristics. Still it is instructive for our purposes to mention them because they make it difficult to continue thinking of individuals simply as agents who freely use the available social resources as they see fit. As we earlier saw, such a conception lies behind both the standard intellectual and social historical accounts of science. On the one hand, the intellectual historian employs the voluntarist premise negatively, as a means of showing that the scientists had the strength of will to resist the temptations of the cultural milieu and to engage, instead, in Kantian feats of self-legislated methodical theory appraisal. On the other hand, the social historian puts the premise to positive work by portraying the scientists as ordinary moral consequentialists, sometimes utilitarian sometimes Machiavellian, who play out the game of science to their maximum advantage. Indicative of the freedom normally, albeit implicitly, attributed to scientists in most historical accounts is the ease with which their actions are susceptible to these kinds of crypto-ethical evaluations.

In light of the preceding remarks, the recent debate between Laudan (1981) and Bloor (1984) over the need for an "arationality assumption" in writing the history of science can be seen as really concerned with "rationality" in Weber's (1954) sense of comprehensive action orientations. Laudan would be taken as maintaining that scientific activity should be explained in purely value-rational *(wertrational)* terms—that is, as following from a steadfast adherence to the dictates of the scientific method—unless it has been shown that the scientists have reached less than exemplary conclusions. In that case, ends-rational *(zweckrational)* considerations start to play an explanatory role, as the "arational" scientists are seen to follow the scientific method, not as an end in itself, but only as long as it facilitates certain extrascientific interests. For his part, Bloor would then appear to be claiming that actual scientific practice does not differ in principle from the other forms of ends-rational activity characteristic of modern Western societies.

Once we see the recent rationality debates from this Weberian perspective, it becomes clear that for all their latent appeals to one or another moral psychology, neither Laudan nor Bloor brings us any closer to understanding the objective features of science. The reason, I submit, is that both philosophical defenders of the alternative historiographies of science focus exclusively on the subjective character of scientific activity—specifically, the scientist's self-understanding of the range of possible actions at his disposal, the choice from which can then be evaluated for its conformity to the preferred model of rational action.

At first glance, this critique does not seem to apply to Laudan and the intellectualists, who, after all, were credited with launching the first objectivist salvo against Forman. However, we must carefully sort out the positive and negative claims in their attack. The negative claim that quantum mechanics "really works" regardless of a physicist's particular social interests is logically independent of the positive claim that quantum mechanics "really works" because it was (and continues to be) the product of methodologically sound practices. As Feyerabend, Hacking, and other realists of an anti-methodological bent frequently point out, while the negative claim may well be true, the positive claim—if tested against the actual practices of scientists—is probably false. Yet it is the latter claim, the one about methodology, that constitutes the core of the intellectualist's thesis. Thus, it seems that the intellectual historian of science can use SOSS against the social historian only on pain of having it used against himself as well.

In contrast, (f) and (g) suggest ways of talking about individuals in social situations without imputing to them a sense of freedom that obscures more than illuminates in understanding the objective character of their actions. Drawing on Pierre Bourdieu's (1981) theory of the circulation of symbolic capital, we may now offer the following dual characterization of an individual engaged in a social practice. On the one hand, there are features of the individual's practice which reenact the practices of earlier individuals. We may think of these features as participating in the "living history" of the culture, with the individual acting as the bearer of tradition. Thus, the "competence" that the audience ascribes to the individual in (f), which earns him their cooperation, is based on enough of his practice being recognizably traditional. This display of competence constitutes the individual's contribution to what is reproduced of the culture. On the other hand, there are features of the individual's practice, including its material consequences, which his successors will have at their disposal when they pursue their own ends. His particular actions may thus be seen as having the effect of extending, restricting, or simply sustaining the practice of which the actions are an instance. These features, highlighted in (g), may be thought of as constituting the "objective historical possibility" (Weber 1964) for action in the culture at a given moment. And so, we may say that the individual here is contributing to what is reproducible in the culture.

While there is likely to be considerable overlap between what is reproduced and reproducible in a society, of more interest to the student of historical change is the often subtle differences between the two. One of Bourdieu's own examples is the gradual stylization of the medieval custom of removing one's helmet as a declaration of peaceful intentions into the modern custom of removing one's hat as a matter of politeness. It would be in these usually small, but sometimes large, changes in practice that the intellectual and social historian would tend to locate the free agency of the individual. However, our Bourdieu-inspired distinction between (f) and (g) aims to counteract this tendency by treating an individual's awareness that he has a certain range of possible actions at his disposal—normally a necessary condition for ascribing free will to that individual (Dennett 1984, p. 36)—as an *effect* of the actions (or potential actions) of others, rather than as the *cause* of his own action. Thus, we are recommending a switch in historical perspective comparable to the reversal of foreground and background in an image, emphasizing the fact that agents are *forced* to make choices.

3. Implications for Rewriting the Forman Thesis

We can apply these Bourdieuan considerations to the present case in the following manner. Instead of seeing the Weimar scientists as making an unconstrained choice from a set of seemingly self-generated possibilities, we propose to see the scientists as maneuvering within a possibility space constrained by a combination of unanticipated consequences of the activities of previous scientists *(the reproducible)* and their own imperfect anticipations of how contemporaries will react to what they do *(the reproduced)*. The result is a dual explanation for why the German physicists of the 1920s felt compelled to agree on an indeterminist interpretation of quantum mechanics. On the one hand, in aligning scientific determinism with the German war effort during World War I, German physicists had failed to anticipate how their discourse would be appropriated against the next generation of physicists, once it turned out that Germany lost the war. On the other hand, as recipients of the discourse of determinism, the physicists of the 1920s failed to contain the effects of this ill-fated historical link (that is, they were unable to define a pure scientific sense of "determinism" that escaped any association with the earlier war effort), largely because they no longer had the authority to control how the discourse was appropriated by movers of public opinion, such as Oswald Spengler, whose message was patently antiscientific. In short, once the discourse of scientific determinism was brought into the public sphere during World War I, it was there to stay, and thus to haunt the next generation of physicists.

However, at this point, we have only proposed a strategy for studying the causes of what individuals take to be the objective features of their social environment. We now need to suggest a further strategy for studying those objective features which the individual is most likely to consider as being non-social in origin. For while Bourdieu's reproduction analysis offers many insights into the maintenance and transformation of social structures, including how they gain a character of permanence and externality to the individuals whose actions reproduce them at a given moment, it offers relatively little insight into why some social structures would *not* appear to the individuals as being social in origin. For as we have claimed, this is the key to understanding the peculiar objectivity that cognitive institutions, such as modern natural science, seem to have.

Marx faced our question squarely with respect to the widespread nineteenth-century belief that the capitalist free market was the "natural" economic order which would result when the social artifices of feudalism and mercantilism were removed. Marx's answer lay in the theory of *reification*—specifically, that the classical political economists, either through a genuine or willful forgetting of history, presented the barely century-old European economy as constitutive of a timeless human nature, whose laws had only been "discovered" by the political economists (Thompson 1984, p. 131). And despite the conspiratorial tone in which some Marxists have described the origins of this phenomenon, reification is probably best seen as an inevitable feature of how a society incorporates its past. As long as a perfect chronicle is economically unfeasible, there will always be the kind of gaps in the historical record that licenses claims of long-term continuities in social practices, even though in fact major, but unrecorded, changes have occurred.

Nowadays only a neoclassicist economic theorist like Friedrich von Hayek (1985) would continue to dispute Marx on the reified nature of capitalism's transsocial objectivity. In contrast, we are clearly far from the point when an account of natural science as the product of reification would go uncontested. But this does not mean there has in fact been much debate on the topic. Rather, we find the relatively undisputed general claim that the origin of a particular scientific belief or theory is irrelevant to its validity. Indeed, by jointly endorsing this claim, historians and philosophers of science manage to respect the boundary between their two disciplines, which, in turn, has had the effect of discouraging historians from studying the reproduction patterns of scientific practices. After all, if a particular scientific theory is valid—so goes the reasoning behind SOSS—nothing of cognitive interest should result from repeated testings of the theory at various moments in history. And so, while Polanyi (1957) and Kuhn (1970a) have given classic accounts of the transmission of scientific expertise from master to novice, neither has undertaken the Bourdieuan task of studying the *long-term* effects of the transmission process—say, through several generations of scientists—on the character of the expertise transmitted. Even at the level of introductory textbooks, although the inscribed sentences and formulae may remain unchanged over the course of many editions, their intended applications and testability conditions may subtly shift.

However, these projects await future historians. As it stands now, we have no hard evidence for an empirical precondition of SOSS's intelligibility, namely, that the theory of quantum indeterminacy accepted by the Weimar physicists (say) is, in the relevant respects, *the same theory* of quantum indeterminacy that most physicists today espouse. "The relevant respects" is, of course, an important qualification, for in the last sixty years the character of quantum mechanics has undergone major change at both the theoretical and experimental levels. Yet SOSS presupposes that certain general principles, such as the indeterminacy of quantum phenomena, have remained sufficiently intact over that period, such that the likes of Bohr and Heisenberg would recognize today's quantum mechanics as a corrected version of the quantum mechanics that they originated, and not as some essentially different theory which bears only a superficial resemblance to their own.

Once again, philosophers of science have not been too helpful in trying to justify SOSS's presumption of theory-identity over time. Undoubtedly, one reason is that they continue to be more concerned with the cognitive difference between two opposing theories supported by the same body of evidence (as in the case of Quine's underdetermination thesis or Hume's and Goodman's problem of induction) than with the cognitive difference between two quite different bodies of evidence which are used to support what are apparently two versions of the same theory, say, at different moments in its history (Fuller [1984]; for one of the few attempts in the philosophy of language to capture the latter concern, see Barwise & Perry (1983), who attribute it to the "efficiency" of language). And whereas the first concern is relevant to the issues faced by the physicists who were comparing determinist and indeterminist interpretations of quantum phenomena in the 1920s, the second is more germane to the historian of physics who wants to compare the data-theory relations in the original quantum mechanics with the more complex versions that today travel under the name "quantum mechanics." Still, despite the neglected state of discussion on this matter, philosophical defenders of SOSS simply presume that, other things being equal, a theory is likely to retain its identity through numerous linguistic formulations and experimental variations. Were we studying *any other* social institution, this presumption would clearly *not* be made.

Michel Foucault's (1975) archaeological approach suggests an explanation for our willingness to presume that the products of scientific and other intellectual practices have an extrasocial objectivity. Most crucially, these products are linguistic in character. Given the relative immateriality and versatility of linguistic artifacts, their reproduction patterns (or "dispersion") cannot be easily traced throughout an entire society over any great length of time. As a result, historians are at pains to locate either a clear origin of a particular word or expression, or precise moments marking changes in usage (that is, differences between the reproduced and reproducible features of the word or expression). The net effect is to lend credibility to the various Platonic entities that are the stock-in-trade of the intellectualists: ideas, concepts, meanings—all essentially ahistorical entities which may take several linguistic embodiments through history. Thus, most intellectual historians consider it naive to search for the "absolute" origins of ideas, largely because any allegedly "original" use of a word or expression is likely to have undiscovered historical antecedents. Not surprisingly, though, Foucault criticizes this attitude on the grounds that it is easily generalizable to the claim that the cognitive content of a word or expression exists regardless of whether the origin is ever discovered. And once this generalization is licensed, philosophers and intellectual historians feel emboldened to claim, for instance, that Western culture has perennially faced "the problem of man," despite the fact that "anthropology," defined as the study of this problem, had to wait for Kant's coinage in 1795. Perhaps the same may be said, on a much smaller scale, for the constancy of "the problem of quantum" and its indeterministic solution over the last century or so.

We may see Foucault's archaeological strategy as offering a counterpart to Marx's theory of reification, only for social practices whose historical traces are more elusive and, hence, more easily thought to be ahistorical. For example, we would be able to account for the confidence with which the Weimar physicists thought they were contributing to a solution to Planck's black body radiation problem or trying to replace Bohr's orbital model of the atom. At first glance, this confidence would seem to be nothing more than part of the everyday unreflective awareness of the working physicist. Yet it is essential to understanding the sense of objectivity that the physicist attaches to his work. And on closer inspection, we can explain the physicist's confidence as the product of superficial similarities between the reproduced and the reproducible features of his discursive practices. In short, we would need to compare the patterns of reading and writing among the Weimar physicists. Are there undetected yet significant changes made in the portions of their reading materials reproduced in their own texts which led them to believe that they were dealing with the same old problems, when in fact they had subtly transformed them? And do these misreadings involve integrating material from other texts, such as Spengler's *Decline of the West* (to use Forman's prime candidate), which were available at the time but not earlier?

But perhaps the most interesting question that might be asked about the reproduction patterns of scientific discourse is whether the surface similarities between linguistic expressions tend to reproduce what we now diagnose (Whiggishly or otherwise) as a "conceptual confusion." The paradigm of studies of this kind is Hacking's (1975b) account of the emergence of "credibility" and "frequency" as competing ways of characterizing the concept of probability. Hacking's main evidence for this concept being confused is that the alternative characterizations are incommensurable: on the credibility reading, probabilities are dispositions to wager, whereas on the frequency reading, probabilities are propensities to behave a certain way under ideal conditions. For our purposes here, a good case of conceptual confusion in this sense is the failure of the Weimar physicists and the general intellectual public to distinguish clearly the possibility of "determining" (by measuring) a quantum particle's momentum and position from the possibility of there being laws "determining" (causally) such a particle's momentum and position at any given moment. (We should note that although Forman provides nearly all the evidence needed to show that the determinism debates were subject to the sorts of conceptual confusions discussed below, he himself is largely oblivious to them. For the original sources, see Kockelmans [1968], part 2.)

Forman (1971, pp. 63-107) begins his account of the debates over determinism in the third quarter of the nineteenth century, with the Neo-Kantian revival and the rise of Machian positivism. At this time, physicists started to incorporate terms like "indeterminate" and "indeterminism," which Kant had introduced as a backhanded way of speaking about reality "undetermined" by our conceptual framework. Ernst Mach continued to understand the terms in this strictly epistemological fashion, namely, as not attributing any properties to reality except our ignorance of its structure. He argued, in Kantian fashion, that science must presuppose that reality has a causal structure, even though it has no way of showing that the presup-position is true.

However, confusion quickly set in with the development of statistical thermodynamics, which suggested to Charles Sanders Peirce and others that *reality as such* may be indeterminate, in the sense of being subject only to probabilistic laws. This suggestion was supported by a strong alternative tradition of metaphysical indeterminism in France that had begun with Pierre Gassendi's commentaries on Lucretius in the seventeenth century and continued in Peirce's time by the economist Charles Cournot and Durkheim's philosophical mentor Emile Boutroux. The French tradition had been sustained largely by philosophical arguments which purported to show that the world seems ordered because our minds are gross instruments, sensitive only to uniformity in the face of diversity. The metaphysical indeterminists believed that even the stability of our immediate sensations was due more to an insensitivity to change on the part of our perceptual system than to some real uniformity that it had perceived. (For more on this neglected tradition, see Mandelbaum [1987], ch. 4.)

Peirce accepted many of these points, which he then proceeded to run together with scientific arguments first suggested by the Maxwell's demon hypothesis, namely, that it may be impossible to "determine" fully the motions of particles in a closed system (especially if the particles are small enough) because in the course of making his measurements, the physicist must interfere with the moving particles. (The quantum physicists were to later associate these arguments with Bohr's formulation of the Complementarity Principle.) Notice that the physicist's inability to "determine" motions of the particles is not quite the same as the metaphysician's inability: whereas the physicist's problem lies in his status as a (massive) intervening variable, the metaphysician's problem lies in a more trenchant cognitive inadequacy that would vitiate his attempts to "determine" nature at any dimension. However, by the 1920s the two sorts of arguments had become linked together, thereby rendering indeterminism a thesis with application well beyond the level of quantum phenomena.

Finally, the difference between Forman's and Hendry's response to the determinism debates is instructive as a key to their tacit philosophies of science. Whereas Forman, in Kuhnian fashion, reports uncritically the physicists' fused usage of "determinism," Hendry (1980, p. 316), following Lakatos, imputes to the physicists a clear, albeit often implicit, understanding of the two senses of "determinism." From our standpoint, both approaches miss the mark, since they present the physicists' usage more as a reflection and facilitator of their thought than as an impediment or constraint. In Forman's case, the emphasis is placed solely on the cultural capital that the physicists can make of a highly undifferentiated concept of "indeterminacy," while Hendry seems to suggest that the physicists had a nuanced understanding of "indeterminacy" but chose (no doubt, for reasons of economy) never to spell out all the nuances. Once again, we find the historians stressing the subjective over the objective features of scientific practice, despite the fact that the physicists themselves found the quantum debates sufficiently confusing to cause Einstein to fret over the prospect that his colleagues would end up convincing the public that electrons had free will (Forman 1971, p. 110).

HAVING THEM CHANGE AGAINST THEIR WILL— POLICY SIMULATIONS OF OBJECTIVITY

How should we go about trying to acquire knowledge, given that the world, independent of our intentions, imposes certain constraints on what we do? To address this question is to engage in a *policy simulation of objectivity*. While it is clear that policy-oriented social scientists would have an interest in answering such a question, it is perhaps not so clear that someone of a philosophical bent would. And so, in order to clarify the project of policy simulation, we shall begin by showing that the concerns of the policymaker and the philosopher may coincide in interesting ways—in this case, in their attempts to make sense of an anthropological field study.

Consider what it would be like to do an anthropological study on a society of knowledge gatherers. The field researcher would note, among other things, the ways in which the knowledge gathering practices of the society are limited by its "environment," broadly construed: the political and economic climate; the cognitive strengths and weaknesses of the members; the modes of producing, distributing, and utilizing knowledge (as well as the means by which the modes are themselves reproduced and distributed over time and space in the society); and interpersonal conventions carried over from the past which may or may not continue to facilitate knowledge gathering. Like so many other products of field research, this catalogue of constraints would leave the reader bewildered as to which ones have a decisive impact on the character of the knowledge gathered in the society. Indeed, the anthropologist may present this feeling of bewilderment as indicative of the thoroughness of his inquiry. He might then point out that the variety of constraints is matched only by the variety of interests that members of the society have in gathering knowledge, which must, in turn, be distinguished from the official ideological line on why the natives *ought* to be interested in gathering knowledge. What the anthropologist has presented us, then, is a sensitive account of the various phenomena associated with knowledge gathering in the society. However, he has yet to engage in a policy simulation of objectivity.

Now say we pose the following question to the anthropologist: "How can your field research be used to control and alter the character of knowledge in the society you have just studied?" We can imagine such a question being asked by a policymaker tied to UNESCO who is interested in introducing certain beliefs and practices into the society which will have the effect of upgrading the natives' standard of living. However, at the same time, the policymaker is concerned that these foreign beliefs and practices be introduced so as to do minimal damage to the integrity of the native culture. Likewise, such a question might be asked by a philosopher—a social epistemologist—who is interested in measuring the conceptual distance between the society under study and his own. And, clearly, one way of measuring this distance would be to specify the means by which one would try to introduce certain beliefs and practices into the society. Perhaps some beliefs and practices would be easy to introduce because the society already has ready-made ways of articulating or using them—but perhaps not. For example, if the society does not have the communication technology for coordinating the findings of the knowledge gatherers, then it would be difficult for the society ever to arrive at certain complex beliefs, say, about weather patterns, which are possible only if the research of several quite disparately placed teams of knowledge gatherers can be integrated. In what follows it will become clear that the crucial "technological gap" separating the natives from ourselves is the subtle material resource of language itself, yo wit the available modes of representation and argumentation.

Given this understanding of the various nuances in the question we have posed, the anthropologist now answers: "On the basis of my field research, I can tell you what sorts of claims and arguments the members of that society will find persuasive, or at least plausible." Now, to what extent would either our UNESCO policymaker or the social epistemologist find this information useful? The answer will depend, in part, on the extent to which knowledge in that society is *reflexive*. In a society with a high level of reflexivity, the natives justify their beliefs in terms that would also best explain why they hold those beliefs. For our purposes, a *justification* is a set of reasons that natives would recognize as an appropriate account of someone's belief or practice, while an *explanation* is a set of causes, knowledge of which could be used to predict the beliefs or practices of the natives. Thus, members of the society with the highest level of reflexive knowledge would see no difference between justification and explanation: the folkways of accounting for oneself and others would coincide with the accounts offered by the best social scientfic theories. We call such a society "reflexive" as a way of suggesting that its members are so critically self-conscious about their epistemic practices that a difference between an *insider's* (justification-oriented) and an *outsider's* (explanation-oriented) perspective on those practices can no longer be discerned.

If the anthropologist is studying a society that is reflexive in the above sense, then he would be an optimal source of information for both policymaker and philosopher. But the odds are against this being the case, if only because modes of justification normally function to stabilize the social order by providing a common standard of rationality (namely, a method for giving reasons for one's own and others' actions), while modes of explanation are indifferent to such a goal and, indeed, lay the epistemic groundwork for changing the social order by specifying the conditions under which certain types of behavior are likely to be maintained and, especially, discarded. For example, the epistemic practices of a society may be so arranged that the only astronomical theories which can be *justified* are those which entail a belief in a flat earth. However, as it happens, one native professes a poorly articulated belief in the spherical shape of planets in general and is promptly declared irrational—or at least arational.

Nevertheless, an *explanation* of the deviant native's belief would reveal how both he and the normal members of his society could have such disparate understandings of the same phenomenon—and why his is probably correct, a fact which has the potential for destabilizing the knowledge base of the society, were it made public.

Even if the knowledge gatherers studied by the anthropologist are as nonreflexive as we have suggested, might there be some other condition under which a detailed understanding of the native justificatory procedures would be of use to the policymaker or philosopher? Yes, namely, if the procedures tend to lead the natives to adopt beliefs (or courses of action) which an outsider would deem true (or rational), even though the best explanations of *why* they are true would completely elude the native justificatory procedures. Policymakers look for situations of this kind as an ideal state for resolving the problem of how to improve the lot of the natives without undermining their cultural autonomy—or, as the social epistemologist would pose it, *the problem of how to maximize a change in beliefs while minimizing a change in how beliefs are justified.*

Consider the following case. In order to set up an efficient agricultural system, it may be necessary that the natives be engaged in more sophisticated land survey techniques than they currently are. Keeping in mind that these are the same natives who believe in a flat earth, the policymaker realizes that the most straightforward means of improving their knowledge—by introducing them to the modern science of geodesy—would challenge so many of their beliefs (to which certain cultural values have been attached over the years) that the very justificatory procedures through which those beliefs have been articulated would come under fire. The natives would respond to this crisis either by uniformly distrusting the foreigners or by disagreeing amongst themselves as to the epistemic significance of geodesy. Clearly, neither case promises to expedite the creation of an efficient agricultural system. However, all is not lost, for the policymaker can capitalize on the fact that the native land survey techniques, for all their error and inefficiency, are still serviceable and justifiable to the natives. His task, then, is to rearticulate the relevant geodesic insights (certainly not the entire science) so that the natives are persuaded that the insights are *a natural extension* of what they already know and do. Although the policymaker would thereby be reinforcing many beliefs he regards as false (such as the flat earth theory) in the name of maintaining native cultural autonomy, he would nevertheless have managed to alter their practices substantially, which will make it possible for some future (better-fed) natives to reflect on whether the traditional justificatory procedures are equipped to expand significantly on the insights which they have now unwittingly been led to incorporate.

At this point, the anthropologist may protest what he takes to be the policymaker's hidden agenda:

> Contrary to my own intentions (and, I would have thought, yours), you are
> interested in the justificatory procedures of the society I have studied, not in
> order to deal with the natives in good faith, but in order to manipulate them.
> Clearly, you are not concerned with respecting the autonomy of their culture.
> For if you were, you would then be forced to recognize that their
> justificatory procedures have been designed to maintain a limited set of
> beliefs and practices which, in turn, stabilize their society. Indeed, the
> natives' resistance to an explicitly Western presentation of geodesic
> knowledge is the ultimate assertion of their cultural autonomy, since they
> are, in effect, suggesting that they would rather stay as they are than to
> surrender the number and kinds of beliefs it would take to incorporate the
> Western discipline. In a sense, you would accord the natives more respect
> than you currently do, were you to make the differences between native and
> Western cultures this obvious. But as it stands, you seem concerned only
> with the natives *thinking* that their cultural autonomy is being maintained,
> while you, as it were, use their own words against their autonomy.

After a somewhat despairing look at the anthropologist, the policymaker
finally decides to make explicit the differences between the epistemology
presupposed by his project and that presupposed by the anthropologist's.

Whereas the anthropologist speaks as the pure insider, the policymaker
speaks as the pure outsider. Consequently, it is not enough for the
policymaker to be told, in Kantian fashion, that he fails to respect the
autonomy of the natives *simply* because he fails to respect the procedures by
which they define and justify their beliefs and actions. In addition, the
policymaker wants to determine the extent to which the words of the
natives match up with their deeds: How well does what they say explain
what they do? If it turns out to be not very well at all, such that the native
society exhibits a low level of reflexivity, then it would seem to follow
that the natives are captive to their own justificatory procedures, oblivious
to the causal structure of their own behavior. This leads the policymaker to
conclude that when the natives make decisions, their deliberations are
sufficiently constrained so as not to exhibit the kind of freedom needed for
ascribing full autonomy to them.

Admittedly, the constraint placed by argumentation formats and other
forms of linguistic representation on one's thought and action seems
somewhat less confining than the more typical examples of constraint, as in
the case of having a gun held to one's head. Nevertheless, for the
policymaker, both are equally "constraints" in the relevant sense. If
anything, the linguistic constraint is the more serious precisely because it is
subtler and more systematic, therefore making it difficult for its limits to
be detected from the inside. (At least, in the case of the gunman, the hostage
can imagine some clear strategies for retrieving his autonomy.) And so, in
response to the anthropologist's charge that the policymaker is concerned
solely with the natives *thinking* that they are autonomous, the policymaker
argues that given the usual discrepancies between justification and
explanation, native autonomy can run *only* thought-deep. Still, by
manipulating the justificatory procedures of the natives, the policymaker
believes he can eventually get them—albeit indirectly—to remove the chief

obstacle to their exercising full reflexive autonomy. But to continue any further along this line of reasoning would be to veer away from epistemology and toward ethics.

Our next epistemic gambit is to regard the policymaker's course of action as simulating the effects of those features of native practice which are not subject to reflexive control. To get at the gambit's significance for the simulation of objectivity, let us first back up a little. In characterizing the epistemic practices of the native society, we have so far understood "constraint" to mean the more or less explicit and monitored justificatory procedures of a society, which routinely allow one individual to recognize another as having competently performed or not. Were societies *completely* constrained in this sense, then the only way in which the procedures could change would be by deliberate legislative effort—the repeal of one set of rules for the purpose of enacting another set. A survey of Wittgenstein, Winch, Kuhn, Foucault, Althusser, and others who fashion social theories after linguistic practice suggests that this conclusion is generally endorsed. Consequently, change tends to be described—when described at all—in terms such as "rupture" and "revolution," implying that the interesting cases of linguistic change are, at the very least, *apparent* to the language users and, very often, *intended* by them. Unfortunately, this image runs afoul of diachronic studies of language, which reveal that in fact very few syntactic and semantic changes occur in this way. Indeed, linguists have identified principles by which such changes occur, largely based on what may be called the "material" character of language: the look and sound of words, their frequency and distribution of utterance—the very features of language most likely to pass without notice in the minds of speakers and writers as they try to express or understand thought and action (Lightfoot 1979). For example, frequently used words tend to acquire a contracted form and an irregular grammar (think of how the verb "to be" is conjugated in various languages), while the meanings of homonyms tend toward some degree of overlap in the long run (in virtue of a kind of "free association" principle). The internal dynamic of these changes seems to be to make articulation more efficient, but their effects clearly run much deeper, as the French linguist André Martinet (1960) first noted. (For opposing views on the philosophical significance of this fact, see Ricoeur [1978, sec. 8].)

We see, then, that language "constrains" thought and action in a subtler second sense, which stems from the mechanism of linguistic change being relatively independent of the intentions of the individuals who use the language as a vehicle of communication. This point has figured prominently in recent deconstructionist philosophies of language, as may be seen from a brief look at Martin Heidegger (1962) and Jacques Derrida (1976).

Heidegger draws on a standard philological account of the origin and diffusion of language, according to which abstract terms begin as metaphors—that is, rooted in concrete images—but gradually come to acquire "literal" meanings, as later speakers forget those origins and define abstractions in terms of other abstractions. However, when speakers are pressed to locate the meaning of an abstract term outside its usual language game (say, in the course of explaining the term to an ordinary speaker), they unwittingly fall back on the primordial metaphorical associations. And so, to borrow from Heidegger, "theory" becomes a way of "seeing" the world, while "truth" is described as something that needs to be "revealed."

Derrida goes beyond Heidegger in challenging the very idea that an abstract term has *one* literal meaning—even in its own language game. He notes that once a term starts to be used outside its original context of utterance, it accumulates local meanings which are the products of negotiation among speakers in particular contexts. Rather than following the Heideggerian route from a metaphorical to a literal meaning (which is ultimately still rooted in the metaphorical), Derrida claims that as the use of a term spreads, its metaphorical meaning yields to an *equivocal* one, whereby the accumulated local senses are indiscriminately run together. As a result of this equivocation, or "dissemination," the term alternatively suggests a deeply hidden essence or a relatively shallow pun. For example, the depth of "the problem of truth" has often been measured by the large number of disparate solutions that have been proposed: correspondence, coherence, semantic, pragmatic, redundancy, etc. However, Derrida would take this fact to indicate that "truth" and its cognates, being heavily used terms in philosophical discourse, have picked up many local meanings over the centuries. In turn, philosophers have mistaken this instance of dissemination as pointing to a common referent, Truth, of which each of the local meanings captures an aspect. Were they fully aware of how simply *using* language can change *usage*, philosophers would be forced to conclude that all that these disparate meanings really have in common is a repertoire of similar looking and sounding terms centering on "truth."

At this point, we are in a position to catalogue the various linguistic constraints—the techniques of objectivity simulation—that accounts for how the policymaker can be as successful as he is in causing the natives to change their epistemic practices *in spite of* their justificatory procedures. We have been implicitly discussing four such constraints, two of which do not require that the philosopher or policymaker know the history of the language community (the *synchronic* constraints) and two of which do (the *diachronic* constraints). Moreover, whatever reflexivity the language community has is more likely to appear at the synchronic than at the diachronic level, if only because speakers are unlikely to have a reliable sense of the trends in usage for fellow speakers in distant times and places.

Synchronic Linguistic Constraints

(A) *Performative Constraints:* Every utterance licenses the audience to draw inferences about the speaker which are independent of the intention that the speaker wishes to express and which significantly color—even to the point of undermining—how that intention is taken by the audience (Silverman & Torode 1980). These inferences arise from the audience recognizing the utterance as a complex social action, the point of intersection for several institutions. For example, aside from the speaker's intention, the utterance simultaneously conveys information about his class background, his emotional state, the responsibilities to which he is committed, the body of knowledge for which he may be held accountable, and so forth. If the speaker is an astute player of the language game in which he utters, then he can express himself so that the audience is able to hold him just to the sorts of inferences which he is prepared to back up by the appropriate follow-up utterances and actions. Reflexive knowledge of this kind is well within the power of the competent speaker, but rarely exercised. And so, the performance of an otherwise competent speaker may be undermined simply because his natural idiom—which suggests, say, working-class origins—is not normally used in expressing the thought he wishes to convey—which concerns, say, some fine point in subatomic physics (Bernstein 1971).

(B) *Expressive Constraints:* Every thought can probably be expressed in every language, but not with the same degree of facility. Given the differences in semantic and syntactic structure among languages, what may be expressed as a simple, readily understandable thought in one language may only be expressed with great complexity and difficulty in another language. For example, until *devenire* was introduced into Latin in the fourteenth century, there was no lexical distinction between the idea of continuous change and the older idea of change from one state to another. *Fieri* had been used indifferently to refer to both, which, from the standpoint of subsequent developments in the history of science, meant that the concept of functional dependence underlying the modern idea of physical law could not be adequately distinguished from the concept of simple proportionality (Waismann 1952). This is not to deny the possibility that Latin speakers prior to the fourteenth century, in some sense, "thought" about the idea of continuous change. However, it *is* to deny that they had much of an incentive to do so, given the great difficulty involved in trying to express the idea. The American linguist Charles Hockett (1954) has gone so far as to reinterpret the Sapir-Whorf Hypothesis (see the postscript of ch. 6) as being entirely about expressive constraints. Moreover, in the absence of a distinct semantic place in Latin for the idea of continuous change, not only would it be difficult for the Latin speaker to think with the idea in combination with other ideas, but even if the speaker succeeded in gaining some private clarity about the implications of the idea, he would still have great difficulty conveying the idea to others. And given its frequent association with confusion, convolution, and even duplicity, the expressive difficulty of an idea may indeed constitute prima facie grounds for an audience devaluing what the speaker says.

Diachronic Linguistic Constraints

(C) *Originary Constraints:* This is the sense in which Heidegger found
the discourse of Western metaphysics "constrained." In order to specify
how this constraint works in more detail, consider the situation of
trying to explain the meaning of an abstract term to someone who is
clearly not familiar with the language game in which the term
normally occurs. Let us say that the explainer must go through
several rounds of explanation before his interlocutor understands the
meaning of the term. We can see the originary constraints getting
tighter each round, as the explainer is forced to revert to more atavistic
forms of expression, until he must resort to appealing to a concrete
image which the interlocutor finally grasps. This shows that while
originary constraints do not operate in normal linguistic usage, where
terms are readily understood in the context of their usual language
games, they do operate in attempts to find one's way either *into* (in the
case of the ignorant interlocutor) or *out of* (in the case of
deconstructive Heidegger) the language game. In that case, what one
might call the *ontoloquy* (that is, the discourse of the inquiring
individual) recapitulates *phyloloquy* (that is, the discursive history of
the language community).

(D) *Process Constraints:* These are the constraints highlighted by
Derrida. They work by linking together the meanings of similar
sounding (or looking) words through a process which is the socio-
historical analogue of Freudian free association. Moreover, the most
important class of homonyms that tend to be converted into synonyms
are words normally said to have multiple meanings, and hence make for
long dictionary entries. A good example is the English verb "behave,"
which in the eighteenth century was treated exclusively as a normative
term, as in "the child *behaved* poorly in class." However, by the late
nineteenth century, the word had acquired the descriptive sense found
in, say, "the *behavioral* consequences of one's beliefs." Nevertheless,
the idea of a "science of behavior" still carries the connotations of being
a study of something rule-governed, whether it be by a moral or a
natural order (Williams 1975, pp. 35-37). This, in turn, allows B.F.
Skinner (1970) to invest the natural order with moral import, as when
he argues that "freedom" and "dignity" are undesirable notions to have
about oneself because they tend cause one to "behave" in ways that
undermine one's social utility.

Taken together, these synchronic and diachronic constraints mark a decisive
shift from how language is normally studied by philosophers and even by
sociologists. Normally, language is regarded simply as a means through
which some end, usually the speaker's intention, is expressed. Much of the

discussion then centers on the possibility of constructing a language that would be a transparent medium of expression. We have shifted the emphasis by looking at the limitations that language places on the speaker's expression of his intention, and how such constraints determine, at least in part, the identity of the intention that the audience ultimately takes to have been expressed. Another way of casting the difference made by focusing on the constraints is that now language is itself being treated as part of the causal order of the community rather than as an ideal representation of that order which remains causally unaffected by it; hence, we see an application of the naturalistic approach to representation originally raised in chapter 2.

PART FOUR

ISSUES IN KNOWLEDGE POLICY-MAKING

CHAPTER ELEVEN

TOWARD A REVIVAL OF THE NORMATIVE IN
THE SOCIOLOGY OF KNOWLEDGE

The disciplinary boundary separating the sociology of knowledge from epistemology has been suspiciously silent for quite some time. An implicit agreement seems to have been made to let the sociologists concern themselves only with what actually passes as knowledge in particular cases, while the epistemologists take care of what ought to pass as knowledge in general. Upon closer inspection, however, it becomes clear that the terms of the agreement have been set by the epistemologists, who typically define the normative standpoint, the realm of the "ought," as a cognitive utopia populated by individuals skilled in deciding between theories which are sufficiently defined and articulated to be translated into a common language for systematic comparison. This legacy of logical positivism remains as robust as ever in the perennial attempts by philosophers of science to design a "logic of justification." As for that other sense of the normative—the one suggested by Plato's *Republic* and Bacon's *New Atlantis*, namely, the ideal regulation of real knowledge systems, to which the sociologist's expertise would likely prove relevant—it has been consigned to the realm of "mere" policy-making and technical applications. How did the sociology of knowledge lose the right to call itself a normative discipline, and how might it regain that right? These are the issues raised by this chapter.

Some opening remarks are in order about what "normative" means in this context. There are three perspectives from which we may regard what one ought to do, which is to say, the domain of the normative: *first person, second person,* and *third person* (Fuller 1984). The first and third person have been the prevalent perspectives in Western moral theory. In the first person, I prescribe norms for my own actions, which invariably entails adopting a certain attitude toward the world. Moreover, the value of that attitude is usually established on "intrinsic" grounds and not in relation to the consequences that having the attitude has on the world. Kant is the clear exemplar here. In the third person, I act as a detached observer or critic of a community of agents, without any direct interest in changing it, but nevertheless with an interest in judging to what extent their actions facilitate their expressed or latent values. In the case of latent values, I would probably have a theory, which may draw on categories unavailable to the community yet can be justified in terms of my general normative theory. Hume is the exemplar in this case. In contrast, we adopt the second person perspective, in which I prescribe norms for my own actions, given that I know how others are likely to act under various conditions. My goal here is not to make myself as I ought to be (contra Kant), nor to judge whether others are as they are ought to be (contra Hume), but to judge whether I am as I ought to be, on the basis of whether I have made others as they ought to be. Plato's philosopher-king is the archetype of the second person perspective, whose pale copies are to be found in the normative posture of executive administrators.

1. Normativity Lost

Sociologists of knowledge generally believe that the epistemological status of a claim is relative to the social group(s) which must certify it before it passes as knowledge. In its first wave, the period between the two World Wars, this point was taken to imply that every knowledge claim had an ideological component, which could be revealed by identifying the social group(s) whose interests would be served by certifying the claim as knowledge. At that time, the sociology of knowledge was dominated by such Marx-oriented thinkers as Lukacs, Mannheim, Horkheimer, and Adorno, all of whom played some part in the development of what has since become known as "The Frankfurt School." The normative project served by this orientation may still be seen in the work of Juergen Habermas, whose "ideal speech situation" is an attempt to allow for the rational evaluation of knowledge claims by having all claimants lay bare their ideological biases for criticism (Geuss 1982). The first wave of the sociology of knowledge has not survived as a coherent and influential body of research. We have so far considered two general criticisms that it failed to address adequately, both of which point to how knowledge acquires its "independent" or "objective" quality:

(a) How does one account for the fact that the social group which first proposes a knowledge claim is not necessarily the one that benefits once the claim is certified? (See ch. 1.)

(b) Even if it is granted that all knowledge claims are proposed in the interest of serving specific groups, how does one account for scientific claims continuing to pass as knowledge long after their original interests have been served? (See ch. 10.)

On the normative front more specifically, the sociology of knowledge foundered on the problems that have generally beset Marxism as a theory of revolutionary practice. In essence, these problems focus on what Marxists would call "the ideality of the real," or the extent to which the way things are is the way they ought to be. Another way of looking at the issue is in terms of Marxism's failure as an objective social science to have any desirable practical payoffs. Its incompetence on this score may be illustrated by the ease with which Marxism has been used against its own interests. For example, while Marx documented capitalism's systemic disorders in order to spur the German workforce to revolt, Bismarck was able to prevent the revolution from ever happening in Germany by reading *Das Kapital* as suggesting the kinds of social welfare programs that would appease the workers. Needless to say, Bismarck's ability to impede revolutionary practice was a direct result of the *truth*, not the falsity or "relativity," of Marxist theory (Heilbroner 1970). Although claims about the normative inertness of the sociology of knowledge are usually confined to Mannheim and said to turn on the intelligibility of a science that treats all knowledge-systems as cognitive equals (see ch. 7), this historical tendency toward normative inertness may be better seen as emerging from the development of Marxism in the years immediately following Marx's death.

During the period of the Second International (1889-1914), the heyday of "Orthodox" (Engelsian, scientific materialist) Marxism, the problem took a particular form. If Marxist social science aspires to lawlike regularities, on the model of the natural sciences, then the prediction of capitalism's demise is true, if true, in virtue of laws of economic change that operate independently of whether the relevant individuals know that their behavior is constrained by those laws. In that case, there is no justification for those individuals, once they have learned of the laws, trying to precipitate what is supposedly an historical inevitability. Indeed, such attempts may be premature to the point of preventing the desired revolutionary outcome. It would seem, then, that Marxism's status as a scientific theory impedes its status as a revolutionary practice. Certainly, this was the political consequence of Marxism prior to the Bolshevik Revolution of 1917. The leading Marxist party in Europe of that period, the Austrian Social Democrats, presumed that all events somehow contributed to the ultimate demise of capitalism—in effect, that the real is taking an ideal course—which led them to see the role of the workaday politician as one of letting history pursue its course and simply attending, via parliamentary means, to the immediate needs of his constituency (Kolakowski 1978, vol. 2).

After 1923, and the publication of Lukacs' (1971) *History and Class Consciousness,* the Frankfurt School began their attempt to overcome the quietism of Orthodox Marxism. They argued that Marxism discovers "dialectical" rather than "mechanical" laws of history, which implies that the relevant sense of "necessity" is not that of the chain of events inexorably resulting in capitalism's breakdown, but rather that of the persistent social relations of production without which capitalism would not be possible. Once the latter have been identified and publicized, especially to the working classes, capitalism may be overcome at any time by intentionally negating those necessary conditions. In that case, the Frankfurt conception of Marxist science as "critical" and not "positive" specifies what needs to be destroyed in order for revolutionary practice to succeed, but it does not identify the next social order, nor does it say how that order will be implemented (Feenberg 1986). The revolutionaries decide these issues for themselves, and hence "create the future," when the time comes. This, in turn, provides a gloss of the Hegelian thesis, invoked by Marx but left unanalyzed by Orthodox Marxists, that freedom requires "the recognition of necessity." In short, then, the real is rendered ideal by the active construction of ideal-creators.

Both Orthodox Marxism and the Frankfurt School were unable to provide a positive account of the future. But whereas the Orthodox Marxists failed because they never had sufficient evidence for predicting the exact moment of capitalism's demise, the Frankfurt School failed because they left any positive account of postcapitalist society entirely up to the collective judgment of revolutionaries. Still, the net effect of both versions of Marxism was to unwittingly support Max Weber's (1964) arguments for the value neutrality, and hence normative inertness, of social scientific theory with respect to social policy. On the one hand, Orthodox Marxism divorced theory of any practical consequences by depicting the laws of economic transformation as proceeding independently of the judgments of those governed by those laws. On the other hand, the Frankfurt School reached a similar conclusion by portraying the laws as open-ended after the fall of capitalism, thus permitting any number of (and hence, no determinate) practical extensions into the future.

A viewpoint that could have sustained the normative thrust of Marxism would negotiate a middle course between Orthodox Marxism and the Frankfurt School, starting with an alternative reading of "freedom is the recognition of necessity," to wit, that revolution is possible only once the proletariat learn how to remove the obstacles that currently prevent history from taking its natural course. In short, the real takes on the appearance of the ideal only through human intervention, but the ideal exists—albeit in a suppressed form—independently of such intervention. This is essentially the attitude that experimental physicists have toward Newton's Laws: the laws always hold, but they can be demonstrated only through specific interventions, the discovery of which is the epistemic goal of science. Roy Bhaskar (1980, 1987) has been preeminent in developing Marxism in this direction.

Over the past fifteen years, the sociology of knowledge has received a new lease on life from several, rather disparate quarters, which we have examined periodically throughout this book. However, we have yet to flesh out the new image of the scientist that has emerged, especially his rather amoral normative orientation, in marked contrast to the morally upright image projected by Robert Merton (1957, chs. 15-16). Admttedly, before Merton, the sociology of knowledge presented the scientist as someone wedded to a particular research program in virtue of the social interests he perceived it as supporting, even to the point of vitiating his scientific judgment. The New Wave, however, tends to present him as being politically less principled but more astute. The scientist now appears to be an accommodating creature, a Machiavellian who moves comfortably from one research program to the next, regardless of the social interests at stake, whenever it seems that he can maximize the use of certain technical skills, which under the right circumstances—say, the successful performance of an experiment—will gain him credibility in the eyes of his peers. Karin Knorr-Cetina (1981) has coined the expression "the logic of opportunism" to characterize the scientist's Machiavellian moves, ones which she believes are likely to increase as it becomes more expensive, both in terms of time and money, to learn new technical skills. A team of sociologists under Michel Callon (1980) at the Paris School of Mines have detected a similar phenomenon as being responsible for successful scientific innovation, namely, the ability to analyze a problem into parts that will permit the most efficient mobilization of resources, especially people.

Perhaps the most interesting feature of this new twist to the politics of science is that, to a large extent, the Machiavellian's judgments simulate those of the fabled "rational" scientist, since in order for the Machiavellian to maximize his advantage he must be ready to switch research programs when he detects a change in the balance of credibility—which is, after all, what philosophers of science would typically have the rational scientist do. To put the point more strikingly, it would seem that as the scientist's motivation approximates total *self-interestedness* (such that he is always able to distance his own interests from those of any social group which supports what may turn out to be a research program with diminishing credibility), his behavior approximates total *disinterestedness*. And so, we can imagine the ultimate Machiavellian scientist pursuing a line of research frowned upon by most groups in the society—perhaps determining the racial component in intelligence is an example—simply because he knows of its potential for influencing the course of future research and hence for enhancing his credibility as a scientist. If Machiavellianism simulates scientific objectivity at the level of the individual scientist, then what simulates objectivity at the level of the scientific community? Arie Rip (1984) of the Amsterdam Science Dynamics Institute has suggested the concept of *robustness*, which pertains to the survival value of particular positions through a series of controversies. Robustness is reminiscent of Kuhn's "Planck Principle" and Noelle-Neumann's "Spiral of Silence," both of which were examined in chapter ten.

2. Normativity Regained

The continuing failure of sociologists of knowledge to address normative issues may be seen in the discussion pages of the leading journal in the field, *Social Studies of Science,* edited at the University of Edinburgh. Originally designed as a general forum for both empirical and normative questions, over the years the empirical has outweighed the normative to the point that normative issues are now deliberately eschewed by the journal. In fact, this trend has probably been the most publicized and abrasive feature of the New Wave of the sociology of knowledge—at least to philosophers such as Larry Laudan who believe that even theories of the social nature of knowledge must face new versions of the normative questions that have traditionally interested epistemologists. As a result, Laudan has engaged in many, largely fruitless exchanges with philosophers who support the sociologists in their avoidance of the normative, such as Edinburgh's Barry Barnes and David

Bloor. Barnes and Bloor would confine the role of the normative in the sociology of knowledge to matters of methodological housecleaning. And by "methodological housecleaning" is simply meant advice on the general structure of research programs most likely to issue in valid and reliable knowledge of the social world. Thus, in order to distance themselves from philosophical questions, Barnes and Bloor will pronounce only on how to regulate the sociology of knowledge, but not on how to regulate any other cognitive enterprise.

However, in all fairness to Barnes and Bloor, the way in which Laudan (1977, ch. 7) poses the normative questions facing the sociology of knowledge leaves much to be desired. Laudan seems to believe, in effect, that the best theory choices made in the history of science—Copernicus, Newton, Darwin, Einstein—are the products of the best method for choosing theories, namely, some version of the cognitive utopia alluded to at the start of this paper. Since this single method can explain all these exemplary episodes, there is no further need to refer to the specific social circumstances in which each theory was chosen. In other words (and this is typical of philosophical responses in general), Laudan thinks that the main challenge to the sociology of knowledge is that the reasoning of the scientific community may be *closer* to an idealized standard of rationality than the sociologists are willing to admit.

Rather than dismissing Laudan's challenge with an "in principle" disdain for normative questions, sociologists would be better advised to start addressing such questions by demonstrating that the various cognitive utopias proposed by philosophers are not only absent from actual scientific practice but, more importantly, are generally unfeasible given the social organization of science. For if what makes a norm "normative" is its ability to be enforced, then a necessary ingredient in the rational selection of a scientific norm is that the scientific community has the resources for enforcing the norm. And, as it turns out, most of the cognitive utopias of the philosophers involve activities such as inspecting the logical structure of arguments and replicating the experiments of one's colleagues, which are simply impossible to enforce on a systematic basis in the world of Big Science (Collins 1985). Therefore, if we assume that "ought implies can" applies equally well to the rational selection of norms in science as elsewhere, then the sociologist of knowledge is in an ideal position to declare the normative pursuits of the philosopher irrational.

However, before the sociologist can celebrate in his newfound cognitive authority over the philosopher of science, he must face an objection from the philosopher of *law*. The philosopher of law wonders whether the "ought implies can" principle can really be used to show that most of the avowed norms of science are irrational. After all, most cases of normative force in the law are ones in which the society benefits in proportion to the norm being obeyed more often, even though no one expects that everyone will ever conform to the norm in *all* the relevant situations. Consequently, it is rational to pass laws against littering, even if they cannot be systematically enforced and only half the population conforms to them, because even that low level of conformity makes the streets that much cleaner. Arguably, all laws have this character, and so the burden of proof is on the sociologist to explain why the norms of the scientific community cannot have it as well.

But, of course, the reason why the sociologist wants to treat science as a special case is that science is regulated mainly by what may be called *norms of coordination:* that is, scientific norms fail to have systemic force if even one part of the system fails to obey them. This feature of the norms reflects the interdependent nature of scientific research. A researcher who "cooks up" his results can vitiate the conclusions of honest researchers who unwittingly incorporate the fraud, largely because there are no obvious signs of the level of conformity to scientific norms. This point is, in turn, explained by the public forum of science being a purely verbal one, consisting in *reports* of what one has presumably done. The contrast with the forum in which civil society is conducted could not be more striking: the degree of conformity to laws against, say, litter can be gauged by a fairly clear behavioral indicator such as amount of garbage on the streets. The contrast here also shows that the relevant issue in designing scientific norms is not whether everyone can obey them, but whether violations can be detected before they infect the entire knowledge production system.

So let us now turn to a positive normative program for the sociology of knowledge. This would involve "sociologizing" traditional epistemological questions. For example, if cognitive progress demands that knowledge be divided into discrete disciplines, does this render obsolete the philosophical ideal of assenting only to claims which one has first tested for oneself? It would seem that growing specialization expands the region of incompetence for any given individual, such that he ends up being able to test fewer of the claims on which his own decisions are forced to rely. This can be readily seen in the increasing role that deference to expert opinion plays. Yet it also opens the possibility of a new version of the "Cartesian demon" (see ch. 2) entering the knowledge system, as individuals defer to experts whose opinions have no real bearing on the claim at hand or have not themselves been properly tested. This can perpetuate and compound errors that may go undetected for long periods of time and may be impossible to correct after a certain point. Just how real is this possibility? And are there appropriate and affordable policy measures for monitoring the flow of information so that such errors can be isolated in time? For example, we might imagine a government bureau designed to determine the standards for the competent use of, say, the authority of quantum mechanics (which suggests that causal determinism breaks down at the subatomic level) in making arguments for the existence of free will. In short, does it pay to centrally coordinate the activities of the various departments of knowledge, or should a laissez-faire attitude prevail, whereby the disciplines monitor their own activities, borrowing and barring where they please? These are the kinds of normative issues stemming from empirical considerations on the social nature of knowledge growth which have been deliberately avoided by the contributors to *Social Studies of Science*, and to which philosophers like Laudan have themselves failed to contribute, since they have focused their efforts exclusively on attacking the sociologists.

3. Freedom and the Administration of Knowledge Production

Despite their studied avoidance of classical philosophical problems, the recent sociologists of knowledge have produced a body of research which points ultimately to a radical critique of the epistemological tradition, one which focuses on demystifying the philosopher's ultimate cognitive utopia: *the free pursuit of knowledge.*

There has been a remarkable amount of agreement among Western philosophers over both the desirability and the feasibility of an institution protected from all other social concerns which would be devoted entirely to the pursuit of knowledge. This utopia is as old as Plato's *Republic* and has been recently reincarnated as Popper and von Hayek's vision of the "open society," as well as Habermas' "ideal speech situation." In each version, the utopia works by abstracting away all the factors which could lead to irresoluble disputes among rational individuals—namely, the particular social interests that would be served by one theory being chosen instead of another—so as to leave at most a difference in evidence base, which can be bridged by the free communication of findings, which will, in turn, be evaluated in terms of a common logic of justification. As with any of these cognitive utopias, one must, at the start, question the exact status of the claim being made. Is it being alleged as a *sociological fact* that all cognitive diversity can be resolved by eliminating differences in social interest? In that case, we have an empirically falsifiable hypothesis, which suggests certain sorts of experiments and historical comparisons. (Indeed, one such falsification may be to show the unfeasibility of even performing those experiments or comparisons.) But perhaps, as is so often the case, it is simply a matter of *philosophical definition* that whatever prevents individuals from agreeing on a common logic of justification will be called "interest-motivated." In that case, all that the sociologist can do is to balk at the philosopher's idiosyncratic usage.

But let us grant for the moment that the philosopher's cognitive utopia has the status of sociological fact. There still needs to be an account of how rational individuals decide that it is time to choose a theory; for while a logic of justification may specify which theory to choose given certain alternatives at a certain time, it does not specify when the time is right for deploying the logic. As we saw in the last chapter, recent sociological research suggests that the interesting question is *not* why one theory was chosen rather than some other; instead, it is why was it thought that a theory choice had to be made *at that time* rather than earlier or later. Moreover, Barnes (1974) has argued that if Quine is correct and theory choice is always underdetermined by the evidence base, then there will never be a time, just given a logic of justification, when it will make optimal sense to decide between theories. One theory may currently appear the best supported only because certain evidence has yet to be provided which would undermine its credibility and tip the scales in favor of an alternative. And left to their own devices, scientists, like the rest of us, would no doubt entertain for an indefinite period of time many incompatible theories at once, since each would have its special virtue in saving the phenomena. But contrary to these idylls of autonomy, deliberations do eventually yield to decisions, and indeed become the centerpieces of philosophical theories of scientific rationality. The sociologist's point would then be that however similarly the scientists justify their theory choices (granting that point for the sake of argument), the decisions themselves turn on such extrascientific exigencies as grant application deadlines, which place the sort of pressure on scientists that could never be generated from within the cognitive utopia of the philosophers.

But should we even grant that the philosopher's cognitive utopia could have the status of sociological fact? A forum for the free pursuit of knowledge seems empirically feasible until we start inquiring into what exactly knowledge *is*, such that it can be "circulated," "extended," "produced," and "distributed." Not satisfied with the usual philosophical metaphors, sociologists take it upon themselves to do a kind of "field ontology" of the cognitive enterprise. They ask: What are the signs that knowledge is present? And although many answers are offered, they all part ways with philosophical approaches by defining knowledge in terms of coded materials which are localizable in space and time. This shift, however slight it may seem, is in fact significant; for no doubt the plausibility of the *free* pursuit of knowledge has rested, at least in part, on an image of knowledge as a set of propositions, whose content is, in principle, accessible to all and independent of any material embodiment—save the few puffs of air it takes to express a proposition as a sentence. Such an image explains why philosophers as otherwise diverse as Popper, Habermas, and Toulmin still take public debate in the Athenian agora as the utopian model of knowledge production in the world of Big Science. In that case, it would seem that knowledge flows freely in its *natural* state (which is essentially as conversation), and that some external force must be applied (say, from particular social interests) before the flow is impeded.

However, the story is quite different once knowledge is seen as suffering from the same problems of scarcity that befall other material goods: to make knowledge more available to one place and time is to make it less available to some other place and time (Machlup [1962] is the pioneering work in this area). To encode quantum mechanics so as to make it accessible to a physicist on the cutting edge of research is, at the same time, to remove it from the first-year physics student or the lay public (not to mention future historians of science). Even if these advanced quantum mechanics texts were readily found in popular bookstores, they would still remain "inaccessible" to lay and student readers, because in order to decode the texts, the nonspecialist reader would need to gain a kind of knowledge—the kind associated with an advanced degree in physics—which requires a relatively long period of cloistered study. In essence, then, the advanced quantum mechanics text tells the nonspecialist how much more knowledge he needs to acquire before he is able to possess the knowledge contained in the text. The same applies vice versa: that is, to encode quantum mechanics so as to make it accessible to the lay reader is to remove it from the professional physicist. If this point does not seem obvious, then consider the prospect of a physicist trying to design a research program on the basis of one of the many available popularizations of quantum mechanics: How would he translate the various slogans, metaphors, and worldviews into empirical operations? He would probably have to do his own amateur history of the popularization, tracking down the texts on which the popularizer draws for his account. And if this example seems farfetched, then consider the more realistic case of someone acquainted with quantum mechanics solely as a program for doing research at the cutting edge of physics being asked about its "cultural implications." He would no doubt draw a blank at first and would start to speak confidently only after having studied the implicit procedures used by Bohr, Heisenberg, Bohm, and others to map quantum mechanics onto the mainstream of Western culture.

At this point, two sorts of objections may be raised. First, someone sympathetic with our general strategy of reinterpreting the problem of knowledge in economic terms may nevertheless wonder whether, *in the long run,* there is necessarily a trade-off between allocating resources for popular texts and for technical science texts. Instead, it would seem that scientists often assume the role of popularizer—especially in government forums—as a *means* of acquiring the time and money needed for conducting research which will ultimately yield a series of technical journal articles or books. Cases of this kind seem persuasive, however, only because they regard the knowledge enterprise from its end state: that is, scientists are presented as having already succeeded in acquiring the resources they needed for continuing research by initially taking the time to show the public the relevance of that research. But when these cases are regarded in terms of the actual sequence of decisions that must be made before that end state is reached, it becomes clear that the scientists indeed recognized the need for making a trade-off, which they did by temporarily redirecting time and effort from technical to popular texts. Admittedly, this strategy was meant by the scientists as a means of buying more time and effort for technical matters, but it was by no means guaranteed that such an attempt at popular support would succeed: for example, the government may decide to fund some other research team. Thus, the seemingly short-term decision to produce publicly accessible texts may turn out to involve an irreversible trade-off.

The second objection arises from the impatience of the classical epistemologist who, having witnessed what has just transpired, wonders whether the only normative questions raised by the above account concern the production and distribution of physics texts—questions better handled by someone familiar with the publishing market than by either a philosopher or a sociologist. But this impatience would reveal a failure to come to grips with a thoroughgoing materialist epistemology. The classical epistemologist clearly has an idealist bias, insofar as he would interpret the points we have been making as being simply about the different ways, popular and professional, in which the basic propositions of quantum mechanics can be embodied. Indeed, the fact that our society embodies quantum mechanics in many different ways, suited to the needs of many different groups of people, may strike the epistemologist as proof that quantum mechanics has been made universally accessible. Unfortunately, as our remarks were meant to suggest, *the crucial epistemological differences occur at the level of the different textual embodiments,* since a popularization of quantum mechanics offers the lay reader no more access to the work of the professional physicist than a state-of-the-art physics text offers the professional physicist access to the general cultural issues which interest the lay public. And here we may define "access" in strictly materialist terms, namely, A has *access* to B's work, if A has the capacity to causally influence B's work. The fact that the layman, through his reading of popularizations, cannot provide the sort of evidence which would either increase or decrease the probability of a standing hypothesis in quantum mechanics demonstrates his lack of access. Likewise, the fact that the physicist, through his professional training in quantum mechanics, cannot inform public opinion on whether the indeterminacy principle bears on the problem of free will demonstrates his own special lack of access.

From the above considerations, it should be clear that normative questions concerning the production and distribution of texts in a society are properly within the purview of an epistemologist who, like the sociologist of knowledge, is inclined to a materialist ontology. Among the most important normative questions that need to be answered involve decisions about the codification of various subject matters, especially taking into account who is likely to obtain access to whose work as a result of producing and distributing a specific codification. A society with few popularizations but many technical texts in quantum mechanics is likely to have a quite different epistemic profile from a society with many popularizations but few technical texts in that field. For example, history would suggest that in the latter society the heyday of quantum mechanics research had passed and that the time had come for the research to be integrated into the mainstream of the culture.

However, the relevant questions here are not simply ones of whether a society can produce and distribute enough technical and popular physics texts. Indeed, economically advanced societies are able to solve these problems with ease. But, clearly, this is not the whole story. Placing an advanced quantum mechanics text in every household in the United States is, by itself, unlikely to increase the average American's competence in technically rendered physics. If a society were interested in raising the public's level of competence in physics to that of the specialist, then it would have to make a major economic commitment to producing and distributing the texts that would be needed to bridge the epistemic gap implicit in the difference between popular and technical physics texts. (Bridging texts could play a similar role in informing members of one discipline of work in another discipline, and would have effects analogous to the ones raised here for the public.) That gap is now filled, rather unsystematically, by the sorts of texts used in teaching introductory and intermediate college courses. I say "rather unsystematically" because, as any college teacher knows, such texts are oriented more to the institutional constraints of college teaching (for example, the text is designed to cover one chapter per week, material is presented so as to serve as the exemplars for self-contained exercises) than to refining and raising the reader's known level of competence. Moreover, in capitalist societies such as the United States, where textbooks are typically published by commercial rather than academic houses, consumer demand is increasing the epistemic gap between what students learn at the elementary and advanced levels. The student's most vivid experience of this gap occurs when he finds that, say, the chapters on sex and drugs that loomed large in his introductory psychology text are not proportionally represented in the content of the upper division courses.

Systematically producing the right kind of "bridging texts" would, in the first place, demand writers with a Piagetian sense of how to get the reader to realize a deficiency in his knowledge which will, at the same time, lead him to a more advanced understanding. Writers of this kind would undoubtedly have a very versatile understanding of physics, one that could be put to equally good use in philosophy, some of the other humanities, or even in advanced theoretical physics itself. They would constitute a new breed of popularizer, half journalist and half pedagogue, who would be contributing to what E. D. Hirsch (1987) has recently called "cultural literacy." While a full-blown commitment to raising the public's level of competence in physics may well seriously divert resources, especially brainpower, from the cutting edge of research, it would likely facilitate the exchange of information among the various sectors of society, thereby distributing power more equitably. Hirsch has stressed this point, which he thinks will lead to a sort of "public science," analogous to Walter Lippmann's (1955, part 2) "public philosophy," which would allow a society to identify itself in terms of the knowledge that its members have in common.

In a period such as the eighteenth-century Enlightenment, when the Newtonian world-system was commonly seen as having extended the frontier of knowledge to its limit, the commitment would be easily made, as many of the best minds believed that they had a choice between correcting popular prejudices by producing bridging texts (the most important being *L'Encyclopedie*) or simply solving the puzzles which remained in subsuming chemical and biological phenomena under Newton's Laws. But it should be recalled that this reallocation of cognitive resources did not simply create a better-informed public. More significantly, once physics was no longer seen as having much of a cutting edge, it was generally inferred that man had finally gained control over nature, and especially himself as part of nature, which, in turn, inspired the various political acts of self-determination culminating in the French Revolution of 1789. The case of the Enlightenment brings to the fore the major points that a sociologized epistemologist must consider when making policy suggestions for organizing knowledge in a society. A policy to make the knowledge posssessed by the special sciences publicly accessible may not only give the impression that inquiry has slowed down, but also that the public may act with confidence on matters where it would not have previously, since—at least from the standpoint of resource allocation—the public's ignorance of the special sciences had been tied to the scientists' own residual ignorance of their domains of inquiry. Once the scientists' ignorance has been eliminated, the resources are made available to enlighten the public. The advisability of utilizing the time, money, and brainpower in this way is, of course, another matter.

In conclusion, we have seen that a key reason why the sociology of knowledge has not been usually regarded as a normative enterprise is that epistemologists have presumed an excessively restricted understanding of "normative" which manages to include the decisions that individual scientists ought to make for regulating their own research practices in idealized settings, yet exclude the decisions that policymakers ought to make for regulating the research practices of the scientific community as a whole in more realistic settings. I have argued that this excessively restricted notion of the normative can be traced to the idealist bias in classical epistemology, which does not take the material instantiation of a proposition—that is, the text which expresses the proposition—to be an essential epistemic property. However, once a more materialist perspective is admitted into epistemology, one in which the problem of knowledge is redefined in terms of the economics of text production, then it is possible to pose, once again, the realistic normative problems which concerned Plato and Bacon and which are tackled most effectively within the general framework of the sociology of knowledge.

CHAPTER TWELVE

SOCIAL EPISTEMOLOGY AND THE PROBLEM ᴄ̣ AUTHORITARIANISM

In the past decade or so, the most convincing arguments within philosophy for the socialization of epistemology have seemed to rest on the unfeasibility of an epistemic norm which requires the knower to justify all of his own beliefs. On the one hand, cognitive psychologists have repeatedly shown that, left to their own devices in relatively unstructured environments (as is normally presented in a laboratory), even highly skilled scientists will commit elementary errors in inductive reasoning (Stich & Nisbett 1984). But luckily, so the psychologists assure us, the collective nature of the scientific enterprise means that each individual's inference will be cross-validated at some point (Faust 1985). On the other hand, social historians of science have increasingly studied the breakdown of the knowledge enterprise into discrete disciplines, which the logical positivists and other reductionists had taken to be an obstacle to "the unity of science." But given the renewed interest in the finitude of human intelligence, disciplinization has suddenly been transformed from a defect to a design feature of knowledge growth (Putnam 1975, ch. 12; Hardwig 1986).

This chapter opens with a critical examination of a tendency that has recently emerged among epistemologists sensitive to these strands in the Science Studies movement, namely, to treat the *difference* between the knowledge of experts and laymen as grounds for conferring absolute authority on the former over the latter. Once we have maneuvered away from this tendency, we shall consider some general strategies by which expertise is "politicized" and "depoliticized." The contrast implied in the last pair of terms is not quite the one that epistemologists would expect (though it is more closely related to it than they would like to admit). For we shall see that to "politicize" expertise is to open the question of cognitive authority to the critical scrutiny of society at large, while to "depoliticize" it is to close the question in favor of the experts.

1. The Lure and Avoidance of Cognitive Authoritarianism

Here is an argument, based on Hardwig (1986), purporting to show that, in most cases, it may be more rational to defer to the authority of experts than to trust one's own epistemic judgments:

(1) The ordinary individual, or "layman," holds more beliefs than he could reasonably be expected to have the relevant evidence for.

(2) However, in most cases, the layman knows of some other individual, an "expert," who through specialized training has acquired the evidence needed for rationally holding the belief.

(3) From (1) and (2) we can conclude either (a) that most of the layman's beliefs are irrationally held, or (b) that it is rational for the layman to hold a belief if someone he recognizes as an expert has the evidence needed for rationally holding it.

(4) Since only (3b) saves the intuition that most of our beliefs are rationally held, it follows that the layman is "epistemically dependent" on the authority of experts for all but the beliefs on which he himself is an expert.

(5) Therefore, for most epistemic judgments, it is less rational to "think for oneself" than to defer to the authority of the relevant expert.

This is the *Authoritarian Theory of Knowledge* (ATK). In a nutshell, it says that the rationality of thinking for oneself diminishes as society's knowledge gathering activities expand to the point of requiring a division of cognitive labor into autonomous expertises. I shall call such a society "knowledge-intensive." I submit that the persuasiveness of ATK and the argument outlined above rests on a conflation of three distinct readings of ATK, which will be surveyed below: *analytical, empirical,* and *normative.*

Analytically, it may simply be a consequence of what it means to be an expert that one defers to his authority. In that case, if a normal member of a society failed to defer to some other member's authority, then it would follow that the latter person did not have the relevant expertise. In this reading, ATK specifies either how one goes about identifying an expert or how one becomes recognized as an expert in the society. Thus, someone opposed to ATK, understood analytically, might then be criticized as follows: "If you don't defer to the authority of experts (on the appropriate occasions), then you defeat (or misunderstand) the very idea of expertise." The skeptic would, therefore, be "irrational" in the sense that someone who violates the rules of a game is (Bennett 1964).

A second reading of ATK is as an empirical generalization about how rational beliefs are formed in knowledge-intensive societies. Much here hangs on the sense given to "rational," which may be taken in one of two ways. In one sense, it would be "rational" for a layman to defer to experts if it increases the likelihood of his achieving his goals, say, by allowing him to conserve on his knowledge-gathering efforts. For instance, as Herbert Simon (1976, pp. 136-139) has shown, when faced with the problem of having to research and implement a policy decision within the same budget constraints, administrators are better off minimizing research costs by deferring to the relevant experts, thereby reserving a larger portion of the budget for implementation. In another sense, it would be "rational" for laymen to defer to experts if the collective effect of their doing so promotes the overall knowledge gathering activities of the society. This fact could then serve as the basis of an invisible-hand explanation for why deference to experts occurs in knowledge-intensive societies such as our own—namely, it tends to prevent redundant research and (perhaps as a result) to stimulate interest in fields where expertise has yet to form. Indeed, these two senses of rationality may operate simultaneously, insofar as the individual who engages in cognitive economy by deferring to experts is also in the best position to increase the society's store of knowledge. In that case, someone opposed to ATK, understood in either of its empirical senses, could easily be charged with "irrationality" in the sense of following a strategy counterproductive to his own and society's goals.

While it may seem that we have now exhausted the possible readings of ATK, we have yet to address the normative question most squarely in the domain of the epistemologist: To what extent is expertise relevant to the sorts of goals which normally cause us to seek knowledge? In step (2) of his argument, the ATK theorist clearly presumes that the epistemic goals of the layman and the expert are sufficiently similar so that the layman may unproblematically build on the knowledge gathered by experts when engaged in his own inquiries. However, the analytical and empirical interpretations of ATK establish only that *if* someone displays the relevant expertise, then we should defer to his authority. But when is such a display of expertise "relevant"? Three considerations may be raised which suggest that even in a knowledge-intensive society there may be rational grounds for "thinking for oneself" and rejecting a general policy of deferring to the authority of experts.

To get at the first consideration, I shall elaborate on an example drawn from Hardwig (1986), which concerns a doctor who advises a patient to visit a cardiologist for treatment of an irregular heartbeat. One reason why the patient may rationally reject the doctor's diagnosis is that his medical judgment is "unreliable." But some care must be taken in defining this last term. Since we are presuming that the advice is being given in a knowledge-intensive society, the patient must accept that the doctor does indeed have some medical expertise. (We shall simply take for granted that this particular doctor is the most competent one the patient could find.) Thus, the fact that the doctor sometimes misdiagnoses an irregular heartbeat does not by itself provide adequate grounds for the patient rejecting the latest diagnosis, since, as an expert in medicine, the doctor gives the correct diagnosis of irregular heartbeats more often than any other expert or layman. Moreover, even if the doctor misdiagnosed irregular heartbeats *most of the time,* he would still be offering expert advice, just as long as no one else had a better track record. Yet, this having been said, the doctor's diagnosis may still not be good enough for the patient, if his threshold level for reliable expert testimony is higher than what the doctor can realistically provide. For example, the patient may have a high reliability threshold because he is averse to spending the amount of time and money it would take to act on the doctor's advice (say, to enter a hospital), unless he is fairly certain that it would have beneficial consequences.

A defender of ATK may at this point try to rebut the first consideration by arguing that the layman's reliability threshold is unduly influenced by a nonepistemic factor, namely, his propensity to spend time and money; if the layman were a pure seeker after knowledge, then he would discount this factor and follow the doctor's advice. The problem with this rebuttal, however, is that it presupposes the very point that the epistemologist needs to prove, namely, that the layman and the expert have sufficiently similar interests in acquiring knowledge so as to make the former's deference to the latter a rational move. A cagier argument for the ATK defender to make would be that the relevance of the doctor's expertise is already built into the lay patient's strategy, such that *if* the doctor were able to offer medical advice on a sufficiently reliable basis, the patient would then gladly take it. Indeed, the patient may even believe that it is only a matter of time before medical expertise will so progress. At least there is nothing in how we have presented the first consideration which suggests the *in*compatibility of the doctor's and patient's interests in acquiring knowledge. For this reason, we must now turn to the second grounds on which the layman may refuse to defer to the expert.

There are many cases in which we routinely make ourselves epistemically dependent on experts, even though we know that their advice is wrong most of time. Aside from the doctor's misdiagnoses, vivid examples include the inability of meteorologists to forecast the weather, the failure of welfare economists to predict consumer behavior, and the ineptitude of hydrogeologists in finding safe sites for dumping nuclear waste (Shrader-Frechette 1983, 1984, 1985). The fact that their expert judgments are still correct more often than the judgments of nonexperts is by itself small consolation. However, as suggested in the rebuttal above, the errors of the expert are tolerated because they are presumably due only to the relative immaturity of his expertise, which in the long run *will* succeed in providing the layman with the kind of knowledge he seeks. Our second consideration for the rationality of overruling expert judgment turns on the likelihood that this belief represents a false account of how and why the cognitive labor of a society—especially our own—becomes divided into autonomous expertises.

If we simplify matters by equating "expertise" with "scientific discipline," we find that the emergence and maintenance of a discipline's autonomy have historically rested on the extent to which a particular set of variables can be systematically isolated and manipulated as a "closed system" (von Wright 1971, Bhaskar 1980, Apel 1984). The test for disciplinary autonomy, then, is whether practitioners have reliable means of preventing extraneous variables from interfering with the demonstration of some specific relation among the discipline's defining set of variables. In terms more familiar to philosophers of science, autonomy comes once the discipline is able to enforce the *ceteris paribus* clause implicit in a fair test of its hypotheses. These matters were examined in more detail in chapter eight, but an example will serve for the general point. Once it became possible to construct a virtual vacuum in the seventeenth century, it also became possible to demonstrate the regularities between mass and acceleration which characterize classical mechanics. And subsequently, expertise in classical mechanics was tied to this ability to make reliable judgments about physical phenomena against the backdrop of a virtual vacuum.

In contrast, personal health, the weather, and rational choice remain difficult phenomena about which to offer reliable judgments, largely because they are the products of several variables whose interrelations are so complex as to render, at least for the time being, any *ceteris paribus* clause unenforceable. For example, an economist may predict that, *ceteris paribus,* when the supply of some commodity increases and the demand for it decreases, the price is bound to fall. This prediction, a theorem in neoclassical economics, turns out to be wrong most of the time. To explain this failure simply in terms of the empirical falsity of the theorem would be to miss the difference between the kind of knowledge which interests the economist as the practitioner of his discipline and the kind of knowledge which interests the layman as an economic agent in the marketplace. The economist would quickly point out that among the conditions implicit in his *ceteris paribus* clause are perfect competition, no government intervention, and ideal utility maximizers. He may then go on to defend the autonomy of economics on one of two grounds: by arguing (i) that a favorable political and economic climate *would* bring about these conditions and their attendant consequences, or (ii) that the theorem's range of application is restricted to "perfect markets," of which real markets are only degenerate versions. However, to the layman interested in arriving at a sound investment strategy, the economist is simply saying that there is no direct extrapolation from the closed systems in which he proposes and tests hypotheses to the complexities of the "undisciplined" environment which prompts the layman to act (Lowe 1965).

Is the situation likely to improve between the economist and the investor in the long run? In other words, would progress in economics entail an improvement in the ability to address the investor's queries? Similar questions may be asked about the doctor, meteorologist, and hydrogeologist to whom laymen are likely to turn for expert knowledge. Insofar as there is such a thing as an "internal history of science" whose problems arise mostly from developments within particular disciplines, there would seem to be little reason to think that a convergence in the epistemic goals of the expert and layman is in the offing. Indeed, it is worth noting that throughout the nineteenth century—the heyday of the division of cognitive labor into disciplines—epistemologists frequently expressed the fear that a Tower of Babel was replacing the Unity of Science exemplified by the Aristotelian corpus. However, Herbert Spencer (among others) managed to allay these fears by arguing that the disciplinization of inquiry is indicative of epistemic progress in the same way as the functional differentiation of organs is indicative of biological evolution (Cassirer 1950). And it may be just this analogy that continues to inform the intuition that a knowledge-intensive society is especially well suited to handling the problems posed by laymen.

Nevertheless, a growing body of empirical research suggests that as disciplines pursue their internally defined problem areas, their practitioners become less inclined to pool together their inquiries in addressing a problem of general public concern. This trend is reflected in the greater financial incentives that government has had to provide in order to lure scientists away from their usual lines of research. And in at least one much-studied case, the reasons are clear. Most of the difficulties surrounding cancer research, both in terms of setting its agenda and in integrating its results, turn on the need for the practitioners of widely disparate disciplines—ranging from molecular genetics to public hygiene—to agree on, for instance, whose research is epistemically dependent on whom else's research, what counts as a solution or progress toward a solution, and even how "cancer" is to be defined and identified (Hohfeld 1983). Since the problematic character of cancer is largely of lay origin, and hence "undisciplined," there are no ready-made answers to these questions. The only course of action seems to be the painful and little-understood process of interdisciplinary negotiation—about which more in the next section.

At this point, the ATK defender, indomitable as ever, may object to our second consideration, arguing that it seems to deny the obvious fact that however reluctant or unsuccessful the experts have been in attending to the epistemic needs of laymen, their presence has certainly made a positive difference toward satisfying those needs. This appears to be a reasonable response, until we take into account the role that experts have had in molding the epistemic interests of laymen—especially in terms of what counts as an acceptable answer to a lay query. However, this molding has been to a large extent unintentional, as much the result of laymen uncritically presuming the appropriateness of the information imparted to them as of experts deliberately passing off such information as appropriate. For example, it is not uncommon for scientists to let politicians make what they will of their research, as long as it leads to continued funding (Haas, Williams & Babai 1977). And given the social prestige attached to such research, politicians are often all too willing to reformulate policy problems to fit the information available, which leads them to declare, prematurely, that the economy is sound or that nuclear reactors are safe. Therefore, before fully conceding that the experts have helped satisfy lay epistemic needs, we must have a way of determining the extent to which these needs have changed because of the presence of experts and whether the changes have indeed been for the better. One way would be through a deconstructive social history of expertise (see Collins [1975, ch. 8] for a start). Another way, perhaps more amenable to the tastes of the epistemologist, would be through procedural guidelines by which laymen and experts can negotiate as equals the relevance of the latter's research to the former's interests. That guidelines of this kind are possible forms the basis of our third and final consideration against adopting a general policy of deferring to the authority of experts.

Max Weber (1964, pp. 50-112) famously restricted the role of social science in social policy to the business of determining the feasibility of alternative means for achieving the goals set by policymakers. The only value judgments that Weber would permit the scientist were endorsements of particular means on grounds of efficiency. But of course, this demarcation of scientists from politicians on the basis of means and ends is much too neat. An economist who showed that all the available means for implementing a balanced budget yielded undesirable byproducts would reasonably be read as offering an implicit argument for abandoning the goal of a balanced budget. This example reveals the core dynamic of lay-expert interaction. In the first round, the layman proposes a desired end state and the expert responds by identifying other states—namely, the intended and unintended consequences of implementing an efficient means—that the layman would probably have to tolerate in bringing about the desired end state. The defender of ATK would end the exchange there, with the layman bound to the recommendations of the expert on pain of being irrational. However, the layman may regain epistemic equality with the expert by deciding whether these additional states are compatible with both his original interest in the end state and other desirable end states which he envisages as coexisting with it. This information—of what an overall desirable future would look like—is not normally available to the expert, yet crucially relevant to the rational use of expertise. Let us dub it *utopian epistemology*. It is the sort of knowledge that might disincline laymen from endorsing nuclear power or undergoing certain medical treatments, no matter how feasible the experts say it is.

2. Expertise Politicized and Depoliticized

Just when the layman thinks that he can now emerge into the public forum as the expert's cognitive peer, he is met by a more intriguing and virulent form of depoliticization. Herbert Simon (1986), the organizational-theorist-turned-cognitive-scientist, is the source of the expert's latest strategy. It applies what may be seen as a *method of exhaustion* to public policy debates, whereby questions of values are converted to questions of fact, until the value question that remains is merely one of technical application. Consider Simon's own vivid example of how we might go about evaluating Hitler's policy of exterminating Jews. This policy is normally challenged for violating the sanctity of human life, as if Hitler can be faulted *only* for going against something that so many of us value so deeply. While no doubt persuasive, these grounds convey the impression that we are hardly more rational than Hitler. For the argument seems to be that since Hitler's values and ours conflict, and there are more of us than of him, therefore our values prevail. A more rational strategy, according to Simon, would be to challenge the *facts* on which Hitler based his policy, granting that *if* the Jews were as big a threat as he maintained, then there would be grounds for extermination. The relevant facts would concern the extent and efficacy of Jewish political and economic activities. What Simon's strategy lacks in human emotion, it makes up in practicality, since it would be presumably quite easy to show that Hitler's factual assumptions are erroneous and thereby conclusively undermine his policy on objective grounds.

Now consider the potential consequences for "rule by experts," once the layman is put in Hitler's position. Whenever the layman presents some desired end-state, the expert need only inquire into the facts about the causal structure of the social world that such an end state presupposes, and then show that those facts do not obtain. After several rounds, the layman's utopia will have been honed down to something clearly within the expert's control. Although Simon does not explicitly draw this conclusion, his strategy strongly suggests the positivist thesis that value disputes are often irresolvable because the parties refuse to argue in a manner that is open to empirical check. In our own terms, this is to say that the parties refuse to depoliticize the dispute, which would involve having it arbitrated by a third party with special access to the facts presupposed by the disputants.

We have just seen how public policy disputes can become depoliticized, once the experts appear to laymen as a "united front." It should be noted, however, that in the face of other cognitive authorities encroaching on their terrain, experts may start to turn *to* politics by establishing themselves as *normative* authorities. Weber (1964, ch. 1) showed this to be the motivation behind the entry of value judgments in economic argumentation. We saw hints of this process earlier. When it became clear that real-world markets did not result from actions taken by ideal utility maximizers, neoclassical economics did not die a naturalistic death. Rather, the economists appropriated the paramoral authority to chastise real-world entrepreneurs and policymakers for failing to approximate the rationality epitomized in their models. And so, from *being evaluated* by the facts as false, neoclassical economics managed to end up *evaluating* those same facts as irrational. In light of the endless and often aimless debates in the human sciences, one is tempted to conclude that, generally speaking, normative authority is the "higher ground" to which disciplines retreat when their theories are in danger of empirical falsification.

In fact, Simon's depoliticizing strategy notwithstanding, there may be an inherent tendency for expertise to become politicized. At least, this would seem to be the lesson proposed by the Australian philosopher of science Randall Albury (1983) in *The Politics of Objectivity*. Albury detects a paradox in the concept of objective knowledge. While objective knowledge is supposed to be the result of rigorous testing on which the scientific community can agree and the society at large can rely, the most pressing social problems that demand the scientists' attention are ones which have not been subject to such testing and hence do not normally elicit consensus in the scientific community. Recalling our earlier example of cancer research, politics is certainly involved in determining which discipline's criteria will be taken to indicate that the disease has been conquered. For example, should one look to a decline in the mortality rate of a target population, or to the actual destruction of cancerous cells under a microscope? The answer that policymakers give to this question has implications not only for the relative cognitive priority of the disciplines cooperating in cancer research but also their relative funding priority. Needless to say, the unholy alliance of opportunism and intellectual myopia render the practitioners of the relevant disciplines ill equipped to deal with these questions of priority.

It would be a mistake to conclude that, because complex cognitive problems require political solutions, it follows that the objectivity of scientific expertise has somehow been compromised. This point has been made most forcefully by the German "Finalizationist" school of Science Studies (Schaefer 1984), who observe that there are two orthogonal directions in which advanced scientific research can go. In essence, these two directions, *intensification* and *extensification*, are the respective social projections of a fundamental trade-off that individuals must make in organizing their own cognitions, namely, to maximize systematicity or retrievability (Hirsch 1987, ch. 2).

On the one hand, research may aim for increased systematicity, or *intensify*, by exploring domains that fall between already existing disciplines (the obvious cases include "sociobiology" and "biochemistry") or are at the extremes of our capabilities for inquiry (such as particle physics and cosmology) in order to, literally, "fill in the gaps" in the system of knowledge that the existing disciplines have been collectively (and often implicitly) articulating. On the other hand, research may aim for increased retrievability, or *extensify*, by drawing together existing disciplines to model phenomena—such as most concrete economic and public health problems—that are more complex than the phenomena that these disciplines normally study on their own. Intensification and extensification correspond roughly to the ways in which basic and applied research draw on existing knowledge to produce more knowledge. Developments in *either* direction may constitute scientific progress. But contrary to positivist folk wisdom, they are not the *same* direction. Indeed, it may be that beyond a certain point in the development of a cluster of disciplines, increased intensification is likely to bring about only marginal cognitive and practical benefits, which would seem to speak on behalf of a knowledge policy of extensification.

Moreover, Albury argues that science's self-image of objectivity is good politics for liberal democracies. The most obvious way of making the case would be that the government, and society at large, reap the benefits of the technological spin-offs from basic scientific research. However, Albury disparages this line of argument as being more myth than reality (Mulkay [1979] offers the evidence). Instead, he argues that liberal democracies benefit from science's objective image, insofar as the tradition of Mill,

Dewey, and Popper has advertised science as the perfect small-scale version of such governments. Thus, if objective knowledge can be produced under the "open society," that fact would seem to legitimate the pursuit of liberal democracy in society at large. Albury is sympathetic to this way of thinking, but he believes that increasing the democratic tendencies of scientific institutions requires dissolving a measure of their autonomy, at least with regard to the lines of research they pursue. On this scheme, which resembles the policy stance of the Finalizationists, research would have to be justified quite explicitly to a forum of interest groups likely to be affected by the various directions that the research might take. Without necessarily compromising the objectivity of the research, this move toward politicization would force scientists to argue for their positions in a forum larger than the strictly professional ones to which they have grown accustomed. To ensure that this increase in democracy is a truly critical exercise, and not simply an exercise in informed consent, not only must the public cross-examine the scientists, but the scientists must also cross-examine each other in order to demystify one another's rhetoric.

In the end, however, it would seem that Albury has struck a rather delicate balance, since democratic politics and cognitive authoritarianism in their pure forms are radically incompatible. For example, Feyerabend (1981b, ch. 4) would commend Albury on seeing the impossibility of a self-governing, "autonomous" democracy embedded within a larger democracy, for this only erects barriers to the free circulation of inquiry—as has indeed been the case in the scientific enclaves of avowedly liberal societies. But Feyerabend would probably then remind Albury that the critical rationalism so emblematic of "the scientific method" originally worked in the forum of the Athenian polis, whose discussion topics were without institutional boundaries; hence, the knowledge gained by the scientific method and the method itself were equally subject to cross-examination. As a result, skepticism became quite pervasive in Greek philosophy. Similarly, the dogged pursuit of critical rationalism in the contemporary world could well undermine the cognitive authority of scientific research—especially by showing that it does not give us what we want or that it does so only as well as alternative epistemic pursuits. Of course, what prevents this from happening is government protection of science, which ensures that public criticism will only have so much efficacy. Albury would extend the efficacy a little further, but why not all the way—in keeping with a pure participatory democracy?

To close on a more authoritarian note, Albury is open to criticisms of a decidedly anti-Feyerabendian sort. Resuming the dialectic, we might say that the reason why the public cannot be entrusted with the task of rationally criticizing the methodological side of science is that people generally exhibit cognitive biases that cause them to make faulty judgments about reliability, validity, and the like. Indeed, the whole point of scientific training is to remove those biases, and *even then* scientists often fall unwitting victims to the same errors; hence David Faust's (1985) call for a tight-knit community of researchers especially sensitive to spotting error in each other's work. Moreover, Albury may be much too generous *even in his estimation of the public's ability to ascertain its own interests and how science might best serve them.* An increasing number of studies from radically unrelated paradigms—experimental social psychology, psychoanalysis, Marxism— point to the marked incompetence of ordinary people in judging their own attitudes and interests, as well as the courses of action that are most likely to cause what they want to happen (Nisbett & Ross 1980). And so, if Albury truly wishes that the public's interests be more adequately represented in the directions taken by scientific research, then he may have to forego the idea that the public can speak competently on its own behalf. Carried to its logical extreme, cognitive authoritarianism of this sort would claim that the only decision that the public is entitled to make is to fund more social scientific research to determine the identity of "the public interest" from the many misleading things that people say and do.

NOTES TOWARD DESIGNING A CORE CURRICULUM FOR A GRADUATE PROGRAM IN KNOWLEDGE POLICY STUDIES

(1) The idea of "knowledge policy" presupposes that academic disciplines can be treated as social institutions whose activities can and ought to be coordinated with one another, as well as with other social institutions. The "knowledge policymaker" is a bureaucrat whose expertise must include not only the usual managerial and administrative skills but also the training normally gained by studying philosophy and "the sciences of science" (Price 1964). Designing a curriculum of this sort ultimately derives its inspiration from Auguste Comte's (1974) "positivist politics." But more than mere philosophical fantasy, such a curriculum has already been implemented in many of the leading social democracies, among them France, Sweden, and the Netherlands. Readers are encouraged to write for the details, which will, of course, differ from *this* philosophical fantasy: Centre de Sociologie de L'Innovation, Ecole Nationale des Mines de Paris, 60 Bd Saint-Michel, 75006 Paris; Swedish Research on Higher Education, National Board of Universities and Colleges, R & D Unit, P.O. Box 4501, S-104 30 Stockholm; Science Dynamics Group, University of Amsterdam, Nieuwe Achtergracht 166, 1018 WV Amsterdam.

(2) "Scientists" (understood broadly, to include all the *Wissenschaften*) have been skeptical of the possibility of knowledge policy because bureaucrats are typically too sensitive to short-term political considerations rather than the long-term interests associated with the pursuit of both theoretical and practical knowledge. However, given their overarching administrative perspective, bureaucrats are potentially in a better position than any individual scientists to understand the collective product of epistemic pursuit. A goal of knowledge policy studies, then, would be to train bureaucrats in the kind of decision making that would instill confidence in scientists that government can have something epistemically interesting to say about how knowledge should be pursued.

(3) In addition, knowledge policy studies would provide a socially constructive outlet for philosophical training, the place of which in the university system has been subject to increasing doubts throughout this century. Philosophers typically learn to reason about normative matters, but too often in a purely aprioristic or "conceptual" manner which either rules out actual situations as "impossible" or includes as "permissible" an indiscriminate mixture of the implementable and the unimplementable. While knowledge policy studies would continue to allow philosophers to reason about what ought to be case, it would be within a thoroughly naturalistic framework in which implementability operates as a constraint on philosophically permissible conclusions.

(4) In fact, it might even be argued that knowledge policy studies would *improve* philosophical reasoning, insofar as without pragmatic constraints philosophers (and practitioners of the humanities in general) tend to be uncritically pluralistic about the pursuit of knowledge, stressing the "inherent value" of pursuing virtually any line of research, rather than pointing out the strengths and weaknesses of the various options for achieving some desirable outcomes. In any case, it is certainly true from pedagogical contexts that students can be made to resist an easy pluralism and to think "deeply" about the relative value of various activities when philosophical problems are posed as practical questions about how some scarce resource, such as time or money, will be distributed among the available alternatives. (Note that by "pragmatic constraints" I mean to be neutral as to Popper's [1957] distinction between "holistic" and "piecemeal" approaches to administration, since one goal of knowledge policy would be to improve the means by which we are able to monitor the consequences of implementing particular knowledge policies, which would thereby extend the limits of implementability.)

By being made sensitive to the pragmatic constraints within which normative judgments must be made, philosophers will also counteract the tendency for their problems to assume lives of their own. A good case in point is the trajectory of philosophical debate over the continuity of scientific development, some of which has already been traced in chapter 3. After Feyerabend (1981a, ch. 4) showed the historical inaccuracy and unfeasibility of scientific progress occurring by a later theory logically subsuming an earlier one, Putnam (1978) and others endeavored to capture the "intuition" behind the subsumptionist view, namely, that some of the earlier theory's content is retained by the later theory; hence was born "the causal theory of reference" (Schwartz 1977). But had Feyerabend's arguments been taken seriously, the intuition that, say, Relativistic Mechanics largely "builds on" Newtonian Mechanics would be treated merely as a datum in our folk history of science, which is to say, a naive (albeit entrenched) belief that probably cannot withstand empirical scrutiny. As it stands, however, philosophers have elevated the intuition to "transcendental" status, a belief without which *any* history of science would be (allegedly) unintelligible. Ironically, then, Feyerabend's case against the leading positivist theory of scientific progress, via logical subsumption, has had only the effect of eliminating that particular theory, since the putative object of the theory (the continuity of science) remains more entrenched than ever in philosophy. This is just one of all too many cases (Strawson [1959] being the most obvious one) in which the threat of empirical falsification has had the effect of booting up a folk intuition to a transcendental condition, thereby creating the illusion that philosophers deal with a special class of objects untouched by the other sciences.

(5) The activities of the bureaucrat are much more philosophical than philosophers would like to admit. Philosophers have always sought ways of

reasoning about incommensurable conceptions, the idea being that each of the incommensurables—whether it be one of the many conceptions of justice or of truth—is attractive in its own way and that somehow, at some appropriate level of abstraction, it can be compared and evaluated with the others. Following Herbert Simon's (1976) model of the administrator as "satisficer," bureaucrats are likewise always forced to weigh considerations—such as efficiency versus accuracy, efficacy versus equity— which can neither be jointly maximized (as desirable as that might be) nor even be compared along some clear metric. A situation of this sort forces the bureaucrat to translate these considerations into some medium which will then enable him to compare the formerly incommensurable notions. Thus, for all their obvious differences, both efficacy and equity would cost a certain amount of time and money to implement, factors which admit of comparison.

(6) When this "bounded" conception of rationality is extended to knowledge policy, the policymaker will need to devise a medium along which incommensurable lines of research can be compared. The nature of this medium will no doubt be affected by the sort of generality dealt with by the policy maker and its attendant type of incommensurability (March 1978). For example, comparing rival research programs in one discipline involves quite different considerations from comparing rival disciplines within, say, the natural sciences, which, in turn, raises quite different concerns from those involved in comparing the natural sciences with the social sciences and the humanities. While the medium in each of these cases would naturally include the usual categories of "costs," "benefits," and "risks," they will be complicated by the fact that when regulating knowledge, *economic* costs, benefits, and risks are complemented by *cognitive* and *political* costs, benefits, and risks, which do not map onto the economic ones on a one-to-one basis. (By "cognitive" I mean the net impact of pursuing a particular line of research on the knowledge production process itself; by "political" I mean its net impact on the balance of power in the society—Who benefits if a particular line of research proves productive?)

(7) Three kinds of courses would form the core curriculum of a graduate program in knowledge policy studies.

(a) *The Art of Transideological Policymaking:* Here students are trained to distinguish the essential from the nonessential features of policy, so that the essential policy features can be accommodated to whichever political ideology happens to come into power. In their ability to divine such essences, Machiavellians have traditionally had a keen sense of the metaphysical in politics. Indeed, Machiavelli *should* be the model, since most policy founders because policymakers become overly wedded to the ideologically tinged language of their original proposals, instead of focusing on the likely empirical consequences of implementing the policy, which could be expressed in less controversial ways. The need for Machiavellian tactics is especially acute in *knowledge* policy-making, where the continuity and retention of research is virtually definitive of the pursuit of knowledge. Continuity and retention, in turn, presuppose that knowledge production can be at least partially insulated from day-to-day political pressures. The Machiavellian twist, then, is to identify *insulation* with *accommodation*. One goal of the course is to realize that by having a clear sense of the difference between the essential and nonessential aspects of a policy proposal, the Machiavellian policy maker can prevent accommodation from turning into mere submission: namely, by defining the essential aspects of his policy proposal so as to include just those areas where he has clear expert authority over the politicians. Of course, definitions of this kind are highly manipulable, which means that the truly successful knowledge policymaker must be able to convert apparently ideological matters (where the politician is the "expert," so to speak) to technical ones (where the policymaker has the final word).

Among the reading sources would be so-called semantic approaches to politics (ranging in technicality from S.I. Hayakawa's [1949] *Language in Thought and Action* to T.D. Weldon's [1960] *The Vocabulary of Politics*), which are good at identifying the occasions when ideological discourse enters gratuitously from the standpoint of cognitive significance. A more general source would be the literature on the law's ability to neutralize the interests of competing parties by forcing the judge cast his decision so as to be universalizable to similar cases in the future, which not only satisfies an obvious ethical end but also serves to advance the law as a codified body of knowledge (Luhmann 1979).

(b) *The Prognostics and Diagnostics of Knowledge Policy:* "Prognostics" considers the general categories and procedures for charting the development of knowledge, while "diagnostics" considers the means by which the policymaker identifies the current situation as an instance of a particular stage in the development of knowledge. This distinction is based on Friedrich von Hayek's (1985, ch. 2) division of economic knowledge into the "theoretical" (what economists strive for—general principles that operate in closed systems) and the "historical" (what economic agents strive for— heuristics for determining at what one point and in which system they happen to be). These two sorts of knowledge need to be separated because often the reason why policy fails is not that the policymaker does not have the right analytic tools or principles for drafting the appropriate proposals, but rather that he does not have a good grasp of the identity of the current state of knowledge: for example, whether a particular discipline is in its "boom" or "bust" phase. Philosophy of science has not helped matters by neglecting the fact that besides selecting a theory, scientists must select a moment at which to select a theory. If selecting a theory is an exercise in prognostics, then selecting the moment is an exercise in diagnostics.

The readings in this course would include such staples of the science of science movement as bibliometrics and other science indicators (De Mey 1982, chs. 7-9), in conjunction with the counterfactual historical analysis practiced by "The New Economic History" and theorized by Jon Elster (1978) in *Logic and Society*. These two sorts of methods have been recently been combined with fruitful results in Irvine and Martin's (1984) *Foresight in Science*. (It should be noted that both philosophers and sociologists of science are generally ignorant of the advances that have been made in recent years by bibliometricians, which now enable them to construct not only a geography of disciplines, but also a "collective narrative" for each discipline on the basis of co-citation analysis. For more, see Small & Garfield [1985] and Small [1986].) The course would also deal with the concerns raised by Popper (1957) in *The Poverty of Historicism* about the self-fulfilling and self-defeating nature of the predictive element embodied in a knowledge policy proposal, as well as the workings of what Robert Nozick (1974, pp. 18-22) has dubbed "hidden" (disorder by design) and "invisible" (order by chance) hands in the production of knowledge. Among philosophical books, Nicholas Rescher's (1979) *Scientific Progress* is unique in treating the issues raised in this category.

(c) *The Administration of Knowledge Policy:* Under this general rubric is included the design and implementation of norms for effective knowledge growth. In dealing with other aspects of social life, administrators have traditionally believed that norms can be beneficial even if they are not systematically enforced (for example, even if every crime cannot be punished, punishing some crime is better than punishing none). However, in the case of knowledge policy the issue is less clear, since real knowledge growth requires that many disciplines and research programs can reliably build on each other's work: fraud or error at some point in the production of knowledge could vitiate the entire process. Thus, a premium may be placed on knowledge policymakers designing norms that are more systematically enforceable than the norms which guide the administration of other parts of society. This may have the effect of drawing attention away from such traditional norms of science as experimental corroboration, which are notoriously difficult to enforce. Another possibility is that rather than increasing the enforcement of norms, the knowledge policymaker follows the lead of successful corporate executives who operate by allowing the maximum amount of local sovereignty in the production process (this might mean that an industrial plant or, in the case of knowledge policy, a discipline manages most of its own day-to-day activities) that is consistent with the corporation's ability to contain and compensate for errors once they arise (Peters & Waterman 1982). One special area where the administration of knowledge policy is likely to raise interesting epistemological issues is the regulation of interdisciplinary borrowing: to take a vivid example, under what circumstances would a metaphysician be allowed to rely on arguments from indeterminacy in quantum mechanics to defend the existence of free will? That is, how should he establish the relevance of the other discipline's research to his own?

The texts in this course would cover the two main areas in which knowledge production needs to be "administered." First is the very process of textualizing and codifying knowledge. By obtaining a sense of the variety of writing styles and citation practices entertained by the disciplines, and the ways in which they have responded to various socio-intellectual needs, students can begin to see how the enforcement of conventions at this basic level can make a difference to the knowledge produced. Charles Bazerman (1988) has been virtually alone in pioneering this very important field. The second area of readings deals with the division of cognitive labor more explicitly and its implications for the production, distribution, and consumption of knowledge. On several occasions, we have cited the work of two sociologists, Richard Whitley (1986) and Randall Collins (1975) on these matters. In addition, an empirical literature is developing on the roles that internal and external criticism play in knowledge production (Campbell 1987, Neimeyer & Shadish 1987). Each area of readings would ideally be complemented by a "practicum," in which students have an opportunity to experiment with alternative writing practices and ways of approaching the channels of distribution (publishers, editors) and consumption (the reading public).

BIBLIOGRAPHY

Aarsleff, Hans: 1982, *From Locke to Saussure*, University of Minnesota Press, Minneapolis.

Abir-Am, Pnina: 1985, "Themes, Genres, and Orders of Legitimation in the Consolidation of New Scientific Disciplines: Deconstructing the Historiography of Molecular Biology," *History of Science*, 23, pp. 73-117.

Adorno, Theodor: 1973, *Negative Dialectics*, Seabury Press, New York.

Adorno, Theodor (ed.): 1976, *The Positivist Dispute in German Sociology*, Heinemann, London.

Albert, Hans: 1985, *A Treatise on Critical Reason*, Princeton University Press, Princeton.

Albury, W. Randall: 1983, *The Politics of Objectivity*, Deakin University Press, Victoria (Australia).

Althusser, Louis: 1970, *Reading Capital*, New Left Books, London.

Anderson, John: 1980, *Cognitive Psychology and Its Implications*, W. H. Freeman, San Francisco.

Apel, Karl-Otto: 1984, *Understanding and Explanation*, MIT Press, Cambridge, Mass.

Arnold, Matthew: 1972, "The Function of Criticism at the Present Time," in C. Ricks (ed.), *Selected Criticism of Matthew Arnold*, Oxford University Press, Oxford.

Austin, John L.: 1962, *How to Do Things with Words*, Harvard University Press, Cambridge, Mass.

Ayer, A.J.: 1952, *Language, Truth, and Logic*, 2nd ed., Dover, New York.

Bachelard, Gaston: 1985, *The New Scientific Spirit*, Beacon Press, Boston.

Baker, Gordon: 1977, "Defeasibility and Meaning," in Hacker & Raz (1977), pp. 26-57.

Baldamus, Wilhelm: 1976, *The Structure of Sociological Inference*, Barnes & Noble, Totowa, N.J.

Barber, Bernard: 1952, *Science and the Social Order*, Collier Macmillan, New York.

Barnes, Barry: 1974, *Sociological Theory and Scientific Knowledge*, Routledge & Kegan Paul, London.

Barnes, Barry: 1977, *Interests and the Growth of Knowledge*, Routledge & Kegan Paul, London.

Barnes, Barry: 1982, *T.S. Kuhn and Social Science*, Columbia University Press, New York.

Barnes, Barry: 1986, *About Science*, Blackwell, Oxford.

Bartley III, W.W.: 1984, *The Retreat to Commitment*, Open Court Press, La Salle, Ill.

Barwise, John and John Perry: 1983, *Situations and Attitudes*, MIT Press, Cambridge, Mass.

Bassnett-McGuire, Susan: 1980, *Translation Studies*, Methuen, London.

Bazerman, Charles: 1988, *Shaping Written Knowledge*, University of Wisconsin Press, Madison.

Bennett, Jonathan: 1964, *Rationality*, Routledge & Kegan Paul, London.

Bernstein, Basil: 1971, *Class, Codes, and Control*, Schocken, New York.

Bhaskar, Roy: 1980, *A Realist Theory of Science*, Harvester Press, Brighton.

Bhaskar, Roy: 1987, *Scientific Realism and Human Emancipation*, New Left Books, London.

Bloor, David: 1973, "Wittgenstein and Mannheim on the Sociology of Mathematics," *Studies in the History and Philosophy of Science*, 4, pp. 173-191.

Bloor, David: 1974, "Popper's Mystification of Objective Knowledge," *Science Studies*, 4, pp. 65-76.

Bloor, David: 1976, *Knowledge and Social Imagery*, Routledge & Kegan Paul, London.

Bloor, David: 1979, "Polyhedra and the Abominations of Leviticus," *British Journal of the History of Science*, 13, pp. 254-272.

Bloor, David: 1981, "The Strengths of the Strong Programme," in *Philosophy of the Social Sciences*, 11, pp. 199-213; also in J. R. Brown (1984).

Bloor, David: 1982, "Durkheim and Mauss Revisited: Classification and the Sociology of Knowledge," in *Studies in the History and Philosophy of Science*, 13, pp. 267-298.

Bloor, David: 1983, *Wittgenstein: A Social Theory of Knowledge*, Columbia University Press, New York.

Bloor, David: 1984, "A Sociological Theory of Objectivity," in S. Brown (ed.), *Objectivity and Cultural Divergence*, Cambridge University Press, Cambridge.

Bloor, David & Barry Barnes: 1982, "Relativism, Rationalism, and the Sociology of Knowledge," in Hollis & Lukes (1982).

Boorstin, Daniel: 1983, *The Discoverers*, Random House, New York.

Boring, Edwin: 1950, *A History of Experimental Psychology*, 2nd. ed., Appleton Century Crofts, New York.

Bourdieu, Pierre: 1975, "The Specificity of the Scientific Field and the Social Conditions of the Progress of Reason," *Social Science Information*, 14, 6, pp. 19-47.

Bourdieu, Pierre: 1977, *Reproduction: In Education, Society, and Culture*, Sage, Beverly Hills.

Bourdieu, Pierre: 1981, "Men and Machines," in Knorr-Cetina & Cicourel (1981).

Boyd, Richard: 1984, "The Current Status of Scientific Realism," in Leplin (1984).

Breal, Michel: 1964, *Semantics: Studies in the Science of Meaning*, Dover Books, New York.

Brown, Harold: 1978, "On Being Rational," *American Philosophical Quarterly* 15, 4.

Brown, James Robert (ed.): 1984, *Scientific Rationality: The Sociological Turn*, D. Reidel, Dordrecht.

Brown, Robert: 1984, *The Nature of Social Laws*, Cambridge Universtiy Press, Cambridge.

Buchdahl, Gerd: 1951, "Some Thoughts on Newton's Second Law of Motion in Classical Mechanics," *British Journal for the Philosophy of Science*, 2, pp. 217-235.

Bullough, Vernon (ed.): 1970, *The Scientific Revolution*, D. C. Heath, New York.

Callon, Michel: 1980, "Struggles and Negotiations to Define What Is Problematic and What Is Not," in K. Knorr-Cetina et al. (eds.), *The Social Process of Scientific Investigation,* D. Reidel, Dordrecht.

Cambrosio, Alberto & Peter Keating: 1983, "The Disciplinary Stake: The Case of Chronobiology," *Social Studies of Science,* 13, pp. 323-353.

Campbell, Donald: 1964, "Distinguishing Differences of Perception From Failures of Communication in Cross-Cultural Studies," in F.S.C. Northrop and H. Livingston (eds.), *Cross-Cultural Understanding: Epistemology in Anthropology,* Harper and Row, New York, pp. 308-336.

Campbell, Donald: 1987, "Guidelines for Monitoring the Scientific Competence of Preventive Intervention Research Centers," *Knowledge* 8, 3, pp. 389-430.

Canguilhem, Georges: 1978, *On the Normal and the Pathological,* D. Reidel, Dordrecht.

Carnap, Rudolf: 1934, "On the Character of Philosophical Problems," *Philosophy of Science,* pp. 5-19.

Carnap, Rudolf, 1956, *Meaning and Necessity,* University of Chicago Press, Chicago.

Carroll, John & John Payne (eds.): 1976, *Cognition and Social Behavior,* Lawrence Erlbaum Associates, Hillsdale, N.J.

Cassirer, Ernst: 1950, *The Problem of Knowledge: Philosophy, Science, and History Since Hegel,* Yale University Press, New Haven.

Cherniak, Christopher: 1986, *Minimal Rationality,* MIT Press, Cambridge, Mass.

Churchland, Paul: 1979, *Scientific Realism and the Plasticity of Mind,* Cambridge University Press, Cambridge.

Churchland, Paul: 1984, *Matter and Consciousness,* MIT Press, Cambridge, Mass.

Cohen, I. Bernard: 1981, *The Newtonian Revolution,* Harvard University Press, Cambridge, Mass.

Cohen, Robert & Marx Wartofsky (eds.): 1964, *Boston Studies in the Philosophy of Science,* vol. 2, D. Reidel, Dordrecht.

Cole, Michael & Sylvia Scribner: 1974, *Culture and Thought,* John Wiley & Sons, New York.

Collins, Harry: 1974, "The TEA Set: Tacit Knowledge and Scientific Networks," 5, *Science Studies,* pp. 165-186. Also in Collins (1985).

Collins, Harry: 1985, *Changing Order: Replication and Induction in Scientific Practice,* Sage, Beverly Hills.

Collins, Randall: 1975, *Conflict Sociology,* Academic Press, New York.

Collins, Randall: 1981, "On the Micro-Foundations of Macrosociologies," *American Journal of Sociology,* 86, pp. 984-1014.

Comte, Auguste: 1974, *The Essential Comte,* Stanislav Andreski (ed.), Croom Helm, London.

Crane, Diana: 1972, *Invisible Colleges,* University of Chicago Press, Chicago.

Crombie, Alistair: 1967, *Medieval and Early Modern Science,* 2 vols., Harvard University Press, Cambridge, Mass.

Crozier, Michel: 1964, *The Bureaucratic Phenomenon,* University of Chicago Press, Chicago.

Darden, Lindley & Nancy Maull: 1977, "Interfield Theories," *Philosophy of*

Science, 44, pp. 43-64.

Darnton, Robert: 1984, *The Great Cat Massacre and Other Episodes in French Cultural History,* Basic Books, New York.

Davidhazi, Peter: 1986, "'Autotelic' Criticism and the Functions of Evaluation," paper delivered at the International Association for Philosophy and Literature, Seattle.

Davidson, Donald: 1984, *Inquiries into Truth and Interpretation,* Oxford University Press, Oxford.

Dawes, Robyn: 1976, "Shallow Psychology," in Carroll and Payne (1976), pp. 3-12.

Degenhardt, M.A.B.: 1982, *Education and the Value of Knowledge,* George Allen & Unwin, London.

De George, Richard & Fernand (eds.): 1972, *The Structuralists from Marx to Levi-Strauss,* Doubleday, Garden City, N.Y.

De Man, Paul: 1971, *Blindness and Insight: Essays in the Rhetoric of Contemporary Criticism,* Oxford University Press, Oxford.

De Mey, Marc: 1982, *The Cognitive Paradigm,* D. Reidel, Dordrecht.

Dennett, Daniel: 1971, "Intentional Systems," in *Journal of Philosophy,* 68, pp. 87-106.

Dennett, Daniel: 1978, *Brainstorms,* MIT Press, Cambridge, Mass.

Dennett, Daniel: 1984, *Elbow Room: The Varieties of Free Will Worth Wanting,* MIT Press, Cambridge, Mass.

Derrida, Jacques: 1976, *Of Grammatology,* Johns Hopkins University Press, Baltimore.

Deutscher, Irwin: 1968, "Public and Private Opinions: Some Situations and Multiple Realities," in S. Nagi and R. Corwin (eds.), *Social Contexts of Research,* Wiley-Interscience, New York.

Dewey, John: 1916, *Democracy and Education,* Macmillan, New York.

Dinneen, Francis: 1967, *An Introduction to General Linguistics,* Holt Rinehart & Winston, New York.

Donnellan, Keith: 1977, "Reference and Definite Descriptions," in Schwartz (1977).

Doppelt, Gerald: 1982, "Kuhn's Epistemological Relativism," in Meiland & Krausz (1982), pp. 113-148.

Dray, William: 1957, *Laws and Explanation in History,* Oxford University Press, Oxford.

Duhem, Pierre: 1954, *The Aim and Structure of Physical Theory,* Princeton University Press, Princeton.

Dummett, Michael: 1976, *Truth and Other Enigmas,* Duckworth, London.

Durkheim, Emile: 1938, *Rules of the Sociological Method,* Collier Macmillan, New York.

Durkheim, Emile: 1951, *Suicide,* Collier Macmillan, New York.

Durkheim, Emile: 1961, *Elementary Forms of the Religious Life,* Collier Macmillan, New York.

Eliot, T.S.: 1948, "The Function of Criticism," in *Selected Essays,* Faber and Faber, London.

Elkana, Yehuda: 1982, "A Programmatic Attempt at an Anthropology of Knowledge," in Mendelsohn & Elkana (1982), pp. 1-76.

Elster, Jon: 1978, *Logic and Society,* John Wiley & Sons, Chichester.

Elster, Jon: 1979, *Ulysses and the Sirens,* Cambridge University Press, Cambridge.

Elster, Jon: 1983, *Explaining Technical Change*, Cambridge University Press, Cambridge.

Elster, Jon: 1984, *Sour Grapes*, Cambridge University Press, Cambridge.

Faust, David: 1985, *The Limits of Scientific Reasoning*, University of Minnesota Press, Minneapolis.

Feenberg, Andrew: 1986, *Lukacs, Marx, and the Sources of Critical Theory*, Oxford University Press, Oxford.

Feigl, Herbert, Michael Scriven, and Grover Maxwell (eds.): 1958, *Minnesota Studies in the Philosophy of Science*, vol. 2, University of Minnesota Press, Minneapolis.

Feyerabend, Paul: 1975, *Against Method*, New Left Books, London.

Feyerabend, Paul: 1981a, *Realism, Rationalism, and the Scientific Method* (Philosophical Papers, vol. 1), Cambridge University Press, Cambridge.

Feyerabend, Paul: 1981b, *Problems of Empiricism* (Philosophical Papers, vol. 2), Cambridge University Press, Cambridge.

Field, Hartry: 1973, "Theory Change and the Indeterminacy of Reference," *Journal of Philosophy*, pp. 462-481.

Fodor, Jerry: 1981, *Representations*, MIT Press, Cambridge, Mass.

Fodor, Jerry: 1983, *The Modularity of Mind*, MIT Press, Cambridge, Mass.

Follesdal, Dagfinn: 1975, "Meaning and Experience," in Guttenplan (1975).

Forman, Paul: 1971, "Weimar Culture, Causality and Quantum Theory, 1918-1927: Adaptation by German Physicists and Mathematicians to a Hostile Intellectual Environment," in R. McCormmach (ed.), *Historical Studies in the Physical Sciences*, University of Pennsylvania Press, Philadelphia.

Foucault, Michel: 1970, *The Order of Things*, Random House, New York.

Foucault, Michel: 1975, *The Archaeology of Knowledge*, Harper and Row, New York.

Foucault, Michel: 1979, *Discipline and Punish*, Random House, New York.

Friedson, Eliot: 1984, "Are Professions Necessary?" in Haskell (1984), pp. 3-27.

Fuller, Steve: 1982, "Recovering Philosophy From Rorty," in Thomas Nickles and Peter Asquith (eds.), *PSA 1982*, vol. 1, Philosophy of Science Association, East Lansing.

Fuller, Steve: 1983a, "A French Science (With English Subtitles)," in *Philosophy and Literature*, pp. 3-14.

Fuller, Steve: 1983b, "In Search of the Science of History: The Case of Wilhelm Dilthey and Experimental Psychology," paper delivered at philosophy department colloquium, SUNY at Stony Brook.

Fuller, Steve: 1984, "The Cognitive Turn in Sociology," *Erkenntnis*, 21, pp. 439-450.

Fuller, Steve: 1985a, *Bounded Rationality in Law and Science*, Ph.D. dissertation, University of Pittsburgh.

Fuller, Steve: 1985b, "Is There a Language-Game That Even the Deconstructionist Can Play?" in *Philosophy and Literature*, 9, pp. 104-109.

Fuller, Steve: 1986, "The Crisis in the Structuralist Paradigm in Experimental Psychology," paper delivered at conference on Testing Theories of Scientific Change, Virginia Polytechnic Institute.

Fuller, Steve & David Gorman: 1987, "Burning Libraries: Cultural Creation and the Problem of Historical Consciousness," *Annals of Scholarship* 4, 3.

Fuller, Steve & Charles Willard: 1986, "In Defense of Relativism: Rescuing Incommensurability from the Self-Excepting Fallacy," paper delivered at the First International Conference on Argumentation, Amsterdam.

Gadamer, Hans-Georg: 1975, *Truth and Method,* Seabury Press, New York.

Gallie, W.B.: 1957, "Essentially Contested Concepts," *Proceedings of the Aristotelian Society.*

Gallie, W.B.: 1967, "The Idea of Practice," *Proceedings of the Aristotelian Society.*

Gellner, Ernest: 1970, "Concepts and Society," in Wilson (1970).

Geuss, Raymond: 1982, *The Idea of a Critical Theory,* Cambridge University Press, Cambridge.

Gibson, James: 1979, *The Ecological Approach to Visual Perception,* Houghton Mifflin, Boston.

Giddens, Anthony: 1984, *The Constitution of Society,* University of California Press, Berkeley.

Gieryn, Thomas: 1983a, "Making the Demarcation of Science a Sociological Problem: Boundary-Work by John Tyndall, Victorian Scientist," in Rachel Laudan (1983), pp. 57-86.

Gieryn, Thomas: 1983b, "Boundary-Work and the Demarcation of Science from Non-Science: Strains and Interests in the Professional Ideologies of Scientists," *American Sociological Review,* 48, 781-795.

Gilbert, Nigel & Michael Mulkay: 1984, *Opening Pandora's Box,* Cambridge University Press, Cambridge.

Glymour, Clark: 1980, *Theory and Evidence,* Princeton University Press, Princeton.

Goffman, Erving: 1959, *The Presentation of the Self in Everyday Life,* Doubleday, Garden City.

Goldman, Alvin: 1986, *Epistemology and Cognition,* Harvard University Press, Cambridge, Mass.

Gombrich, Ernst: 1979, *The Sense of Order,* Phaidon, Oxford.

Goodman, Nelson: 1949, "On Likeness of Meaning," *Analysis* 10, pp. 1-7.

Goodman, Nelson: 1955, *Fact, Fiction, and Forecast,* Bobbs-Merrill, Indianapolis.

Gould, Stephen J.: 1983, *The Mismeasure of Man,* Norton & Sons, New York.

Graham, Loren: 1981, *Between Science and Values,* Columbia University Press, New York.

Graham, Loren (ed.): 1983, *The Functions and Uses of Disciplinary History,* D. Reidel, Dordrecht.

Grandy, Richard: 1973, "Reference, Meaning, and Belief," *Journal of Philosophy,* 70, 1973.

Granger, Herbert: 1985, "The Scala Naturae and the Continuity of Kinds," *Phronesis,* 30, 2, pp. 181-200.

Grant, Edward: 1977, *Physical Science in the Middle Ages,* Cambridge University Press, Cambridge.

Greene, Judith: 1972, *Psycholinguistics,* Penguin, Baltimore.

Grice: Paul: 1957, "Meaning," *Philosophical Review,* 66, pp. 377-388.

Grice, Paul: 1975, "Logic and Conversation," in P. Cole and J.L. Morgan (eds.), *Syntax and Semantics,* vol. 3: *Speech Acts,* Academic Press,

New York.

Grunbaum, Adolf: 1984, *The Foundations of Psychoanalysis: A Philosophical Critique*, University of California Press, Berkeley.

Guerlac, Henry: 1965, "Where the Statue Stood: Divergent Loyalties to Newton," in E. Wassermann (ed.), *Aspects of the Eighteenth Century*, Johns Hopkins University Press, Baltimore.

Guttenplan, S.D. (ed.): 1975, *Mind and Language*, Oxford University Press, Oxford.

Haack, Susan: 1978, *Philosophy of Logics*, Cambridge University Press, Cambridge.

Haack, Susan: 1980, "Is Truth Flat or Bumpy?" in D.H. Mellor (ed.), *Prospects For Pragmatism*, Cambridge University Press, Cambridge.

Haas, Ernest, Mary Williams & Don Babai: 1977, *Scientists and World Order*, University of California Press, Berkeley.

Habermas, Juergen: 1971, *Knowledge and Human Interests*, Beacon Press, Boston.

Habermas, Juergen: 1975, *Legitimation Crisis*, Beacon Press, Boston.

Hacker, Peter and Joseph Raz (eds.): 1977, *Law, Morality, and Society*, Oxford University Press, Oxford.

Hacking, Ian: 1975a, *Why Does Language Matter to Philosophy?* Cambridge University Press, Cambridge.

Hacking, Ian: 1975b, *The Emergence of Probability*, Cambridge University Press, Cambridge.

Hacking, Ian: 1979, "Michel Foucault's Immature Science," *Nous* 13.

Hacking, Ian (ed.): 1981a, *Scientific Revolutions*, Oxford University Press, Oxford.

Hacking, Ian: 1981b, "Lakatos' Philosophy of Science," in Hacking (1981a), pp. 128-143.

Hacking, Ian: 1982, "Language, Truth, and Reason," in Hollis and Lukes (1982).

Hacking, Ian: 1983, *Representing and Intervening*, Cambridge University Press, Cambridge.

Halliday, Michael: 1982, *Language as Social Semiotic*, University Park Press, Baltimore.

Hallpike, C.R.: 1979, *The Foundations of Primitive Thought*, Oxford University Press, Oxford.

Hansen, Bert: 1978, "Science and Magic," in Lindberg (1978).

Hanson, Russell: 1958, *Patterns of Discovery*, Cambridge University Press, Cambridge.

Hardwig, John: 1986, "Epistemic Dependence," *Journal of Philosophy*, 82, 7, pp. 335-349.

Harre, Rom: 1970, *The Principles of Scientific Thinking*, University of Chicago Press, Chicago.

Harrison, Bernard: 1979, *An Introduction to the Philosophy of Language*, Collier Macmillan, London.

Hart, Herbert: 1948, "The Ascription of Responsibilities and Rights," *Proceedings of the Aristotelian Society*.

Hart, Herbert: 1961, *The Concept of Law*, Oxford University Press, Oxford.

Hart, Herbert & Anthony Honore: 1959, *Causation in the Law*, Oxford University Press, Oxford.

Haskell, Thomas (ed.): 1984, *The Authority of Experts*, Indiana University Press, Bloomington.

Haskell, Thomas: 1984, "Professionalism versus Capitalism: Tawney and Peirce on the Disinterestedness of the Professional Community," in Haskell (1984).

Haugeland, John (ed.): 1981, *Mind Design*, MIT Press, Cambridge, Mass.

Hayakawa, S. I.: 1949, *Language in Thought and Action*, Harcourt Brace, New York.

Hearst, Eliot (ed.): 1979, *The First Century of Experimental Psychology*, Lawrence Erlbaum Associates, Hillsdale.

Heelan, Patrick: 1983, *Space-Perception and the Philosophy of Science*, University of California Press, Berkeley.

Hegel, G.W.F.: 1964, *Reason in History*, Bobbs-Merrill, Indianapolis.

Heidegger, Martin: 1962, *Being and Time*, Harper and Row, New York.

Heilbroner, Robert: 1970, *Between Capitalism and Socialism*, Random House, New York.

Hempel, Carl: 1965, *Aspects of Scientific Explanation*, Collier Macmillan, New York.

Hendry, John: 1980, "Weimar Culture and Causality," in C. Chant and J. Fauvel (eds.), *Darwin to Einstein: Historical Studies on Science and Belief*, Longmans, London.

Hertz, Henrich: 1899, *Principles of Mechanics*, J.T. Walley, London.

Hesse, Mary: 1963, *Models and Analogies in Science*, University of Notre Dame Press, South Bend.

Hirsch, E. D.: 1967, *Validity in Interpretation*, Yale University Press, New Haven.

Hirsch, E. D.: 1976, *The Aims of Interpretation*, Yale University Press, New Haven.

Hirsch, E. D.: 1987, *Cultural Literacy*, Houghton Mifflin, Boston.

Hockett, Charles: 1954, "Chinese vs. English: An Exploration of the Whorfian Thesis," in H. Hoijer (ed.), *Language in Culture*, University of Chicago Press, Chicago.

Hofstadter, Richard & Walter Metzger: 1955, *The Development of Academic Freedom in the United States*, Columbia University Press, New York.

Hohfeld, Rainer: 1983, "Cancer Research: A Study of Praxis-Related Theoretical Developments in Chemistry, the Biosciences, and Medicine," in Schaefer (1983), pp. 93-126.

Hollis, Martin: 1982, "The Social Destruction of Reality," in Hollis and Lukes (1982).

Hollis, Martin & Steven Lukes (eds.): 1982, *Rationality and Relativism*, MIT Press, Cambridge, Mass.

Horton, Robin: 1970, "African Thought and Western Science," in Wilson (1970).

Irvine, John & Ben Martin: 1984, *Foresight in Science: Picking the Winners*, Frances Pinter, London.

Jarvie, Ian: 1970, *Concepts and Society*, Routledge & Kegan Paul, London.

Jarvie, Ian: 1984, "A Plague on Both Your Houses," in J.R. Brown (1984).

Jones, Robert Alun: 1983, "On Merton's 'History' and 'Systematics' of Sociological Theory" in Graham (1983).

Jones, Robert Alun & Henrika Kucklick (eds.): 1981, *Knowledge and*

Society: Studies in the Sociology of Culture Past and Present, JAI Press, Greenwich, Conn.

Kelsen, Hans: 1949, *The General Theory of Law,* Harvard University Press, Cambridge, Mass.

Kitcher, Philip: 1978, "Theories, Theorists, and Theoretical Change," *Philosophical Review,* 87, pp. 519-547.

Knorr-Cetina, Karin: 1981, *The Manufacture of Knowledge,* Pergamon Press, Oxford.

Knorr-Cetina, Karin: 1982, "Scientific Communities or Transepistemic Arenas of Research? A Critique of Quasi-Economic Models of Science," *Social Studies of Science,* 12.

Knorr-Cetina, Karin & Aaron Cicourel (eds.): 1981, *Advances in Social Theory and Methodology,* Routledge & Kegan Paul, London.

Kockelmans, Joseph (ed.): 1968, *Philosophy of Science: The Historical Bakckground,* Collier Macmillan, New York.

Koehler, Wolfgang: 1971, *The Selected Papers of Wolfgang Koehler,* Liveright, New York.

Kolakowski, Leszek: 1978, *The Main Currents of Marxism,* 3 vols., Oxford University Press, Oxford.

Kordig, Carl: 1971, *The Justification of Scientific Change,* D. Reidel, Dordrecht.

Koyre, Alexandre: 1964, *From the Closed World to the Infinite Universe,* Johns Hopkins University Press, Baltimore.

Koyre, Alexandre: 1969, *Newtonian Studies,* University of Chicago Press, Chicago.

Krige, John: 1980, *Science, Revolution, and Discontinuity,* Harvester Press, Brighton.

Kripke, Saul: 1977, "Identity and Necessity," in Schwartz (1977).

Kuhn, Thomas: 1970a, *The Structure of Scientific Revolutions,* 2nd ed., University of Chicago Press, Chicago

Kuhn, Thomas: 1970b, "Reflections on My Critics," in Lakatos and Musgrave (1970).

Kuhn, Thomas: 1977a, *Essential Tension,* University of Chicago Press, Chicago.

Kuhn, Thomas: 1977b, "Second Thoughts on Paradigms," in Suppe (1977).

Kuhn, Thomas: 1981, "A Function for Thought-Experiments," in Hacking (1981a), pp. 6-27.

Lakatos, Imre: 1970, "Falsification and the Methodology of Scientific Research Programs," in Lakatos and Musgrave (1970), pp. 91-196.

Lakatos, Imre: 1981, "The History of Science and Its Rational Reconstructions," in Hacking (1981a).

Lakatos, Imre & Alan Musgrave (ed.): 1970, *Criticism and the Growth of Knowledge,* Cambridge University Press, Cambridge.

Lamb, David & Susan Easton: 1984, *Multiple Discovery,* Avebury Press, Trowbridge.

Latour, Bruno: 1981, "Insiders and Outsiders in the Sociology of Science, or How Can We Foster Agnosticism?" in Jones & Kucklick (1981).

Latour, Bruno & Steve Woolgar: 1979, *Laboratory Life: The Social Construction of Scientific Facts,* Sage, Beverly Hills.

Laudan, Larry: 1977, *Progress and Its Problems,* University of California Press, Berkeley.

Laudan, Larry: 1981, "The Pseudo-Science of Science?" *Philosophy of the Social Sciences,* 11, pp. 173-198; also in J.R. Brown (1984).

Laudan, Larry: 1983, "The Demise of the Demarcation Problem," in Rachel Laudan (1983), pp. 7-36.

Laudan, Larry: 1984, *Science and Values,* University of California Press, Berkeley.

Laudan, Larry: 1984a, "Explaining the Success of Science," in J. Cushing, C. Delaney, and G. Gutting (eds.), *Science and Reality,* University of Notre Dame Press, South Bend.

Laudan, Rachel (ed.): 1983, *Working papers on the Demarcation of Science and Pseudo-Science,* Virginia Tech Center for the Study of Science in Society, Blacksburg.

Laymon, Ronald: 1984, "The Path from Data to Theory," in Leplin (1984).

Leech, Geoffrey: 1983, *Principles of Pragmatics,* Longmans, London.

Lemon, L.T. & M.J. Reis (eds.): 1965, *Russian Formalist Criticism,* University of Nebraska Press, Lincoln.

Leplin, Jarrett (ed.): 1984, *Scientific Realism,* University of California Press, Berkeley.

Le Pore, Ernest (ed.): 1986, *Truth and Interpretation,* Blackwell, Oxford.

Levi, Isaac: 1984, *Decisions and Revisions,* Cambridge University Press, Cambridge.

Levi-Strauss, Claude: 1964, *The Savage Mind,* University of Chicago Press, Chicago.

Lewis, David: 1969, *Convention,* Harvard University Press, Cambridge, Mass.

Lightfoot, D.W.: 1979, *Principles of Diachronic Syntax,* Cambridge University Press, Cambridge.

Lindberg, David (ed.): 1978, *Science in the Middle Ages,* University of Chicago Press, Chicago.

Lippmann, Walter: 1955, *The Public Philosophy,* New American Library, New York.

Lowe, Adolph: 1965, *On Economic Knowledge: Toward a Science of Political Economics,* Harper & Row, New York.

Lugg, Andrew: 1984, "Two Historiographical Strategies: Ideas and Social Conditions in the History of Science," in J. R. Brown (1984).

Luhmann, Niklas: 1979, *The Differentiation of Society,* Columbia University Press, New York.

Lukacs, Georg: 1971, *History and Class Consciousness,* MIT Press, Cambridge, Mass.

Lukes, Steven: 1982a, "Relativism in its Place," in Hollis & Lukes (1982).

Lukes, Steven: 1982b, "Comments on David Bloor," in *Studies in the History and Philosophy of Science,* 13, pp. 313-318.

Lyons, John: 1977, *Semantics,* vol. 1, Cambridge University Press, Cambridge.

Lyotard, John-Francois: 1984, *The Post-Modern Condition,* University of Minnesota Press, Minneapolis.

MacDonald, Graham & Philip Pettit: 1981, *Semantics and Social Science,* Routledge & Kegan Paul, London.

Machlup, Fritz: 1962, *The Production and Distribution of Knowledge in the United States,* Princeton University Press, Princeton.

MacIntyre, Alasdair: 1970a, "The Idea of a Social Science" in Wilson (1970).

MacIntyre, Alasdair: 1970b, "Is Understanding Religion Compatible with Believing?" in Wilson (1970).

MacIntyre, Alasdair: 1984, *After Virtue*, University of Notre Dame Press, South Bend.

Macquarrie, John: 1965, "Rudolf Bultmann," in Marty and Peerman (1965).

Maher, Brendan and Winifred Maher: 1979, "Psychopathology," in Hearst (1979).

Makkreel, Rudolf: 1975, *Dilthey: Philosopher of the Human Sciences*, Princeton University Press, Princeton.

Mandelbaum, Maurice: 1987, *Purpose and Necessity in Social Theory*, Johns Hopkins University Press, Baltimore.

Mannheim, Karl: 1936, *Ideology and Utopia*, Routledge & Kegan Paul, London.

Mannheim, Karl: 1940, *Man and Society in an Age of Reconstruction*, Routledge & Kegan Paul, London.

Mannheim, Karl: 1971, "On the Interpretation of *Weltanschauung*," in K. Wolff (ed.), *From Karl Mannheim*, Oxford University Press, Oxford, pp. 8-58.

March, James G.: "Bounded Rationality, Ambiguity, and the Engineering of Choice," *The Bell Journal of Economics* 9, pp. 587-608.

Martinet, Andre: 1960, *A Functional View of Language*, Oxford University Press, Oxford.

Marty, Martin and Dean Peerman (eds.): 1965, *A Handbook of Christian Theologians*, Fontana, Cleveland.

Maruyama, Magoroh: 1968, "The Second Cybernetics: Deviation-Amplifying Mutual Causal Processes," in W. Buckley (ed.), *Modern Systems Research for the Behavioral Scientist*, Aldine, Chicago.

Masterman, Margaret: 1970, "The Nature of Paradigm," in Lakatos & Musgrave (1970), pp. 68-76.

Mauss, Marcel: 1979, *Sociology and Psychology*, Routledge & Kegan Paul, London.

McCarthy, Thomas: 1978, *The Critical Theory of Juergen Habermas*, MIT Press, Cambridge, Mass.

McCauley, Robert: 1986, "Intertheoretic Relations and the Future of Psychology," *Philosophy of Science* 53, 2, pp. 179-199.

McCole, John: 1985, "Benjamin's *Passagen-Werk:* A Guide to the Labyrinth," *Theory and Society*, 14, 4, pp. 497-509.

McGuire, J.E. and P.M. Rattansi: 1966, "Newton and the Pipes of Pan," *Notes and Records of the Royal Society of London*, 21, pp. 108-143.

McInerny, Ralph: 1983, "Beyond the Liberal Arts," in Wagner (1983), pp. 248-272.

Meiland, Jack & Michael Krausz (eds.): 1982, *Relativism: Cognitive and Moral*, University of Notre Dame Press, South Bend.

Mendelsohn, Everett: 1964, "Explanation in Nineteenth Century Biology," in Cohen and Wartofsky (1964), pp. 127-150.

Mendelsohn, Everett and Yehuda Elkana (eds.): 1982, *Sciences and Cultures*, D. Reidel, Dordrecht

Merquior, J. G.: 1986, *From Prague to Paris*, New Left Books, London.

Merton, Robert: 1936, "The Unanticipated Consequences of Purposive Social Action," *American Sociological Review*, 1, pp. 894-904.

Merton, Robert: 1957, *Social Theory and Social Structure*, 2nd ed., Collier

Macmillan, New York.

Merton, Robert: 1976, *Sociological Ambivalence*, Free Press, New York.

Miller, Neal: 1959, "The Liberalization of Basic S-R Concepts: Extensions to Conflict Behavior, Motivation, and Social Learning," in S. Koch (ed.) *Psychology: A Study of Science*, vol. 2, McGraw-Hill, New York.

Moore, Ronald: 1978, *Legal Norms and Legal Science*, University of Hawaii Press, Honolulu.

Mulkay, Michael: 1979, "Knowledge and Uitlity: Implications for the Sociology of Knowledge," *Social Studies of Science* 9, pp. 69-74.

Mulkay, Michael: 1984, "The Scientist Talks Back: A One-Act Play, with a Moral, about Replication in Science and Reflexivity in Sociology," *Social Studies of Science*, 14, pp. 265-282.

Mulkay, Michael, Nigel Gilbert & Steve Woolgar: 1975, "Problem Areas and Research Networks in Science," *Sociology*, 9, pp. 188-203.

Munevar, Gonzalo: 1981, *Radical Knowledge*, Hackett, Indianapolis.

Nagel, Ernest: 1968, *The Structure of Science*, Routledge & Kegan Paul, London.

Needham, Rodney: 1972, *Belief, Language, and Experience*, Blackwell, Oxford.

Neimeyer, Robert & William Shadish: 1987, "Optimizing Scientific Validity," *Knowledge* 8, 3, pp. 463-485.

Neurath, Otto: 1962, *Foundations of the Social Sciences*, University of Chicago Press, Chicago.

Neurath, Otto: 1983, "Encyclopedia as 'Model,'" in *The Selected Papers of Otto Neurath*, D. Reidel, Dordrecht.

Newell, Allan & Herbert Simon: 1972, *Human Problem Solving*, Prentice-Hall, Englewood Cliffs, N.J.

Newmark, Peter: 1981, *Approaches to Translation*, Pergamon, Oxford.

Nickles, Thomas: 1980, "Introduction," in T. Nickles (ed.), *Scientific Discovery, Logic, and Rationality*, D. Reidel, Dordrecht.

Nida, Eugene: 1964, *Towards a Science of Translation*, E.J. Brill, The Hague.

Nisbett, Richard & Lee Ross: 1980, *Human Inference: Strategies of Social Judgment*, Prentice-Hall, Englewood Cliffs, N.J.

Noelle-Neumann, Elisabeth: 1982, *The Spiral of Silence*, University of Chicago Press, Chicago.

Nowotny, Helga: 1979, "Science and Its Critics: Reflections on Antiscience," in H. Nowotny and H. Rose (eds.), *Countermovements in the Sciences*, D. Reidel, Dordrecht.

Nozick, Robert: 1974, *Anarchy, State, and Utopia*, Basic Books, New York.

Ong, Walter: 1963, *Ramus, Method, and the Decay of Dialogue*, Harvard University Press, Cambridge, Mass.

Oppenheim, Paul & Hilary Putnam: 1958, "Unity of Science as a Working Hypothesis," in Feigl, Scriven & Maxwell (1958), pp. 3-36.

Passmore, John: 1966, *A Hundred Years of Philosophy*, Penguin, Harmondsworth, Middlesex.

Pauck, Wilhelm: 1965, "Adolf von Harnack," in Marty and Peerman (1965).

Perelman, Chaim & L. Olbrechts-Tyteca: 1969, *The New Rhetoric*, University of Notre Dame Press, South Bend.

Peters, Thomas & Robert Waterman: 1982, *In Search of Excellence*, Warner

Books, New York.

Pitkin, Hannah: 1972, *The Concept of Representation*, University of California Press, Berkeley.

Poincare, Henri: 1905, *Science and Hypothesis*, Science Press, New York.

Polanyi, Michael: 1957, *Personal Knowledge*, University of Chicago Press, Chicago.

Popper, Karl: 1957, *The Poverty of Historicism*, Harper and Row, New York.

Popper, Karl: 1963, *Conjectures and Refutations*, Harper and Row, New York.

Popper, Karl: 1970, "Normal Science and Its Dangers," in Lakatos and Musgrave (1970).

Popper, Karl: 1972, *Objective Knowledge*, Oxford University Press, Oxford.

Popper, Karl: 1981, "The Rationality of Scientific Revolutions," in Hacking (1981a), pp. 80-106.

Price, Derek de Solla: 1964, *Little Science, Big Science*, Penguin, Harmondsworth, Middlesex.

Prigogine Ilya & Isabelle Stengers: 1984, *Order Out of Chaos*, Bantam, New York.

Putnam, Hilary: 1975, *Mind, Language, and Reality* (Philosophical Papers, vol. 2), Cambridge University Press, Cambridge.

Putnam, Hilary: 1977, "Meaning and Reference," in Schwartz (1977).

Putnam, Hilary: 1978, *Meaning and the Moral Sciences*, Routledge & Kegan Paul, London.

Putnam, Hilary: 1981, "The 'Corroboration' of Theories," in Hacking (1981a), pp. 60-79.

Putnam, Hilary: 1982, *Reason, Truth, and History*, Cambridge University Press, Cambridge.

Putnam, Hilary: 1983, *Realism and Reason* (Philosophical Papers, vol. 3), Cambridge University Press, Cambridge.

Putnam, Hilary: 1984, "What is Realism?" in Leplin (1984).

Quine, W.V.O.: 1953, *From a Logical Point of View*, Harvard University Press, Cambridge, Mass.

Quine, W.V.O.: 1960, *Word and Object*, MIT Press, Cambridge, Mass.

Quine, W.V.O.: 1969, *Ontological Relativity and Other Essays*, Columbia University Press, New York.

Rawls, John: 1955, "Two Concepts of Rules," *Philosophical Review*, 64.

Reichenbach, Hans: 1938, *Experience and Prediction*, University of Chicago Press, Chicago.

Rescher, Nicholas: 1977, *Dialectics*, SUNY Press, Albany.

Rescher, Nicholas: 1978, *Peirce's Philosophy of Science*, University of Notre Dame Press, South Bend.

Rescher, Nicholas: 1979/8, *Scientific Progress*, Blackwell, Oxford.

Ricoeur, Paul: 1978, *The Rule of Metaphor*, Routledge & Kegan Paul, London.

Rip, Arie: 1982, "The Development of Restrictedness in the Sciences," in N. Elias et al. (eds) *Scientific Establishments and Hierarchies*, D. Reidel, Dordrecht, pp. 219-238.

Rip, Arie: 1984, "Controversies as Informal Technology Assessment," Report to the Science Dynamics Institute, Amsterdam.

Rorty, Richard: 1972, "The World Well Lost," *Journal of Philosophy,* 69.
Rorty, Richard: 1979, *Philosophy and the Mirror of Nature,* Princeton University Press, Princeton.
Rosch, Eleanor: 1973, "On the Internal Structure of Perceptual and Semantic Categories," in T.E. Moore (ed.), *Cognitive Development and Acquisition of Language,* Academic Press, New York.
Rosenberg, Alexander: 1980, *Sociobiology and the Preemption of Social Science,* Johns Hopkins University Press, Baltimore.
Rosenthal, Peggy: 1984, *Words and Values,* Oxford University Press, Oxford.
Ryle, Gilbert: 1949, *The Concept of Mind,* Barnes & Noble, Totowa, N.J.
Sacksteder, William: 1986, "Some Words Aristotle Never Uses," *The New Scholasticism* 60, 4, pp. 427-453.
Sartre, Jean-Paul: 1976, *Critique of Dialectical Reason,* New Left Books, London.
Schaefer, Wolf (ed.) 1984, *Finalization in Science,* D. Reidel, Dordrecht.
Schlick, Moritz: 1977, *General Theory of Knowledge,* Springer-Verlag, Vienna.
Schnaedelbach, Herbert: 1984, *Philosophy in Germany: 1831-1933,* Cambridge University Press, Cambridge.
Schneider, Louis: 1971, "Dialectic in Sociology," *American Sociological Review,* 36.
Schofield, Robert: 1970, *Mechanism and Materialism,* Princeton University Press, Princeton.
Schutz, Alfred: 1962, *Collected Papers,* vol. 1, Martinus Nijhoff, The Hague.
Schwartz, Stephen (ed.): 1977, *Naming, Necessity, and Natural Kinds,* Cornell University Press, Ithaca.
Schweber, Silvan: 1982, "Demons, Angels, and Probability: Some Aspects of British Science in the Nineteenth Century," in A. Shimony and H. Feshbach (eds.), *Physics as Natural Philosophy,* MIT Press, Cambridge, Mass.
Scriven, Michael: 1958, "Definitions, Explanations, and Theories," Feigl, Scriven & Maxwell (1958), pp. 99-195.
Searle, John: 1969, *Speech Acts,* Cambridge University Press, Cambridge.
Segall, Marshall: 1979, *Cross-Cultural Psychology,* Wadsworth, Belmont.
Segall, Marshall, Donald Campbell & Melville Herskovitz: 1966, *The Influence of Culture on Visual Perception,* Bobbs-Merrill, Indianapolis.
Serres, Michel: 1972, *L'Interference,* Editions de Minuit, Paris.
Serres, Michel: 1982, *Hermes: Literature, Philosophy, Science,* Johns Hopkins University Press, Baltimore.
Shapere, Dudley: 1981, "Meaning and Scientific Change," in Hacking (1981a), pp. 28-59.
Shapin, Steven: 1982, "History of Science and Its Sociological Reconstructions," in *History of Science,* 20, pp. 157-211.
Shapin, Steven and Simon Schaffer: 1985, *Leviathan and the Air-Pump: Hobbes, Boyle, and the Experimental Life,* Princeton University Press, Princeton.
Shrader-Frechette, Kristin: 1983, *Nuclear Power and Public Policy,* D. Reidel, Dordrecht.

Shrader-Frechette, Kristin: 1984, *Science Policy, Ethics, and Economic Methodology*, D. Reidel, Dordrecht.

Shrader-Frechette, Kristin: 1985, *Risk Analysis and Scientific Methodology*, D. Reidel, Dordrecht.

Silverman, David & Brian Torode: 1980, *The Material Word*, Routledge & Kegan Paul, London.

Simon, Herbert: 1976, *Administrative Behavior*, 3rd ed., Collier Macmillan, New York.

Simon, Herbert: 1981, *The Sciences of the Artificial*, 2nd ed., MIT Press, Cambridge, Mass.

Simon, Herbert: 1986, "Alternative Visions of Rationality," in H. Arkes & K. Hammond (eds.), *Judgement and Decision Making*, Cambridge University Press, Cambridge, pp. 97-113.

Skinner, B.F.: 1970, *Beyond Freedom and Dignity*, Alfred Knopf, New York.

Skinner, Quentin: 1969, "Meaning and Understanding in the History of Ideas," in *History and Theory*, 8, pp. 3-53.

Skinner, Quentin: 1970, "Conventions and the Understanding of Speech Acts," *Philosophical Quarterly*, 20, pp. 118-138.

Skorupski, John: 1976, *Symbol and Theory*, Cambridge University Press, Cambridge.

Small, Henry: 1986, "The Synthesis of Specialty Narratives from Co-Citation Clusters," *Journal of the American Society for Information Science* 37, 3, pp. 97-110.

Small, Henry & Eugene Garfield: 1985, "The Geography of Science: Disciplinary and National Mappings," *Journal of Information Science* 11, pp. 147-159.

Smart, Barry: 1983, *Foucault, Marxism, and Critique*, Routledge & Kegan Paul, London.

Smith, William Cantwell, 1977, *Belief and History*, University of Virginia Press, Charlottesville.

Sorokin, Pitrim: 1928, *Contemporary Sociological Theories*, Harper & Row, New York.

Sperber, Daniel: 1982, "Apparently Irrational Beliefs," in Hollis & Lukes (1982).

Stern, Fritz (ed.) 1956, *Varieties of History*, Meridian Books, Cleveland.

Stich, Stephen & Richard Nisbett: 1984, "Expertise, Justification, and the Psychology of Inductive Inference," in Haskell (1984), pp. 226-241.

Strawson, Peter: 1959, *Individuals*, Methuen, London.

Suppe, Frederick (ed.): 1977, *The Structure of Scientifc Theories*, University of Illinois Press, Urbana.

Suppes, Patrick: 1962, "Models of Data," in E. Nagel (ed.), *Logic, Methodology and the Philosophy of Science--Proceedings of the 1960 International Congress*, Stanford University Press, Palo Alto.

Swift, Jonathan: 1960, *Gulliver's Travels*, New American Library, New York.

Thackray, Arnold: 1970, *Atoms and Powers*, Harvard University Press, Cambridge, Mass.

Thiem, John: 1979, "The Great Library of Alexandria Burnt: Towards the History of a Symbol," *Journal of the History of Ideas*, 40, pp. 507-526.

Thompson, John: 1984, *Studies in the Theory of Ideology*, University of
    California Press, Berkeley.
Tocqueville, Alexis de: 1955, *The Old Regime and the French Revolution*,
    Doubleday, Garden City, N.Y.
Toulmin, Stephen: 1972, *Human Understanding*, Princeton University Press,
    Princeton.
Tourtoulon, Pierre de: 1922, *Philosophy in the Development of the Law*,
    Macmillan, New York.
Tversky, Amos & Daniel Kahneman: 1981, "The Framing of Decisions and
    the Rationality of Choice," *Science* 221, pp. 453-458.
Tweney, Ryan, Michael Doherty & Clifford Mynatt (eds.): 1982, *On
    Scientific Thinking*, Columbia University Press, New York.
Ullmann-Margalit, Edna: 1978, "Invisible-Hand Explanations," *Synthese*
    39, pp. 263-281.
Ullmann-Margalit, Edna: 1983, "On Presumption," *Journal of Philosophy*
    80, pp. 143-162.
van Fraassen, Bas: 1968, "Presupposition, Implication, and Self-Reference,"
    Journal of Philosophy 65.
van Fraassen, Bas: 1980, *The Scientific Image*, Oxford University Press,
    Oxford.
Vartanian, Aram: 1973, "Man-Machine from the Greeks to the Computer,"
    in P. Wiener (ed.), *Dictionary of the History of Ideas*, Charles
    Scribner's Sons, New York, vol. 3.
von Hayek, Friedrich: 1973, *Law, Legislation, and Liberty*, University of
    Chicago Press, Chicago.
von Hayek, Friedrich: 1985, *New Studies in Philosophy, Politics,
    Economics, and the History of Ideas*, University of Chicago Press,
    Chicago.
von Wright, Georg: 1971, *Explanation and Understanding*, Cornell
    University Press, Ithaca.
Wagner, David (ed.): 1983, *The Seven Liberal Arts in the Middle Ages*,
    Indiana University Press, Bloomington.
Waismann, Friedrich: 1951, "Verifiability," in A. Flew (ed.), *Logic and
    Language*, Blackwell, Oxford, first series.
Waismann, Friedrich: 1952, "In Defense of New and Uncommon Uses of
    Language," *Analysis* 13, 1.
Watzlawick, Paul: 1977, *How Real is Real?* Random House, New York.
Weber, Max: 1954, "Basic Concepts of Sociology," in M. Rheinstein (ed.),
    Max Weber on Law in Economy and Society, Harvard University
    Press, Cambridge.
Weber, Max: 1964, *Methodology of the Social Sciences*, Collier
    Macmillan, New York.
Weisheipl, J. A.: 1978, "The Nature, Scope, and Classification of the
    Sciences," in Lindberg (1978).
Weldon, T. D.: 1960, *The Vocabulary of Politics*, Penguin, Harmondsworth,
    Middlesex.
Whitley, Richard: 1986, *The Intellectual and Social Organization of the
    Sciences*, Oxford University Press, Oxford.
Whittaker, Edmund: 1929, *A History of Theories of Aether and Electricity*,
    Cambridge University Press, Cambridge.
Willard, Charles: 1983, *Argumentation and the Social Grounds of*

Knowledge, University of Alabama Press, Tuscaloosa.

Williams, L. Pearce: 1967, *The Origins of Field Theory*, Doubleday, New York.

Williams, Raymond: 1975, *Keywords*, Oxford University Press, Oxford.

Wilson, Bryan (ed.): 1970, *Rationality*, Blackwell, Oxford.

Winch, Peter: 1958, *The Idea of a Social Science*, Routledge & Kegan Paul, London.

Winch, Peter: 1970a, "Comment on Jarvie," in R. Borger and F. Cioffi (eds.), *Explanation in the Behavioral Sciences*, Cambridge University Press, Cambridge.

Winch, Peter: 1970b, "Understanding a Primitive Society," in Wilson (1970).

Wittgenstein, Ludwig: 1958, *Philosophical Investigations*, Oxford University Press, Oxford.

Wittgenstein, Ludwig: 1961, *Tractatus Logico-Philosophicus*, Routledge & Kegan Paul, London.

Wittgenstein, Ludwig: 1967, *Remarks on the Foundations of Mathematics*, MIT Press, Cambridge, Mass.

Woolgar, Steve: 1983, "Irony in the Social Study of Science," in K. Knorr-Cetina and M. Mulkay (eds.), *Science Observed*, Sage, Beverly Hills, pp. 239-266.

Woolgar, Steve & Dorothy Pawluch: 1984, "Ontological Gerrymandering: The Anatomy of Social Problems Explanations," manuscript.

Wright, Crispin: 1980, *Wittgenstein and the Foundations of Mathematics*, Duckworth, London.

Yates, Frances: 1968, "The Hermetic Tradition in Renaissance Science," in C.S. Singleton (ed.), *Art, Science, and History in the Renaissance*, Johns Hopkins University Press, Baltimore.

Young, Robert M.: 1985, *Darwin's Metaphor*, Cambridge University Press, Cambridge.

Zilsel, Edgar: 1945, "The Genesis of the Concept of Scientific Progress," *Journal of the History of Ideas*, vol. 6.

Zuriff, Gerald: 1985, *Behaviorism: A Conceptual Reconstruction*, Columbia University Press, New York.

INDEX